THE OMBUDSMAN

THE OMBUDSMAN
Citizen's Defender

EDITED BY

DONALD C. ROWAT

Professor of Political Science
Carleton University
Ottawa

LONDON: GEORGE ALLEN & UNWIN LTD.
TORONTO: UNIVERSITY OF TORONTO PRESS
STOCKHOLM: P. A. NORSTEDT & SÖNER

FIRST PUBLISHED IN 1965
SECOND IMPRESSION 1965
THIRD IMPRESSION 1966
SECOND EDITION 1968

SBN 04 351023 X *Cloth bound ed.*
SBN 04 351024 0 *Paper bound ed.*

PUBLISHED IN GREAT BRITAIN BY GEORGE ALLEN & UNWIN LTD
PUBLISHED IN CANADA BY UNIVERSITY OF TORONTO PRESS
PUBLISHED IN SWEDEN BY P. A. NORSTEDT & SONER

PRINTED IN GREAT BRITAIN
by Photolithography
BY JOHN DICKENS AND CO LTD
NORTHAMPTON

PREFACE TO SECOND EDITION

NEW DEVELOPMENTS

The short time since this symposium first appeared has seen a remarkable growth of world-wide interest in 'Ombudsmanship.' The idea that legislatures should appoint an Ombudsman—an officer to receive and investigate complaints from citizens against unfair administrative action—is gaining wider and wider acceptance. In an article written in 1964, I argued that conditions had become ripe for the adoption of the system in most democratic countries of the world;[1] and in the concluding essay of this symposium, I stated that 'the Ombudsman should be regarded as an important new addition to the armoury of democratic government.' Since then, many articles have appeared on the subject, three books have been published, and two more symposia will appear in the United States early in 1968.[2] Also, Ombudsman plans have been adopted in several countries, and many Ombudsman proposals have been made in other countries. Four of the new plans—those for Britain, Alberta, New Brunswick and Hawaii— were approved in the first half of 1967.

Indeed, the situation is changing so rapidly that it was thought desirable to revise the first edition of this book in order to include the most important of the new developments. It would have been too difficult and costly to revise the whole of the book at this early stage. The original edition, including the Introduction, has therefore been left untouched except for minor corrections, and the up-dating has been done. by altering the Appendix to include important new acts, bills and proposals, and by adding this preface on new developments.[3]

The Appendix has been extended by adding the British Parliamentary Commissioner Act, the Ombudsman Act for Alberta, Hawaii's Ombudsman Bill and an extract from a special report of the Indian Administrative Reforms Commission in October 1966, proposing Ombudsmen for India. Since the Norwegian Act is outlined fully in the essay by Mr Os, Senator Long's Bill of March 1967, proposing an

[1] 'Ombudsmen for North America', XXIV *Public Administration Review* (Dec. 1964), 231.

[2] The books are: Walter Gellhorn, *Ombudsmen and Others: Citizens' Protectors in Nine Countries* and *When Americans Complain: Governmental Grievance Procedures* (both published by Harvard University Press, Cambridge, 1966); and a monograph by Stanley V. Anderson, *Canadian Ombudsman Proposals* (Berkeley, Institute of Governmental Studies, 1966). One of the symposia will be based on the October 1967 conference of the American Assembly, and the other will appear in the *Annals*, probably in May 1968.

[3] Based on my article, 'Recent Developments in Ombudsmanship', X *Canadian Public Administration* (March 1967), 35-46. I should like to thank the editor for permission to reprint portions of that article.

Administrative Ombudsman for the United States, has been sub-stituted for it. Also, the Connecticut Bill has been replaced by a model law for a state Ombudsman, produced by the Harvard Student Legis-lative Research Bureau in 1965.[4] I should like to thank the authors of these documents for permission to reproduce them.

Before proceeding with my commentary on new developments, I wish to mention a mistake, which Sir John Whyatt has drawn to my attention, in the third paragraph of my Introduction to the first edition. This mistake was particularly unfortunate because it introduced in a misleading way a quotation from the Whyatt report which I then criticized. By unintentionally omitting the words 'in Sweden' before the quotation, I left the impression that the report's claim regarding wide publicity in all stages of an Ombudsman's investigation applied also to the other Scandinavian countries. I should like to apologize to the authors of the report for giving this misleading impression.

My contributors from countries which had Ombudsman systems in 1965 have been good enough to send me reports on any important new developments. No significant changes have been made in these systems. In Finland and Sweden, however, there seems to be a feeling that the Ombudsman is becoming overloaded and needs assistance. At the beginning of 1967 a third full-time lawyer, an expert in military law, was added to the staff of the Finnish Ombudsman, and a private Bill was introduced in 1966 proposing that the legislature should elect a full-time Assistant Ombudsman (instead of the Deputy Ombudsman, who acts only when the Ombudsman is absent). In order to increase the efficiency of his inspections, the Finnish Ombudsman has begun to concentrate on a special topic or area each year. In 1966, for instance, he investigated the method of handling juvenile deliquents.

A proposed change in the Swedish system is even more far-reaching. In 1965 a governmental committee recommended that, in order to reduce the load on the Ombudsman for civil affairs, the supervision of judges, prison officials and police should be transferred to the Ombudsman for military affairs. As an alternative solution, Mr Bexelius, the Ombudsman for civil affairs, has proposed a system of three Ombudsmen to divide among themselves the tasks of the two existing Ombudsmen. Early in 1967 the Government introduced a Bill in which these alternatives were set forth. As it is up to Parliament alone to decide about its own Ombudsmen, the Government did not make any recommendation as to which solution should be preferred. The Swedish Parliament had not yet made its decision by the fall of 1967.

The fact that no important revisions of the newer schemes in Norway and New Zealand have been found necessary is a good indication that these schemes have been working successfully. Indeed, the only

---

[4] For an explanation of the detailed provisions of this model law, see *Harvard Journal on Legislation* (June 1965), 226-238.

significant proposal for change has been to extend the Ombudsman's jurisdiction. In both countries his power will probably be extended within the next year to include local government administration, as in the older systems. Both Norway and New Zealand seem pleased with their Ombudsmen. In Norway, where the Socialist Government was defeated in the fall election of 1965 after twenty years in power, the new Parliament re-elected the first Ombudsman for civil affairs to a second term. And in New Zealand, the Ombudsman's position was the only senior one for which a recent Royal Commission considering civil service salaries recommended a salary increase.

The number and disposition of complaints received in New Zealand has not changed significantly in recent years. In the fiscal year 1966, the Ombudsman handled 799 complaints. Only 444 of these were actually investigated. Of the 351 in which the investigation had been completed, 56 were found to be justified. Thus, of total complaints handled, slightly more than half required investigation and of investigations completed, 16% required some sort of remedial action. Compared with the previous year, a larger proportion of total complaints required investigation and a slightly larger proportion were justified (7% versus 6%).[5] This perhaps indicates that the people of New Zealand are becoming more sophisticated about what type of complaint should go to the Ombudsman.

NEW ADOPTIONS AND PROPOSALS

United Kingdom

Among the new developments elsewhere, the most outstanding, of course, has been the adoption of the plan in the United Kingdom. In the fall of 1965, the new Labour Government issued a White Paper setting forth the general principles of its proposed plan.[6] It followed this up in July 1966, by presenting its Bill to Parliament and announcing the appointment of Sir Edmund Compton, the retiring Comproller and Auditor General, as Britain's first Parliamentary Commissioner. This announcement was greeted with consternation by many members of Parliament, not because of the person named—nearly all agreed that the choice was excellent—but because the appointment had been made by the Government before the Bill had been approved by Parliament. However, the Bill was approved in principle on October 18, Sir Edmund was granted funds for an office and staff on October 19, and the Bill was referred to a standing committee for study. Incorporating amendments proposed by the standing committee, the Bill was reported to Parliament in November, was approved by Parliament with further amendments in March, and Sir Edmund took office

---

[5] New Zealand Ombudsman, *Report for the Year Ended* 31 *March* 1966, and 1967, Appendix B.
[6] *The Parliamentary Commissioner for Administration*, Cmnd. 2767 (London, H.M.S.O.).

April 1, 1967, with about fifty assistants, all drawn from the civil service. Compared with the established systems, the new British scheme places a number of serious limitations upon the Ombudsman's powers. The most important of these, stemming from the unnecessarily conservative proposals of the Whyatt report, are the provisions that complaints must be referred to him by members of Parliament and that he reports the results of investigations to them rather than to the complainants. These provisions were made to reduce the load on the Ombudsman in such a large country, and to make the scheme more palatable to MPs who feared loss of contact with their constituents. However, many people, including myself, feel that this is an undesirable restriction on the plan, because many complainants will not wish to take their case to a partisan politician, and he will be an extra screen between them and the administration. Also, a complainant should have the right to be a direct party in his own case. This latter point will be met to some extent if, after a case has been referred to the Commissioner, he is allowed to deal with the complainant directly.

A schedule to the Act provides a list of the departments and authorities subject to investigation by the Commissioner. Included are all ministries and departments and such agencies as the Civil Service Commission and the Central Office of Information. Another schedule, however, lists matters not subject to investigation. Among the most important of these are relations or dealings with foreign governments, security matters, police action, and personnel matters in the civil service and the armed forces. Also excluded are the public corporations, government contracts, Regional Hospital Boards, the government of Northern Ireland, and local government. Although the Commissioner is appointed by the Government, he holds office during good behaviour, can be removed only by Parliament, and is expected to be an independent officer of Parliament comparable to the Comptroller and Auditor General. He will have access to all departmental documents (including internal minutes) but not Cabinet or Cabinet committee papers. Ministers will not have the right of Crown Privilege to refuse the disclosure of documents, as they have in courts now, because the Commissioner's investigations will be private. When they think it in 'the public interest,' however, they may instruct him to refrain from the subsequent publication of documents and information. Also, he is debarred from matters for which there are remedies in the courts. Since Ministers can refuse to submit testimony to the courts, this provision has been criticized as intending to protect civil servants from embarrassing probings. On the other hand, a complaint can be made by a corporate body as well as an individual, and visitors from abroad are included among possible complainants.

An important amendment to the revised Bill, moved by the Government, provided that the Commissioner might not 'review by way of appeal any decision taken by a government department or other authority in the exercise of a discretion.' This amendment was attacked on the ground that it would emasculate the Bill altogether by making it impossible for the Commissioner to investigate any of the thousands of decisions where departments have a discretion. The Government spokesman, however, claimed that the Commissioner should not have the power to review the merits of a discretionary decision, and the amendment would not exclude him from reviewing the fairness of the method by which the decision was arrived at. Hoping to satisfy the criticism, the Government later moved a substitute amendment in the House of Lords to say that he may not question the merits of a discretionary decision 'taken without maladministration in the exercise of a discretion vested in any department or authority.' This is still a far cry from the provision of the New Zealand legislation which allows the Ombudsman to review a decision if he thinks it is simply 'wrong.'

The limitations placed upon the Commissioner's scope and powers by the Government were greeted with a good deal of criticism by the Press in Britain. He was amusingly described as a 'muzzled watchdog,' a 'crusader without a sword,' an 'Ombudmanqué,' and an 'Ombuds-mouse.' Because the 'Ombudsomissions' were so blatant, it was even suggested that the date he took office, April 1, was significant. Certainly Britain seems to have adopted the plan in an unnecessarily truncated form. To the argument that the Commissioner's powers can always be extended later, the answer is that, once approved or created, a law or institution acquires a great deal of inertia which makes it difficult to change. In view of Labour's enthusiasm for a strong institution before it came to power, this case is a further illustration of a serious defect in the parliamentary system of government: because the executive proposes all important Bills, and because it dominates the legislature, it is in a strong position to resist any provision that may limit its own powers. Scholars like J. D. B. Mitchell continue to argue that the need for fundamental reform of British public law is so great that a Parliamentary Commissioner will be of little consequence.

An abortive proposal to create an Ombudsman for local government should also be mentioned. This was in a Bill presented by Lord Wade to the House of Lords[7] and given second reading in October 1966, the same month in which the Government's Parliamentary Commissioner Bill received its second reading in the House of Commons. It would have provided Regional Commissioners for Administration with powers to investigate complaints direct from the public against maladministration by local authorities in England and Wales. After a brief debate and little public discussion, it was quickly defeated on the ground that the Government had already declared its intention in the White Paper to consider eventually extending the Parliamentary Commissioner's powers to local government.

[7] *Local Government (Rights of the Public) Bill* [H.L.] (London, H.M.S.O., 6 July 1966).

A *

Canada

Canada had two provincial Ombudsmen in operation by the end of 1967, with several more in the offing. By the time the first edition of this symposium had appeared, private members' Bills proposing an Ombudsman had been introduced not only in Canada's federal Parliament but also in the provincial legislatures of British Columbia and Ontario. In addition, the Alberta Bar Association had drafted a model Bill for that province. The scheme had also been discussed in the legislatures of Saskatchewan, Manitoba, New Brunswick and Nova Scotia and was being studied by the Ontario Commission on Human Rights. This meant that the Ombudsman idea had been at least placed officially before all of the provincial Governments except in Newfoundland, Prince Edward Island and Quebec. But private members' Bills are not very significant in Canada, and proposals are a far cry from adoption. The important thing is to have Government acceptance for the idea.

By the end of 1965 the plain fact was that, after several years of discussion and numerous proposals from various sources, no Government in Canada had publicly committed itself to creating an Ombudsman. Except for a resolution adopted unanimously by the Legislative Assembly of Prince Edward Island in April 1966, instructing the Government to consider the appointment of an Ombudsman, no other official action was taken on the subject until the end of 1966. In fact, by that time interest in the proposal actually seemed to have flagged. Although a federal parliamentary committee had recommended the scheme in February 1965, and the Prime Minister had announced in the April Speech from the Throne that the Ombudsman idea would be referred to a new Royal Commission on administrative bodies, the Commission was not appointed, and the subject was not even mentioned in the Speech from the Throne for the 1966 Session. Near the end of the year, I was half-seriously thinking of writing a piece called, 'Whatever happened to the Ombudsman?'

Meanwhile, two events had occurred which were destined to revive the idea. The Labour Party in Britain and the Union Nationale in Quebec, both of which were committed to the idea, had been elected to office. Suddenly, at the end of 1966, the Governments of Quebec, Alberta and Manitoba all announced that they intended to introduce the plan. In fact, in January 1967 the Government of Alberta ran a large advertisement in newspapers across Canada headed 'Ombudsman, Commissioner of the Legislature,' seeking applications for an appointment to be made before July 1st at a salary of $20,000 per annum. The qualifications sought were 'a substantial record of formal education and related experience, preferably in law and the social sciences.' Alberta's Ombudsman Bill was given final approval on March 30th, and on April 7th it was announced that the new Ombudsman, chosen from among 230 applications, would be the retiring head of the federal

Royal Canadian Mounted Police, who was to take office in September 1967. Alberta's Act, the first to be adopted in North America, is based largely on the New Zealand legislation. It is thought that one important aspect of the Ombudsman's work in Alberta will be to hear appeals from the decisions of the relevant provincial boards where landowners or occupants believe that, in cases of disputes with petroleum or pipeline companies, they have not been fairly treated by the boards.[8] At present there is no appeal from these boards to the courts.

In December 1966 the Government of Manitoba issued a White Paper, *Citizen's Remedies Code*, which indicates that its proposed Legislative Commissioner for Administration will act only at the request of a member of the legislature, as in Britain and in Congressman Reuss's Bill. However, unlike Alberta's Ombudsman, his jurisdiction will extend to local government.

It should also be noted that at the end of 1966 the Government of Newfoundland announced in its Speech from the Throne that the Ombudsman idea would be referred for study to a select committee of the legislature. By this time then, the proposal had received some kind of formal consideration by either the Government or the legislature of all ten provinces. In addition, at the beginning of the year the Government of Nova Scotia inaugurated a system of twenty so-called Welfare Ombudsmen. These are three-man, lay tribunals scattered throughout the province—roughly one for each county—appointed by the Minister of Welfare to hear and decide appeals against decisions made by the Welfare Department on social assistance benefits. Unlike Ombudsmen, however, they will have the power to reverse decisions.

The Governments of Manitoba and Quebec have not as yet presented a Bill to the legislature, and it now seems unlikely that they will do so before 1968. Indeed, the first Ombudsman in Quebec may be created at the municipal rather than the provincial level, in the newly-created city of Laval, which combines 14 former municipalities on Jesus Island and is now the second largest city in Quebec. The victorious civic party in Laval's first election had included an Ombudsman plank in its campaign platform, and plans to present a Bill to the Quebec legislature establishing the office for Laval. Also, in January 1967 the Lemay Commission in Quebec included the office as part of its proposal for a new regional government to encompass the suburbs opposite Montreal's south shore.

At the end of April the Government of New Brunswick suddenly introduced an Ombudsman Bill sponsored by the Premier. Before the end of May it had passed in the legislature. Like the Alberta Act, it is modelled on that of New Zealand. A few weeks before the provincial election in October (in which the Liberal Government was returned), a former university president was appointed as Ombudsman.

[8] News story by Edward Romaine in *Financial Post* (Jan. 7, 1967), 18.

At the federal level, in response to questions in the House of Commons, Prime Minister Pearson stated in the fall of 1966 and again early in 1967 that his Government was conducting discussions with the provinces regarding a federal Ombudsman plan, and hoped to make an announcement on the subject shortly. Although the subject was not mentioned in the Speech from the Throne in May, and no announcement had been made by October, the adoptions in Britain, Alberta and New Brunswick will no doubt accelerate action on a federal plan for Canada.

United States

The most remarkable burgeoning of interest in Ombudsmanship has occurred in the United States. Indeed, one might almost call it 'Ombudsmania.' As one commentator put it, 'The Word this year is *Ombudsman!*' On December 2, 1966, *Time* magazine ran a story headed 'The People's Watchdog,' featuring the two new books on the subject by Walter Gellhorn, eminent Professor of Law at Columbia University. Accompanying the story was a photograph of the 'Om-' column from Webster's unabridged dictionary, to which were added a red insert mark and the word '*Om-budsman*,' written into the appropriate place in the column. *Time* claimed that 'so far, the word does not even appear in U.S. dictionaries.' To its dismay, it received letters from Funk and Wagnalls and Thorndyke-Barnhart pointing out that the word appeared in *their* dictionaries! Quoth red-faced *Time* in its next issue: '*Time* is wordless. *Ombudsman* can also be found in the addendum of Webster's third, unabridged.' Also significant is the fact that in Congressman Reuss's Bill, re-introduced as HR 3388 on January 23, 1967, the proposed Administrative Counsel is now called the Congressional Ombudsman.

In the Introduction to this book, I predicted that, even though Canada and the United States had taken an interest in the Ombudsman plan more recently than had Britain, they were likely to adopt a version of it more quickly because it could be adopted at either the national or the provincial or state level of government. In the event, this turned out to be true, but only partly true, because I had not anticipated that the first adoption might be at the local level. The first jurisdiction to create a version of the office in North America was Nassau County, N.Y. On May 31, 1966, the County Executive, a Democrat, appointed to the office of Commissioner of Accounts a person to act as Public Protector, and gave him authority to 'protect the public and individual citizens against inefficiency, maladministration, arrogance, abuse, and other failures of government.' The person appointed was formerly a judge and chairman of the County Board of Ethics. By the end of May 1967, he had handled about 500 cases. Meanwhile, however, the County Board of Supervisors, which was predominantly Republican, had appointed an Advisory Committee on the Ombudsman, with the

County Prosecutor as Chairman. After a trip to Scandinavia, he recommended that the Public Protector should become an agent of the legislative rather than the executive branch of the County's government; he should be appointed by the Board of Supervisors and, to ensure his political neutrality and independence, should be removable only by a two-thirds vote of the Board[9]. Although popularly referred to as an Ombudsman, the Public Protector does not meet the essential qualification of being an independent agency of the legislature.

More significant has been the recent adoption of a genuine Ombudsman plan by Hawaii, the first American state to do so. Hawaii's Ombudsman Bill was approved by the legislature on April 30, 1967, and sent to the Governor for signature. Under the provisions of Hawaii's Constitution, since the Bill was approved within the last ten days of the session, it automatically became law on June 24th, even though Governor Burns refused to sign it. His refusal, however, may delay the implementation of the plan. Since the Ombudsman is to be appointed by the legislature, the scheme cannot come into operation until the 1968 session in any case. He is to be appointed for a term of six years, and a two-thirds vote in both houses will be needed to remove him from office. Late in 1965, Hawaii's Legislative Reference Bureau had produced a brief report on the Ombudsman which reprinted the Acts for Denmark and New Zealand, the Bill for Connecticut, and the Harvard model Bill. As can be seen in the Appendix, Hawaii's law is based mainly on the Harvard Bill, except that in the latter the Ombudsman is to be appointed by the Governor.

In addition to this actual adoption, proposals are now being made thick and fast in the United States for all levels of government. In March 1967 Senator Long introduced his Bill to create an Administrative Ombudsman for the United States, initially with jurisdiction over such agencies as the Social Security Administration and the Veterans' Administration. Earlier, Senator Long and two co-sponsors had re-introduced a Bill for an Ombudsman in the District of Columbia. Also, Senators Magnuson and Long re-introduced their so-called Tax Ombudsman Bill, but this is really a proposal to create regional tax commissioners within the Tax Court to decide appeals on small tax claims.

In February Congressman Reuss decided to dramatize his Ombudsman Bill and test the idea for the federal level by appointing a personal assistant as a temporary 'Ombudsman' for his Milwaukee constituency. Professors Gellhorn and Anderson and I agreed to be consultants on the project. The assistant held office hours at six postal stations as well as in a central office. Over a four-month period he received nearly 500 complaints and enquiries requiring some form of action. Most of these were by telephone or personal call, with very few

---

[9] William Cahn, *Report on the Ombudsman* (Mineola, N.Y., Nov. 1966), pp. 28 mimeo.

by mail. Surprisingly, 40% of them concerned state or local government. A large number of the complaints were justified, many of them cases of administrative delay. Backed by Mr Reuss's influence, the 'Ombudsman' had good success with remedial action. At the end of the project the assistant prepared a brief analysis of the results, in which he not unexpectedly recommended the Reuss Bill.

Because of the magnitude of the problems encountered at the federal level, however, a full-scale Ombudsman plan is not likely to be adopted for some years. Much more likely will be further adoptions at the state or local levels. In 1967, legislators filed Ombudsman Bills in over half of the states, including such important states as California, Illinois, Michigan and New York. Legislators in many other states had shown a definite interest in the plan. It will be only a matter of time before some of these states establish legislative Ombudsmen. Meanwhile, so-called Ombudsman plans have been created in two states, Michigan and Colorado. Like the Nassau plan, however, they are part of the executive arm of government. In July 1966, Michigan's Secretary of State appointed a special complaints officer for his department with the title of Ombudsman, and at the end of 1966 the newly elected Lieutenant Governor of Colorado, a Democrat in a predominantly Republican state, announced that he was prepared to receive and investigate complaints. By the end of May 1967, he had received about 500 complaints and enquiries. Although these schemes seem to have been set up partly to give a push to the idea of a legislative Ombudsman, unfortunately they and the Nassau scheme are likely to be influential as precedents. Some of the Bills filed in the New York legislature, for instance, propose an Ombudsman in the executive branch.

At the local level, of great significance have been the recent developments in New York City. In November 1966, the Civilian Review Board for the police was abolished in a bitterly fought referendum. The Policemen's Benevolent Association, which took the stand that a review board should not single out the police, is reported to have spent $400,000 in the campaign against Mayor Lindsay's support of the Board. After the Board's defeat, both sides agreed that a version of the Ombudsman institution, which would be prepared to review complaints against *any* part of the civic administration, might be a suitable compromise. The Ombudsman idea was already well known there because Judge Bexelius, Sweden's Ombudsman, and Sir Guy Powles, New Zealand's Ombudsman, had crossed paths in New York during tours of the United States early in 1966. In the course of his tour Judge Bexelius had also given evidence before committees of the Congress and the California legislature. In New York, the two Ombudsmen appeared simultaneously at a meeting chaired by Professor Gellhorn in a kind of all-star show before the powerful local bar association. Bills on the subject had also been submitted to the City Council.

Mayor Lindsay therefore referred the idea to a team of City officials to draft a plan. Later, however, he re-introduced his scheme for city-wide Neighborhood City Halls, which would be run by the executive branch on a budget of $250,000. The Democratically controlled City Council opposes this scheme for fear it will be used for political purposes. In May 1967 the local bar association produced a draft Bill for an independent Ombudsman, to be appointed with the advice and consent of two-thirds of the Council and removed only for cause by a three-quarters vote. The President of the Council immediately supported and introduced the Bill, but Mayor Lindsay's reaction was to favour instead expanding the present office of the Commissioner of Investigation, who is an executive officer, and making his appointment subject to Council approval.

Other developments have also given a strong push toward Ombudsman adoptions for cities. In July 1966 the law school at the University of Buffalo began a pilot project under two professors as unofficial Ombudsmen for the city of Buffalo. Early in 1967 Professor Gellhorn produced a model Ombudsman Bill for state and local governments, and in March the President's Commission on Law Enforcement and Administration of Justice recommended replacing local Police Review Boards with 'Ombudsman-type' review agencies. As a result, Ombudsman proposals are now being made for other cities, such as Kansas City, San Francisco and Oakland. The Oakland proposal, however, made by the mayor in March 1967, is for an executive officer under the city manager, like the Citizens Assistance Officer appointed in the same month for San Diego.

The Ombudsman idea has become so popular in the United States that so-called Ombudsmen are now being proposed and appointed for universities, school boards, and other public and private organizations. For example, in April 1967 an 'Ombudsman committee' of three professors was appointed by the administrator for the State University of New York in Stony Brook to hear complaints from students or professors, and in June the appointment of a professor half time as an Ombudsman for student grievances was approved by the Berkeley Senate of the University of California. Also, at the end of 1966 the President of the Michigan Bar Association appointed all seventeen Past-Presidents as 'Ombudsmen' to hear complaints from lawyers against action taken by any official of their Association. The name Ombudsman has even been given to the person handling customers' problems in a San Francisco department store. In Canada, too, the idea is spreading to universities and other organizations. At the new Simon Fraser University in Burnaby, B.C., for instance, since 1965 the student body has elected a student as a so-called Ombudsman, but he acts as an advocate for the students rather than an independent investigator of complaints.

There has also been a rapid growth of 'newspaper Ombudsmen' in the United States. These are complaint columns run by newspapers which, though prepared to handle any personal grievance, play a role surprisingly like Ombudsmen when investigating complaints against official action, especially if they have been given a big budget for investigations. The first such column, 'Watchem,' was begun by the editor of the Houston Chronicle in 1961. Interestingly, he knew about the Ombudsman at that time and thinks this may have influenced his decision to start the column.[10] By 1967 more than two dozen big dailies had complaint columns. Some have large staffs which handle hundreds of letters a week and thousands of telephone calls. Their action on complaints is often reported directly to complainants. Only a small portion actually appear in print. Similar columns now exist in several Canadian and Australian cities.

As this survey shows, a serious problem connected with implementing the Ombudsman plan in the United States will be how to preserve the precise meaning of the Ombudsman concept. Other problems will be how to prevent the Ombudsman from becoming an arm of the executive, and how to keep him independent and non-partisan. Because of the strong tradition of executive and partisan appointment in the United States, special qualifications and techniques for appointment must be adopted to help solve these problems.

Other Developed Democracies

It is not surprising that Australia, with its close cultural ties to New Zealand, became interested in the Ombudsman at an early date. Indeed, since Australia is a federation, the mystery is why the plan has not already been adopted there at either the federal or state level. The only adoption has been at the local level, by the Albert Shire Council, Gold Coast, Queensland. Although there have been numerous proposals over a period of several years for the state and federal levels, as yet no Government has been willing to commit itself to adoption. Again, the explanation seems to be the dominance of the executive over the legislature in the Commonwealth parliamentary system. Most proposals have been made for the state level. In the case of Victoria, they go back to October 1962 when the Opposition leader returned from overseas convinced that Victoria should have an Ombudsman. By October 1963 the Government of Victoria had set up a parliamentary committee to look into the question but later allowed the enquiry to lapse.

Other states in which the proposal has been actively discussed over a period of years are South Australia, New South Wales and Western Australia. In New South Wales, the Government has referred the idea to a Law Reform Commission, set up in 1966, and has requested a draft Bill. In Western Australia, the first newspaper complaint column in Australia was begun in Perth's *Daily News* in April 1965. In its

[10] Letter to the author from W. P Stevenson, former editor, Feb. 27, 1967.

first two years it received about 3,500 complaints, many of them against state and federal agencies. The column is actually called 'The Ombudsman,' and has been influential in promoting the idea. Yet a Minister of the Government in Western Australia has argued that a state plan is unnecessary now because the 'Ombudsman' column is meeting the need. The *Daily News* itself is convinced that real parliamentary Ombudsmen are needed in Australia.[11] Although Prime Ministers Menzies and Holt have both insisted that a federal Ombudsman is unnecessary, it is likely that a state plan will be adopted before long in Australia.

In Europe, the Ombudsman continues to be discussed in Ireland. Mr Abrahamson reports that the idea is being considered by the Public Services Organization Review Group, appointed by the Minister of Finance. The other European democracies, perhaps because their systems of administrative courts partly meet the need, have not taken as much interest in the Ombudsman plan as has the English-speaking world.[12] Dr Crince Le Roy has reported that in the Netherlands an Ombudsman was proposed for the city of Rotterdam, but rejected by its Council in 1964. The same year, following a study of the Scandinavian plan by J. G. Steenbeek, a commission of the Society for Administrative Law recommended a general plan for the Netherlands, and included a draft Bill in its report (Publication No. L 11 of the Society). This report was discussed at the Society's annual meeting in September 1964, and most of the speakers were in favour of the plan. However, the Government has taken no action on the proposal. In February 1967, the Committees for Petitions of both chambers of Parliament proposed measures designed to increase the effectiveness of these two Committees in handling complaints. They proposed that they should be given the same powers as a Parliamentary Commission of Inquiry to inspect documents and to hear public officials, and that an office should be set up to prepare the reports of the two Committees.

[11] Letter to the author from J. R. Davies, Assistant Chief of Reporting Staff, April 5, 1967.

[12] Among the recent articles in German is a long review of my book by Walter Haller, 'Der Ombudsmann', NF 85 *Zeitschrift fur Schweizerisches Recht* (Basel, 1966), 355-72; an earlier article in French by Goerges Langrod is 'Le control parlementaire de l'administration dans les pays nordiques', 12 *Revue Administrative* (Paris, 1959), 664-73. I should like to thank Drs. H. Thierfelder and W. Haller for information on Germany, Switzerland and Austria, and for the following list of publications: Georg Hahn, 'Der Justizbevollmächtigte des schwedischen Reichstages, I: Entstehung und Entwicklung des Amtes', 87 (NF 48) *Archiv des offentlichen Rechts*, 389-467; Hans Marti, 'Die aufsehende Gewalt', in *Verfassungsrecht und Vergassungswirklichkeit, Festschrift fur Hans Huber* (Bern, 1961), 174-189, and *Pladoyer fur controllierte Macht* (Bern, 1964), 33; Hans Thierfelder, *Zum Problem eines Ombudsmans in Deutschland* (Köln und Berlin, Grote, 1967), pp. 48; Aktionsgemeinschaft Deutscher Ombudsmann, *Der Ombudsmann* (München, Lohmüller, 1966); Fritz Bauer, *Die neue Gewalt* (München; Lohmüller, 1964), pp. 24; René Helg, *La haute surveillance du Parlement sur le gouvernement et l'administration* (Bâle, Helbig und Lichtenhahn, 1966), pp. 89.

There has been continuing interest in the Ombudsman plan in Western Germany, but no real enthusiasm for its adoption. This is partly because the successive military Ombudsmen in that country have tended to damage the prestige of their office by getting involved in controversial issues. Since about 1965, however, there has been a sharp upswing in interest. A society has been formed to support the idea of Ombudsmen for civil affairs, and unofficial proposals have now been made for the "city-states" of West Berlin, Bremen and Hamburg. The Hamburg proposal is in the form of a detailed draft bill modelled on the Danish plan, and was published in *Mensch und Staat* (No. 1, 1967), a journal of opinion which strongly supports the Ombudsman idea. In August 1967, Willi Weyer, Minister of Interior for North-Rhine Westphalia, the largest state in the federation, proposed that the idea should be considered by the permanent Interstate Conference of Ministers of Interior, and on September 1 one of the most widely-read weeklies, *Christ und Welt*, published an article entitled, "When Will a West German Ombudsman Come?" The federal Minister of Justice, Gustav Heinemann, favours an Ombudsman plan for civil affairs, but feels that it should be tried out first in one or two of the smaller states. Others feel that an independent office, especially at the federal level, would itself turn into an unwieldy bureaucracy. They propose instead that, in order to strengthen the legislature, an expert staff be appointed to serve the Committee on Petitions.

Other European countries which have taken an interest in the plan are Switzerland and Austria. It has been discussed in Switzerland since 1960, when the Danish Ombudsman made a speech in Bern on the invitation of the Swiss Society for the Rule of Law and Individual Freedom. The chairman of the Society subsequently published a paper proposing that the system should be introduced by an amendment to the Swiss Constitution. In 1962 a commission of the Society proposed the appointment of both civil and military Ombudsmen. This proposal was widely discussed in the press. In 1964 a Swiss scholar, Dr Walter Haller, produced a book in German on the Swedish Ombudsman.[13] In the same year, Switzerland experienced its own version of the British Crichel Down Affair, and a special parliamentary Commission of Investigation had to be appointed. This has naturally enlivened the discussion of the subject. In Austria, discussion appears to have begun with an article published in 1961. In 1963 the Danish Ombudsman made a speech in Vienna, and since then the idea has been repeatedly discussed. Because Switzerland and Austria are both federations, there is a possibility of the plan being introduced there at either the federal or state level.

---

[13] *Der schwedische Justitieombudsman* (Zurich, Polygraphischer Verlag, 1964), pp. 320.

Developing Countries

In contrast with the mild interest in Europe, the Ombudsman idea has been spreading rapidly among the developing countries of the world. In Israel, the cities of Tel-Aviv and Jerusalem in 1966 appointed complaint officers who are popularly styled Ombudsmen, but who are really part of the executive. In its first full year the Tel-Aviv office received over 1,000 complaints, of which over half were considered justified.[14] More important, the Israeli State Comptroller has gradually taken on the functions of an Ombudsman. This development came naturally because the Comptroller, an officer of the legislature with no authority to control the administration, had been given broad powers to audit not only financial propriety but also general legality, efficiency and morality. From the outset in 1950, the first State Comptroller deemed it right to handle complaints from the public as an aid to his supervision of the administration. It was only gradually, however, that his complaint-handling function became widely known. As a result, the number of complaints has steadily risen, from 1,300 in 1961 to 3,100 in 1966.

The handling of complaints, which of course is only a small part of the Comptroller's functions, is under the supervision of a senior officer, who co-operates with the legal adviser and the division in charge of inspecting the body against which the complaint is directed. The system has the advantage of making use of the large corps of experienced investigators and efficiency experts in the Comptroller's office. The procedure for handling complaints is very much like that of the Ombudsman schemes and in recent years may have been influenced by them. Indeed, the increasing popularity of the Ombudsman idea in Israel has resulted in proposals that the complaint-handling function should be especially recognized either by creating a separate Ombudsman or by making specific legal provision for this function in the Comptroller's office. A special committee of the legislature was set up in 1965 to consider these questions, and is expected to report late in 1967. It will probably favour the second alternative because the Comptroller's office, like the Swedish Ombudsmen, successfully combines the functions of both efficiency inspection and complaint-handling. In any case, this interesting native Israeli variation of the Ombudsman plan deserves careful study. In few other countries of the world has the legislative auditor been given such broad powers to inspect and supervise general administration.

Other developing countries in which the Ombudsman plan has been adopted are Guyana and Mauritius. The British Guiana Independence Conference of November 1965 made provision for the plan in the

14 I should like to thank the Tel-Aviv complaint office for this information, and Mr. J. E. Nebenzahl, the State Comptroller, for the information on his office; he has also put out a useful brochure, *The State Comptroller of Israel and his Office at Work* (Jerusalem, 1963), pp. 92.

Constitution for the new State of Guyana,[15] and the first Ombudsman, formerly the Director of Public Prosecutions, was appointed on the eve of independence in May 1966. The plan was also included by the 1965 Mauritius Constitutional Conference in the new constitution for an independent Mauritius.[16] The effective date of this constitution was delayed, however, until after an election in 1967. In both countries the Ombudsman is appointed by the Government only after consultation with Opposition leaders, and in Guyana he can be removed only for cause upon the recommendation of a special tribunal. Both countries have a racially mixed population, and in both cases it was thought that an Ombudsman would be especially useful for investigating complaints of racial discrimination by officials. In his first full year in office, Guyana's Ombudsman received only about 150 complaints, and only one of these was an allegation of racial discrimination. However, his office got off to a slow start, and it is too early to judge how effective it will be. Both schemes are important precedents for racially heterogeneous developing countries.

In January 1966, the Ceylon Colloquium on the Rule of Law, which was attended by about a hundred jurists from the Asian and Pacific region, recommended the institution for that region, and in April-May 1967 the United Nations held a seminar in Jamaica on human rights, with the Swedish civil Ombudsman as a guest expert.[17] The Latin American delegates agreed that the institution would suit their conditions, and urged the U.N. to publicize it in Latin American countries. These recommendations have added considerable weight to the idea of Ombudsmen for developing countries. For instance, in July 1967 the Jamaican section of the International Commission of Jurists proposed the plan for Jamaica. It has also been proposed for Hong Kong and is being considered in Malaysia. After Singapore's break with Malaysia, a constitutional commission for Singapore, headed by the Chief Justice, in December 1966 recommended constitutional provisions for an Ombudsman much like those for Guyana and Mauritius.[18] The Government of Singapore has so far

[15] Cmnd. 2849 (London, H.M.S.O.), 17-18. See also British Guiana Commission of Inquiry, *Racial Problems in the Public Service Report* (Geneva, International Commission of Jurists, Oct. 1965), which reprints the section on the Ombudsman from the Report of the Constitutional Commissioner for Mauritius (Prof. S. A. de Smith).

[16] Cmnd. 2797, 28-9. See also Constitutional Commissioner for Mauritius, *Report* (Mauritius Legislative Assembly Paper, No. 2, 1965).

[17] 'The Need for an Ombudsman in the Asian and Pacific Region', 26 *Bulletin of the International Commission of Jurists* (June 1966), 7; United Nations Human Rights Seminar on the Effective Realization of Civil and Political Rights at the National Level, *Extracts From Draft Report* (Georgetown, Guyana, 1967), 19; Alfred Bexelius, 'Background-paper on the Swedish Ombudsman's Institution' (pp. 48 mimeo.).

[18] Republic of Singapore, *Report of the Constitutional Commission 1966* (Singapore, Government Printer), 18-22.

refused to accept the plan on the ground that there has been insufficient experience with it yet in Commonwealth countries. More significant is the comprehensive Ombudsman scheme proposed for India by the federal Administrative Reforms Commission. The Ombudsman idea had been discussed in India for several years, and proposals had been made at both the state and federal levels. As early as 1963, for instance, the institution had been proposed by an official commission for the State of Rajasthan. Several other states have set up Ombudsman-like Vigilance Commissions to deal mainly with the problem of corruption. These Commissions, however, are appointed by and responsible to the executive. Early in 1966 the Punjab Administrative Reforms Commission recommended that 'in order to increase the utility of the Vigilance Commission, it should be made independent of government or ministerial influence.'[19]

At the federal level, a Committee on the Prevention of Corruption had in 1964 recommended the creation of a Central Vigilance Commission, headed by a single Commissioner and composed of three Directorates: General Complaints and Redress, Vigilance, and Central Police. The Commissioner would be appointed for a six-year term and would have the same independence as the Auditor-General. His functions and powers would be somewhat like those of New Zealand's Ombudsman, except that he would also inspect for corruption and could initiate a prosecution against an official if he were not satisfied with the action taken by the Government on his recommendation.[20] The Government, however, accepted only part of the Committee's recommendations. It did not make the Commission independent of executive influence, and it rejected the proposal for a Directorate of General Complaints and Redress. Instead, in January 1966 it appointed a Commissioner for Public Grievances in the Ministry of Home Affairs to supervise the handling of grievances and the work of new complaints officers in the ministries and departments, and to receive and review grievances himself. To the end of March 1967, he had received about 1,400 complaints, and had obtained remedial action on many of them. The Commissioner and the departmental officers, however, are part of the administration itself. In October 1966, the Administrative Reforms Commission, in a special interim report, therefore proposed a new scheme for independent, Ombudsman-like grievance officers.[21]

[19] 'Digest of Reports', 12 *Indian Journal of Public Administration* (April-June 1966), 20; for additional commentary on the Vigilance Commissions, see earlier issues of the *Journal* (e.g. 11, 1965, 124).

[20] For details of this proposal, see J. B. Monteiro, 'Comment', *Public Law* (Summer 1965), 81-88; see also R. K. Swamy, 'The Case for a Permanent Tribunal of Inquiry', *Modern Law Review* (April 1964), 257-68.

[21] Government of India, Administrative Reforms Commission, *Interim Report on Problems of Redress of Citizens' Grievances* (New Delhi, Oct. 1966), 18 plus an annexure, which is a draft Bill for the Lokpal.

The new proposal is unusual in that it would include both levels of government and at the same time divide the top from the lower levels of administration. There would be a sort of super-Ombudsman (the Lokpal) with jurisdiction over both federal and state Ministers and Secretaries, and also a lower order of Ombudsman (the Lokayukta), one for the federal government and one for each state, to cover the levels below the federal and state Secretaries. These officers would all be appointed by the President of India. They would be answerable only to him and to the federal or state legislatures, and would be independent of the federal and state Cabinets. The Lokpal would be appointed on the advice of the Prime Minister, but only after he had consulted the Chief Justice and the leader of the Opposition. The state Lokayukta would be similarly appointed on the advice of a state's Chief Minister.

The Commission claims that, though a constitutional revision would be desirable, the scheme could begin without such a revision. To an outside observer it is difficult to see how such a scheme could be effected in a federal system without a constitutional revision. It is also difficult to see how the super-Ombudsman could be made answerable to both the federal and state legislatures, or how he and the sub-Ombudsmen would be able to sort out their respective functions in a hierarchial system of administration for which Ministers at the top are held responsible. However, the proposal represents an interesting attempt to divide up the heavy work of an Ombudsman in a huge federal country. The first chairman of the Commission became Deputy Prime Minister a few months after the interim report was issued, and in August the Government accepted in principle the proposal for a Lokpal.

Influenced by these recent adoptions and proposals, many other developing countries will no doubt take up the idea. The application of the system to developing countries, however, will run into special problems. A number of commentators, including myself, have argued that 'the institution will work well only in a reasonably well-administered state; it cannot cope with a situation where the civil service is riddled with patronage or corruption.'[22] Also, it may fail if it is adopted in a truncated form, or in a form that subjects it to too much partisan pressure. Unfortunately, in many developing countries the civil service *is* riddled with patronage and corruption. And the need for rapid development has put a premium on a strong executive, which is not likely to endow an Ombudsman with sufficient independence or powers of investigation, even where two or more political parties are allowed to exist. Where one party is dominant, the independence of an Ombudsman would no doubt be limited. In a one-party state the Ombudsman would almost inevitably be dominated by the executive.

---

[22] 'Ombudsmen for North America', *op. cit.*, 233.

Nevertheless, as Professor Gellhorn's chapters on the Communist states show, one-party states, too, have the problem of ensuring that minor bureaucrats in the field adhere to central policy and do not make decisions in accordance with their own personal whims or interests. For this reason, one-party states have an interest in one of the unique features of the Ombudsman system, that of providing a feedback from the people at the bottom of the administrative hierarchy to the politicians at the top. One-party states which do not have a Russian-style Procurator may therefore become interested in adopting a version of the Ombudsman plan. However, this version is likely to be a far cry from the existing schemes. It will be an arm of the executive rather than the legislature, and will probably be more like an administrative control bureau than an independent investigator.

There has already been some discussion of the Ombudsman plan for the one-party states in Africa, and one of them, Tanzania, has actually adopted a scheme influenced by the plan.[23] Tanzania's One-Party State Commission recommended in April 1965 that a five-man commission be appointed 'to enquire into allegations of abuse of power by officials of both Government and Party alike.' Accordingly, an Act was passed in March 1966 providing for a three-man Permanent Commission of Enquiry. This Commission receives complaints direct from the public and has the power of access to government documents. However, its members are appointed by the President for only two-year terms, and its first Chairman is a former Minister. It reports only to the President, he may stop any investigation, and the results of important investigations may not be made public. At the same time, the Act creating it was strongly influenced by the New Zealand model, and during their first months in office the Chairman and Secretary visited both New Zealand and Israel. The Commissioners also toured the country to publicize the scheme, and in the last half of 1966 dealt with more than 1,000 complaints.

Although there are reasons for concluding that the Ombudsman plan would not work as successfully in the developing countries, at the same time the case for its adoption is stronger there. The pressure for rapid development means that individual rights and the fine points of fair legal procedure are more likely to be disregarded in the interests of speed, efficiency and the broader public interest. The bureaucrats in many former colonies have inherited from their colonial masters an attitude of superiority rather than service, an 'insolence of office' which

[23] See Tom Sargant, Correspondence: 'The Ombudsman and One-Party States in Africa', 8 *Journal of African Law* (3, 1964), 195-7, and further correspondence by E. V. Mittlebeeler (3, 1965), 184-5, and N. M. Hunnings (2, 1966), 138-9; on the Tanzanian scheme, see United Republic of Tanzania, Presidential Commission on the Establishment of a Democratic One-Party State, *Report* (Dar Es Salaam, Government Printer, 1965); 'Tanzania: A One-Party State', *Bulletin of the International Commission of Jurists* (August 1965); and *African Recorder* (Jan. 1-14, 1966), F1245.

often leads to arbitrariness. And the people are often illiterate, with little consciousness of their legal and human rights. Even if an Ombudsman plan in these countries were to work with only half the effectiveness of the original schemes, its adoption would be well worthwhile.

In sum then, within the period since the first edition of this book the Ombudsman scheme has been adopted in five widely scattered countries: Guyana, Mauritius, the United Kingdom, Canada and the United States. Counting the previous five general systems, the military Ombudsman in Western Germany, and the Israeli State Comptroller, this means that a version of the plan now exists in twelve countries. Its likely adoption soon in many more jurisdictions in Canada and the United States, and the growing number of proposals and adoptions in other countries, lead me to believe that my tentative prediction in the concluding paragraph of this book may not be far off the mark: 'The Ombudsman institution or its equivalent will become a standard part of the machinery of government throughout the democratic world.'

Through its growing public popularity, however, there is a sense in which the Ombudsman idea may become its own worst enemy. Any kind of new complaint or appeal officer in any kind of organization is now likely to be mistakenly dubbed an Ombudsman in order to gain popular support for his activities. It is becoming all too easy to lose sight of the three essential features of the original Ombudsman systems.

These are:

(1) *The Ombudsman is an independent and non-partisan officer of the legislature, usually provided for in the constitution, who supervises the administration;*

(2) *he deals with specific complaints from the public against administrative injustice and maladministration; and*

(3) *he has the power to investigate, criticize and publicize, but not to reverse, administrative action.*

To avoid public confusion in discussing the Ombudsman idea, the use of the term 'Ombudsman' should therefore be restricted only to institutions which have this unique combination of characteristics. Otherwise, the vital importance of one or other of these characteristics may be forgotten when so-called Ombudsman plans are being proposed.

D. C. R.

October, 1967.   *Ottawa*

INTRODUCTION

In recent years the Scandinavian office of Ombudsman has gained widespread attention in the democratic world as a device for controlling bureaucracy. The Ombudsman is an officer of Parliament who investigates complaints from citizens that they have been unfairly dealt with by government departments and who, if he finds that a complaint is justified, seeks a remedy. The institution was so successful in its home countries of Sweden and Finland at helping to protect citizens against arbitrary authority that neighbouring Denmark adopted it in 1955. From there it spread to Norway and New Zealand in 1962, and now is being actively considered or discussed in countries as far apart and as different in constitutional structure as Canada, Britain, Holland, India, Ireland and the United States.

A major difficulty in discussing the scheme outside Scandinavia, however, has been the lack of full and accurate information about its actual operation. This has been largely due to language barriers. No doubt the willingness of the first Danish Ombudsman to write and to speak in English about his office has helped greatly to overcome this difficulty. His paper to a United Nations seminar held at Kandy, Ceylon, in 1959, for example, stimulated New Zealand's interest in the idea, and when it was first discussed in Britain he very willingly appeared there to give speeches and to be interviewed on television. Despite this, some misinterpretations of how the scheme actually works have managed to creep into the discussions in the English-speaking world and have been partly responsible for its rejection to date in Britain. For instance, the notion has become fixed in many people's minds that the Ombudsman is some kind of Super Administrator who has power to overrule the decisions of officials, even Ministers, and thus may interfere with ministerial responsibility to Parliament. In fact, the Ombudsman's main powers are only to investigate and recommend.

Unfortunately, even as comprehensive a study as the recent report of Justice, the British section of the International Commission of Jurists, contained inaccurate information about the scheme. It claimed that in Sweden 'all documents are made available to the Press and wide publicity is given to [an Ombudsman's] investigation in all its stages'.[1] This is simply not true. In Denmark and Norway the documents are of course not made available to the Press. But even in Sweden and Finland, where there is public access to most official documents, many files are secret (e.g. those on security matters, trade secrets and the treatment of inebriates or the mentally ill). The Press do not normally investigate the documents in other cases beyond the letter of

[1] *The Citizen and the Administration* (London, 1961), 52.

complaint, the explanations given by officials, and the Ombudsman's decision. The Ombudsman seldom holds oral hearings, and when he or some other official designated by him does so, the minutes are released but the hearings themselves are never open to the public. The names of complainants and officials involved are not ordinarily released, and the Press co-operate to prevent unnecessarily injurious publicity. The 'Justice' report may have left the impression that to adopt the Ombudsman institution would be to turn the flood-lights of publicity upon the inner workings of the administration. Actually, an Ombudsman usually conducts his investigations with far less injurious publicity than results from investigations under the Inquiries Acts in the Commonwealth countries.

It is in order to correct wrong impressions such as these, and to provide a fuller background of information and discussion for debating the Ombudsman scheme on its true merits in the many countries where it is now being considered, that this book is presented. I have assembled the present collection of essays in the belief that an adequate understanding of the Ombudsman institution can be gained only by studying the explanations of experts living in each of the countries that now has the Ombudsman institution. I have been fortunate in being able to persuade Sten Rudholm, the Swedish Chancellor of Justice, Alfred Bexelius and Hugo Henkow, the present Ombudsmen for civil and military affairs in Sweden, Paavo Kastari, a former Ombudsman in Finland, Miss I. M. Pedersen, an eminent Danish judge, Arthur Ruud, the Norwegian Ombudsman for military affairs, and Audvar Os, one of the architects of the new Ombudsman scheme for civil affairs in Norway, to write extended essays on the Ombudsman institutions in Scandinavia.

These essays reveal that significant variations exist among the Scandinavian countries in their arrangements for protecting the citizens against arbitrary authority. Sweden has no fewer than three 'guardians of the law'—the Chancellor of Justice, who is an official of the Crown, and the parliamentary Ombudsmen for civil and military affairs. Finland, like Sweden, has a Chancellor of Justice, whose office to a large extent overlaps that of the Ombudsman, but there is no separate Ombudsman for military affairs. In both of these countries, unlike Denmark and Norway, the Chancellor and the Ombudsman have the power to prosecute officials, and their work includes complaints against the courts. Norway, like Sweden, has a separate office of Ombudsman for military affairs, which was created in 1952, ten years before the adoption of the more comprehensive office for civilian affairs, and four years before the office of military Ombudsman was set up in West Germany. Of considerable significance is that Sweden and Finland have a system of administrative courts, while Denmark and Norway do not. It might have been argued that the system of administrative law in Sweden and Finland is so different from the system in the common-law countries that the Ombudsman scheme could not fit into the latter. But the cases of Denmark and Norway make this argument lose its force, as does the recent adoption of the institution in New Zealand. Contrariwise, the argument that the Ombudsman would not fit into countries that have administrative courts loses much of its force in relation to Sweden and Finland.

The Nordic democracies are not the only countries that have entertained or experimented with the idea of a 'tribune of the people' or 'inspector general'. K. C. Davis cogently argues that the same basic idea has a long tradition in the United States,[2] and W. M. Evan demonstrates in his essay the interesting parallel that exists in the office of Inspector General in the US Army. In the Philippines President Magsaysay created a Presidential Complaints Committee in 1954, and I have succeeded in persuading Professor Viloria to outline the work and success of that Committee. Another related institution is the European Commission of Human Rights, described by J. F. Smyth.

By now proposals for an Ombudsman have been made in a number of countries other than those that have already adopted the scheme, and I thought it would be of value to have these proposals presented and discussed by their supporters in these countries. The country that has discussed the idea for the longest period of time is the United Kingdom, but the only detailed proposal has been the semi-official one put forward in the 'Justice' report and rejected by the Conservative Government. The new Labour Government, however, has announced that it plans to introduce the scheme. Canada and the United States, although they have taken an interest in the institution more recently, may adopt a version of it more quickly. This is partly because they have federal governments and it can be adopted either at the national level or by the states or provinces. Indeed, it has also been advocated for large cities in these countries. In Canada a private member's Bill proposing the scheme has been introduced in the last three sessions of Parliament, and several provincial governments are actively considering the idea. Similarly in the United States, the scheme has already been proposed in some of the state legislatures, an official body has advocated it for the city of Philadelphia, and Congressman Reuss in 1963 introduced a Bill into the House of Representatives to establish an Administrative Counsel similar to the Ombudsman. Congressman Reuss and his legislative assistant have been good enough to contribute an essay outlining this proposal.

For the benefit of readers in countries interested in considering the Ombudsman system, I thought it would be helpful to include sets of contending essays which present some of the arguments for and against transplanting the institution. These countries fall naturally into three groups—those with a well developed system of administrative courts such as France and West Germany, common-law countries that have

[2] 'Ombudsmen in America', *Univ. of Penn. Law Rev.* 109 (June 1961), 1057–76.

inherited the British parliamentary system, and countries with a congressional system of government involving a separation of the exective and the legislature like the United States and the Philippines. I have therefore arranged the essays in accordance with these three groups.

A book of this nature represents a real effort in international co-operation. It includes essays by twenty-nine contributors from thirteen nations and one international authority, and involves eight languages. The difficulties of international communication become fully apparent when one works on a project of this kind. I can only hope that I have done a reasonably adequate job of putting into readable English the essays by the contributors whose mother tongue is not English, and of finding equivalent English terms where necessary. I must say, however, that I was helped immeasurably in this task by the excellent command of English possessed by most of these contributors. In the few cases where they had their essays translated for them, their knowledge of English was usually good enough for them to improve upon their translator's version!

I should like to take this opportunity to thank Carleton University for its financial support of publication and the Canada Council for a senior research fellowship and a grant that made possible visits to Europe in 1961 and 1962 and personal contacts with most of the European contributors. Above all, I should like to thank the contributors for their willing co-operation in this project. Their generosity in offering to write essays, their conscientiousness in meeting deadlines, and their patience in reviewing 'revisions of revisions' is evidence of their belief in the value of the Ombudsman idea and of their dedication to finding a solution to the problems of bureaucracy in the democratic world.

D. C. R.
Ottawa

February, 1965

CONTENTS

LIST OF TABLES

I

EXISTING OMBUDSMAN
SYSTEMS

SWEDEN'S GUARDIANS OF THE LAW

THE CHANCELLOR OF JUSTICE
by Sten Rudholm*

The office of Chancellor of Justice might be said to have been introduced by King Charles XII through his Order of the Chancery, issued in 1713. The office thus came into existence during Sweden's war with Russia under Czar Peter I. But even before 1713, in both Sweden and Finland (since the thirteenth century linked to Sweden), there were offices which to a certain extent could be considered as predecessors to the Chancellor of Justice. Thus, during the latter part of the sixteenth century, the so-styled Crown Provost supervised the public prosecutors and functioned, on behalf of the King, as the chief prosecutor. These duties were later undertaken by the Crown's Attorney at the Svea Court of Appeal in Stockholm.

The most important function of the office created in 1713—originally styled Supreme Procurator (*Högste Ombudsmannen*)—was to exercise a general supervision to ensure that laws and regulations were complied with, and that public servants discharged their duties properly. Particularly in grave matters, such as treason, the Supreme Procurator himself was to conduct the case in court. Through an additional Order of the Chancery in 1719, the name of the office was changed to the still-used Chancellor of Justice (*Justitiekansler*, in Sweden generally referred to as JK). The change of name did not signify any change in function; the institution was still to serve as a general means of controlling the state's administration from the legal point of view. Subsequent legislation, regarding the Chancery in general, as well as later instructions setting forth the duties of the JK, has to all intents and purposes maintained his original functions in regard to control and supervision. However, this does not mean that his duties in other respects, nor his general position in the administration, have always been the same. For a brief interval in the middle of the eighteenth century, the JK's position was altered in that he was no longer to be appointed by the King but by the then existing representative bodies: the four Estates. The JK's office was thereby transformed from serving

* Sweden's Chancellor of Justice.

as an agency for the King and the Councillors, to holding a post of confidence for the Estates. The office of JK during this period, from 1766 to 1772, may be regarded as the predecessor to the office of Ombudsman (*Justitieombudsman*, or JO), founded in 1809 as an institution of the four Estates. However, as a result of the *coup d'état* in 1772—staged by King Gustavus III and shifting to him the political power which since the death of King Charles XII had rested with the four Estates—the JK again became an official holding a post in the confidence of the King and the Council. And during the years just preceding 1809, the JK also served as a Councillor and acquired a position somewhat like that of a Minister of Justice.

The new polity as introduced by the Constitution of 1809—in substantial parts still in force—was founded on constitutional experience from earlier times. A division of the state's authority between the King and the Estates was established in order to prevent a one-sided wielding of power, whether by an absolute monarch as under Charles XI and Charles XII, or by the Estates as had been the situation during the eighteenth century. The executive power was left to the King and Council, while the exclusive authority to levy taxes was granted to the four Estates, and legislative power was entrusted jointly to the King in Council and the Estates. The judicial power was, as before, vested with independent courts. The control over public offices and officials was to be exercised by two separate institutions: the JK on behalf of the King and Council, and the JO on behalf of the Estates (later the *Riksdag*, or Parliament, which in 1866 succeeded the four Estates).

Through the new Constitution, the office of JK again became an independent authority under the King and Council, but without being linked to a simultaneous holding of posts as Councillor or Minister. Thus the political aspect of the JK's office, resulting from his additional duties during the years immediately preceding 1809, was removed and from then on his strictly non-political position has been maintained. Up to 1840, however, the JK as well as two Supreme Court Justices had to be present at Cabinet meetings when matters of a legal nature were to be dealt with.

A special clause in the Constitution of 1809 (paragraph 27) lays down the fundamental provisions for the office of JK. It starts with stating the general qualifications for the holder of the office: he has to be an able, impartial person, versed in the law and having had experience as a judge. The clause continues by describing, in general, the functions of the JK: in his capacity of the King's principal law officer, he must represent the Crown, or cause the Crown to be represented, in cases affecting the rights of the state, exercise supervision on behalf of the Crown over the administration of justice, and take action against judges or officials in case of dereliction of duty.

Since 1809 there have been only two changes of major importance in the JK's position and duties. One was that in 1840, mentioned above. The other resulted from the modernization in 1948 of the Swedish court procedure, which introduced oral proceedings in appellate courts, including the Supreme Court. The reformed procedure entailed a substantial increase of functions for the JK as the state's principal prosecutor. In view of his other heavy duties he was relieved of his function to prosecute in ordinary criminal cases, but he retained the power to prosecute higher officials for offences involving dereliction of duty or abuse of authority. The prosecutorial functions thus detached from the JK's office were entrusted to the newly-established office of Chief Crown Prosecutor (Riksåklagare, in Sweden generally referred to as RÅ), who at the same time became the chief administrative authority for the country's public prosecutors.

A detailed prescription of the JK's duties are set forth in an office-instruction issued by the King in Council, which was last revised in 1947. The duties could be classified in four main groups: (1) to act as the Council's principal legal adviser; (2) to represent the Crown as Attorney-General in cases affecting the state's interest; (3) to exercise supervision on behalf of the Crown over all public servants and to take action in case of abuse; (4) to carry out specific duties as detailed in the office instruction.

As the principal legal adviser, the JK gets his tasks mainly from the Council, or a member thereof as head of the Ministry concerned, requesting him to state his opinion on a matter that is subject to consideration and decision by the King in Council. The requests concern a great variety of matters, for example, questions of inalienable estates in tail, proposed changes affecting endowed funds, and generally matters where legal appraisements are to be taken into account before reaching a decision. Sometimes the subject requires elaborate juridical examination, perhaps involving legal history. And the JK is frequently requested to give his opinion on draft bills that have been prepared within the Ministry concerned or by specially assigned commissions or draftsmen. The number of matters dealt with by the JK in his capacity of legal adviser has amounted in recent years to about 200 per year.

The JK's function of representing the state's interest in civil suits where the Crown has been made a party, is not very onerous because many of the central administrative boards and agencies are authorized themselves, each in its own field, to represent the Crown in controversies. In such instances, however, the JK is to superintend the activity of the agency and, when requested, to assist with advice and instructions. The number of lawsuits in which the JK himself has represented the Crown has amounted in recent years to 25–50 per year.

Ever since the JK's office came into existence the supervision of public servants has had the leading role among the various functions of the office. This particular function is performed in a manner and form corresponding to the Ombudsmen's equivalent functions, as described in the following essays by Mr Bexelius and Mr Henkow. All officials—central as well as local—are subject to the JK's supervision, provided only that the official holds a post qualified to incur a public servant's particular responsibility as defined in the Penal Code. Exempted from his supervision are the civil and military Ombudsmen (JO and MO)—just as he is exempted from their supervision—and members of the King's Council. In regard to the latter, Sweden maintains the rule that Ministers cannot be prosecuted for offences related to their official function, unless otherwise decided by Parliament's Standing Joint Committee on the Constitution.

If by means of a complaint against an official, or if by other means such as through the press, the JK becomes aware of an act of mismanagement, he is bound to have an inquiry made and, if justified by the investigation, to have the official prosecuted in court. If the fault committed is of a lesser significance, the JK—as well as the JO and MO in their fields—might let the matter stand as it is after an explanation has been given by the official, or after a correction has been brought about. To enable the JK to exercise his supervisory task, he is provided with the same means of power as are the JO and MO. Thus he may inspect courts and public offices, attend their sessions and deliberations, and examine their records and files. Every public office and official must furnish him with any information requested. An additional aid to his supervisory function is the examination of reports submitted to him yearly by governmental branches and organs on their activities. Primarily, this examination aims to ensure that matters are being handled and decided without unnecessary delay.

What has been said indicates not only that the JK, the JO and the MO exercise a general supervision over public offices and officials, but also that these three supervisory institutions carry out their functions, broadly speaking, by similar means applied in parallel ways. It might seem strange and irrational that almost identical functions are executed by different supervisors: the JK on one side, and the JO and MO on the other. The explanation of this situation, however, is to be sought in the historical background already outlined. In order to avoid unnecessary overlapping in their activities, the JK, the JO and the MO communicate informally. This applies particularly to questions of when and where their inspection tours are to take place. Some years ago an expert commission, in examining the three offices, recommended that the JK and JO should inspect every public agency at least once during a period of ten years. Thus each agency would be visited every fifth year on an average. However, due to the extent of the JK's other functions and the growth of the state's administration, it has not been possible during the last few years to maintain the inspections on the scale recommended.

Regarding action to be taken on complaints or reports in the press, too, there are often informal contacts among the three offices in order to avoid double initiatives. The JO's activity on complaints from individuals is of considerably greater proportions, of course. When a citizen considers himself treated unjustly by a public office or official, he will as a rule find it more natural to apply to the Ombudsman as the Parliament's and the voter's own spokesman. If, on the other hand, a governmental office desires to have some action examined and verified as to its correctness, it is usually the JK who is approached as the counsel of the office's superior authority. It is certainly in the nature of things that complaints from individuals against public offices are more frequent than applications from public offices questioning their own actions or those of other public offices. Summing up, one could say that in practice there have been no real inconveniences caused by the fact that the supervisory duties of the three offices mainly coincide.

The number of cases concerning the JK's supervisory functions in recent years has averaged more than 200 new ones per year (about 40 per cent of his total number of new cases). Out of these, a good many are taken up by the JK on account of his observations at inspection tours or otherwise; the remainder emanate from reports or applications made by public offices, or from complaints lodged by individuals.

As for the fourth category of the JK's functions, his specific duties are of a rather diverse character. Here will be described only two groups of these duties, both of a certain interest in point of principle.

One group is connected with the JK's function as prosecutor for infringement of the Freedom of the Press Act (1949). The Minister of Justice is to supervise the observance of the Act, but this supervision does not include any right whatever of censorship. However, if the Minister considers that public proceedings should be instituted for an offence under the Act, he is to notify the JK and deliver to him the printed matter in question. Also, without such notification, the JK may bring an action provided that the offence constitutes a case for public prosecution. The authority for such prosecution is vested exclusively with the JK and no other prosecutors—not even the RÅ, JO or MO. It should also be noted that a private person who considers himself offended by an accusation or other libellous item published in a newspaper or otherwise, is entitled to institute proceedings even if the JK has decided not to prosecute. If the offence does not come under public prosecution—which is the case in most instances of defamation —it is always up to the aggrieved party himself to institute the proceedings. Only a few indictments per year have been made by the JK for offences under the Act. During recent years they have mainly concerned pornographic magazines.

The second main group of the JK's more specialized functions derives from the procedural reform of 1948 and its stipulations in regard to legal practitioners. Their organization, the Swedish Advocates' Association, is a private society with a charter approved by the King in Council. The professional use of the designation *advokat* is restricted by law to members of the Association. Supervision to ensure that advocates adhere to principles of prudency and professional ethics is exercised, in the first place, by the Association itself through its governing board. Disciplinary sanctions to be administered by the board are expulsion from the Association or, in less severe cases, the issuance of warnings or reminders. According to the provisions of the Law of Procedure, the JK may request disciplinary action against an advocate neglecting his duties. The JK is further authorized to appeal to the Supreme Court against the board's decision in disciplinary proceedings. In order to enable the JK to perform his task in this area, the board must submit to him all of these decisions. Although their number amounts to well over 100 per year, only in a few instances has the JK found cause to appeal to the Supreme Court.

Of course, the quantity and variety of the JK's functions make it impossible for him alone to take charge of all the matters for which he is responsible.[1] The permanent staff at his disposal is, however, not particularly numerous: for the time being, five lawyers and a few other employees. For dealing with special matters one or more expert assistants (usually lawyers with experience as judges) are occasionally called upon for limited periods of time.

The account just presented shows that the duties and functions of the JK's office are manifold and diverse. During its existence, it has been relieved of some duties but others—mainly for the protection of the citizen's legal security—have been added. Nevertheless, the JK's functions as legal adviser and as supervisor of public offices and officials are essentially the same nowadays as they were when his office was first created 250 years ago.

[1] See table in Appendix summarizing the main groups of the JK's cases.

THE OMBUDSMAN FOR CIVIL AFFAIRS
by Alfred Bexelius*

Sweden, like many other countries, has long been confronted with the problem of how best to protect her citizens from undue interference, negligence and errors by government officials. Sweden has met the problem in a number of different ways.

The right to appeal to higher authorities is the most important process for rectifying erroneous decisions. Within the various fields of government administration there is a system of appeals equivalent to that found in the judicial system. This system of appeals dates back to the days when everyone had the right to appeal unfavourabel decisions to the highest judge in the land—the King. Today this right

* Sweden's Ombudsman for Civil Affairs.

of appeal, once exercised by the King personally, extends to the highest judicial court in the nation, the Supreme Court of Justice, or in administrative matters to the Government or to the Supreme Administrative Court. The number of appeals allowed on a decision varies from one administrative are? to another. But in most cases at least two appeals are guaranteed and often as many as three can be made. In the case of income and property taxes, there are no fewer than four instances (i.e. three levels of appeal). This appeal system, as can be clearly seen, gives the citizen adequate opportunity to test the legality and fairness of any administrative decision.

In many nations it is possible to test the legality of administrative rulings in the ordinary courts. In Sweden, however, this opportunity is limited to only a few cases. In principle, the legality of administrative decisions cannot be tested in the courts. But this limitation is, of course, directly related to the number of possibilities available to appeal the rulings of subordinate administrative officials to the Government or to the Supreme Administrative Court.

One very effective means of protection Swedish citizens enjoy is that, for centuries, every judge or official has been liable to a penal responsibility, which probably goes further than in any other country. This responsibility is now expressed in this way: if a judge or a civil servant through neglect, imprudence or want of skill disregards his duties according to statutes, instructions, or the nature of his office, he shall be condemned in the ordinary courts to a fine or to suspension for neglecting his duty. This means that a Swedish civil servant can be held responsible if he acts in conflict with the nature of his service even if there are no special instructions.[1] This wide area of criminal responsibility of public servants—combined with their obligation to compensate for the damages caused by any error—has naturally developed to restrain them from submitting to any undue interference. It has also induced them to follow the letter of the law.

Further protection for the citizens was provided for in an ordinance passed in Sweden in 1766. According to the principle there established, all documents from which government officials make their decisions are public. They are available not only to the parties concerned but also to any other citizen who wishes to consult them. This privilege allows anyone to check whether the administrative rulings have been made on sufficient grounds. There are several significant exceptions to this law. One is that papers dealing with a person's private life are not available to the public. Neither are the papers where special provisions decree they must be kept secret. But there is a wide range of freedom, even in these cases, for the individual involved to acquaint himself

---

[1] *Editor's note:* The Swedish Penal Code draws a distinction between civil servants occupying entirely subordinate posts and those holding a position of some importance and independence. The latter group are subject to a particularly strict official and penal responsibility.

B *

with the relevant documents. The privilege of checking official actions is limited, however, in another way. Even given the chance to go through the papers concerned, the average citizen is hardly qualified to judge whether or not a particular ruling is legal or not. There is, therefore, need for another means to supervise administrative actions in addition to what the citizens themselves can do.

As Mr Rudholm has already pointed out, in 1713 King Charles XII, who had been out of the country at war with Russia and other lands for twelve years, decreed that there should be a supreme representative of the King—later called the Chancellor of Justice—to supervise government officials. It was soon maintained, however, that the Chancellor was not independent enough from the Government to be in a position to protect the citizens sufficiently. It was therefore held that the public authorities should also be controlled by an office entirely independent of the Government.

The response to this opinion was the creation of the post of '*Justitie-ombudsman*' (JO)[2] when the new Constitution was adopted in 1809. In this Constitution, which was influenced to a certain extent by the theories of Montesquieu, the powers of the state were divided between the King and his Council, Parliament and the courts. To balance the wide powers afforded the King and his Council, Parliament was given far-reaching means of exercising control over governmental activities. One of these means was the power to appoint an Ombudsman to make certain that the laws were adhered to by the administrative authorities and by the courts.

However, little is known in detail about what was behind the creation of the office of JO, or even with whom the proposal originated. Certainly the office was established against the wishes of the Government of that time. It was framed during discussions in the parliamentary committee that—in a few hectic weeks in the spring of 1809, when the nation was at war with Russia—was drafting the new Constitution for adoption by Parliament. Regarding the new office, the committee announced only that the general and individual rights of the people should be protected by a guardian appointed by Parliament, who should see that judges and other officials followed the laws. Thus, the office was to guarantee civil rights.

Powers of the Ombudsman

The powers of the JO as defined in the Constitution have generally remained unchanged since they were first set down. They are to supervise how judges, government officials and other civil servants observe the laws, and to prosecute those who have acted illegally or neglected their duties.

2 The Swedish word '*ombud*' refers to a person who acts as a spokesman or representative of another person. In his supervisory position the JO is a representative of the Parliament, and thereby of the citizens.

To perform his supervisory duties the J O has access to all documents
—even the secret ones—and the right to be present at all deliberations
at which judges or administrative officials make their rulings. The J O
is thereby assured a complete view of all legal and administrative
activity. Furthermore, on request all officials are obliged to provide
the J O with the information they have on a matter in question. The J O
also has the right to ask for the assistance of any official for the purpose
of making necessary investigations, and all prosecuting attorneys must
perform any prosecution the J O may decree.

Since this point is so often missed by foreign observers, it is important
to note that the J O does not have the authority to change the decisions
of courts or administrative officials. He is not a judge. In fact, according
to the early conception, he was considered to be a prosecutor. In
principle he is still a prosecutor in cases of undue interference or errors
on the part of the nation's officialdom. But the power to prosecute a
case is seldom used by the J O nowadays. In the majority of the cases
he handles, he finds that a public reprimand or criticism of the decision
is all that is necessary.

The presentation of an annual official report to Parliament is included in the duties of the J O. This report—usually 400–500 pages
long—contains an account of the work he has done, and of the investigation he has made of the 'condition of the administration of the law
of the Kingdom', including a summary of the most important cases
upon which the J O has made a ruling during the past year. It is distributed to all administrative officials, and is probably the J O's most
important means of influencing the application of the laws in Sweden.

At least formally the powers of the J O do not appear to be particularly great. The influence of the office on the legal security of the
citizens is not based on far-reaching powers. Instead, his influence is
felt as Parliament's representative and through the weight of the
arguments he cites to support his statements.

The Status of the Ombudsman

The Ombudsman is, of course, both formally and in reality entirely
independent of the Government. A remarkable feature of the office, in
the form given to it by the Parliament of 1809, is its independence not
only of the Government but also of Parliament itself. As expressed by
the first holder of the office, the J O is made dependent only on the law.
He decides for himself which subjects he shall investigate and makes
his own decision on what action should be taken. This means that he
does not receive any instruction as to which cases he should investigate.
Nor will anybody in Parliament try to influence him to act in a certain
direction when he is investigating a particular case. Throughout the
history of the office there is no evidence whatsoever in the annual
reports to support an assumption that undue influences have ever been
exerted on the Ombudsman.

The political parties in Parliament always try to unite in the selection of an Ombudsman.[3] This is done to ensure that the JO's decisions are made without regard to political pressure and that the general public may have full confidence in his political independence. With very few exceptions, the Ombudsman has been chosen from the justices of the courts; and the JO's office staff, which includes six jurists, are appointed by the JO himself.

Officials Under the JO's Jurisdiction

In principle and with few exceptions the JO's supervision embraces all national and municipal officials. Members of the Government, however, are exempt from his control. This stipulation relates to a constitutional provision that only the King decides executive matters. The Ministers are, at least formally, only his advisers. Under present conditions, however, it is the Ministers who exercise the real power.

In Denmark and Norway the Ministers are under the supervision of the Ombudsman. In Sweden, however, no opinion has been expressed that the JO's authority should be extended to the Ministers as well. To maintain public confidence, the JO must avoid political conflicts. This is an essential advantage in his work. If he were required to intervene against the Government he could easily become involved in the struggle between the political parties. Moreover, how the Ministers perform their duties is controlled by Parliament. Parliament may also order the prosecution of a Minister before a special court. The JO acts as prosecutor in cases of this kind. However, since 1854 no legal proceedings have been initiated against a Minister.

Before judging whether there is any real need to extend the JO's control to Ministers, it must be kept in mind that in Sweden the administrative departments are independent of the Ministers. A Swedish Minister cannot give administrative officials binding orders when dealing with particular matters. The officials have only to follow the laws; their position of independence is almost the same as that of the courts. In principle the Government can influence administrative officials only by issuing general orders and instructions in Council. Consequently, in Sweden the Ministers have no political responsibility for the measures that are decided upon by subordinate, but independent, officials. Accordingly, it is only the Ministers themselves and things which are done under their direct responsibility that do not come under the JO's jurisdiction.

From the beginning the JO's supervision also embraced all military commanders and officers of lower rank. Since 1915, however, these officers have been under the jurisdiction of a separate Ombudsman—the *Militieombudsman* or MO. His field—described more fully in a later section—is much the same as the JO in the civilian sphere.

With regard to members of the Supreme Court of Justice and members of the Supreme Administrative Court, the control of the JO is limited in such a way that action can be instituted against a member of one of these courts only when a serious misdemeanour has been committed. No such action has ever been instituted.

There is no such limitation on other judges. It has been suggested —although not in Sweden—that this arrangement might endanger the independence of the courts, that the threat of intervention by the Ombudsman might cause a judge to act contrary to what otherwise he would have done. Experience shows, however, that Swedish judges are not influenced in their decisions by the power of the JO to survey the activities of the courts. The JO cannot change the decisions of a court. Once it is accepted that a judge should be punished by a higher court for an abuse of his powers, his independence cannot be harmed by the additional fact that the prosecution of the offence may be made on the initiative of the JO. The claim to an independent position does not necessarily mean that a judge should be free from responsibility or criticism when acting against the law. From the JO's annual reports of the past 150 years, anybody may see that there has been a need for the supervision of judges as well as other officials. It is to be noted that only the King's Chancellor, the JO and the MO may order the prosecution of judges and other high officials for neglect of duty. When the JO has intervened, it has been a case of clear and obvious infringement of the law, delay in trying a case, or improper conduct by the judge against the parties or witnesses concerned. A few years ago, for example, a judge was condemned after the JO had indicted him for extensively helping a lawyer friend in cases which were outside his own jurisdiction as judge.

Where the error is of lesser significance, the JO criticizes the judge instead of initiating prosecution. Criticism of judges is of course made with the greatest caution. The criticism is seldom directed against the actual decision in a case. It refers more generally to the way the case was dealt with. This criticism in no way harms the independence of the judges in arriving at a just decision.

One example can be given, however, in which criticism was directed against the decision itself. Swedish law states that a person under 18 years of age may be sentenced to prison only under aggravating circumstances. Recently the JO was called upon to review a case where a judge had sentenced two boys—aged 15 and 16—to six months' suspended sentence for the theft of a pair of unlocked motor scooters of little value. The boys had never been in trouble before. In reviewing the case the JO could not find any 'aggravating circumstances' to warrant disregarding the principal theme of the law. He therefore asked the judge for an explanation of his sentence. The judge explained that he thought the boys should know what to expect if they did not behave themselves in the future. However, the preamble to the law had stated that this was not reason enough to circumvent the principle that minors under 18 years of age should not be sentenced to jail. In this case the JO could not avoid criticizing the judge. The criticism amounted to a reference to the foundations for the law, and a reminder of how the framers of the law had intended the courts to handle a matter of this kind.

Until recently officials of municipal governments were exempt from the JO's supervision. In 1957 this was changed. Now all municipal boards and officials—but not elected members of municipal councils—are subjected to the JO's attention. However, where there is no question of actions against personal liberty or evident abuse of powers, the JO is not to interfere until the possibilities of correction by municipal authorities or by appeal have been tried.

How the Supervision Is Carried Out

The JO has great freedom to decide the direction of his supervisory activity. Actually, it is determined principally by the complaints that are brought to him by the citizens. In earlier days, his interventions were seldom based on complaints. Only about 70 a year were received in the first 100 years of the office's existence. But in recent years the number of cases has risen to about 1,000 a year. Probably there would be fewer appeals if administrative officials would explain their decisions in greater detail. In a good many cases the petitioner does not understand why the official ruled as he did and therefore imagines he has been discriminated against; all the JO needs to do is explain to the petitioner the reasons for the decision.

Complaints must, of course, be conveyed in writing. However, this does not stop someone displeased with an official decision from calling on the JO or one of his assistants and presenting his grievance orally. The complainant usually draws up his appeal without the help of a lawyer; the JO and his assistants have extensive experience in figuring out exactly what the petitioner is aiming at.

The first step taken in handling a complaint is to request from the authorities concerned the documents in the case. It is usually possible to judge from these documents alone if there is sufficient cause for the complaint. The JO must not unnecessarily overload officials with statements and investigations. However, if it is not clear that the complaint is unwarranted, he requests further written information from the authority concerned. Yet more than half of all petitions are dismissed without burdening the official with any further statement.

If the written material—the complaint, the documents, and the statement from the official involved—does not indicate sufficient foundation for a judgment on the official's ruling, the JO may ask the police for a closer investigation and questioning of the persons involved. The JO himself may also hold a hearing, or assign the questioning to one of his assistants. If the judgment demands knowledge of some special field, the expert relevant governmental authority is obliged to assist the JO in his investigation, and to render an opinion.

The JO often initiates investigations without being motivated by a complaint. He frequently undertakes these on the basis of reports on the activities of the courts or administrative officials that appear in the newspapers. Moreover, a great many matters are taken up as the result of observations made during inspections. Checking the work of officials while he is on inspection tours is probably the most important sphere of the JO's activity. Every year he and/or his assistants visit courts, prosecutors, police authorities and government officials of all types. By talking with the officials and by examining random documents, they check to see that the cases have been legally tried and decided upon, and that prompt action has been taken. The JO also personally inspects jails, guard rooms, mental hospitals, institutions for alcoholics, and homes for wayward children. Through conversations with the officials and inmates he meets on each visit, he can ascertain for himself whether or not the inmates are being properly treated.

During the past few years an important phase of the JO's supervisory activity has been to conduct special investigations of administrative practices in various fields. These investigations include the study of a great number of documents requested from different authorities but dealing with similar cases and rulings. The investigations have been aimed at two objectives in particular. One is to study the administrative authorities' explanations of their decisions. The other is to see whether the party concerned has had a chance to comment on the material upon which the official has based the decision. Special investigations have also been made of compulsory admissions to mental hospitals and work houses; and the courts' application of the laws on drunken driving has also been the object of a very extensive investigation that included the co-operation of the nation's foremost medical experts. Finally, a similar investigation has been made of the authorities' inconsistent practices in revoking driving licences.

The information revealed by these nation-wide investigations is placed at the disposal of the country's officials so they can judge for themselves what is the best practice. Unfortunately the JO's resources do not allow investigations of this type to be done to the extent that seems desirable.

Steps Taken When Faults Are Found

By means of the supervision just described, many faults and acts of negligence are of course found, against which action has to be taken in various ways. At first the JO almost exclusively ordered prosecution before the courts. Even minor faults, which had caused no harm to private citizens, were dealt with in this manner. Soon, however, entirely outside the JO's instructions, a practice was developed in minor cases to replace prosecution with a reminder to the official concerned that his handling of the case had been faulty or improper. Today, therefore, prosecution is much less frequent than before. During the last few years the number of prosecutions before the courts has not amounted to more than five cases a year. Giving reminders is, consequently, the manner of proceeding against faults and negligence which the JO now uses in the great majority of cases.

The power of prosecution is used whenever a case of arrogance or improper conduct appears. These cases were common in the nineteenth century but are rare today. What is prosecuted, above all, is the disregard of legal rights, the maintenance of which is essential in a democratic society. If the individual sustains damages because of an error, the JO usually prosecutes for the mistake in order to give the individual an opportunity to file for damages.

It should be pointed out that too great a tendency to waive prosecution for obvious errors is dangerous. There should be no doubt in the public's mind of the general will to protect the citizens from undue interference and serious faults by the authorities. The satisfactory functioning of the complex machinery of society demands that private individuals be judged in court on all kinds of insignificant violations of the rules of order; and the circumstances are taken into consideration only in setting the extent of the punishment.

It therefore appears to be a neglect of the principle that everyone is equal under the law when cases coming under the criminal law for official errors are not prosecuted, especially if they concern high officers who, with their intelligence, education and experience, ought to know how to act properly.

If it is not a question of errors which appear to be serious from this point of view, a reminder is the most common form of intervention nowadays. The aim of such a reminder is not only to give the erring official a reprimand, but also to achieve the longer-range effect of protecting the legal security of the citizen through preventing a repetition by other officials. As all the more important cases are presented in the JO's annual report, the reminders help to spread a knowledge of the contents of the law and of desirable procedural principles of justice. In this manner the JO can contribute considerably to greater legal security. As a prerequisite, however, he must not be content simply to state his opinion about what is right. He must support his statements with clearly stated, convincing reasons.

Over the years the JO's practice of issuing reminders has sometimes aroused the indignation and irritation of the civil servants and their reaction has frequently won support in the press. The argument has been advanced that the official subject to criticism by the JO has no opportunity to have the legitimacy of the criticism tested before a court. It has also been disputed whether the JO should have any duties other than to prosecute and to recommend alterations of the law. In 1908 this conception also found support within Parliament. However, on that occasion an MP gathered a number of other members for a motion of confidence in the JO and in the general practice of the office. It was argued then that the whole supervision of the observance of the law would be meaningless if the JO were not allowed to render statements on the legal understanding of the law. Later, in 1915, the JO's old practice of giving reminders in connection with errors and negligence was written into the formal instruction for the office.

It should be noted that this practice of giving reminders is mainly in the interest of the public officials themselves because a reminder is considered a lesser evil than being prosecuted for the fault. In cases of admitted errors and negligence there should, therefore, be no apprehension against this form of intervention. If, however, the official concerned disputes that he has acted in error, the JO usually feels obliged to refer the case to the courts by prosecuting for the fault. But such protests from public officials who have been reprimanded are rare.

Intervention by the JO is not limited to dealing with the mistakes and acts of negligence that have been committed. He also follows up to see if the injured parties have been compensated. When ordering a prosecution, the JO always instructs the prosecutor, whom he appoints, to give the wronged party free legal aid in claiming damages. When a fault appears excusable, and the JO therefore wants to avoid a court prosecution, the JO gives the erring official an opportunity to give redress to the wronged party. This may obviously give rise to the justified remark that the JO thereby exercises constraint upon the official concerned, a situation which may seem unfortunate because no appeal can be made against the JO's decision. However, this procedure is seldom resorted to, and only in cases where rather small amounts of damages are involved. Such cases are always accounted for in the annual report.

The JO may also appeal to the Government for compensation to a complainant and such an appeal is nearly always successful. For example, a few years ago when the police were rounding up a gang of hooligans that had been making a disturbance, a photographer who had just come out of a restaurant was hit by a police sword and had to be treated at the hospital. He then appealed to the JO. A follow-up investigation could not determine which police officer had inflicted the wound. The JO therefore wrote to the Government requesting compensation for the photographer, and the request was approved. In another case a court had unjustly ordered an arrested person to pay costs of his own return from the USA to Sweden for trial. The party had complained to the JO on another aspect of the case. But in his review the JO discovered that the complainant had been erroneously made to pay his own transportation costs. Since the law was not clear in regard to the obligation to repay transportation costs, the judge could not be held responsible for the error. But the JO wrote to the

Government and requested that the man be reimbursed. This request was also granted. In cases of unjust punishment the JO has tried to help the convicted person either to get a new trial or to appeal to the Government for clemency.

Faulty but not Punishable Interpretations of the Law

The laws regulating the activity of administrative authorities are often vaguely worded and provide a wide scope for varied interpretation. Through appeals, however, uniform practices are gradually formed. In the course of his supervisory activity the JO frequently discovers individual officials diverging from established practice. However, officials in Sweden are not bound by precedent. It is impossible to say, then, that an official who diverges from the generally accepted practice of the law has committed a punishable error. Yet the importance of a uniform application of the law has made it desirable for the JO to intercede in such cases, even though the instruction governing his office does not specify such action.

As an example, the JO noticed on an inspection trip a few years ago that one county board had been interpreting the law on the treatment of alcoholics in a much stricter sense than other county boards. In several cases the county board had ordered compulsory confinement to homes for alcoholics. This appeared to be in conflict with the origin and purpose of the law and the practice of the Supreme Administrative Court and the other counties. It did not conflict with the letter of the law, however. The officials had committed no punishable error. Yet if the JO had not intervened in this case, he would hardly have been acting in accordance with his duty to watch over the rights of the citizens. He must try to prevent compulsory confinement when this is not in harmony with the intent of the law and its interpretation as generally accepted in practice. The JO therefore wrote to the county board and reviewed the motivation for the law and the high court's interpretation. He pointed out that the board's rulings did not agree with the accepted application of the law. The JO thus avoided the impression that the board's action constituted a punishable error. He simply stated that this conception of how the law should be interpreted ought to be considered in future cases of a similar nature.

The common interest in avoiding any deprivation of freedom that conflicts with the practice of the Supreme Administrative Court and with the purpose although not the letter of the law, has justified the JO's action in such cases. He calls the official's attention to what may be considered to be the valid legal position. The JO's annual report also contains a series of statements on how certain laws should be properly interpreted and applied. Without asserting that an opposing interpretation constitutes an error in the performance of duty, the JO can expound in some detail the basis of the law and case practice. Usually the JO avoids taking up doubtful interpretations of the law.

Moreover, he seldom criticizes a court's interpretation of the law except for cases in which the application is so obviously incorrect that it involves a punishable fault. And in regard to administrative officials, the JO usually avoids raising the issue of interpretation of the law (except in cases of error, of course) when the question can be solved by a ruling from the Supreme Administrative Court.

The boundaries are vague, however. Sometimes it is difficult to avoid taking a stand on certain interpretive questions when the complaint is directed at the interpretation of the law itself. In cases where it seems desirable to take a position, the JO usually gathers material for a correct decision by drawing on the experiences and viewpoints of other officials and organizations. He feels it is sufficient to illuminate the legal question—without directing any criticism—and to express his own opinion. To local authorities who are not able to gather similar statements in the same way, this type of clarification of legal questions can often be valuable. In such cases—where the question is not one of error—the influence of the JO's statement is completely dependent on the reasons he cites for his opinion. If an official has a different opinion he is, of course, free to follow it. And it must be remembered that since the JO's activity is controlled by Parliament, an improper statement on his part is always subject to criticism. It would not be wise to deny the JO the chance to give a legal interpretation that can help alleviate errors and hardships for the private citizen. The need of the citizens for legal protection should be given great weight in this evaluation.

Recommended Changes in the Law

When considering complaints or on inspection tours, the JO frequently observes shortcomings in legislation. It is his duty to comment on these and to recommend improvement. In the nineteenth century successive Ombudsmen recommended several important reforms. Their requests were not always acceded to, it is true, but the various holders of the office were undaunted and often returned to the charge. One of them, Mr Landin, was particularly successful. Thus, it was upon his proposal that, in 1840, Parliament enacted a reform to the effect that persons unable to pay fines should no longer be flogged but given a term of imprisonment on bread and water. At the same time, the rules concerning such imprisonment were mitigated, likewise on the initiative of Landin. He was also successful in obtaining the abolition of a statute of 1752 according to which the Courts of Appeal could order the drawing of lots in cases of manslaughter in which more than one person had participated and it could not be found out which of the accused was responsible for the physical impact actually causing death. Another Ombudsman proposed joint deliberations of the divisions of the Supreme Court in order to avoid frequent changes of judicial practice. In 1879 the JO demanded the creation of an institution to which the courts should send reports on convicted persons, and from which information about such persons could be given to courts and prosecutors. This reform had to wait until 21 years later, when the Register of Convicted Persons Act was passed.

In our days—when reform work is carried on with greater intensity— this part of the JO's task has less significance. Yet every year he still makes several petitions for change to the Government.

Let me give an example of how the Ombudsman acts in this connection. A couple of years ago a Stockholm paper reported that an alcoholic in a drunken condition had stabbed his wife to death, yet four days before this the wife had notified the police that her husband was a dangerous alcoholic and that she felt threatened. The JO saw the newspaper report and began to investigate whether the police ought to have taken care of the man after the wife had complained about him. The investigations showed that the police had immediately taken the man into custody and questioned him on his alleged danger and threats to his wife. The law did not permit the police to keep the husband in custody more than 24 hours unless legal grounds existed to force him into an institution for alcoholics. No such conditions appeared during their scanty investigation, and they were powerless to hold him as a dangerous alcoholic. They had to release him after 24 hours, and the tragic consequences followed. The JO found that the police should have been able to make the necessary investigation in the time allowed. He considered, however, that their negligence did not constitute a punishable fault, due to special circumstances surrounding their investigation. He therefore found it necessary only to criticize the police, and to give his opinion on how the case should have been handled. In addition, however, he wrote to the Government and suggested a change in the law that would give the police increased power to hold anyone suspected of being a dangerous alcoholic in order to give them enough time to make an investigation. The suggestion made by the JO was, of course, designed to increase the legal protection of citizens threatened by alcoholics.

Typical Groups of Cases

The legal control of official decisions is often considered to be only a question of whether an official has the formal authority to make the decision under discussion. But the legal supervision by the JO includes the question of whether a decision is materially justified, that is whether the decision is founded on the actual facts in the particular case. Because of greatly varying conditions the law must give officials sufficiently wide latitude to act in accordance with the circumstances. For this reason the authority of the JO to interfere in cases where the law has delegated to an agency the power to make discretionary decisions, has been questioned. But the purpose of the JO's office—to be a guardian of the citizens' public and individual rights—cannot be achieved if he is not allowed to control discretionary decisions. In many cases it is impossible to distinguish between legal and discretionary questions. When the law gives an official the right to act according to discretion, it does not mean the official may act arbitrarily in that area. It means only that the authority may make its decision with regard to the circumstances in the particular case. In this connection only such circumstances may be taken into account as have been ascertained by objective evidence.

Even when there is a rather wide margin for administrative discretion, there are certain limitations that must not be overstepped. If, for instance, an official neglects to take action when action is called for, he has undoubtedly proceeded contrary to the law. This can be illustrated with an example. A few years ago the JO saw fit to prosecute a district judge because he failed to appoint defence counsel for a person charged with a crime. According to Swedish law, the judge in uncomplicated criminal cases has a certain latitude for deciding if a defence counsel is to be appointed. The accused was a 16-year-old German girl, a maid, who did not speak Swedish and who was prosecuted for having taken a few minor things valued at about 80 crowns. The girl, who admitted having taken the things, did not know anybody in Sweden from whom to obtain advice. Further, how her offence was to be labelled in the law seemed very uncertain. The solution of this point of law carried fundamental consequences with regard to the punishment for the offence and, especially, to the possibility of expulsion from the country. The girl was condemned to two months' work under the supervision of a probation office, and to expulsion from the country. To the JO, it was evident that in the circumstances the failure of the judge to appoint defence counsel was against the spirit of the law, that the judge had no right to use his discretionary powers in this way and that, therefore, he had acted wrongly.

Now and then the JO is compelled to act on a decision that formally agrees with the law but which has been taken to fulfil another aim than that foreseen in the law. This can happen when an official is charged with granting permits. The following may be mentioned as an example. Foreigners are not as a rule allowed to have work in Sweden without a special permit. The aim of the law is to prevent foreigners from working where there are many Swedish unemployed. The central board, which had to give such permits, gave them on condition that the foreigner join the trade union concerned. This condition was not in accordance with the aim of the law, and the JO had to criticize the board.

The JO's control embraces not only the nature or content of decisions. It also of course covers the procedural handling of cases, i.e. questions of due process. This is of special importance with regard to the administrative agencies, since the administrative process—as already mentioned—is largely not regulated by law but has been developed by practice instead. Therefore, it is important that the JO, possessing a general survey of the entire administrative field, takes up questions of principle for discussion on the basis of practical cases. When inspecting administrative agencies, usually the JO and his assistants first investigate, by random selection of cases, how the agency observes the fundamental principles of justice in the administrative process. Thus, the JO specially investigates whether sufficient evidence has been collected, whether a party has been given an opportunity to answer evidence against him, and whether the agency, when this is called for, has sufficiently explained the grounds of a decision. Quite frequently grave and surprising defects are found, which are to be seen against the background that administrative procedure is not regulated by law.

What Faults Have Caused Intervention

During the nineteenth century the control by the JO was chiefly directed against courts, prosecutors, the police and the prisons. It is quite natural that the controlling activity of the Ombudsman should have been concentrated in this way. Throughout this period the local civil service was small. The members of the old rural community had few contacts with public servants other than the officers of justice. Thus, it was natural that inspections should be essentially confined to the courts of justice. Gradually, however, the civil service increased, and as early as 1904, in the course of its examination of the JO's activities, the Standing Parliamentary Committee on Legislation pronounced it desirable 'that, in so far as his other official duties allowed, the Ombudsman should pay attention also to the way in which administrative authorities discharged their duties. If this could be done, there would be reason to expect sound proposals for such reforms in the administration as are necessary and useful to the public.' However, this advice effected no significant change in the Ombudsman's range of activity, possibly because the holders of the office were taken from the judiciary and were therefore not well acquainted with civil service practices. It is only during the last few years that the administration has become the main subject for the activities of the JO.

When perusing the yearly reports, one is astonished at the insignificant number of really flagrant violations of the law which have caused intervention. The explanation would seem to be that such crimes are rare among Swedish officials, and also that the JO's control does not concern, and is not intended to concern, the administration of public money entrusted to public servants. Abstractions of money have, therefore, normally been the subject of action by other prosecutors.

Some time ago an American journalist who was preparing to write an article about the Ombudsman repeatedly asked whether the holders of the post had ever done anything really remarkable. He was not greatly impressed by some of the cases mentioned to him. Indeed, there have been no sensational inquisitions of corrupt officials through-out the history of the JO's office, nor can its activities be described as a dangerous struggle against injustice and oppression. There is no reason, however, to blame the Ombudsman for this. Apart from social injustice outside his sphere of action, such cases of real maladministration have simply not existed. This does not mean, however, that the office has been unnecessary. Just as a drop wears away a stone by falling repeatedly, so the innumerable comments on the proper meaning of the law which have emanated from the JO's office during the past 150 years have influenced the way in which public officials perform their duties.

It is only natural that, ever since the creation of the office, control over imprisonments should have been one of the JO's most important tasks. The yearly reports give an account of innumerable actions against imprisonments which have been held unlawful for one reason or another. Many actions have been brought against judges who have committed accused persons to arrest on the basis of insufficient investigation. The requirement that a person should not be arrested unless the charge against him is founded upon evidence of some plausibility was not upheld as strictly in the old days as it is now. The truth of this statement appears in the report of an earlier Ombudsman who reported that both the Court of Appeal and the Supreme Court had dismissed an action brought by him against a borough court. In 1880 that court had heard an accusation against a woman charged with attempting to utter a false coin, and in two separate sessions had ordered her to be kept in prison although no examination of the coin had taken place. The coin turned out to be genuine, and had merely been in contact with quicksilver. The outcome of his action against the members of the borough court gave the Ombudsman reason to draw the attention of the legislature to the need for appointing lawyers as counsel for the defence in cases where the accused had been arrested.

A great number of actions have further been directed against prosecutors, judges and county courts for neglecting to hear and decide with sufficient speed cases where the accused has been arrested. In this respect, things have improved enormously since the last century. Whereas nowadays the standing question when inspecting courts and prosecutors' offices is how many *months* elapse between the crime and the punishment, the corresponding length of time was earlier calculated in years. This slowness was partly caused by the rules of procedure. In the course of the years the Ombudsmen have made numerous requests for measures intended to hasten legal proceedings. In many cases, however, the slowness was due to neglect. One can understand that diligence and order could be lacking when one finds in old records of inspections that there were judges who had neglected for years to hand down their decisions in chronological order as prescribed by law. Such neglect was, of course, prosecuted.

Prison administration has been the object of the JO's never-failing attention. All prison establishments have been inspected repeatedly, and on these occasions the prisoners have always been allowed to speak to the Ombudsman. This tradition began with the first Ombudsman, who took a great interest in the more humane treatment of prisoners, as his numerous requests on this topic to the Government bear witness. He denounced the demoralizing influence of prison life on the convicts, and demanded a thorough reorganization of the methods of punishment.

An extreme example of what faults could be discovered in an inspection of a prison in earlier times may be mentioned. During an inspection of the debtor's prison at Stockholm, in January 1825, the JO observed that among the prisoners was a brewer who had been kept there since December 1803. In February 1805 he had been sentenced to imprisonment for fraud by the Court of Appeal, but had lodged an appeal with the Supreme Court. The documents of the case had accordingly been delivered to the Masters of the Supreme Court in April 1805, and the case had been entered on the lists. However, in 1807 it had been removed, allegedly because the documents had disappeared. At the action of the Ombudsman, the King in Council saw fit 'graciously' to exempt the man from any further penalty!

Another illustration of how little respect the authorities had for the liberty of the individual may be given. At one time persons without an independent livelihood had to pursue a 'lawful occupation'. Otherwise, they were liable to be arrested as vagabonds and set to work. A woman who had obviously been a vagabond in her earlier days was given a hearing in order to find out whether she had a lawful occupation. She then gave incorrect information about herself and her circumstances. On this ground, a county board in 1838 ordered that she should be committed to the prison of Gothenburg and there be kept in a private cell until reliable information about her could be found—an order which was perfectly lawful at the time. Ten years later, when examining the prisoners' lists, the JO discovered that the woman was still being kept in prison. After he had demanded information about the matter, the county board took steps in December 1848 to settle the affair, and after handling it with the normal speed of that time was able, in August 1849, to decide that the woman should be released. The governor of the county was prosecuted by the JO for neglecting during the long period from 1838 to 1848 to gather information about the woman.

During the latter part of the nineteenth century and the first two decades of the twentieth, the Ombudsman had to intervene on innumerable occasions, in his capacity as custodian of civil rights, against violations of the freedom to hold public meetings. In our days, when we have grown accustomed to the idea that anyone may freely express his opinion on any subject, we are apt to be surprised at the sensitiveness of the authorities in those days. Thus, in 1887 the mayor and aldermen of a town saw fit to issue a prohibition against a speech by a celebrated economist on the subject: 'The Increase in Sweden's Population and its Dangers for Public Welfare and Morals.' In the opinion of these magistrates his well-known views on these matters were repugnant to good morals and the law of the land. As the meeting had been duly announced to the authorities and no permit was required under the law, upon the action of the JO the magistrates were fined 20–30 crowns each. Another speaker was forbidden by the magistrates of another town to lecture on the subjects: 'Is There a Life Beyond the Grave?' and 'Is Christianity a Religion for our Time?' In this and other similar cases the Ombudsman intervened, and the responsible magistrates were fined. The penalties imposed in such actions were small, but there can be no doubt that these interventions of the JO, with the support of the superior courts, put an end to further attempts to encroach upon the freedom of public meetings.

In Sweden the principal local authorities may issue certain ordinances. Throughout the history of the Ombudsman's office, its holders have always had to intervene against local regulations which had been issued without statutory support or which curtailed the freedom of the public without sufficient reason. An example—only a few years old—helps to illustrate the nature of the JO's vigilance in this area. In Sweden the general traffic regulations are issued by the Government under laws passed by Parliament. The local police authorities, however, have the authority to issue traffic safety ordinances as dicated by local conditions. In a little town in south Sweden, where young boys used to drive around on motorcycles without silencers and make a terrible noise to the annoyance of ordinary people, the chief of police got the idea of issuing a traffic ordinance to put an end to the noise. He decreed a general prohibition against driving motorcycles in the town between the hours of 9 o'clock at night and 6 o'clock in the morning; this prohibition did not include travel to and from the place of work or other journeys deemed absolutely necessary. At the same time, the police were instructed to stop only those who used their vehicles in such a manner as to cause a disturbance, i.e. young motor enthusiasts. The prohibition immediately became popular with the general public and the newspapers praised the chief of police, which caused chiefs of police in other cities to hasten to issue similar prohibitions. It was then the JO's duty to explain to the police chiefs that they were not allowed to use their power to issue a traffic ordinance for a purpose other than traffic security. To put an end to the noise was a purpose which fell outside the legislation giving the police chiefs the power to issue traffic ordinances.

However, a national committee had at about the same time proposed an amendment to the law which would give the police chiefs express power to decree such prohibitions. The proposal was recommended by all the administrative agencies which had to give their opinion on the committee's report. This caused the JO to write to the Government and advise against accepting the committee's proposal. The problem of the noise made by the young motorists could be dealt with by other means, and from the point of view of protection of rights it was important that the legislator should not, without very strong reasons, give the administration powers to introduce general restrictions on the citizen's movements—powers that were liable to lead to prohibitions for which there was no real cause. Of course, this action was not popular, and the papers carried harsh comments on the JO. However, the Government accepted his opinion, and the committee's proposal was rejected.

Throughout the history of the office the Ombudsmen have had to interfere against improper behaviour towards petitioners and the abuse of official positions. To judge from the yearly reports, the need for intervention has diminished as the years have passed. But the JO can still be required to intervene in cases of abuse of power by higher officials. A few years ago he had to prosecute a bishop who had exceeded his authority towards a subordinate priest. The priest, who wanted to be elected rector in a parish, had had voting papers printed with his name on them, and these were distributed to parish members before the election. This in itself does not constitute an offence under Swedish law. But it does conflict with the practice that a priest may not work for his own election. Upon hearing about the episode, the bishop wrote to the priest that he was to announce in the local newspapers that, for reasons for which he was not without guilt, he was no longer a candidate for the election. The bishop also wrote that if the priest did not comply he would take disciplinary action. The JO heard of the affair when it came out in the press, and began an investigation. The result was that the bishop was prosecuted for exerting unauthorized pressure on the priest. The bishop disputed the prosecution, maintaining that civil authorities may not intervene in the fulfilment of his duties. The Supreme Court ruled, however, that since Sweden has an established Church the bishop came under the court's jurisdiction, and so he had to pay a fine for his error.

A Summary of the JO's Aims

When the office of Ombudsman was instituted in Sweden it was intended that the JO should act as a guardian of the people's common and individual rights. In other words, he should try to prevent the abuse of powers by the authorities and, in this way, be a protector of the citizen's security under the laws. This purpose remains the same today as 150 years ago. However, in the society of today his duty is discharged in a different way. Initially the role of the Ombudsman was thought of as that of a prosecutor in proceedings taken against judges and civil servants. Thus, the purpose was to be achieved by means of the general preventive effect of the prosecution. However, quite early it became the practice in minor cases to substitute public prosecution with a reminder.

The mere existence of an Ombudsman, independent of the bureaucracy, to which anybody may carry his complaints, will act to sharpen the attention of the authorities in dealing with cases and to counteract tendencies toward abuse of powers and arbitrary decisions. Of necessity this preventive function supposes energetic activity on the part of the Ombudsman. No official likes to be exposed before the general public and his colleagues. Awareness of the fact that an official action may be questioned by the Ombudsman will certainly ensure that officials take greater pains in doubtful cases.

This preventive effect of the existence of the office—which is of great importance for legal security—is certainly strengthened by the Ombudsman having power to institute public prosecution for faults and negligence of a serious nature that cause general insecurity with regard to citizens' rights. Fortunately nowadays such faults are rare. However, when they appear they are always prosecuted in court. Because of the attention devoted in the press to cases prosecuted by the Ombudsman, and because of the detailed account of such cases given in the Ombudsman's annual reports, the extreme importance of not overstepping proper limits is very forcefully brought home to the civil service.

The tremendous expansion of government activities and the great number of statutes and rules make it impossible, of course, for officials to entirely avoid making errors or oversights in the fulfilment of their duties. A number of the mistakes committed, however, are not of a serious nature and do not cause a loss of legal rights to the party concerned—for instance, neglect of certain procedural rules, or failure to give information regarding decisions taken. In particular cases oversights of this kind may seem trifling and inconsequential. On the side of the officials, it is often maintained that the Ombudsman should not concern himself with such errors. However, it would be unfortunate and damaging to legal security if they were consistently left without criticism. Procedural rules are necessary to safeguard important public and private interests, and their neglect may, in the long run, add up to a serious loss of the citizens' rights. To avoid this it is necessary to criticize errors and to remind administrative agencies of the regulations in force. By doing this the Ombudsman prevents faults and oversights damaging to individuals without having to resort to public prosecution of the guilty official.

When the Ombudsman criticizes an official at fault, the criticism is worded in such a way as to serve as information to other officials. Knowledge of the law is disseminated due to the fact that all important faulty decisions are accounted for in the Ombudsman's annual report. The JO thus makes a substantial contribution to better practice and this improves the legal security of the citizens.

Nowadays statutes cannot always contain clear and exhaustive directions to the administration. Often there is left a rather wide margin of freedom of action to the agencies. As a result, actual practice in the treatment and judging of similar cases may differ between various agencies. Yet it seems highly desirable that this varying practice should, as far as possible, become uniform. Consistency in the application of the law is of importance to prevent the impression on the part of the general public that cases are arbitrarily decided and that exceptions are made to the principle of everybody being equal before the law. The Ombudsman's actions help to achieve this consistency.

To the citizens it is of great value that there is an independent office that may take up questions of legal security against the background of actual cases. In the administrative field—where there is no counterpart to the civil law statute on court procedure—there are many questions of principle which in order to be treated by statute have to be investigated in the light of actual practice. The JO has undertaken many investigations of this kind in connection with inspections and the examinations of complaints, and these have resulted in petitions for legislative action to strengthen legal security in the administrative field.

One important aspect of the Ombudsman's activity that is frequently overlooked is the rejection of unwarranted complaints. Obviously it is of great interest to the official attacked that accusations of abuse are not left open, and that it is made evident by an impartial agency that the complaints were not justified. Also, it is of great importance that accusations made in the press, or otherwise, regarding abuse by the authorities are taken up for investigation by an agency free of bureaucratic influence, and that these investigations are available and the true facts made known to the general public. Since the Ombudsman nowadays gives the grounds for decisions rejecting complaints, the petitioner will receive an explanation of what to him appeared to be wrong. By the rejection of unwarranted complaints after proper investigation and on grounds clearly stated, the Ombudsman contributes to strengthening public confidence in the authorities and thus to the feeling of well-being in the society.

The task of the Ombudsman's office is not limited to interfering after faults and errors have been committed. The foremost object of the office has always been, and still is, to work for a better protection of rights and to try to prevent faults by directing attention to the true substance of the law and to improvements in practice and in the statutes for the benefit of the general public. Hence the Ombudsman's office is definitely positive in character.

A Glance Ahead

The experience gained so far in the JO's work does not justify a demand for a change in the general functions of his office. The extension of the activities of the society to new fields and the enormous enlargement of the administration during the last decades, however, have resulted in a call for an intensification of the JO's control of the administration. The desirability of such an intensification has been suggested on several occasions. In this connection it has been recommended that special Ombudsmen be appointed for the tax system, for social affairs (children's care, temperance care and social welfare), and for the municipal authorities. Whether or not such a far-reaching proposal is adopted, an intensification of the control can be achieved only by enlargement of the inspection work. The need for such an enlargement is beyond all doubt. By increasing his inspections, the JO could effectively contribute towards greater legal security. During the most recent years the inspections of the local state administration have been increased a great deal. However, the extensiveness desired has not been achieved. Time has not allowed inspections of the central state administrative authorities.

During the last seven years the number of complaints has almost doubled. Because of this it has not been possible for one Ombudsman to find time to increase the inspections sufficiently and at the same time handle all of these complaints. Furthermore, the organization must be such that the Ombudsman has liberty to decide when to intervene, and to choose ways of intervention.

These problems of organization, which have been created by recent developments, could be solved in several ways. One way to gain necessary relief in the work connected with complaints would be to turn over to the superior office in question complaints which are directed against minor officials, and which concern only trifling offences. After investigation and trial of the complaints the superior office would report the results to the JO. Since a great deal of work is required for trials of minor complaints, a great relief could thus be attained. No doubt the most important function of the JO is to take necessary action against senior officials.

Probably such a reform, however, would be insufficient. During the last few years it has become increasingly evident that it is not possible for one Ombudsman to handle the supervision of both the judicial system and the administration. Since certain advantages are gained by combining the supervision of both, it would be advantageous to strengthen this supervision by appointing an Assistant Ombudsman who would handle those cases which the JO does not handle himself. Against such a solution it has been argued that the personal character of the Ombudsman's office would be lost. It is considered to be of importance that complainants should know who is going to decide on their complaints. This speaks for a division into two separate offices, one for the judicial system (courts of justice, prosecuting attorneys, police, and prison authorities) and another for the administration. Finally it is quite conceivable—since the amount of work assigned to the MO is not of the same magnitude as that of the JO—that the MO might undertake some of the JO's tasks.

In the spring of 1963 the problems outlined above caused the Swedish Parliament to decide upon an investigation of the organization and activities of the offices of both the JO and the MO, with a view to bringing about an intensification of their supervision. This investigation has been entrusted to a committee in which, except for the Communist party, all the political parties are represented.

COMMENTS ON THE OMBUDSMAN FOR CIVIL AFFAIRS
by Ulf Lundvik*

I shall comment on some aspects of the Swedish institution that are likely to be of interest to foreign readers yet have not been treated fully by Mr Bexelius.

Election and Tenure of Office

The Ombudsman is elected, on behalf of Parliament, by a body of 48 electors who are, themselves, chosen by and from among the members of both Houses (24 from each). Originally the election was to take place on the very day that the electors were themselves appointed. This, of course, left little time for them to deliberate and find a man of their choice, and so it became customary that the election was discussed and more or less arranged beforehand by the party leaders and other prominent members of Parliament. This system, however, was resented by many members, who held that the election should be left entirely to the electors. In 1941 the law was amended in order to do away with the prearrangements. The electors were given 10 days within which the election must be made. This, however, brought about no real change. Prearrangements were still made. It is known that on one occasion the electors tried to find a candidate of their own but failed for lack of time since the man they first asked did not accept the candidature. They then elected the man proposed by the party leaders. In 1961 the time limit was extended to 15 days. It remains an open question whether this will be enough.

In the nineteenth century and the first two decades of this century, the votes sometimes were divided among two or more candidates. Since World War I the elections have been unanimous, except occasionally for some blank ballots. (In 1933, however, a Military Ombudsman was elected with 24 votes against 23 cast for the re-election of his predecessor.) As a rule the elections have not aroused great interest

* Swedish judge and former Deputy Ombudsman for Civil Affairs.

among the public or been much commented upon in advance by the press.

For a long time it has been customary to take the Ombudsman from among the judges of the courts of appeal or lower courts. There has been a strong tendency to take the former Ombudsman's Deputy as he already has some experience of the work. The Deputy is elected in the same way as the Ombudsman himself, and what has been said above in the main applies also to this election.

Before 1941 the election was for a term of only one year. Although the Ombudsman could be re-elected any number of times, and actually very often was re-elected, there were frequent changes of Ombudsman. The main reason for this was that an Ombudsman after some years usually was offered a seat in the Supreme Court or some other high office, which gave him better pay and a more secure position, and he then resigned. The frequent changes were resented by Parliament, so in 1941 the law was amended. Since then the Ombudsman has been elected for a term of four years, though of course Parliament has the right to dismiss him before the expiration of his term in exceptional cases. At the same time his salary was raised to the level of that received by a judge in the Supreme Court. It was understood that an Ombudsman should be prepared to serve for at least two periods of four years. On the other hand, it has been thought that the Ombudsman should not hold office too long. After two or three periods it would be suitable to have a new man with fresh ideas. As the Ombudsman's work is very strenuous it has also been feared that his alertness and initiative might flag if he were to hold office for too many years. Although there is no law as to how many times an Ombudsman may be re-elected, recent events seem to show that Parliament will not re-elect an Ombudsman after twelve years' tenure. It may be added that he receives a full pension after that time.

Parliament's Control

The Ombudsman's yearly report to Parliament is referred to one of the standing committees—the First Law Committee—to which the Ombudsman also delivers his records and minutes for examination. The report is discussed at several meetings. Sometimes the Ombudsman, at the Committee's request, will attend a meeting for a discussion of some matter. The examination of the records and minutes is mainly left to the Committee's secretary, who reports if he finds anything that he thinks should be brought to the Committee's attention. During the examination the Committee normally will ask for the complete file of documents on some cases which have attracted its interest or where complaints have been made against the Ombudsman's decision. The whole work seldom takes more than three weeks, during which time the Committee also has other duties to discharge. The scrutiny therefore cannot be said to be very close. Still it does not lack importance as a means of controlling the Ombudsman's activity. When reporting to Parliament on the examination made, the Committee on a few occasions has criticized one or more of the Ombudsman's decisions or the general planning of his work, for example holding that he should pay greater attention to certain fields of the law. Such observations have also sometimes been conveyed to the Ombudsman orally and in private. They are certainly considered by him most carefully. The Committee may even propose that Parliament should dismiss the Ombudsman before his term of office is out. Such a proposal, however, has never been made. Yet in the past, when the elections were yearly, sometimes an Ombudsman failed to be re-elected when there had been discontent with his work.

The Committee's report, which is considered by both Houses, does not usually cause a debate, and general debates on the report are rare. Sometimes, however, a member or two will rise to make some remarks, perhaps criticizing the Ombudsman for a decision or for alleged lack of zeal. The members may also use the opportunity to comment upon facts disclosed by an investigation. They are then normally answered by the Chairman of the Committee or another of its members. The Ombudsman himself has no right to the floor. Generally, then, one can conclude that Parliament's control over the Ombudsman is exercised mainly by the Committee and that the nature of this control depends upon the quality of the members and the effectiveness of the Committee's work.

Right to Appeal Against the Ombudsman's Decision

As has been explained in Mr Bexelius's essay, the Ombudsman nowadays seldom resorts to prosecution when intervening against illegal or improper conduct by an official. In most cases he only gives the official an admonition. Often the Ombudsman does not even say that he finds the official at fault, but simply gives his opinion on how the relevant provisions of the law should be applied. It has been held by some observers that the official concerned should have a right to appeal against such an admonition or opinion as it usually gains great publicity and thus may harm his reputation and prejudice his possibility of obtaining promotion. Even a public interest has been held to be involved. Although the Ombudsman's expressed opinions on questions of law are not binding, they enjoy great authority and are usually followed. Therefore, some people think, there should be the possibility of having such opinions revised in some way.

To some extent it is already possible to have the Ombudsman's decisions reconsidered. Firstly, nothing prevents the Ombudsman himself from retrying a case. It happens now and then that, after the Ombudsman has left a complaint without action, the complainant brings in further evidence which causes the Ombudsman to reopen the case and intervene. Similarly, after giving an admonition, the

Ombudsman may—on further evidence or on finding that he has overlooked some provision of the law—change his opinion and revoke the admonition. Such incidents have occurred, although very rarely.

Secondly, the official, when dissatisfied with the admonition, may ask the Ombudsman to prosecute him and so let the court decide whether he has committed a fault. There is no legal obligation for the Ombudsman to comply with such a request, but in the very few cases where an official has asked to be prosecuted the Ombudsman has ordered prosecution. The possibility of bringing a case to court by way of prosecution is, however, limited. Although Swedish law goes very far in punishing officials for fault or negligence committed in their official capacity, in practice punishment is not inflicted by the courts for minor errors, especially if they are caused by some excusable mistake about the meaning of the law. Since under Swedish law the ordinary courts have no general control over the administration, the Ombudsman cannot go to court asking simply for a statement that the official has committed a fault. He must claim to have the man punished. Thus, if the Ombudsman does not himself consider the fault punishable, he cannot bring the case before a court. Many of the cases where the Ombudsman expresses criticism are of this character. In these cases, therefore, it is not possible to have the Ombudsman's decision reconsidered by a court.

Thirdly, the official concerned may turn to the parliamentary committee charged with the examination of the Ombudsman's administration and complain about the Ombudsman's decision. Such complaints have been made on several occasions, but they have not been mentioned in the committee's reports and seem to have caused no action. It may be supposed, however, that if the committee should find the complaint well founded it would take some form of action, such as stating in its report that it considered the Ombudsman's decision to be wrong.

Some years ago a private member of Parliament moved that an official who had been given an admonition should have a formal right to appeal to the committee. The bill was rejected, however, since it was considered inappropriate and inconsistent with the nature of the Ombudsman's office to allow appeal against his decisions to a parliamentary committee. At the same time it was remarked that everybody has a right to bring any supposed erroneous decision of the Ombudsman to the attention of the committee, which would consider such complaints while examining the Ombudsman's administration.

To allow a formal right to appeal against the Ombudsman's decisions would, in my opinion, meet many difficulties. A parliamentary committee is hardly the right body to try such cases. To let the appeal lie to the ordinary courts would not be consistent with the tendency of Swedish law to withhold the control of the administration from these courts and would also involve other problems. It would perhaps be less

C

incongruous to allow appeal to the Supreme Administrative Court, although objections can be made also against that suggestion.

The Deputy Ombudsman

Whenever the Ombudsman is on leave, for his yearly vacation, for sickness or for any other reason, his duties are discharged by the Deputy. Moreover, while on duty the Ombudsman may delegate part of his work to the Deputy. This system of dividing the work between the Ombudsman and the Deputy was introduced in 1941 and was then meant to be used only occasionally and for short periods. The increasing amount of work in later years, however, has made it necessary for the Ombudsman to let his Deputy take over more and more of his duties. Recently the Deputy has been acting for the Ombudsman nearly eight months of the year (six months while the Ombudsman is on duty and about two months when he is on leave). Even this has proved to be inadequate, so in 1963 the law was amended to allow the Deputy to act for the Ombudsman the whole year round.

The Ombudsman usually handles the more important cases himself, e.g. cases where far-reaching questions of principle are involved or where bona fide complaints are made against a high official such as a director general or a county governor. Minor cases are left to the Deputy. Sometimes a case will concern a field of the law with which either the Ombudsman or the Deputy is particularly well acquainted. It will then normally be handled by the one who is familiar with the problems involved. Furthermore, when any personal interest of the Ombudsman or the Deputy is involved, or the case concerns a relative of one of them or a personal friend, the case will be handled by the other. The Ombudsman naturally is anxious to avoid even the suspicion of being biased. The work of inspecting the courts and the administrative bodies is also divided between the Ombudsman and the Deputy. The Ombudsman usually takes about two-thirds of it, including the inspection of the higher administrative bodies (central bodies and county governors' offices).

The Deputy is answerable for his decisions directly to Parliament and not to the Ombudsman. There is no provision in the law regulating the relations between the Ombudsman and the Deputy. Yet close co-operation between them is necessary, particularly in order to avoid contradictory decisions. For this purpose, while holding office as Deputy from 1956 to 1961, I usually conferred with the Ombudsman before starting an investigation on my own initiative, and I used to discuss with him cases delegated to me about which I felt that we might take different views. If—as happened on rare occasions—we could not agree, I referred the case to the Ombudsman for his own decision. It must naturally be left to the Ombudsman to organize the work—to decide what inspections are to be made and at what time, which members of the staff are to work for the Ombudsman and which for the Deputy, and so on. In my opinion the Ombudsman should also have the right to give certain directives to the Deputy, e.g. concerning what questions special attention should be paid to and what principles should be followed when deciding whether an official should be prosecuted or not.

Administrative Publicity

Under Swedish law every citizen has free access to all official documents, except those which have been expressly declared secret by statute. Several groups of documents have been thus declared secret, yet the great majority of the files and minutes are public. From a practical point of view this means that they are open to the press. The publicity rule also applies, of course, to the documents received or drawn up by the Ombudsman. With very few exceptions all letters of complaint, explanations given by officials and the Ombudsman's own minutes and decisions are public. In some cases, however, departmental files produced at the Ombudsman's request are secret.

Every day a representative of the main newspaper agency calls at the Ombudsman's office to examine the inward and outward correspondence of the day. The documents are laid out on a table in advance to facilitate his work. The reporter selects cases of general interest and circulates the information to the newspapers. Often a case is of merely local interest and the information is sent only to the local newspapers concerned. At a rough estimate the press representative reports upon one-third of the total number of cases and only a minority of these are considered to be of interest to the main newspapers. Usually he will not report upon a case until the Ombudsman has rendered his decision. Cases of great interest, however, are reported upon earlier, especially if they concern topics which have been previously discussed in the newspapers.

Individual newspapers seldom send reporters to examine the Ombudsman's documents but mainly rely upon the central news agency. Sometimes, however, a complainant will send a copy of his letter to a newspaper, asking to have it published. Such demands are often complied with.

Some of the Ombudsman's more important decisions are commented upon in leading articles. Such articles often contain criticism—based upon the facts disclosed by the Ombudsman's investigation—of the Government, the practice of administrative bodies, or the content of some statute. Sometimes the Ombudsman is criticized for the way he has handled or decided a case.

There has been some resentment among officials against the extent of this publicity. It has happened that grave accusations have been reported in the newspapers which afterwards have been found groundless. The harm already done to the official's reputation is hardly redressed by the subsequent acquittal which often gains little publicity in the press. Some years ago a member of Parliament moved for an amendment of the law so that letters of complaint would be kept secret until cases had been decided by the Ombudsman. But the parliamentary committee that considered the matter held that the interest of publicity must prevail and so the bill was rejected. Nowadays, however, the press tries to avoid groundless accusations. There is an agreement among the newspapers not to report complaints if they do not seem to be well founded and to avoid as far as possible mentioning the names of the officials concerned. Even after decisions have been rendered, usually officials' names are not published except for cases where their identity would be revealed anyhow by the facts reported, e.g. when the Ombudsman intervenes against a county governor or a director general for some maladministration in his office.

As for the complainants and other private persons involved in a case, generally their names are not mentioned by the press. In some cases— for example, complaints concerning the treatment of alcoholics, where the disclosure of their identity would be highly detrimental to their interests—care is taken not even to mention the name of the town or village where the occurrences concerned have taken place. Still, a complainant has no right to have his case kept secret. Whether a request for secrecy should be complied with or not is entirely left to the discretion of the press.

The publicity given to the Ombudsman's activity should not be looked upon merely as a consequence of old Swedish traditions. For the proper functioning of the Ombudsman system a considerable amount of publicity seems indispensable. The Ombudsman's decisions on questions of principle would lose most of their importance if they were not brought to the attention of all those officials who may have to deal with similar questions. Furthermore, no Ombudsman would be able to discharge his duties effectively without the confidence of the people, and in order to gain that confidence he must exercise his activity openly and not withhold his decisions from the scrutiny of the public.

In my opinion, therefore, it is of vital importance that the Ombudsman's decisions should be public, save for exceptional cases where interests of state security, etc., are involved. With the long-established traditions of administrative publicity in Sweden, we find it natural that most documents received or drawn up by the Ombudsman are also open to the public. Experience in Denmark, however, seems to show that this is not indispensable. In Denmark the Ombudsman's decisions are public, but not other documents. Yet the Ombudsman scheme has had considerable success in that country.

THE OMBUDSMAN FOR MILITARY AFFAIRS
by Hugo Henkow*

Originally, the *Justitieombudsman* was the Swedish Parliament's sole Ombudsman. It was not until 1901 that the establishment of an additional office was suggested. In that year a new national defence organization was being legislated, and a member of Parliament proposed the establishment of a military Ombudsman responsible solely to Parliament. His position and powers would be the same as the *Justitie-ombudsman* but limited to matters regarding national defence. However, this proposal was not accepted by Parliament; neither were similar proposals in the years 1903, 1904 and 1908.

Although Parliament at this time did not seem convinced that a special instrument of control was needed for the armed services, the Government had a divergent view. It had become evident to the Government that antimilitaristic propaganda was gaining ground and causing widespread distrust of military administration. In 1908 the Government therefore appointed a committee of civil members with the instruction to investigate military administration and expenditures, and to report as well on the treatment and welfare of the conscripts. The activity of the committee was from the outset meant only as a temporary solution to the question of civil control in military matters.

When the first world war broke out in 1914, Sweden reformed her national defence. The country did not get involved in the operations of war, but the reform naturally meant an increase in the number of military personnel as well as augmented allocations for defence. The Government now found it expedient finally to settle the question of a better parliamentary control over military matters. The military administration had not been excluded from supervision by the *Justitie-ombudsman*, but the growth of the state's administrative functions had made it virtually impossible for him to give detailed attention to all governmental branches. As to national defence, his activity had been reduced to observing sentences pronounced by courts-martial, examining records of military prisons, and investigating matters particularly called to his attention. Public opinion, however, was demanding a more efficient control in this vast field, especially since compulsory military service made citizens for long periods subject to conditions differing from those of other citizens. Thus, the application by summary procedure of the comparatively severe military law seemed to require careful observation that the real aim of this legislation was not thwarted. Further, allocations for military purposes made up a considerable part of the state's budget and needed closer supervision. Even though complaints were often based on misconceptions, it was considered

* Sweden's Ombudsman for Military Affairs.

essential to forestall such misconceptions and, generally, to prevent
any public distrust in the military administration.

Mainly for these reasons it was decided to transfer the supervision
of the military administration to a new official—the *Militieombudsman*
(MO)—whose office was to be built on the same principles as that of
the JO, and who, like the JO, was to be a jurist. A previous suggestion
that the new officer ought to possess expert military knowledge was
thus repudiated; the intention was not that he should interfere with
purely military technicalities. It was considered essential that the position
of the new officer should be of a strictly non-military character as the
aim of his office was to strengthen public confidence in the national
defence organization. This could best be done by an independent
institution which could provide continuous supervision, impartial
investigation of complaints, and intervention in cases of abuse.

Parliament accepted the Government's proposals along these lines
and approved the amendments to the Constitution and the legislative
instructions that were necessary to provide for the office of *Militieombudsman*. The institution came into existence May 19, 1915. The
original legislation has not been affected in any material way by later
amendments or by pertinent changes in the Constitution.

The MO, like the JO, is appointed by Parliament for a four-year
term, and with rare exceptions the appointment is renewed at the end
of each term. The appointment is made by ballot, taken by a group of
48 members of Parliament. This group also appoints a Deputy *Militieombudsman*, who is to replace the MO whenever he is off duty. In
order to enhance the prestige of the MO and JO, their remuneration
now corresponds to that of a Justice of the Supreme Court, and they are
entitled to a pension after only three periods of service. The MO's
permanent staff consists of three other jurists and three clerks, but
now and then other officials are attached to his office for special tasks.

The position and powers of the MO are in all essential respects the
same as those of the JO. Thus, within the limits of the relevant provisions
of the Constitution and of the above-mentioned instructions, the MO
performs his duties independently of both the executive and Parliament.
Even Parliament does not give directions on particular cases or matters
to be investigated. However, he must submit yearly to Parliament a
printed report on the activity of his office. The report, together with all
registries, diaries, and pertaining documents are examined by the First
Committee of Law, the same standing committee as supervises the JO.

The MO's main duty is to ensure that statutes, regulations and rules
are observed by officers and other officials charged with functions
pertaining to military administration. The Minister of Defence, like
other Cabinet Ministers, is exempted from this supervision. Otherwise,
anyone above the rank of a corporal is subject to his scrutiny. As to
non-military personnel, his jurisdiction applies to anyone in a position
of such responsibility that he can be prosecuted for dereliction of duty.

Therefore, it also applies to judges, prosecutors and policemen when they deal with cases of military concern. This feature is partly due to the fact that, as a result of a reform in 1948, Sweden has no courts-martial in time of peace. If a military commander, by virtue of his disciplinary rights, inflicts a penalty of arrest upon a soldier, an appeal lies to the ordinary courts. Such courts, as well as public prosecutors and ordinary police, are in charge of all cases regarding military offences.

It may well happen that either the MO or the JO is faced with a case which he finds to be more properly within the jurisdiction of the other. This overlapping, however, is foreseen in their instructions, and they are entitled, at their own discretion, either to hand over the case to the other, or to continue with it. A similar conflict of jurisdiction may arise with the Chancellor of Justice. In such an event, the MO and the Chancellor make an informal agreement as to who will be in charge. Should the Chancellor have investigated a matter without taking further action, the MO is not prevented from taking up the case again.

Of course the MO cannot possibly supervise everything that happens in military court cases as well as in the military administration, especially since he is expected to decide personally on the cases investigated by his office. Although a formal complaint, unless anonymous, always causes his office to make an inquiry, most investigations arise from findings in connection with random checks of files, records, and reports from the various branches of the military administration. During the last ten years, only about 80 out of 700 yearly entries in the MO's registry have referred to complaints. Previously, complaints took a greater portion of the entries. Thus by the end of the 1920's, the complaints numbered about 100 of 250 yearly entries. During the second world war, when Sweden was non-combatant but maintained a strong military force, the MO dealt with about 2,000 cases yearly, out of which as many as 1,400 were complaints.

Although complaints account for a relatively modest portion of the MO's activities nowadays, there is no doubt that the public view is still that the MO's main function is to deal with complaints. It is very important, of course, that complaints should be dealt with, but it is also of importance to a public feeling of legal security that judicial or other official errors do not pass unremarked, even if not complained against. The lodging of a complaint does not necessarily mean that an error has been committed, but when a person believes that he has suffered injustice, and is unable to seek formal recourse, it is important that his complaint should be conscientiously dealt with. Even if the ground for a soldier's complaint might sometimes be trivial, there is no doubt that his grievance, if not consoled, may in the long run prove detrimental to his unit and, subsequently, to the community. The welfare organization within the military forces endeavours to relieve the soldier of his personal problems. However, military routine and discipline, necessary as they are, may hamper the soldier's full confidence in the solution to his problem.

Any person is entitled to lodge a complaint with the MO but more than half of the complainants are conscripts. The majority of complaints concern conditions of service, such as questions of length and kind of special assignments, leave and other favours, respites and exemptions from service. Another sizeable group of complaints concerns illness or injury by accident as, for example, when a soldier complains that the medical officer—in spite of a sick report—failed to examine or give treatment, or when, after decampment, a soldier claims damages for injuries inflicted during service. Soldiers may also complain that they were insulted or assaulted by superiors, or that an officer was intoxicated or otherwise neglected his duty. Lastly, it should be mentioned that some of the complaints concern the exercise of disciplinary power, including disciplinary punishments.

To a certain extent officers and others regularly employed in the defence organization, including civilians, also make complaints to the MO. Usually these complaints concern promotion. If the appointment in question is made by the Government, the complaint does not fall within the MO's competence, of course. Since failure to promote is usually the result of such factors as recommendations and ratings by the complainant's superiors, the complaint usually aims at how these were handled. Regarding the conditions of service, not only the conscripts but also the regular personnel sometimes lodge complaints, and it may even happen that a commander will complain against his subordinates. For instance, a commander once alleged that a warrant-officer had neglected his duty to honour the reputation of his regiment by stating at a public meeting on the wages of warrant officers that the statistics did not correctly indicate the amount of work incumbent on warrant officers. In another such case, a regimental commander asked for the MO's decision when two medical officers held partly contradictory views as to whether the disciplinary confinement of a conscript should be carried out in view of the soldier's mental condition.

Complaints from persons outside the military administration occur to approximately the same extent as complaints from the regular (as distinct from the conscripted) defence personnel. A conscript's parents may complain, for example, that their son was not treated properly, but more often such complaints regard infringements on private property: a fisherman reports that a marine vessel destroyed his nets; a farmer states that his woodlot was set afire because military personnel did not take due precautions during a field manœuvre.

Investigations not caused by complaints are taken up by the MO on his own initiative. These arise in three different ways. First, the MO's office examines monthly reports submitted by military prisons at regimental and equivalent military units. These reports list everyone being confined as a disciplinary punishment or while awaiting trial for a military offence. The reports also indicate the length of time of the confinement and on what decision it was based. By this examination, the M O is enabled to observe continuously a great part of the administration of justice within the forces, whether exercised by public prosecutors and common courts or by military commanders; it is deemed particularly important that the right not to be deprived of one's liberty except by a legally well-founded decision should be scrupulously upheld.

Secondly, the M O pays attention to accounts in the press of military incidents and other matters connected with national defence. Apart from informative articles on manœuvres, installations, equipment, etc., now and then there appears an article depicting in sensational colours accidents or incongruities, sometimes followed up by critical comment. The article may lead the M O to demand a report from the military authorities concerned. If justified by this report, a further investigation is made and sometimes it is directed towards something other than the point raised by the article, as, for example, when an account of a fatal accident causes an inquiry as to the suitability of the existing security provisions. The press is thus a distinct asset to the M O's supervisory task.

The third and most important source of questions taken up on the M O's own initiative is his inspection tours. During a total of about 40 days per year, the M O tours approximately one-fifth of the military units and installations. At the same time he visits prosecution offices and tribunals in the area concerned. The primary objects of the inspections are files and documents relating to military jurisdiction as well as registries of disciplinary or other penalties inflicted on soldiers. In connection with this part of the inspection, questions of principle are taken up for discussion and, when necessary, information about the correct application of pertinent rules is given to officers and other officials. As it is incumbent upon the M O to supervise not only the treatment and welfare of conscripts and other soldiers but also the general administration of the unit, he extends the inspection to buildings and other installations. Particular attention is paid to the condition of quarters, mess-halls, rest-rooms, canteens, etc., and information is gathered through informal talks with commanders, representatives of the conscripts, welfare officers and others. Soldiers under arrest are asked how they are treated in respect of privileges, such as reading and fresh-air breaks. Registries of military hospitals are likewise subjected to examination. With the assistance of special experts, personnel rolls and mobilization files are inspected. Experts also assist in the inspection of commissariat and ordnance.

Defects exposed by the inspection lead to a close investigation of the matter, whether governed by regulations or not. The M O's duty to ensure observance of the laws and regulations was never meant to be taken literally. Therefore, when express rules do not exist, the M O is entitled, as is the J O, to see that officials act in accordance with the aim and spirit of the law, for the benefit of the public weal and individual rights. Nor is the MO's activity restricted by the secrecy provisions with respect to military administration. Although in principle all official files are open to the public in Sweden, there are several exceptions, some of which relate to national defence. The MO, however, has access to secret documents and is entitled to visit military installations in restricted areas, etc. The control exercised by the MO in this sphere has particular merit because he is able to represent the public in a field where the normal controls, such as scrutiny by the press, do not apply. This superintendence of the MO forms a barrier against injudicious or even purely arbitrary actions in domains where public observation is cut off.

Nearly all matters taken up by the MO—whether by complaint or on his own motion—are subjected to further inquiry, starting by explanations being asked from the official concerned. If needed, further information is gathered from other persons familiar with the matter. Because of the MO's limited staff, he usually requires the authority primarily concerned to arrange the necessary hearings. All official institutions and agencies are obliged to give the required assistance. If necessary, part of the investigation is carried out by the police. Sometimes the MO himself conducts a hearing, and often expert opinion is asked for, say from the Medical Board. Also, private organizations are at times given an opportunity to express their views.

Naturally, an investigation does not always fully elucidate the factual situation. Such an outcome is particularly unsatisfactory in cases where the investigation was instigated by a complainant: he will not get redress of his grievance, nor on the other hand will the official get his desired confirmation that he was not at fault. When the MO decides to close such a case, he does so by a written statement in which he sets forth, as minutely as the matter requires, what the investigation has established and why he has found no error committed. Even such a decision as this might give some satisfaction to a complainant, particularly when he is seeking no direct redress. It now and then happens that a person, before formally lodging his complaint, calls upon the MO for a discussion of the matter and then abstains from pursuing his complaint; he is contented with the oral explanation of the facts and legal aspects of the case and realizes that nothing further is to be gained from a formal complaint.

The means at the MO's disposal for correcting faults are the same as for the JO. These have been discussed fully by Mr Bexelius and Mr Lundvik and will only be summarized here. The MO, like the JO, has the power to prosecute only for an indictable offence and has no direct power to order an official to correct his mistake or to compensate for a loss. Barely ten cases per year reveal such serious errors that criminal proceedings are instituted. However, like the JO, his power to prosecute and his authoritative position, founded on Parliament's confidence, offer him considerable opportunity to bring about corrections and to exact obedience without bringing a case to court. The guarantee against his acting arbitrarily lies with the control of his administration by Parliament.

During his inspections of buildings and other installations the MO often finds defects, such as lack of repairs, which are due not to any failure on the part of an officer but to lack of funds. In such cases the MO usually restricts himself to pointing out the defect to the commander who, with reference to the MO's observation, will ask for the necessary amount to be appropriated by the authorities. Only in certain instances, such as alarming sanitary conditions, does the MO communicate his observations directly to the Government.

The MO is not entirely restricted to applying the existing law. Like the JO, he may propose changes in the law. For instance, a proposal has been made designed to make disciplinary fines more effective in order to reduce the use of disciplinary confinement. Even if the MO himself has not taken the initiative in proposing changes, now and then he is requested to give his opinion on a proposal prepared by the Government. Though the JO gets similar requests, the MO is far more in demand for this purpose because he is the only official in the country having all-round experience in the military-legal field.

One of the arguments against the creation of the office of *Militie-ombudsman* was that discipline would be harmed by offering a soldier the opportunity to complain against his superiors. Such misgivings did not prove to be correct, however. It is true that at first the MO's office did encounter scepticism from the officers. But with the lapse of time they have come to a better understanding of both their own and the soldiers' rights; they now consider it only natural that military discipline should conform to procedural rules designed to protect the rights of the individual. It can nowadays be said that the MO's office is generally respected from the officers' side. Most of today's officers—not the least those of higher ranks—are fully aware of the benefits arising from the existence and activity of the institution.

In conclusion, it should be emphasized that the MO does not belong to the official hierarchy; rather, he forms an institution parallel to it. An indictment made by him could be preferred by a public prosecutor as well; and the superintendence exercised by him in respect of judges and officials is, in principle, incumbent on their superiors, ultimately on the Government. The fact remains, however, that the MO does receive complaints and otherwise finds that conditions demand correction. These circumstances, whatever their reason, point to the justification of the institution: it acts as a legal safeguard and contributes to a public feeling of safety and of confidence that the Rule of Law prevails; it provides an independent, impartial, and juridically qualified body to whom an aggrieved citizen can apply; and it gives the officials an additional reason for scrupulous discharge of their duties. Finally, one could say that the MO's office fulfils its most important task by its mere existence.

2

FINLAND'S GUARDIANS OF THE LAW

THE CHANCELLOR OF JUSTICE AND THE OMBUDSMAN*

by Paavo Kastari†

Recently interest has been awakened in the establishment of the office of parliamentary Ombudsman in so many countries that one can almost speak of its being in fashion. When public authorities interfere more and more in the circumstances of an individual's life, it is only natural that the need grows for some kind of guardian for the legal protection of the individual which would be swiftly and authoritatively available for help when someone alleges that his rights have been unjustly encroached on by officials.

The existence of guardians such as this in Finland does not seem to have attracted any special attention among the innovators, either in the Nordic countries or elsewhere.[1] Indeed, the lively international interest which has arisen in political circles and in professional periodicals has been to such an extent directed to Denmark's new Ombudsman that even Sweden has been left almost unconsidered. Yet Sweden is the home country of this institution, which is based on lengthy tradition and practice there.

Naturally such an institution cannot simply be transferred from one country to another. It must be moulded to fit the legal system and traditions of each particular country, and this is rarely an easy task. Consequently, although the legal systems in Sweden and Finland have a common origin extending into a distant past, the special organs to guarantee the safeguarding of the law, which in these two countries

* A revised and extended version of 'The Parliamentary Ombudsman: his Functions, Position and Relation to the Chancellor of Justice', *International Review of Administrative Sciences*, XXVIII (No. 4, 1962), pp. 391–8. The author and editor wish to thank the editor of the *Review* for permission to reprint portions of that article.

† Professor of Constitutional Law, University of Helsinki, and former Ombudsman.

[1] The only foreign commentator is Donald C. Rowat, 'Finland's Defenders of the Law: the Chancellor of Justice and the Parliamentary Ombudsman', *Canadian Public Administration*, Toronto, 1961, pp. 316–25 and 412–15.

are traditionally related, have developed rather differently since the connection between the two countries was ended a century and a half ago. In Sweden the safeguarding of the legal position of the individual has been concentrated in two parliamentary Ombudsmen, in comparison with whom the Chancellor of Justice, who is appointed by the King, seems to have been rather neglected. In Finland, on the other hand, there is only one parliamentary Ombudsman, and the Chancellor of Justice, who is appointed by the President, still has a very important position in safeguarding the rights of the individual.

Finland's Chancellor of Justice originated from the corresponding office in Sweden. When Finland was separated from Sweden in 1809 and became attached to the Russian Empire as an autonomous constitutional Grand Duchy, she inherited the legal system that had existed under Sweden's Constitution of 1772. Thus Finland had its own Chancellor of Justice, or Procurator, as he was called during the Russian period.

In 1812 the Procurator received his own rules of procedure in accordance with which he not only had to ensure the legality of the acts of all officials and courts but, as guardian of the law, he was to be present in the sessions of both chambers of the so-called Senate—the legal division, which acted as the Supreme Court, and the economic division which acted as the Government of the country. The power of the Procurator actually extended even higher up the official hierarchy. Since the Emperor was usually outside the country in St Petersburg, he was represented in the Finnish capital by a Governor General, who was also the chairman of the Senate and both its divisions, although in actual practice he did not do much in this capacity. The Procurator assisted the Governor General in ensuring the observance of the law but, in spite of his subordinate position, he also saw to it that the Governor General himself observed the law. If the Procurator noticed something illegal in the acts of the Governor General or the Senate, he was empowered to remind them of it and, if this did not result in any correction, he could report to the Emperor himself.

Successive Procurators made use of their prerogatives in actual practice, especially towards the end of the last century when the period of Russification began. In fulfilling their difficult and responsible task, they played an important role during this period. While defending the Constitution and laws of the country, they got into difficult conflicts with the Governor General and some were even expelled from office by the Emperor, being replaced by Russian-minded persons and in the end by a Russian jurist. But as defenders of justice the Finnish incumbents had built around this post an excellent tradition. This was shown, for instance, by the nomination of P. E. Svinhufvud, the first and leading figure of the constitutional struggle, to this post after the Revolution of 1917 upon his return from Siberia where he had been sent by his predecessor.

Position of the Chancellor and Ombudsman

As an indirect result of the Russian era, which lasted for over a hundred years but had no direct effect on the Finnish legal system, the Chancellor of Justice—a title adopted in the new Constitution of independent Finland in 1919—attained a considerably different position from his Swedish counterpart. The Finnish Chancellor's duty is to see that the Government observes the law. He must be present at its sessions and 'in particular he has to be present when matters are presented to the President of the Republic in the Council of State' (Rules of Procedure, 1957, sec. 2). Although he is not a member of the Council of State, either he or his deputy regularly attends every meeting of this body whether presided over by the President of the Republic or the Prime Minister. With a few exceptions, the President is competent to take action only when presiding over meetings of the Council of State. Thus the Chancellor of Justice can keep a check on his official activities, as well as on those of the Council of State. Of course the Chancellor has no veto power, either absolute or suspensive, and no right to participate in the voting, but his presence and authoritative opinions on legal matters have an important practical influence on the actions of the Government. If a Cabinet member acts in a manner contrary to the law, it is incumbent upon the Chancellor of Justice to make a representation to the member concerned or to the Council of State upon the subject, and at the same time to indicate in what respects the act is illegal. If no heed is taken of the representation, the Chancellor must have his opinion recorded in the minutes of the Council of State. This has, in fact, occurred on certain occasions. He also has the right to advise the President of the matter and if the President finds that there is no ground for prosecution against the member of the Cabinet, the Chancellor ultimately may report on the case to Parliament (Constitution, Art. 47). His right to comment on any illegality is an important part of the mutual guarantee system by means of which the Constitution (Arts. 35, 41, 45 and 47) seeks to ensure the legality of the actions of the highest government organs. Indicative of the status of the Chancellor as a consultative member of the Government is the fact that if he is to be prosecuted for any illegal actions of his own this prosecution must be in the same manner as for Ministers of State, that is, in a special court, the High Court of Impeachment, on the initiative of the President of Parliament.

Like the Ministers, the Chancellor receives advance agenda and memoranda of all matters coming before the Council of State. If any item on the agenda arouses his attention, he can demand further details from the Minister or official introducing the item. If the information he receives gives cause for doubt, he informs the Minister concerned and comments on the legality of the matter. The item is then removed from the agenda for further preparation, or else the

Minister bows to the Chancellor's opinion or informs the Council of the Chancellor's views before presenting the matter. If the Council concurs with the Chancellor's view his intervention in the matter is generally not mentioned in the minutes.

To avoid surprise intervention by the Chancellor of Justice, his asistance is often sought nowadays in preparing matters for the agenda. In fact, he is obliged to render advisory opinions to the President and the Council of State upon demand. Recently he has even given such opinions to other officials, provided there are good grounds for their request, i.e. they are not merely too lazy to take the trouble to familiarize themselves with the matter. In addition to opinions from the Chancellor, then, preliminary consultations with him have become ever more frequent. In the Chancellor's work with the Council of State, the emphasis is nowadays on preventing illegality before it occurs.

It is important to note that the Chancellor's tenure of office does not end with a change in the Government. From a legal point of view his position is not as strong as that of judges and other so-called irremovable officials, for the President may relieve him of his duties if he thinks that the common good requires it. But in actual fact the Chancellor would not be expelled because of an attitude hostile to the Cabinet or for political reasons. By virtue of the traditional concepts formed during the years of Russian oppression, his position is very independent and authoritative. Thus it would be very difficult for the Cabinet to defend before public opinion an action which the Chancellor had declared to be illegal and this does not seem to have happened in actual practice.

In a way the Chancellor's position has been strengthened by the fact that the legality of the acts of the Cabinet is also safeguarded by the parliamentary Ombudsman. Like the Chancellor of Justice, he receives advance agenda and memoranda of all matters coming before the Cabinet. He also has the right to be present at sessions of the Cabinet although in practice he seems to have attended only once. This happened on February 2, 1923, and, from the point of view of the activity of the two guardians of the law, created a *cause célèbre*. The Chancellor and the Ombudsman together so contrived it that an important law, energetically supported by the Cabinet and accepted by Parliament but regarded by the guardians of the law as unconstitutional, was sent to the Supreme Court for an opinion. Since the Court also shared their view, the President used his right of veto and did not ratify the law.

The parliamentary Ombudsman does not have such old and hallowed traditions as the Chancellor. Following the Swedish example, the institution was included in the Constitution Act in 1919 and at first had no great practical importance; indeed, its abolition was suggested in 1932. Since then, however, its importance has grown to be comparable with that of the Chancellor of Justice. Indeed at times, depending upon the situation and the personal qualifications of the holders of these posts, its importance may even be greater than that of the Chancellor's office. The importance of the institution in recent times is indicated by the fact that in 1961 a law was passed guaranteeing the Ombudsman the right to pension and dependant's pension and giving to the officials in his department salary and pension rights similar to those of other permanent officials.

From a legal point of view, the Ombudsman has a power of safeguarding the law similar to that of the Chancellor of Justice. They receive the same salary and both belong to the highest paid group of government officials. The real source of the Ombudsman's authority, however, is Parliament—which elects him, on whose behalf in a way he is acting, and to whom he gives a yearly report on his activities. Initially he was elected for one year only, but in order to protect his independence his term was extended to three years and in 1957 to four years. His independence is further emphasized by the fact that Parliament cannot dismiss him during his term of office. However, on two occasions since the second world war Parliament, being dissatisfied with some of the actions of the Ombudsman, has not re-elected him. Since the present Ombudsman is the eleventh, the average tenure has been four years. The Ombudsman having the longest period of office served for 14 years.

Promotion to the post of Chancellor of Justice has come almost solely from the ranks of the judges, often from members of the Supreme Court or the Supreme Administrative Court, and from this post promotion has frequently been to the presidency of these highest courts. On the other hand, the group of jurists from which the Ombudsman has been elected has been more varied. In general the highest judges have not been willing to undertake this job and therefore the more outstanding younger jurists have had to be called upon. Moreover, political expediency has often played a part in the selection. These factors have, to some extent, had a negative influence on the position and prestige of the Ombudsman. Recently several Ombudsmen have been promoted to membership in the Supreme Administrative Court. This hardly signified any promotion, but was considered worth while because of the permanency of the office. Some Ombudsmen have, after their resignation, participated in political life. The present Minister of Justice is a previous Ombudsman. In addition to him, three former Ombudsmen later became Cabinet Ministers, one of them Prime Minister.

Functions and Powers of the Chancellor and Ombudsman

Because of the aforementioned historical factors, both the Chancellor and the Ombudsman have been regarded as supreme guardians of the law; hence they have naturally been led to superintend the activity of the whole body of public officials, the courts, the municipal and Church organs of self-government, and the state's highest officials.[1] No field of public activity lies outside the scope of their guardianship.[2] However, neither of them safeguards the interests of the state in the sense of being entitled to represent the state in a civil action against an individual. The Rules of Procedure for the Ombudsman (1920, Sec. 4) prohibit him from interfering with the official acts of the Chancellor of Justice. Since the latter similarly refrains from interfering with the work of the Ombudsman, no conflicts arise. If one of them is aware that a case is pending with the other, he refuses to deal with it. But if one has already given a decision, the other may investigate a complaint dealing with the same matter and may even reach an opposite conclusion, but of course they try to avoid this.

The main difference between the Ombudsman and the Chancellor of Justice derives from the fact that the former is elected by Parliament while the latter is appointed by the President. Because of his close contact with the Government, the Chancellor acts as legal adviser to the Government and the ministries, in much the same sense as does a crown jurist, who should be wholly objective but who is frequently partisan in his representations. This characteristic the Ombudsman cannot be said to possess at all. Another difference is that the Chancellor is the head of all official prosecutors and even appoints them to the city courts. In case of need he may also nominate an assistant prosecutor or a special prosecutor in a disciplinary action. The Ombudsman may, but does not have to, act as the prosecutor in the cases he brings up. Instead he often orders a prosecutor of either the court of the first instance or a superior court to present the charges arising out of the material which he furnishes. The Ombudsman can only bring charges for an offence committed by someone in office, while the Chancellor of Justice can also bring them in the case of a crime or misdemeanour by a private person.

A noteworthy difference in practice has also arisen from the efforts to make their work more equal. The task of the Ombudsman, and also the number of complaints directed to him, had initially remained rather meagre. So in 1933 the Chancellor of Justice was, without circumscribing his powers, relieved from the duty of enforcing compliance with the law in the military forces, in penal camps and penitentiaries, and in regard to people otherwise imprisoned or detained.

---

[1] The Supreme Administrative Court, however, expressed the opinion (1956 I 16) that it does not belong to the duties of the Ombudsman in accordance with Art. 49 of the Constitution Act to superintend the official acts of the President, and that consequently he had no right to make a proposal that a nomination made by the President should be rescinded.

[2] In actual practice their activity has not turned out to be like that of the procurators provided with wide powers in some East-European countries. Compare Glenn G. Morgan, 'The Soviet Procuracy's General Supervision Function', *Soviet Studies*, 1960, pp. 143–72; and 'Le concept de la légalité dans les pays socialistes', *Polska Akademia Nauk*, 1961, pp. 107–8.

This led the Chancellor to refer almost all complaints against officials connected with these fields to the Ombudsman. As a result, nowadays most of these complaints are addressed directly to the Ombudsman. However, as will be seen later, the Chancellor still has an important task in enforcing compliance with the rules governing detentions by checking documents dealing with the execution of sentences.

The Chancellor of Justice rarely makes inspection tours of the offices under his guardianship. In the work of the Ombudsman, however, such inspections play a considerable part. He inspects courts, police stations and different administrative offices, and is specially mindful of the need to investigate prisons, penal camps and other closed reform institutions. In fact, making inspection tours, particularly of the prisons, has been specifically mentioned in the Rules of Procedure for the Ombudsman (sec. 10) as his special duty. These inspections are usually made without previous warning and during them prisoners or other inmates of institutions are usually offered an opportunity to talk to the Ombudsman without any member of the staff being present. Special attention is paid to the use of disciplinary power, to the investigation of documents concerning its application, and to medical care.

During the last decade almost forty institutions or offices yearly, including approximately six prisons, have been inspected by the Ombudsman. He has usually inspected the same prison at an interval of 2–3 years. Prisoners have on the whole been fairly ready to utilize the possibility of talking to the Ombudsman. However, they have rarely presented complaints on prison conditions, and even more rarely have such complaints been justified. In general their inquiries have been concerned with the carrying out of the sentence, such as the allegedly incorrect summing up of multiple sentences or the beginning of the period of parole. Many prisoners have inquired about the possibility of remitting their sentences as a result of new evidence or presumed errors of judgment. In those cases where a prisoner can base his oral complaint on facts which indicate that it may be justified, he is generally told to send his complaint in written form to the Ombudsman's office. However, the Ombudsman may, if necessary, take immediate action on an oral complaint by requiring statements and by taking oral testimony. Letters addressed by a prisoner to the Ombudsman or the Chancellor have to be forwarded sealed and the prison officials have no right to read them.

Since the Chancellor of Justice also has the duty of superintending the administration of punishment, here the tasks of the two guardians of the law directly coincide. Every six months the courts send the Chancellor their lists of persons sentenced to imprisonment, and every four months the county administrations forward to him extracts of the diary kept on prison sentences. He also obtains directly from the prisons monthly lists of all prisoners serving sentences. In addition he orders yearly from two of the county administrations extracts from the list of fines sent in by the courts. By investigating these documents he can effectively check the activities of the prosecutors, the courts and the executive officials concerned. Most of the actions and admonitions mentioned in the Chancellor's annual report result from these documentary investigations.

Another way in which the activity of the courts is followed by the Ombudsman and the Chancellor is that the higher courts send them yearly statistics concerning pending, decided and postponed cases. Also, both of them obtain a copy of all verdicts given by the courts in cases concerning crimes and misdemeanours in office. In such cases the Chancellor is entitled to ask the prosecutor to appeal to a higher court. The Ombudsman may do this only in cases which he himself has initiated.

The difference in the nature of the work done by the two guardians of the law may be seen best from the way they carry out their tasks regarding the administration of punishments. It is characteristic of the Chancellor, as part of the executive, that his main aim is to ensure that the laws are enforced and to prosecute or take other action when observing negligence or mistakes. The Ombudsman, on the other hand, is more concerned with the rights of the individual, and tries to safeguard the rights of those subject to official acts.

Thus, local government officials sometimes present complaints to the Ombudsman on the activities of higher state officials. These generally concern the application of the provisions on social help from state funds. The professional organizations of state officials have also presented complaints to the Ombudsman on actions concerning their members. In one decision on such a complaint the Ombudsman criticized a head office for wrong and unjustified action in filling certain vacancies and offices. A more recent example is a complaint from the organization representing academic officials in which they argued that in the spring of 1963 the Cabinet acted against the provisions of a law guaranteeing state officials the right to negotiate with the Cabinet on salaries before the budget proposals on them are made to Parliament. In his decision the Ombudsman conceded that the menace of a strike called for rapid action, but he criticized the Minister who had presided over the negotiations for not giving the organization a legitimate time to prepare for the negotiations.

Supervision of the Armed Forces

The fact that historically the Ombudsman is an offshoot of the same institution as the Chancellor of Justice still has importance for the former's work. This we notice by directing attention to the armed forces. This field of state activity, by its nature and especially since the transfer of supervision over it to the Ombudsman in 1933, ought to be one of the main foci of investigation. Yet in the regiments themselves and elsewhere within the armed forces the Ombudsman has rarely made inspections. (In the last few years, however, more inspections have been undertaken than in previous years, and they also seem to have been more effective.) Similarly, complaints coming from the armed forces, except for the years immediately after the second world war, have been few, and from conscripts very rare.

As an example of the type of complaint received from the forces let me describe a case decided in 1962. The commander of a unit had ordered a soldier to guard-room detention for continued and needless visits to the doctor. But the soldier attached to his complaint a statement by a highly esteemed medical professor that he suffered from a very rare and hard to define rheumatic disease. After the Ombudsman had acquired this and other explanations, the Commander of the Defence Forces rescinded the punishment because the guilt of the soldier could not be proved conclusively, as the use of disciplinary punishment presupposes. The Ombudsman then said in his decision that the matter did not give rise to any further action.

Conscripts are naturally entitled to by-pass their commanding officers and the regular official channels in order to present complaints directly to the Ombudsman or to the Chancellor. In 1926 the Chancellor sent a communication to the Commander of the Defence Forces in which he emphasized the possibility for a soldier to make a complaint direct to the Chancellor if 'he has been denied his legal rights'. The Chancellor stressed the importance of this matter by adding: 'Every effort by the military officers to prevent their men from turning to the Chancellor of Justice is therefore an offence committed in office, which I shall regard as indictable' (Report, 1926, p. 35). But for one reason or another the attitude within the army seems to be that use of the right of direct complaint is inappropriate, and this has limited its application. It is also clear that conscripts have not been using the opportunity during the Ombudsman's inspections to present oral complaints without the presence of the commanding officer. The ensuring of compliance with the law has been centred mainly within the armed forces themselves and, in the last resort, in the legal branch of the General Staff. The legal branch exerts its supervision by such means as checking orders of the day in which disciplinary punishments must generally be recorded.

Thus in regard to the armed forces the work of the Finnish Ombudsman has not developed on lines at all similar to the work of the Swedish military Ombudsman. In a recent report by a committee investigating the legal protection of conscripts, no recommendations were made to alter the position of the Ombudsman, nor was the establishment of a special military Ombudsman proposed in accordance with the Swedish example. So in fact the Ombudsman in Finland is very much like the Swedish civil Ombudsman, except that the former's superintending powers include not only the Ministers and the Cabinet but also the armed forces. In both countries the Chancellor of Justice is in a sense senior to the Ombudsman, but in Sweden the Ombudsman seems to have surpassed him in range of authority whereas in Finland the Chancellor has maintained his original position.

Methods of Supervision

Material for action by the Finnish Chancellor and Ombudsman is gathered in many different ways. Both of them make use of their own initiative as a result of incidents published in the papers. Although this happens rather infrequently, two recent examples may be of interest. In the first case it was claimed that one of the mathematical problems in the matriculation examination for 1963 was chosen from outside the school course. As a result of comments in the press the Ombudsman asked the board choosing the problems for an explanation. The board admitted its mistake and the Ombudsman thereupon criticized it. In the second case, it seemed apparent from a news story that a policeman had acted incorrectly in detaining a drunken man by hitting him with a bottle taken from the man's pocket. The policeman's superior officer was of the opinion that the policeman had not acted wrongly, taking into account the special circumstances. Nevertheless, the Ombudsman ordered charges to be brought against the policeman and he was punished. News stories and comments sometimes create a demand for explanations from the officials concerned. After receiving these explanations it is often possible for the Chancellor or Ombudsman to state that the official has already remedied the matter or that there is no reason for further action.

Most occasions for the use of the Ombudsman's own initiative arise from his inspection trips, while the Chancellor's use of his initiative mainly arises from checking reports on the administration of punishments. The State Auditors, who are elected by Parliament and who on Parliament's behalf watch over public finances, have in some cases informed the Ombudsman of misdemeanours noticed by them. In this way was initiated the case mentioned later in which two former members of the Cabinet were fined. Joint action between the State Auditors and the Ombudsman, who between them take care of the different sides of parliamentary surveillance of the Government, has in other respects been close. Officials of the courts and ministries, however, after having observed what appear to be illegalities would send the necessary information to the Chancellor of Justice for a decision. According to the reports for 1962 the Chancellor had 64 cases belonging to this group and 317 cases arising from the exercise of his own initiative, while the Ombudsman handled only 121 cases based on his own initiative.

Complaints and petitions made by private persons constitute the largest group in the yearly records of both officials. In 1962 the Chancellor handled 493 of these while the Ombudsman had 858, including 105 referred to him by the Chancellor. The great majority of the complaints, even of those leading to some investigation, ultimately prove to be unfounded. Apart from the inspection of the written complaints, most of them result in no action except sending back, along with the reasons, the decision of their rejection. Thus in 1962 the Chancellor made 437 rejections and the Ombudsman 632. Prisoners especially present many unfounded complaints, particularly during inspection trips. A great majority of these can at once be rejected for want of evidence or other obvious reasons. Among people complaining there are always some professional litigants, but it is nevertheless important that all complaints be resolved by an authoritative decision coming from one whose position sets him apart from the official machinery against which the complaints are made. Confidence in the courts and the administration is increased by the mere fact that the man in the street and even the man who has lived on the shady side of the community have the possibility of presenting their views to the Chancellor or the Ombudsman on the wrong they presume themselves to have suffered.

Some examples of complaints by people other than prisoners may be mentioned. The parents of a boy lost in the war made a complaint to the effect that they had been refused a pension on account of their son because of wrongful interpretation of the law. In his decision the Ombudsman said that the official handling the matter had acted wrongly and the pension was granted. A farmer insisted that charges be brought against an official because a road under his jurisdiction had been extended illegally to encroach the farmer's property. Similarly, charges have been brought against local government officials acting as members of a road committee for mistakes in the committee's work concerning private roads. During recent years there have been many complaints in which the father of a child born out of wedlock, or a divorced father, who has been sent to a correctional institution to refund the maintenance of his child, has complained about the severity of the conditions of probation under which he would be freed.

A general idea of the nature of the Ombudsman's work may be gained from a perusal of his annual reports. The report for 1962, for example, states that of the 805 matters he brought to a conclusion in that year, 201 concerned requests for the reversal of court decisions or rehearings, 70 dealt with other court proceedings, 99 with the enforcement of penalties, 128 with prison conditions and the conduct of prison officials, 60 with the conduct of the police and public prosecutors, 67 with the commitment of persons to public institutions, 27 with the activity of welfare officers, 9 with the conduct of military officers, 93 with the conduct of other officials, and 51 with other matters. In his report for 1960 he made proposals of a general nature to the authorities regarding such matters as the removal of defects in law on taxation and accounting, the checking of regulations on forced labour, and a clarification of the provisions of the Welfare Subsidies Act. He also requested the Supreme

Court to reconsider a sentence because the accused was subsequently found to be mentally deficient. Among those prosecuted was a tax collector for charging an excessive fee, a warden who physically maltreated a prisoner, a judge who fined an accused in his absence although the latter had been misinformed in his summons of the place in which the session was to be held, a municipal medical officer who refused to attend a patient brought to him in urgent need on the grounds that the latter came from another locality, and three former Ministers of the Government accused of malfeasance. Examples of actions for which the Ombudsman issued admonitions, or criticisms, are the appointment of non-qualified officials by the Board of Post and Telegraphs; the misinterpretation by certain tax collectors of a presidential decree concerning their fees; and the issue by the Finance Ministry of a doubtful interpretation of a certain act.

The work of the guardians of law in Finland, like these same officers in Sweden, differs considerably from that of the institution which, inspired by the Swedish example, has been adopted in Denmark and Norway. In both Finland and Sweden, the Ombudsman and the Chancellor of Justice, having the same historical background and traditions, are the foremost guardians of justice and this is especially reflected in their activities as prosecutors. There are several reasons for this. Nearly all of the activities of officials in both Finland and Sweden have always been closely regulated by statutes, instructions or orders published in the law codes and by rules of procedure. In accordance with this legalistic tradition charges for a crime or misdemeanour in office are swiftly brought in the courts or in the administrative disciplinary procedure. The latter may result in either a fine or a warning comparable to a punishment. Since a misfeasance nearly always can be considered an offence in office, strictly speaking, charges should always be brought in such cases when there is sufficient evidence. However, this would be excessive.

In the light of this information it may be easier for a foreigner to understand that in 1962 the Chancellor of Justice prosecuted officials in 29 cases and initiated disciplinary procedure or gave an admonition 31 times. In most cases (20 and 21) his action arose from checking the previously mentioned lists of prisoners and fines. As a result, the charges were mainly brought against judges. Neither in Sweden nor in Finland has the superintendence of the courts by the guardians of the law detracted from the independence of the courts. Yet this consideration in Denmark and Norway, as well as in the Anglo-Saxon countries, seems to be regarded as a hindrance to extending the competence of the Ombudsman to the courts.

The willingness of the Chancellor to prosecute was even more in evidence formerly; and not even to this day is a difference made in the statistics between the disciplinary procedures and his admonitions. In contrast, this distinction is made in the Ombudsman's statistics, and one notices that in 1962 he brought charges for an offence committed in office only 10 times, and gave 39 admonitions, but did not initiate any disciplinary procedures.

The admonition system was developed at first in practice and was not legally recognized until afterwards. It may be related to the notifications which the Chancellor of Justice used to present during the Russian period in the sessions of the Senate and which both he and the Ombudsman may now present at the sessions of the Cabinet by virtue of Article 47 of the Constitution. Admonitions were given to officials of inferior status at an early date but only obtained official recognition as substituting for charges or disciplinary action in the Rules of Procedure for the Chancellor of Justice issued at the end of 1957. In principle, an admonition does not signify a punishment at all, because neither the Ombudsman nor the Chancellor has the final decision-making power in regard to the matter; they merely express in the form of an admonition for the future their views concerning an official's action or statutory interpretation which, in their opinion, has been incorrect. This may, of course, be interpreted as a criticism. However, admonitions are often given only in the form of a rejection of a complaint, a copy of which is sent to the official concerned. Although the complaint itself is rejected, the reasons given may contain a criticism or admonition.

When criticizing a faulty action neither the Ombudsman nor the Chancellor pronounces on its suitability but refers only to illegalities in the action itself or in the procedure leading to it. The line cannot be clearly drawn but the attitude taken may be described by saying that they pay attention to *détournement de pouvoir* but not to such aspects of injustice as e.g. whether a decision was unreasonable. In recent years there has been an increasing tendency to try to avoid a prosecution and to be satisfied with a criticism or admonition, especially in cases of minor offences or when the official himself has later corrected his error or admitted his mistake. There are even signs of the Chancellor and Ombudsman playing a more active advisory role with the administrative officials, in order to prevent them beforehand from taking illegal action. Also, if a case is still pending or may still be taken to a higher court, it will not be interfered with. In this connection it should be pointed out that, in general, the decisions of administrative officials may be appealed on both procedure and content to administrative courts and ultimately, as may the decisions of Ministers and the Cabinet (but not the President), to the Supreme Administrative Court.

There is no time limit or formula for making complaints, but as a rule they have to be in writing and anonymous ones are not dealt with. A complaint may be dealt with even if the plaintiff himself has suffered no injury and is not directly concerned. If a complaint is not immediately rejected, it will be sent for an explanation to the official concerned or, in case of an offence in office, for a personal statement by the official. Additional explanations and documents may naturally be required later, and the Ombudsman and Chancellor are entitled to familiarize themselves with all documents of the office concerned even if they are only internal. If necessary a police officer or the superior official concerned may be called upon to make a survey of the case under investigation. Only in an important or special case does the Ombudsman's office, where there are only two full-time and one part-time legal officers, investigate the case directly. This is also true of the Chancellor of Justice because he and his assistant and his six legal officers are fully occupied with negotiations on legal questions and statements to the Cabinet as well as inspecting the enforcement of sentences, supervising prosecutors, etc.

In Finland, as in Sweden, official documents are generally open to the public. This applies, of course, to the documents gathered in the offices of the Ombudsman and the Chancellor. Making official documents public has not caused any harm in the case of either these guardians of the law or other officials. The possibility of demanding view of the documents has been used to a rather minor extent, but by its mere existence this principle of access intensifies the exactness of the officials' actions in the applications of law and justice, and thus adds to legal security.

In addition to the prosecution of charges and the issuing of admonitions, both guardians may take other action as well to safeguard the law. If the illegal situation can no longer be corrected by the official concerned because the decision has become legally binding, they may ask the Supreme Court or the Supreme Administrative Court to annul the decision. The annulment proposals have often been concerned with cases where it has been found that a person was at the time of committing a crime not fully responsible and should therefore have been more leniently sentenced. At other times a criminal may have been sentenced as a habitual criminal to a heavy sentence, although he had not suffered earlier sentences which would define him as a habitual criminal. Wrongful summing up of multiple sentences has also caused anulments or corrections of sentences. Several fines for wilful non-appearance in court are yearly annulled when it has become clear that the reason for the non-appearance was outside the control of the accused. Also, a prisoner was granted a new period of time for making his appeal when, because of the action of a prison official, his written appeal was not duly forwarded.

In general, the Chancellor and the Ombudsman do not try only to amend situations *ex post facto* but also to prevent injustice. For example, in the preliminary negotiations and when dealing with a case in a session of the Cabinet, in addition to any clear illegality the Chancellor of Justice may pay attention to a conflict with general principles of law such as the legal unjustifiability of the intended decision, but it is not intended that he refer to the political or expedient (perhaps unreasonable yet not illegal) factors concerned in the meetings of the

Cabinet. Also, the Ombudsman is entitled to be present at the meetings of administrative officers and the sessions of the courts to express his opinion during the handling of a case; but in practice this has very rarely happened.

Both guardians of the law have the duty of making proposals to amend conflicting and defective laws. In actual practice they sometimes make such proposals to the Cabinet, although not in the form of detailed draft bills. Similarly they may make suggestions to officials to correct omissions in the procedure or in the rendering of justice—on matters similar to those concerning admonitions. Nevertheless, they do not present detailed analysis and criticism as does the Danish Ombudsman.

Role of Parliament and Public Opinion

Annually both present to Parliament, and the Chancellor of Justice also to the President, reports concerning their activities, in which their most important work is described. These reports are distributed to the most important offices and courts, and by this means the decisions and criticisms are expected to have an influence as expressing authoritative interpretations and as evidence of the vigilance of the guardians of the law. In Parliament these reports are handled by the Constitutional Law Committee which usually wants to review the documents connected with certain complaints and which as a rule invites the Ombudsman and the Chancellor to be present for oral explanation. Now and then the Committee presents a criticism in its statement on the reports or expresses its belief and concern—since Parliament cannot give any binding advice or orders to either of them—that the author of the report should intensify his activity or pay special attention to certain matters. In the full session of Parliament the reports only rarely cause any discussion and even more rarely do the Ombudsman and the Chancellor participate in the discussion. Although they cannot be members of Parliament, in fact they possess a right to speak similar to that of Cabinet members (that is, they are given priority over members of the Parliament). The Ombudsman has sometimes used this right to report his findings on illegality or to speak on legislative matters closely connected with the rights of Parliament and its members, or the position of the Ombudsman.

It should also be mentioned that the Ombudsman in a way checks how well the Cabinet has fulfilled the wishes of Parliament. He must include in his report a statement of those wishes and suggestions expressed by Parliament to the Cabinet but which the Cabinet is still considering at the end of the reporting year. Such a statement may include, for instance, a suggestion that a proposal to amend a certain law or to build a new railway, bridge or port should be prepared and laid before Parliament. In order to prepare this statement the Ombudsman asks the officials of the departments concerned to present a short review of each such case at the end of the reporting year. When considering this particular section of the report, the Committee has sometimes required a detailed explanation from the official concerned and, where the explanation has not been satisfactory, a criticism or other statement has been presented in the Committee's report.

To sum up it may be said that the Chancellor of Justice and the parliamentary Ombudsman are the highest guardians of the law, and have extensive powers which are comparable and to a great extent overlap. Experience has shown that their use of these powers—be it directed towards the highest grades in the administrative or judicial systems or towards the independent local governments and self-governing Churches—is an important and positive part of the judicial system, the guardianship of the law, and the guarantee of the rights of the individual. Their powers are so great that their use involves, besides expert legal knowledge, complete objectivity, good judgment and tact, and at times also the courage and energy to deal with important matters and with the alleged offences or mistakes of even the highest officials. For example, as a result of the Chancellor's investigations and on his initiative the President on one occasion decided to let a Cabinet member stand trial for misbehaviour on account of the drawing up of a Cabinet protocol. Similarly, on the initiative of the Ombudsman, Parliament in 1952 decided to present charges against four Cabinet members, of whom two were punished and two acquitted. In a decision issued in 1953 the Chancellor of Justice struck out a complaint in which a previous Cabinet member had been accused of having misused his official position in order to have the direction of a road changed to favour his own farm. Recently, too, as a result of a complaint the Chancellor asked for charges to be brought against the heads of the Old Age Institute for having granted loans on more favourable conditions than normal to some building associations established by the employees of the Institute. In this process several people were sentenced in 1962 to punishments and to the payment of reparations.

In addition to their normal functions, public opinion expects from the guardians of the law something of the work of the investigating commissions which the Parliaments of several other countries may set up but which the Parliament of Finland cannot because such investigations are interpreted as belonging to the executive power. As their unlimited powers of investigation include also the power to press charges, these wide powers might themselves prove dangerous if carelessly used on the basis of a hasty judgment or insufficient investigation, for instance, to satisfy too great an ambition or on account of motives removed from strict objectivity. The strength of the tradition connected with the office and the high moral level of the men concerned, however, have generally been sufficient to prevent such happenings. Some of their actions have naturally been criticized, but as a rule public opinion generally has accepted them. When they avoid issues of expediency and limit themselves strictly to the law, their actions readily enough find support because of the people's traditional respect for law.

The importance of the parliamentary Ombudsman has gradually increased—although hardly evenly. This institution now has an assured place in the Finnish system of law and a special importance in the system of guaranteeing the legal position of the individual. In weighing the relative importance of the two guardians of the law, it depends simply on the development of circumstances whether and to what extent the scale will tip in favour of the Ombudsman, but it is hard to believe that the situation will ever become comparable to that in Sweden. The activity of the Chancellor of Justice gains both in esteem and importance by his presence at Cabinet meetings. There is some feeling, however, that his work as legal adviser to the Government is not completely in accord with his duties as guardian of the law on the Council of State and as the citizen's defender. It has therefore been suggested that part of this work should be taken over by a new officer, an Attorney General, who would also be a general representative of the state in civil actions.

It seems probable that progress in regard to both guardians of the law will, as in Sweden, be typified by a diminishing number of charges against officials and a growth in the number of admonitions and criticisms. But the limiting of their activity to defence against outright illegalities is based on such strong traditional views that it is difficult to imagine this situation changing in the future. Finnish experience, therefore, does not coincide with the practice of the Ombudsman in Denmark where the activity of officials is sometimes criticized solely because it is considered unjustifiable or unreasonable.

3

DENMARK'S OMBUDSMAND*

by Miss I. M. Pedersen†

Denmark has had a democratic constitution since 1849. The King is the nominal head of the executive, but he has no personal responsibility and performs his functions through responsible Ministers. The legislative assembly, which is unicameral, is called the Folketing. The judiciary is independent of the administrative authorities as well as of the Folketing. Part of the public administration is performed by the local municipal authorities. Under section 82 of the Constitution the municipal authorities are independent, but the central government is entitled to supervise their activities.

The Ministers are responsible to the Folketing for the efficient administration of their departments. This means that they are responsible for the activities of civil servants and other state employees as well as for their own personal acts. Also, Ministers may be censured in the Folketing. They may even be charged and brought before the Rigsret, a special court composed of members of the Supreme Court and the Folketing. This has happened, however, only a few times.

It is obvious that in the normal case a citizen who has a grievance against the administration will have to think of remedies other than this if he wants to obtain redress. If he is dissatisfied with the decision of one of the lower administrative authorities he will usually have a right to lodge a complaint with the Minister. In some cases he may have a right of appeal to a special administrative board or tribunal. If the decision has been made by a ministry and he has no right of appeal to an administrative tribunal, he may try to make the ministry reconsider its decision. Some applicants seek a personal interview with the Minister himself. This is easier in Denmark than in most other countries, because it is a time-honoured custom that Ministers receive applicants every Thursday morning. It is not necessary to have a previous appointment or to show that your case is of special importance.

If it turns out during the investigation of such a complaint that a public employee has committed some act of negligence or maladminis-

---

* Part of this essay has already appeared as 'Ombudsmandsinstitutionen i Denmark', in *Nordisk Administrativt Tidsskrift* (1962), 248–73. The author and editor wish to thank the editor of *N.A.T.* for permission to reprint portions of that article.

† Judge of the City Court of Copenhagen.

tration he may, if the circumstances are sufficiently grave, be prosecuted before the ordinary courts. This power is only made use of in exceptional cases. It is also possible to take disciplinary action against the permanent civil servants. Even this power is used sparingly. But disapproval may be expressed by the Minister or by a superior official either orally or in writing to any public employee. Nevertheless, the complainant has no personal right to institute proceedings. He is dependent on the decision of the Minister or the administrative heads of departments and cannot force them to take action against negligent state employees.

In many cases complainants will have a further remedy, however. They may sue the public authorities and/or their employees in the ordinary courts. (There is no system of administrative courts in Denmark.) A plaintiff in a case concerning an administrative act or decision may claim damages or ask for a declaration as to its legality. He may also ask the courts to annul a decision, if he can show sufficient grounds. However, the courts do not have general powers to set aside the decisions of the administrative authorities. For one thing, they are never entitled to review the purely discretionary aspect of administrative acts, but only to deal with questions of fact and law. Yet this must be understood in a fairly wide sense. *Détournement de pouvoir* (use of power for an unintended purpose) is sufficient ground for annulment. Another example is grave faults of procedure.

It has frequently been a subject of public discussion whether these remedies offer sufficient protection to citizens against mistakes or abuse of power by administrative authorities. The public interest in the problem has been steadily growing, because the functions of administrative authorities have been increasing rapidly. Although this increase has frequently been in response to demands from the public and in the best interests of the citizens, it is not without its dangers. In a great number of cases the authorities must necessarily interfere in the sphere of private interests, and often they will have to restrict the rights and activities of citizens in favour of another citizen or group of citizens. This, of course, means that conflicts between administrators and citizens are more frequent and often more serious than in former days.

In these circumstances it was natural that by the end of the second world war the problem of how to protect the reasonable interests of private individuals and at the same time make it possible for the administration to do its work efficiently, had become a main problem in both administrative and constitutional law. It was admitted that the control exercised by the independent courts was of considerable importance. Danish courts have not been afraid of criticizing the administration, and they have been strongly supported by the modern development of administrative law as an academic subject (which started in 1924 when Professor Poul Andersen published his famous thesis 'Invalid Administrative Acts'). Nevertheless, many people held that the remedies described above were not sufficient. It is therefore not surprising that this problem was taken up by the parliamentary committee set up in 1946 to consider amendments to the Constitution.

One of the solutions discussed was the adoption of an Ombudsman on the Swedish model, and many arguments were put forward for and against the plan. One question was whether the Ombudsman could be fitted into the Danish constitutional system, whether it would not interfere with the system of ministerial responsibility. The Swedish experience was of little use in this connection: the Swedish Ministers are not subject to the control of the Ombudsman. Another problem was the position of the civil servants. The scheme was the subject of much discussion among state employees, and very few were in favour of it. It was maintained that the introduction of an Ombudsman would tend to make civil servants afraid to take responsibility without being protected by written rules. This, it was argued, would result in less flexibility in the attitude of the civil service, to the disadvantage of the public. Also, many opponents of the institution argued that the Ombudsman's office would be swamped with frivolous complaints and that his time would be taken up mostly by cranks.

In spite of all these arguments the parliamentary committee decided in favour of the Ombudsman institution. It was of the opinion that the Ombudsman's supervision over the Ministers would create no insurmountable difficulties as to ministerial responsibility. Since the majority of the members of the committee were or had been Ministers, their opinion carried considerable weight. But the arguments put forward by the civil servants led to some amendments in the original scheme.

As a result of the proposals of the committee, section 55 of the revised Danish Constitution of 1953 reads:

Legislation shall provide for the appointment by the Folketing of one or two persons, who shall not be members of the Folketing, to supervise the civil and military administration of the state.

The detailed rules were laid down in the Ombudsmand[1] Act of September 11, 1954, later supplemented by Directives adopted by Parliament on March 22, 1956. The first Ombudsman, Professor Stephan Hurwitz, was elected on March 29, 1955, took office on April 1, 1955, and has held office since then, as he has been re-elected after each general election.

Eight years are not a long time in the history of a public institution. Even at this early stage, however, the student will find much material to consider, principally in the Ombudsman's annual reports. Naturally it is still too early to predict how the Ombudsman's work will influence

[1] The Danish term is *Ombudsmand*, but in the interests of uniformity and ease of pronunciation in English, henceforth I shall use the Swedish word.

the Danish constitutional and administrative system in the long run, but an analysis of the cases shows definite trends. It is the purpose of this essay not only to describe the system created by the Ombudsman Act, but also to try to analyse these trends in order to show how the Ombudsman has actually used his powers within the flexible limits of the Act and the Directives.

I. JURISDICTION

Control Over State Administration

Under the Act the Ombudsman has powers to supervise all state administration, civil and military. This means that he is entitled to control all persons acting in the service of the state, Ministers included. As might have been expected, some questions as to the limits of his jurisdiction have arisen from time to time. The functions of some public institutions are not clearly defined, and certain institutions or persons carry on *some* activities that are clearly within the Ombudsman's jurisdiction and others that are outside it.

Institutions and Persons with Political Functions. The Folketing itself is of course outside the Ombudsman's powers. Also, in a case reported in the annual report for 1961 (p. 75) it was held that the activities of a committee of the Folketing on a Bill were not within the Ombudsman's jurisdiction. But members of the Folketing are not exempted from control when they are acting in other capacities. In a case in 1955 (p. 76) a member was criticized for his behaviour as a member of the Government's Agricultural Land Board.

The Ministers are also subject to control. The prediction of the parliamentary committee that such control would not interfere with ministerial responsibility has turned out to be true. One of the reasons for this is that the Ombudsman has categorically refused to let himself be used, directly or indirectly, as a tool of the politicians or as a weapon in the hands of the opposition parties in the Folketing. His position was made clear in several test cases put before him during his first year. In one of them (case 1955, p. 64) he states his principles in no uncertain terms. The case concerns the right of the Government to overdraw its account with the National Bank. The Ombudsman says:

It must be conceded that there is a limit to the powers of a Government to draw upon its account . . . to cover expenses granted by the Folketing, but where this limit is to be drawn must depend upon political not legal factors. For this reason I am not competent to give an opinion on the subject.

The rule of ministerial responsibility must afford protection . . . against abuses.

In a later case too (1959, p. 76, the Blechingberg Case), the Ombudsman held that he had no jurisdiction to criticize a statement made in the Folketing by the Prime Minister on his usual ministerial responsibility.

But if the complaint dealt with is a non-political issue, something to do with the administration of the Minister's department, the Ombudsman is competent. For example (1956, p. 119), an applicant had had a personal conference with the Minister of Finance. After-wards he wrote to the Minister and stated that, relying on an alleged promise from the Minister, he intended to import some specified goods. The point in issue was whether the ministry ought immediately to have informed the applicant that he was mistaken and that no such promise had been given, or whether the ministry was justified in not having corrected the mistake until the case was finally decided. The Minister held that his department had acted correctly in spite of the Ombuds-man's opinion that *in the circumstances* the applicant ought to have had immediate information.

An interesting borderline case was one reported in 1960 (p. 94). Before an election the Prime Minister had sent letters to voters on paper having the same design as that provided for him as Minister of his department for informal letters (the so-called 'underhaandsbreve'). The Ombudsman asked the Prime Minister to consider whether Ministers ought not to avoid using the above-mentioned design on letters sent to voters during an election campaign.[2]

The Courts. Judges were from the beginning kept completely outside the Ombudsman's competence, although Sweden and Finland have a different system. The reason for the Danish rule—which has now been accepted in Norway—is that supervision by the Ombudsman is thought to be against the principle of the independence of the judiciary. It is not because judges are considered infallible. On the contrary, they are subject to control by the Court of Complaints; when sitting in cases against judges this Court has three members: a Supreme Court Judge, an Appeal and District Court Judge, and a County Court Judge. At first the activities of deputy judges were within the control of the Ombudsman, but this resulted in some practical difficulties. After an amendment of the Act, the deputy judges are now subject to the Court of Complaints but not to the Ombudsman. Administrative tribunals, however, are within the Ombudsman's competence. Members of these bodies are *not* subject to the jurisdiction of the Court of Complaints. Many of the cases reported by the Ombudsman deal with the functions of such tribunals.

The Church. The Lutheran Church in Denmark is not a state Church

---

[2] The question of ministerial responsibility and the Ombudsman's control has recently been dealt with in a report of the Committee on Ministerial Responsibility [*Betænkning om ministrenes ansvar for regeringens førelse*, Statens Trykningskontor, Copenhagen, 1962].

in the proper sense of the word, but it has a very close connection with the state. Civil servants employed by it are subject to the Ombudsman's control, except in matters which directly or indirectly involve the tenets and preachings of the Church (the Directives, section 2).

Privately Owned Institutions. There have been some cases where the Ombudsman has held that he had jurisdiction over institutions that are not owned by the state. Such questions are decided according to the circumstances in each case. For example (1957, p. 164), the Ombudsman held that he was competent where a complaint was lodged against the head and the board of an independent home for children, since the Government paid all ordinary expenses of the institution, appointed the members of the board and had the final decision in the appointment of the head. Also, the National Bank of Denmark, which is not owned by the state but has many functions under modern currency and trade legislation, has until further notice agreed that it falls within the jurisdiction of the Ombudsman in all cases where it has powers to exercise a public function in relation to citizens (1957, p. 146). The question of the Ombudsman's jurisdiction in this field has not yet been finally decided.

Other Questions. The Danish Government holds shares in the Scandinavian Airlines System and appoints some members of its board. Two civil servants who held these appointments had failed to inform Ministers about developments in the financial situation of the company. Their activities in this respect were held by the Ombudsman to be within his jurisdiction (1961, p. 156).

Control Over Municipal Administration

As from April 1962 the Ombudsman's jurisdiction was extended to persons acting in the service of municipal authorities in all matters concerning which an appeal may be lodged with a government authority. But the municipal councils themselves acting as a body are, generally speaking, outside the Ombudsman's competence, although he *may* on his own initiative start an investigation if the decision of a council appears to involve a violation of essential legal interests.

Before the amendment was made, many representatives of municipal government interests maintained that to give the Ombudsman even a limited right of supervision would be detrimental to the important principle of local self-government. It is still too early to decide whether this dismal prediction will turn out to be true, although it does not seem very likely in view of the fact that in 1962 the Ombudsman did not receive more than three complaints within the scope of the amendment. It is, however, quite clear that the amendment will have one advantage. Formerly it often happened that the Ombudsman received complaints in cases which had been dealt with by the municipal authorities in the first instance and by a government authority upon appeal. It was

obviously unsatisfactory that the Ombudsman was competent to deal
only with the activities of the appellate body.

II. REMEDIES

The Ombudsman cannot *annul or amend* an administrative order, but
he has a number of other powers (secs. 9 and 10 of the Act and sec. 9
of the Directives as amended in 1962):

(a) If he finds that a Minister or a former Minister ought to be held
responsible under civil or criminal law he may submit a recommendation to this effect to the Folketing.

(b) If he is of the opinion that any other person within his jurisdiction
ought to be held responsible for a criminal offence he may order the
prosecuting authority to institute a preliminary investigation or to
prosecute such a person before the courts.

(c) If he considers there are sufficient grounds for instituting disciplinary proceedings he may order the competent administrative
authorities to start such proceedings against civil servants.

(d) He may state his views on the matter to the person whom the
complaint concerns.

He has never *ordered* a criminal prosecution or the initiation of
disciplinary proceedings. In one case (1961, p. 174) he *recommended*
to the Minister of the Interior to put a case before the Director of
Public Prosecutions, asking him to consider whether a member of the
National Service Board ought not to be prosecuted for violating his
duty to secrecy as to matters brought before the Board; but the Director
decided not to prosecute. This means that the powers dealt with under
a–c above have never been used. On the other hand, the Ombudsman
has very frequently made use of his powers to state his views on a case.
This has turned out to be at one and the same time a very flexible and
efficient instrument, through which he has exercised considerable
influence. He has used a great variation of expressions suited to both
the type of case and the gravity of the errors committed. Some examples
will be given below. If major mistakes or acts of negligence have been
committed, he not only states his opinion to the person concerned, but
he also makes a report to the competent Minister and *to the Folketing*.
He also makes a report if he is of the opinion that Acts or statutory
instruments ought to be amended (secs. 10 and 11 of the Act).

III. HIS INDEPENDENT STATUS

Although according to sec. 3 of the Act the Folketing may issue general
directives to the Ombudsman, it cannot interfere with the way in which
he deals with individual cases. This principle was stressed by the
Folketing in a case reported in 1959 (p. 76) when the majority of its

members held that as a matter of principle the Ombudsman ought not
to be asked to investigate a specified case. In 1955 (p. 105) the Ombudsman refused to comply with a request from the Minister of Agriculture
to investigate a case concerning the Royal Veterinary and Agricultural
College—one that had attracted much public attention. In his discussions with the Minister he stressed that, if he took up the case, he would
also have to consider whether the Minister or his department had
committed any faults. Actually the Ombudsman decided to investigate
both these cases on his own initiative. This meant that he was entirely
free as to which aspects of the case he wanted to deal with.

It is very important to keep this principle in mind: the control
exercised by the Ombudsman is not political. He acts as an independent
authority, although he must possess the general confidence of the
legislative assembly and may be dismissed if he loses it.

IV. PROCEDURE

According to section 6 of the Act any person may lodge a complaint.
There is no need to prove a special interest. If, however, the complainant has no *reasonable* interest in the case at all the Ombudsman may be
rather reluctant to institute an investigation. The complainant must
give his name and make his complaint within a year. The Ombudsman
may, however, always investigate a case on his own initiative and does
so quite frequently. This means that if there are real grounds for
investigation these formal rules will not prevent a case from being
dealt with.

Even if a complaint is lodged within a year and concerns a matter
within the jurisdiction of the Ombudsman, it will not necessarily be
formally investigated. Under section 6 of the Act the Ombudsman, on
receiving a complaint, decides whether there is sufficient occasion for an
inquiry. This means that he is entitled to dismiss the case at once—and
often does—when the statement of the complainant in itself is sufficient
evidence that there are no good grounds for complaint, or when the
complaint concerns certain groups of discretionary decisions where
experience has shown that the Ombudsman will not usually be competent to comment. Before dismissing the case, however, he will
frequently make a sort of preliminary investigation; e.g. he may study
the administrative file or hold an informal discussion with the officials
concerned.

These powers of summary investigation and rejection are of course
necessary. Otherwise there would not be sufficient time for the Ombudsman to concentrate on the really important cases, on matters of principle.
The institution must *not* develop on the model of government departments where the Minister sees only a small number of the cases. It is
also important that there should be no undue delay in answering
complainants.

Some recent figures will show how many cases are dealt with in this summary way:

	1958	1959	1960	1961	1962	1963
1. Total case load	1,101	873	1,100	1,065	1,080	1,130
2. No action taken or cases dismissed (incl. item 3)	809	692	891	891	928	979
3. Cases dismissed after summary investigation	249	253	288	307	239	254
4. Cases formally investigated	292	181	209	174	152	151
5. Critical comments made	60	39	49	48	36	53
6. Recommendations, etc.	17	18	12	16	14	10

These figures derive from the Ombudsman's official statistics. Items 1–4 show cases *initiated* in the relevant years, and items 5–6 are cases *closed* in these years. One reason the figures showing no action are so high is that the Ombudsman receives many complaints concerning matters that are outside his competence or where the prescribed time limit has been exceeded.

The real case load of the office is shown by the figures in categories 3 and 4: these are the cases within the Ombudsman's normal jurisdiction. It is interesting to note that the number of cases where a formal investigation has been considered necessary has decreased.

The term formal inquiry may be somewhat misleading, as it is much less formal than court procedure. According to section 7 of the Act the complaint must, as soon as possible, be put before the department concerned with a request for a statement. The department and the civil servants are under a duty to give the Ombudsman the information that he asks for and to provide him with the necessary documents. He may also summon witnesses to give evidence before a court, but it has never been necessary for him to do so. On the other hand, it quite frequently happens that he personally interviews the complainant or other persons concerned with a case. The Act makes applicable some of the rules restricting the duty to give evidence that apply in the ordinary courts. No formal decision about the scope of this section has ever been made. Nor has a formal decision been made on the important question whether the administrative authorities are under duty to submit their internal minutes to the Ombudsman. However, he is quite often given access to such minutes. He also has wide rights to inspect public premises.

The person against whom a complaint is directed is protected by the rule that his defence must be stated if the case is reported to the Folketing or if it is included in the annual report. If he is a permanent civil servant, he may ask for the complaint to be dealt with under the rules governing disciplinary investigations. This right has never been invoked. On the other hand, many civil servants have brought complaints against their superior officers.

The Ombudsman is under a duty to keep information secret if the circumstances of the case make this necessary (sec. 8 of the Act). This is a factor that has probably been of the greatest importance in his relationship to departments. It is easier for a public authority to release confidential information to him if it is known that it will be kept secret, and especially that it will not be communicated to the complainant or any other private persons or to the press.

V. ADMINISTRATIVE APPEAL AND ACCESS TO THE COURTS

Until the Act was amended in 1959 complaints could be taken up by the Ombudsman even if there was a right of appeal to a higher administrative body. Now such complaints are dismissed summarily. But if the complaint deals not with the decision itself but, for example, with the conduct of the subordinate authorities, the Ombudsman still has jurisdiction. He may also decide to investigate the decision itself on his own initiative (section 6 of the Act).

The Ombudsman is competent even if the subject matter may also be dealt with by the courts. And he may advise complainants as to the possibility of instituting a lawsuit (sec. 6 of the Directives). He may also recommend to the competent authorities that they grant free legal aid. Such recommendations have, until now, always been followed. In several cases the Ombudsman has recommended to administrative authorities to cause difficult legal problems to be brought before the courts. If a lawsuit has already been instituted before the Ombudsman receives a complaint, he does not usually make any comments, but he has now and then commented on problems of law (see, for example, 1958, p. 48, and 1960, p. 95).

VI. PROBLEMS DEALT WITH

According to section 3 of the Directives the Ombudsman is obliged to 'keep himself informed as to whether any person under his jurisdiction pursues unlawful ends, makes arbitrary or unreasonable decisions or otherwise commits mistakes or acts of negligence in the discharge of his duties'. This rule has given the Ombudsman a very free hand and has opened wide possibilities. It is interesting and useful to study the cases in the annual reports in order to see how it has been applied in practice.

1. Qualifications of Officials Making Decisions

Normally there are no general rules within departments as to which officials are entitled to make decisions or orders. The Ombudsman has dealt with the question in several cases.

Case 1956, p. 213: A building loan was partly revoked by a civil servant of a fairly low status. The Ombudsman held that a decision of this type ought to have been made by an official in the administrative class (the majority of whom hold law degrees).

Case 1960, p. 55: The Ombudsman did not criticize that an Under-Secretary had decided a case instead of putting it before the Permanent Secretary or the Minister.

2. Bias

Case 1957, p. 63: The Ombudsman recommended to the Minister of Finance that he consider an amendment of the taxation legislation to avoid some taxation officials sitting as members of appellate bodies and hearing cases that these officials had decided in the first instance.

Case 1956, p. 196: The Director of the Industrial Injuries Directorate is chairman of the Council of Industrial Injuries Benefits, although appeals against a number of the decisions made by the Directorate have to be lodged with the Council. The Ombudsman held that this was not compatible with fundamental legal principles.

Some of the cases show how difficult it may be to procure unbiased expert advisers. A typical case is 1960, p. 102: The permanent expert on questions of water supply employed by the Ministry of the Interior was the Director of the Copenhagen Water Supply Board, which is a party to a considerable number of the cases concerning water supply decided by the Ministry. The Ministry pointed out that it would be impossible to find a qualified expert who was not connected with some water supply board. The Ombudsman, therefore, did not criticize the Ministry for appointing the Director as its permanent expert, but he held that the Director ought not to have been consulted in a case which might have resulted in an action against the Copenhagen municipal authorities.

Cases dealing with bias on personal grounds are rare. In one, however (1958, p. 116), a professor had taken part in his faculty's discussion about a medical thesis by his son-in-law and in the University Council's discussions concerning the son-in-law's application for a research grant. This was naturally not approved by the Ombudsman, who made several recommendations to the faculty and the university for their future guidance.

3. Evidence

The evidence in an administrative case must be complete and correct. This is stated especially clearly in case 1958, p. 48, concerning a plumber who had been refused unemployment benefit. The Labour Exchange which had dealt with his case in the first instance had omitted some information in its memorandum to the Labour Directorate. 'The Exchange ought to have realized that it was of the utmost importance that in a case like this the Labour Directorate should receive exact information about all relevant circumstances.'

Hearsay evidence is not excluded, but if such evidence is communicated by a subordinate authority it must draw the attention of the deciding authority to the fact that the information is not based on direct evidence. In cases 1955, p. 76, and 1957, p. 231, information collected by subordinate authorities for the Agricultural Board later turned out to be inaccurate. In other cases the Ombudsman has insisted that evidence of importance to a case should be preserved in memoranda, reports, etc.

Authorities may in some circumstances be expected to make investigations to ensure that key evidence before them is correct. In the above-mentioned case concerning the plumber's unemployment benefit the Ombudsman says, in his letter to the plumber, 'I must regret that the Labour Directorate which on the basis of your letter of Oct. 17, 1955, must have known that the information given by the Labour Exchange (that you had not called there until Oct. 28) could hardly be true, did not before finally deciding the case try to clear this matter up'. The Ombudsman found special cause for disapproval in the fact that the Directorate had referred to this date in the reasons it had given for refusing the plumber's application.

Normally the authorities are also responsible for seeking supplementary relevant evidence not presented by the complainant himself. A typical example is 1957, p. 62: The Health Board had received a complaint about inconvenience caused by soot and smoke from a laundry. It did not take statements from three neighbours, whose names had been given by the complainant, and it did not order observation of the local conditions without previous notice to the owner of the laundry. It was held that these things ought to have been done before the Board decided the case. On the other hand, cases must not be delayed because the authorities want to collect irrelevant material (1957, p. 175). Nor are the citizens entitled to demand the assistance of the authorities to provide information that concerns issues other than those dealt with in the case concerned (1961, p. 77).

4. Failure to Give Applicants Information about the Evidence and the Opportunity to Argue Their Case

The Ombudsman has often dealt with these questions. Case 1957, p. 194, is especially interesting, for it concerned not an official but a private lawyer, the permanent counsel for the Government. He was criticized because he had not given the legal adviser of a private soldier, who was suing the Ministry of Defence for damages, sufficient access to the file of the case concerning the accident which had given rise to the lawsuit.

It is also important that applicants should be given sufficient opportunity to argue their case. The situation is, of course, clear if an Act or statutory instrument lays down that some matter must be put before an applicant. But the Ombudsman has made critical comments even in the cases where the authorities were under no statutory duty. For example (1957, p. 138), the Emigration Office ought to have informed an employer about the complaints of a young foreign girl working with him as a trainee, before allowing her to give up her employment. In 1960 (p. 55), he criticized the Ministry of Housing for only giving a municipal council the opportunity to argue its case through a telephone conversation between the chairman of the council and a junior official in the Ministry. (The case dealt with a matter which the council held to be a question of principle.) And in 1961 (p. 75), he held that a ministry ought to have granted an applicant an oppotunity for an oral conference even if there was no reason to think that the conference would have influenced the final decision.

5. *Other Procedural Rights of the Applicants*

Applicants are entitled to be informed about the final decision of a public authority. This rule applies even if it is decided to take no action at all. Case 1959, p. 41, illustrates this very well. Every year the Ministry of Works grants money for new roads to municipal authorities. Successful applicants are naturally informed about the grant, but formerly no information was given to authorities that did not get a share. Even though the Ministry had established this practice for a number of practical reasons, the Ombudsman held that as a matter of principle it was desirable that the Ministry should answer even unsuccessful applicants. If a case cannot be brought to its final conclusion within the normal time, for example because the department is considering legislative amendments or making a general investigation of the subject matter, applicants ought to be informed about the reason for the delay (1956, p. 177, and 1960, p. 105). In case 1958, p. 186, the Ombudsman held that a postman was entitled to have the final decision in a disciplinary action communicated in writing. It was not sufficient that the order of the authority had been made known to him by his superior officer.

A rather interesting problem was raised in case 1958, p. 255. The National Bank had decided that a business man who frequently had to send applications to the Bank, should not be allowed to communicate in person with the Bank, but only in writing or through other persons (employees or lawyers). The reason was that the complainant had over a long period been violent and abusive when discussing his cases with the officials of the Bank. In view of this the Ombudsman did not criticize the Bank; he informed the complainant that the question was within the jurisdiction of the ordinary courts.

6. *Information about Reasons for Decisions*

There is no general legal duty for administrative authorities to give reasons for their refusals. The Ombudsman has always been of the opinion, however, that it is important for the good relationship between citizens and the administration that the authorities show no reluctance to inform applicants about the circumstances on which they base their decisions. It will often be necessary for the citizen to have this information when he has to decide whether he wants to bring the case before the courts or lodge an administrative appeal. In 1956 (p. 218), it was stated that it was not sufficient for the authority to make a general and unspecified reference to the evidence in the case.

7 Information about a Right to Appeal

In 1958 (p. 40) the Ombudsman recommended the Ministry of Social Affairs to consider whether applicants should not always be made acquainted with the rules of the Industrial Injuries Benefit Act concerning their right of appeal. 'It must thus be held to be in accordance with administrative practice that the citizens are, as far as possible, advised and informed about rights of appeal.' If this refers to the general right of appeal to higher administrative authorities, which is an unwritten law in Danish administration, practice does not go quite as far as stated by the Ombudsman. But advice as to a right of appeal is probably always given when the special circumstances of the case demand it. And if there is a *statutory* right of appeal there is undoubtedly a growing tendency to inform applicants about their rights.

8. Administrative Standards

Administrative functions ought to be exercised in such a manner that the citizens are not inconvenienced more than is strictly necessary, and that no undue offence is caused. The last problem has been discussed in some cases where the activities of individuals or institutions have been made the subject of general investigation. It will often be felt as a special hardship if the investigation is conducted by the police. But even if a police investigation does not lead to a prosecution for a criminal offence, the Ombudsman does not criticize if it is shown that there were grounds for starting the inquiry (1957, p. 96, and 1955, p. 93). Civil servants must never be rude or arrogant, neither when they are in the right nor when they are in the wrong (1955, p. 55). A specially interesting case is 1961, p. 74, in which a complaint had been lodged about some comments made by the Director of the State Railways concerning the policy of the motor car industry especially in relation to the railways. He had also made some comments on the attitude of the newspapers to this problem. It was held that the Director had not exceeded the bounds of what must be considered permissible.

9. Unnecessary Delay

A very great number of the reported cases deal with this problem, which the Ombudsman considers of the highest importance. He has made general investigations of the problem in the General Taxation Tribunal and other institutions. Thus the question of how to avoid undue delay in the future has always held his attention as much as the matters which have caused particular complaints to be made.

10. *Other Errors*

Other errors drawn to the Ombudsman's attention have been extremely varied. For example, some documents had not been returned to an applicant who had asked for them (1958, p. 177); an answer to an application was sent to a lawyer who did not represent the applicant (1956, p. 212); incorrect information was given concerning the valuation of a house (1956, p. 151); illegible signatures were placed on public documents (1957, p. 186). In 1958 (p. 85), the Director of a Copenhagen bank which was the object of a number of press reports (and which later failed), untruthfully told some newspapers that the Inspectorate of Banks had endorsed its activities. The Ombudsman held that it would have been more correct if the Inspector had publicly denied the truth of the Director's statement instead of only calling its inaccuracy to the attention of the Director himself.

11. *Questions of Law*

It is quite clear that the Ombudsman will always comment adversely if the administrative authorities have acted against the law, whether statute or unwritten law. His cases on questions of law deal with a great variety of subjects, but the problems do not vary much from those in civil lawsuits dealing with the question whether the administration has acted *ultra vires*.

The 1961 report is especially rich in cases concerning fundamental principles of administrative law. Several cases deal with different aspects of the problem of *res judicata* (pp. 48 and 51), and one (p. 85) questions whether a department that has issued a statutory instrument is entitled to grant a dispensation from its rules even where there is no express provision made for such dispensations.

12. *Discretionary Powers*

As might be expected, many complaints concern the exercise of discretionary powers. In deciding these the Ombudsman has naturally been guided by the rules laid down in the Directives: he is to keep himself informed whether any person 'makes arbitrary or unreasonable decisions'.

The Ombudsman has done much to fix the limits within which discretionary powers must be exercised. He has often stressed that cases should be decided according to the prevailing practice, although this must not make the attitude of the official inflexible to such an extent that there is no longer any exercise of discretion (1958, p. 150). Also, similar cases must be decided in the same way; citizens have a right to expect equality before the administrative authorities as well as equality before the law. But often an analysis of the relevant factors will show that two cases are not really similar. If this happens the Ombudsman, of course, does not comment adversely. And if one applicant has obtained a permission because of an error by the administration, this does not give later applicants a right to succeed with similar applications. There have been surprisingly few cases concerning *détournement de pouvoir*. One of these is 1957, p. 169, which dealt with an application for taking over a taxi-cab owner's business. The Ombudsman was of the opinion that the Chief of Police, when deciding which applicant was to obtain the licence, was not entitled to take into consideration the price offered by the applicants to the former holder of the licence as payment for the good-will of the business.

But these are problems that the courts, too, have dealt with. It is therefore of central interest to study the Ombudsman's attitude to the *purely* discretionary element in administration—to the cases where he has found none of the above-mentioned defects. The reason for this is that even if he does not have *unrestricted* powers in this field, yet they are wider than those of the courts, which may not set aside unreasonable decisions.

In quite a number of the reported cases the Ombudsman only draws the attention of the complainants to his restricted powers. But even in such circumstances the reasons for the administrative decisions are often the object of much more detailed discussion than is normally found in a court judgment. A typical example is 1956, p. 86, concerning a dispensation from two sections in an Act. The Ombudsman says: 'Even if the arguments on which the dispensation from section 8 is based are not as weighty as those on which the dispensation from section 9 is based, I do not find that there are sufficient grounds for criticizing the decision of the Ministry of Trade.' In case 1958, p. 188, a civil servant had been dismissed because he had committed theft and had lost his right to a state pension. The Ministry of Social Affairs refused to grant him a normal old-age pension. The report makes it quite clear that the Ombudsman, during a personal conference with the Minister, argued strongly in favour of the applicant, but to no avail. In this case the Ombudsman contented himself with the statement in his report that 'he did not fully agree with the point of view of the Ministry'. (The applicant did obtain his pension later through the intervention of the Financial Committee of the Folketing.)

But there are also cases where the Ombudsman has expressed quite clearly that he found the exercise of discretion unreasonable. This happened in a recent case (1961, p. 54) in which he held that some discretionary decisions concerning payment of duty on imported goods could not, in the circumstances, be considered reasonable. In 1960 (p. 60), the police authorities decided, without previous notice, to order a man who had failed to pay a fine, to serve the optional term in prison fixed by the court when the fine was imposed. The Ombudsman did not find this decision reasonable. In cases like this the ordinary courts would not have been able to criticize the administrative authorities.

A number of cases involve expert opinion. Naturally the Ombudsman is very reluctant to disagree with the opinion of experts. But he has done so from time to time. In 1957 (p. 106) he criticized the opinion of the medical experts of the Industrial Injuries Directorate, who held that the state of health of a patient must be considered stationary—which meant that his claim for damages could be settled without awaiting further developments. The reason for the Ombudsman's attitude was that in the near future the patient would probably have to have one more of his fingers amputated. In the same year (p. 142) the Ombudsman also expressed his opinion upon whether a literary composition acquired by the Danish Broadcasting Company was a 'monodrama' or a short story.

The printed cases concern matters in which the Ombudsman has had to make formal decisions. But it is important to keep in mind that much of his influence is based on his direct contacts with the civil service through correspondence, conference, telephone conversations, etc. He has probably exerted considerable influence on the exercise of discretion by these methods—in contrast with the courts, which have no similar opportunities.

VII. CONCLUDING EVALUATION

The purpose of the preceding detailed analysis of the Ombudsman's work has been to attempt to show how he has made use of the wide powers granted to him by the Folketing. It is important to know what may technically be achieved in practice by this and other types of controlling authority. Of course, it is a political question what system of controls a country wants to have, but it is important that lawyers and political scientists provide sufficient material for the politicians and the public to make the best possible choice. Before undertaking the final evaluation of the Ombudsman's work, therefore, it may be useful to stress what may be achieved by judicial control.

It is worth noting that the courts cannot take any initiative on their own: they are not entitled to make general investigations, but must decide the issues put before them by the litigants. Their function is, moreover, to settle questions of fact and law, not of discretion. Law must, however, be taken in a fairly wide sense. For example, Danish courts, like the French Conseil d'État, can quash a decision because of *détournement de pouvoir*. If an administrative decision is based on an allegation that a citizen has acted dishonourably or in bad faith, the courts would normally also be competent. On the other hand, beyond such flexible but, after all, fairly objective standards they have no power. If a Minister has exercised a discretionary function and there is no error of procedure, no *détournement de pouvoir*, no unjust discrimination or any other violation of the rules of natural justice, judicial control is powerless. Even if the courts decide that an administrative error in law (in the wide sense indicated above) has been committed, this does not necessarily result in a court order setting aside the administrative decision or awarding damages. In many cases the error must be of a certain importance or have influenced the final decision of the authority. These principles of Danish law do not differ fundamentally, of course, from the principles of court jurisdiction in most other countries.

Two important areas of administration are, therefore, outside the courts' jurisdiction: (1) the purely discretionary element in decisions, and (2) minor errors of procedure and conduct, and similar questions of organization and efficiency. There are very strong reasons for restricting the powers of the courts like this. Discretionary decisions are normally made within fields where there are few or no objective standards. This means that a wider competence for the courts would make it very difficult for officials to plan a long-term policy because they would find it impossible to predict the attitude of the courts in cases brought before them by dissatisfied citizens. This problem would be still more serious if it were a question of government policy of central importance. It might in certain circumstances make it very difficult to plan a state budget or for the Government to pledge itself in Parliament to adhere to a certain economic policy.

To take an example: At present the Danish Government is cutting down public expenses very strictly. This must necessarily cause considerable hardship, e.g. to people who before the new economic policy was introduced, might reasonably have expected to obtain a public building loan. If an unsuccessful applicant for one of these loans were able to challenge the decision of the Ministry of Housing before the courts, the judge might possibly think that the Ministry had taken too strict a view and quash its refusal. This would force the Ministry to revise its refusals in similar cases and also to revise its future policy and thus cause an increase of public expenditure at a time when the responsible political bodies have come to the conclusion that the state budget must be cut down.

There are not the same practical reasons for excluding the Ombudsman's control, because he has no power to annul any administrative decision and thus upset a carefully planned policy. But he can discuss the underlying principles of practice and policy, and this will undoubtedly be extremely useful within many fields of administration. In actual practice—as shown above—he has had considerable influence within the field of pure discretion: in some cases he had made the authorities change their minds, but—what is just as important—in many cases he has caused a much more thorough discussion of the principles of the exercise of discretion than any case brought before the courts would have done. And it must be kept in mind that this influence is exercised to a much wider extent than may be deduced from the reported cases. Any step in this direction must be considered a highly useful development.

Are the Ombudsman's decisions concerning minor questions of official procedure, conduct and efficiency of the same importance? Is it necessary to set up an institution to tell officials that applications must not be left unanswered for months on end, that citizens are entitled to meet with civil behaviour when they visit a public office, etc.? In my opinion many civil servants tend to undervalue or disregard the importance of such problems, maintaining that what matters is that the final decision is right. They are apt to consider rules of procedure a stone in the path to efficient administration and hold that such rules may quite often be a disadvantage to the citizens themselves, as they tend to make administrative machinery less flexible. This point of view is to a large extent a mistake. Rules of procedure and carefully planned administrative techniques very often promote efficiency, as shown by the experience of the ordinary courts, where they ensure that the judge obtains the best possible evidence and that the cases are fully argued before they are decided. But even if formal rules do not make for better decisions, it is necessary to introduce them in order to protect the interests of the citizens. Such rules also tend to promote a good relationship between the administrators and the citizens. This is an advantage to both parties, since it will make citizens more willing to co-operate and more willing to accept an adverse decision without lodging an unnecessary complaint.

For these reasons it is useful that the Ombudsman has taken up this type of problem. It would give a wrong picture of the Danish administration, however, if it were not stressed that many of the principles laid down by the Ombudsman are already practised in government departments and by other public bodies. An Ombudsman appointed by the civil service might well have reached, in the majority of cases, the same decisions as the Folketing's Ombudsman.

The British Whyatt Report raises the question whether control by the Ombudsman will not hamper the efficiency of the administration. 'Under our constitution', it says, 'a Minister is responsible for the efficient administration of his Department and it might well be said that he would find it difficult, if not impossible, to discharge this duty if an independent body could, as of right, enter his Department and investigate allegations of maladministration without his permission.'[3] As noted above, nobody feared such consequences in Denmark, and experience has shown that there are no grounds for such fears. Neither has there been any tendency in civil servants to be less inclined than before to take responsibility without being protected by orders from the heads of the departments or by written rules.

It is indeed difficult to see how the Ombudsman's investigation of

[3] *The Citizen and the Administration: the Redress of Grievances—A Report* (Director of Research, Sir John Whyatt; London, 1961), 74.

a case might hamper the administration of a department. He cannot order the Minister or the officials to change any decision. Why should it prevent them from discharging their duties if the Ombudsman asks for a statement concerning the case, for permission to look through a file, or for a conference either with the officials or the Minister? If no error has been committed, nothing worse ensues than the trouble of having to write an additional letter or to fit an additional conference into a crowded programme. If any error has been committed, there is no reason to spare the feelings of Ministers and officials and no reason for them to complain that they have to spend their time on the matter. The only thing they may reasonably ask for is that the error should be dealt with in the proper perspective. There is a considerable difference between real misconduct in the service and the committing of an error which might happen to any busy and overworked official, and he would be the first to admit that it should not have happened.

From a Danish point of view the conclusion must therefore be that the Ombudsman's office has proved to be an extremely useful institution: it has supplemented the control without hampering the efficiency or independence of the administration. This has, moreover, been done with a small personnel and complaints have been answered quickly. The Ombudsman has been able to raise matters of principle even in cases where no formal complaint has been made, and he has a well developed technique which enables him to dismiss frivolous or unimportant complaints summarily. This means that, to a large extent, he has been able to concentrate on matters of more general interest or of importance to the future conduct of public business.

But the Ombudsman's work has not made judicial control super-fluous—in fact, he himself has from time to time recommended that questions of law concerning the exercise of administrative powers and other problems be brought before the courts, and the Law Reports contain as many and as important decisions concerning administrative law as they did before 1955. It is fortunate that the introduction of the Ombudsman system has not lessened the influence of the judiciary upon the development of the principles of administrative law. Instead, it has increased public discussion and interest in these vital problems and created opportunities for a more detailed control over executive authorities.

4

NORWAY'S OMBUDSMEN

THE OMBUDSMAN FOR CIVIL AFFAIRS
by Audvar Os*

I. THE BACKGROUND

1. *The proposal of the Expert Commission on Administrative Procedure*
The initiative to establish an Ombudsman in Norway was taken up by an Expert Commission on Administrative Procedure appointed by the King in Council to examine the question of more appropriate safeguards in public administration. This Commission published an extensive report in 1958. According to its terms of reference, it was to consider and make recommendations on:

(1) administrative procedure, both as regards adjudication and delegated legislation, and
(2) the control of administrative powers, comprising judicial review as well as parliamentary control.

Regarding the second item, the essential part of the Commission's considerations in dealing with parliamentary control was the question of establishing an Ombudsman corresponding to the Swedish and Danish institutions. The Commission unanimously agreed that such an institution was desirable, and put forward a Draft Bill for an Ombudsmann[1] to be based on the Swedish and, especially, Danish systems.

In discussing this proposal the Commission strongly emphasized that the benefit to be derived from the Ombudsman system would depend essentially upon the Storting (Parliament) finding the right person for the office. He ought to be a highly qualified lawyer and should be so well paid that the Storting could engage the best man. Moreover, he must possess such insight and authority that administrative organs and private persons as a rule would defer to his opinion.

The report of the Commission, together with the Draft Bill, was submitted for consideration to the Government, to its subordinated and affiliated agencies, and to many private organizations and associations. The great majority of opinions later received by the Government

* Assistant Attorney General of Norway.
[1] Hereafter the Swedish spelling will be used.

gave support to the proposal. In many cases, however, this was only lukewarm support, the agency concerned declaring that it had no adverse comments to make. Only a few institutions directly opposed the reform, and no central administrative agency took this point of view. Many agencies did, however, express serious doubts as to the advisability of the proposal. The Ministry of Commerce, for example, clothed its scepticism in these words:

Speaking on its own behalf, the Ministry of Commerce, all facts being considered, seriously doubts whether it is advisable to establish an Ombudsman system in Norway. Many facts tend to show that the rules of law in force, and those now proposed, concerning appeal to an administrative authority of higher rank, together with judicial and parliamentary control, give the individual sufficient protection against unfairness, fault and negligence in the exercise of administrative authority.[2]

On the other hand, the proposal was strongly supported by the National Associations of Commerce and of Industry, and by the Bar Association. And—what is more remarkable—the unions of civil servants had no objection. In Denmark the proposal met rather strong opposition from the civil servants. To avoid the same reaction in Norway, the Commission took great care to stress that the Ombudsman would not be 'the people's prosecutor' as against the officials. The activity of the Ombudsman was not intended to be directed *against* the administration. Instead, in dealing with the complaints submitted to him he would act as a neutral and impartial organ.

2. *The Government's View*

The Government accepted the Commission's proposal and in the early spring of 1961 introduced a Bill in the Storting. According to the Government's statement in support of the Bill, the motives behind the proposal were chiefly as follows:

The system of an Ombudsman may be of great help to anyone who feels that he has been subject to abuse of power by administrative authorities. To bring a suit at a court of justice may appear to be difficult and expensive. Not everybody will have the opportunity of having a case debated in the Storting by interpellation and question. Many people will also shrink from the idea of going to the newspapers with a case. By bringing the matter before the Ombudsman, the person concerned may have it examined in a simple and inexpensive manner.

The system will probably be advantageous to the public service also, as the Ombudsman will clear up and eliminate complaints which have no firm bases. In this way he may turn out to be a protector of govern-

[2] Government Bill no. 30 (1959–60), 6.

ment employees as against querulous and other quarrelsome persons. Further, the Ombudsman may lessen the burden of work for the members of the Storting, who now constantly get complaints from private persons concerning the activities of some administrative authority. . . .

With the standard our administration has today, it is indeed not likely that the Ombudsman will find a basis for criticism in any considerable number of cases. Experience both in Sweden and Denmark has shown that only in a relatively small number of the complaints is a basis found for further procedure. But the system may to some extent contribute to a higher degree of vigilance in public administration. And through a longer period of time its effect may be to strengthen confidence in the public service, and to create a feeling of security in the individual regarding his relations to the public service.[2]

Although basically the same, in one essential respect the Government's Bill differed from that of the Commission: the Government did not find it advisable to empower the Ombudsman to review the reasonableness of administrative decisions. During the public debate that followed its publication, the Bill was subjected to severe criticism on this point. (The detailed arguments are considered later, in part V of this essay.)

The Bill did not come up for reading during the session of 1961, it being a year of parliamentary elections, and a new Bill had to be introduced in 1962. The criticism against the 1961 Bill had been considered and rejected by the Government and the new Bill was presented in unchanged wording. But at the committee stage in the Storting the representatives were exposed to strong arguments from influential sources. It was pointed out that the Danish Ombudsman had the power to review administrative discretion. And the Danish Ombudsman himself, Professor Hurwitz, in an article in a Norwegian law review gave a short survey of his experiences in this respect, and stated as his opinion that such a competence had to be considered as a real advantage to the system.

The result of the discussion in the Storting was a kind of compromise: the final Bill gave the Ombudsman the right to scrutinize the exercise of administrative discretion, but only in so far as he should find the decision in question to be unlawful or *clearly unreasonable*. In this form the Bill was passed unanimously and the Act was promulgated on June 22, 1962. In November 1962, the Storting adopted the Instructions governing the Ombudsman's activity. At this time the discussion in the Storting was concentrated upon the question of the authority of the Ombudsman in relation to the Storting.

[2] Government Bill no. 30 (1959–60), 6.

II. POSITION IN RELATION TO THE STORTING

The Ombudsman is, of course, elected by the Storting. Only in this way is he thought to get both the necessary independence of the administration and the necessary degree of authority that is implied in his position as a delegate of the Storting. During the discussions in the Storting considerable attention was directed to this matter of his authority in relation to the administration and to the Storting. It was strongly emphasized that the Ombudsman should not be established as an organ for constitutional control with the power of calling persons to account. Nor should he be empowered to issue injunctions against the administration or to alter any administrative decision. Moreover, it was stressed that the Ombudsman should not be engaged in political questions. The Government, therefore, rejected a proposal that the Ombudsman ought always to be elected from supporters of the opposition parties in the Storting.

It is expressly stated in the Act that the Ombudsman shall carry out his task independently of the Storting. This independence, however, is somewhat limited. In the first place, the Storting lays down general regulations for his activity, as it has already done by the Instructions of November 1962. Secondly, the Storting may on certain conditions deprive the Ombudsman of his commission (see the Act, sec. 1, para. 2). The Norwegian law is, on this point, in accordance with the Swedish and Danish systems. The Commission had not put forward a corresponding provision, as it was of the opinion that such a rule would be of minor practical importance and, in addition, be at variance with the general Norwegian rules as to public commissions. The Government, however, felt that instances might occur when it would be desirable to discharge an Ombudsman who for some reason disappointed the confidence shown him. He might even violate the Storting's rules governing his activity. The Storting agreed with the Government on this point, but as a safeguard against a misuse of the majority party's power it was provided in the Act that the Ombudsman can be discharged only by a majority vote of two-thirds. This provision should enable the Ombudsman to act independently of any purely partisan opinion of the majority party in the Storting.

A special relationship between the Ombudsman and the Storting is established by the Ombudsman's submission of annual reports to the Storting (see also IV below). These reports will be handled by one of the permanent parliamentary committees, probably the Protocol Committee, since it already has the task of supervising the administration. Thereafter the reports will be subject to discussions in the Storting. It is to be expected that during these discussions the Ombudsman will sometimes be criticized, either because he has been too severe in his judgment or because he has not acted with sufficient energy on certain matters.

When the Instructions were up for discussion there was some anxiety among the members as to the authority of the Ombudsman in relation to the Storting. Much care was taken to make it clear that the Storting itself should still be free to take up for discussion or decision any complaint that might be sent to the Storting or to any of the representatives. On the other hand, the members excluded the Ombudsman from reviewing matters that previously had been dealt with by the Storting, by either of its chambers (the Lagting or the Odelsting), or by the Protocol Committee. In this respect the Instructions are in harmony with the fundamental idea of the new institution.

The Storting went further, however, by adding a provision in section 5 to the following effect: 'In cases that are submitted to the Ombudsman from the Storting or the Odelsting, he shall give his opinion, which shall be placed before the Storting or the Odelsting for decision.' Thus a special procedure was established, which deviates from the Ombudsman's regular procedure in two essential respects: firstly, he seems to be *under a duty* to take up and express his opinion on matters submitted to him by the Storting in this way; secondly, his opinion will not appear in the regular annual report, but in an *ad hoc* report, which will be discussed separately in the Storting. In such cases there is an evident risk that the Ombudsman will not only be opposed or criticized for his opinion, but even plainly repudiated by the Storting. Even if this is not likely to happen, it does not harmonize well with the principle of independence for the Ombudsman. On this point the Norwegian system differs from that in Denmark, where the legislature has no authority to enjoin the Ombudsman to take up certain matters.

III. COMPETENCE

1. *Which Public Authorities Come Within the Ombudsman's Competence?*

The province of the Ombudsman is the administrative agencies of government. It excludes the strictly municipal administration and, as in Denmark, the judiciary. The exclusion of the judiciary applies not only to the judicial but also the administrative functions of the courts, since it would be rather difficult to distinguish between these functions. The activity of the Storting and its divisions is, of course, outside his province. Decisions made by the King in Council (the Cabinet) are also outside his control. In this respect the political and constitutional control exercised by the Storting itself is thought to be sufficient. The Ombudsman has, however, authority to scrutinize a member of the Cabinet in his capacity as head of a ministry.

As to governmental administration, the Ombudsman's field of competence is rather extensive. It comprises all branches of the public service and concerns not only the exercise of public authority but also business-like activity managed by the state and services rendered in connection with education, research and health. The armed forces are technically within his jurisdiction too. But since Norway has had an Ombudsman system for the armed forces since 1952 (see next essay), it is not expected that he will be very active in this area.

Whether the Ombudsman's competence should also include municipal administration was a matter of concern during the preparation of the Act. This question was thoroughly discussed in the report of the Commission and its conclusion was that for the time being municipal administration should not be included: Norway should first gain some experience with the Ombudsman system. It proposed, however, that the Ombudsman might be given the power when dealing with a case at a higher level that had been decided in the first instance by a municipal organ, to examine the procedure applied by that organ. And if the case concerned or was connected with the deprivation of personal liberty, the Ombudsman should have authority to deal with any administrative level, including decisions made by municipal agencies.

The Government concurred in the Commission's proposal in these words:

It seems right to proceed with some care, and consequently natural to delimit his main province to the administrative agencies of the central government. Subsequently, experience may show the necessity for a general extension of the Ombudsman's province to municipal administration. To some extent, however, decisions by subordinate municipal authorities should be subjected to the Ombudsman. In Sweden as well as in Denmark it has been felt as a disadvantage that the Ombudsman, when controlling the superior administrative authority, has been precluded from investigating the procedure of the lower municipal agency.[3]

Attention was drawn to the system in the other Nordic countries in this respect. Both in Sweden and Denmark the law had recently been amended to extend the Ombudsman's province to parts of the municipal administration. In Finland this area of administration had always been within the Ombudsman's control. The Government felt that the practical solution was to let the Storting—according to the need from time to time—determine in the Instructions which lower municipal authorities should come within the competence of the Ombudsman. And the Instructions of 1962 gave the Ombudsman a rather free hand in this respect. There is really no limit other than the Ombudsman's own judgment on the necessity of extending his investigations to municipal organs. Where the deprivation of personal liberty is involved, it is quite clear from the Act (sec. 4) that the Ombudsman can control any municipal organ.

In practice many borderline questions will arise as to the scope of the expressions 'Government administrative organs' and 'other public servants', as used in section 4 of the Act. For instance, it is not possible

[3] *Loc. cit.*, 8.

today to draw a clear line of distinction between governmental and municipal administration. It will therefore not always be evident if an official or a commissioner is in the 'service of the state' or in the service of a county municipality. Also, the line of distinction between administrative activity and other kinds of state activity, particularly of a business character, may be dubious.

Realizing these specific problems, the Government chose the solution of having the Act give the Storting competence to resolve such border-line questions in the Instructions. Even if agencies undoubtedly should be regarded as belonging to the 'governmental administration' or 'state service', the Storting is entitled to determine that they shall not fall within the Ombudsman's control where this is thought to be un-necessary—particularly agencies which do not make decisions of any importance to the individual citizen, and where the control exercised by the Auditor of Public Accounts may be regarded as sufficient. The Storting may also decide if a particular organ is to be regarded as a 'court of justice'.

In the same way the Act gives the Storting power to determine that particular parts of a government institution's functions should be excepted from the Ombudsman's supervision. In the rules for the Danish Ombudsman it is determined that servants of the established Church are within his competence except for questions which directly or indirectly concern the Church's confession and preaching. A similar exception may turn out to be desirable in Norway. So far, however, the Storting has not acted under this provision of the Act. On the other hand, it has expressly stated in the Instructions that certain county organs shall be regarded as part of the Government's administration for purposes of the Ombudsman's supervision.

2. What Matters May the Ombudsman Investigate?

The Ombudsman's control is not limited to administrative activity in regard to private citizens, but also applies to internal personnel administration—appointments, disciplinary measures, dismissals, etc. Thus a public employee has the right to complain to the Ombudsman if the appointing authority proceeds illegally against him or commits procedural errors. Moreover, the Ombudsman's control comprises not only decisions in particular cases but also the exercise of rule-making power. The main bulk of his activity, however, will certainly apply to particular cases. As for the rule-making power, his main job will be to call the administration's attention to procedural defects in rules and regulations as well as substantive defects such as inadequate wording that results in an unreasonable application of a rule.

3. Under What Conditions May the Ombudsman Act?

Although the Ombudsman may raise a case on his own initiative, the principal cause of action is expected to be a complaint from an injured citizen. According to the Commission's Draft Bill, a complaint could have been submitted by anybody, but the Government tightened the Bill by demanding a certain *party interest* as a condition for an actionable complaint. This is not, however, carried further than that the complainant himself *must be affected* by the matter he brings before the Ombudsman. Requiring a party interest is expected to reduce the number of complaints from cranks and from those who would like to exploit the Ombudsman system for purposes of propaganda. For instance, certain organs of the press might otherwise try to profit by putting cases before the Ombudsman in order to 'blow them up'.

The formal requirements for a complaint are in other respects modest: the complaint has to be signed, and it must be rendered not later than a year after the action complained of took place or ceased. If the time is overdue, the Ombudsman is not required to look into the matter, but neither is he prevented from doing so on his own initiative. Also, he is always completely free to decide whether a duly filed complaint gives sufficient grounds for any action at all on his part.

It has been a matter for consideration whether administrative appeal should be exhausted before a case can be taken up by the Ombudsman. The Government was of the opinion that he should not ordinarily deal with *decisions* as long as the right to make appeal to a superior authority is open. However, sometimes it can be an advantage if the Ombudsman may interfere at once and examine the matter when fresh. It might also give the Ombudsman a better opportunity to conciliate if he is brought into the picture before the decision is 'final' and has become a matter of prestige. When the complaint relates to procedural matters—e.g. neglect to answer applications or other tardiness—it is quite clear that the Ombudsman should not have to wait until the case has been dealt with by the superior authority.

The Government left this whole question to be settled in the Instructions, which now state that the exhaustion of remedies is to be the general rule, but at the same time that the Ombudsman may deal with a complaint right away if he finds a special reason to do so. He may also intervene when appeal to the King is the only remedy available. Because appeal to the King means in practice to the Cabinet, to require appeal first in such cases would actually prevent the Ombudsman from dealing with them, because decisions of the Cabinet are exempt from his competence.

IV. PROCEDURE

The Ombudsman is given wide freedom to choose the procedure he may find appropriate in each particular case. Two important rules, however, govern his procedure. If he decides to proceed with a complaint, ordinarily he must submit it to the agency or public servant concerned. It is expected that the only exception to this rule will be when such a procedure clearly would prevent the enlightenment of the case. Another basic rule is that the Ombudsman must inform the complainant of the result of an investigation. However, it is up to the Ombudsman to decide to what extent the information he has gathered will be placed before the complainant for his comments.

The Ombudsman has a wide authority to demand information and the production of documents and records from all officials and public servants. This authority also applies to municipal servants in those cases where the Ombudsman's competence is extended to municipal organs. If he should need information from others not willing to give it voluntarily, he may order evidence to be taken by the courts. A provision substantially corresponding to this also applies in Denmark and in Sweden.

The Expert Commission had suggested that the Ombudsman should also have access to the internal working papers of the civil service. But several administrative agencies expressed doubt as to such an extensive right to demand information—having in mind the manner in which the administration performs its duty today. It was feared that such a right would entail a new and cumbersome routine in the execution of public business. Today officials may use an informal mode of expression, knowing that it will be read only by superior officials. Should all files be open to the Ombudsman, it was argued, officials would be compelled either to phrase memoranda in a more formal and less informative way, or to avoid committing themselves in writing by giving opinions orally. Frankness and confidence between superior and subordinate officials would be especially likely to be injured.

In accordance with such arguments it was agreed that the expression 'documents' in section 7 of the Act does not include the internal working papers, but only the 'official' documents. This means letters, declarations and the like forwarded to an administrative authority or procured by it from others, and letters from the administrative authority occasioned by the case. The expression 'records' means especially records which the administrative authority concerned, *according to statutes or regulations*, is required to use. But the Ombudsman will also have power to demand records used according to established practice, unless they are kept only for internal use.

The Government agreed with the Commission that the Ombudsman should have at least the same right as the courts to demand information hedged by the rules of secrecy about official or business matters (see secs. 204–209 in the Civil Procedure Act). The Commission had proposed that government officials should give the Ombudsman information without hindrance by the rules of secrecy. In judicial proceedings, however, an official must have permission from superior authority in order to give evidence about restricted matters. And the Government held that there was no reason to have a different system for the Ombudsman. This would also accord with the principle that the

Ombudsman should not unconditionally have access to internal documents. Part of the official's professional secrecy is not to divulge information on his own stand in a case to persons who are not concerned with it. Since the Ombudsman has no right to see the official's written recommendations, it was agreed that he should not be able to enjoin the official to give oral testimony on the matter. However, the authority concerned may permit the official to give oral testimony. Thus the Ombudsman in this regard is placed in the same position as are the courts. The Ombudsman himself and his employees are also under the secrecy rules unless he considers the divulging of certain information to be 'necessary for the performance of his duty'.

It is not intended by the Norwegian Act that the Ombudsman should undertake inspections at random. Although he has the right of access to all official establishments, his right must only be exercised while investigating individual cases. It will depend upon the Ombudsman whether he is content with having the material on a case transmitted or finds reason to visit the authority concerned. A visit may especially prove valuable when the complaint relates to treatment in a prison or other institution.

It is assumed that the press will take a great interest in the work of the Ombudsman. In all probability his annual report will not satisfy the press, which wants to have fresh news about cases pending before the Ombudsman. To meet this problem the Act states that the Ombudsman himself shall decide 'whether and if so in which manner he shall inform the public of his action in the case'. The chief purpose of this provision is to protect the Ombudsman against aggressive newsmen and other curious people. He is free not only to choose the form of publication he may find appropriate, but also to decide not to publish anything about it at all. Cases might appear, of course, which are not suitable for publication—for instance, cases where the security of the state is involved or where the complainant does not wish any publicity.

To enable the Storting and the administration to follow the work of the Ombudsman, he must submit a printed annual report, and he may also submit a special report to the Storting and the ministry concerned if he 'becomes aware of negligence or errors of major significance or far-reaching importance'. According to the Instructions the annual report must give a survey of the proceedings in cases which are of general interest. If he has found no basis for a complaint, neither the name of the complainant nor of the administrative agency or official is to be mentioned in the report. Names may be omitted in other cases, too, when the Ombudsman finds a particular reason for doing so. For instance, a complainant may have good grounds for wishing to be kept anonymous. The report must not contain information regarding trade, business or official secrets.

An important rule is that in mentioning a case the report must always contain a summary of the statement given in defence by the agency or official concerned. In this way the administration will be able to justify its action or omission. Experience from Sweden, Finland and Denmark, where reports are issued according to corresponding provisions, shows that the important cases will be edited more or less like court decisions. The report of a case will contain a summary of the complaint, followed by the arguments of the administrative agency, then the results of supplementary investigations, and finally the opinion and conclusion of the Ombudsman. If he has found reason to express criticism, the report will usually give information on the reaction to this by the agency concerned. As in the other Nordic countries, it is expected that the annual reports will become valuable sources of information on administrative law.

V. POWERS

1. Power to Proceed Against an Official?

An important problem in the preparation of the Act was the powers to be given to the Ombudsman. The Swedish as well as the Danish Ombudsman are entitled to order prosecution of or disciplinary proceedings against an official. They may not, however, annul a decision, but may express their opinion as to how a decision should have been made and how a statue should be interpreted. This power is often exercised. In Sweden proceedings are in some instances instituted against officials. But this is mainly due to the rigid Swedish laws on official liability. The Danish Ombudsman has not as yet used his power to demand proceedings against any official.

The Commission concluded that it was not necessary to vest in the Ombudsman himself authority to prosecute or order prosecution or disciplinary proceedings. It was further argued:

Considering the Ombudsman system contemplated in the Draft, it is assumed that the Ombudsman's position will be as strong, if not stronger, when he does not become a party to the proceedings but bases his work on his confidence and authority. After having made his investigation, he will express his opinion to the administrative authority and the private person or organization concerned. He may point to any illegal or neglectful conduct discovered. Having in mind the Ombudsman's knowledge and authority and his highly trusted position, one may assume that the administration and the citizen will generally defer to his opinion.

It goes without saying that if he so wishes he may also express his opinion on how a particular case should have been decided. If after completing his investigations he thinks that anybody has been subjected to injustice and has suffered damage, he will not have to stop at pointing to this. He may also—if he considers it right—state that damages ought to be paid. If he considers it justified according to the circumstances of the case, he may also recommend that the authority concerned either compensate the injury or render another decision.

One might ask whether the Ombudsman may recommend that the public prosecutor indict an official, or that the appointing authority dismiss or take disciplinary measures against him. As already mentioned, the Ombudsman should not have authority to order such measures. But if he considers it justified, he should be at liberty to express his opinion as to what should be done.[4]

No objection was raised against this view of the Commission. In fact, it was further pointed out that if the Ombudsman should be given power to order the prosecuting authority to indict or the appointing authority to take disciplinary measures or instigate proceedings for dismissal, the character of his position would change. This would, among other things, raise constitutional problems. In Norway the King is the highest prosecuting authority as well as the head of the state's administration. Hence the Ombudsman's instructions to the prosecuting or appointing authority would be binding on the King in Council (or Cabinet). According to our constitutional practice, although the Storting may interfere in particular administrative cases and make decisions binding on the administration, this has to be done by a formal vote in plenum. And it is assumed that the Storting may not generally delegate this power. Hence it would be considered necessary to amend the Constitution in order to enable the Storting to vest in the Ombudsman power to give instructions binding on the administration, even though this control would not directly include the King in Council. This constitutional problem did not arise in Denmark because the Constitution itself declares that there shall be a parliamentary Ombudsman to supervise the nation's civil and military administration. In Sweden, too, the principal provisions governing the Ombudsman are inserted in the Constitution. Because of the limited powers proposed for the Norwegian Ombudsman, it was not necessary to amend the Constitution.

The Ombudsman's power, then, is limited to expressing his opinion on cases or matters brought before him. It is a fundamental assumption, however, that the complainant as well as the administrative authority will usually defer to the Ombudsman's opinion. The Ombudsman's decision will have its effect mainly through his strong personal authority.

2. Power to Review Discretionary Decisions?

The main fields of the Ombudsman's concern are expected to be incorrect applications of the law, wrong evaluations of the evidence, administrative mistakes, omissions or delays, and errors in administrative procedure. But, as noted earlier, he was also given the power

[4] *Loc. cit.*, 10.

to criticize abuses in the exercise of administrative discretion. In this respect his competence is similar to that of the courts. Although the Commission would have given the Ombudsman a wider competence, enabling him also to review the reasonableness or wisdom of administrative decisions, this proposal was put forward with some hesitation:

Objections of considerable weight may be made to letting the Ombudsman also deal with the exercise of the purely discretionary part of the administrative decision. The Ombudsman is not intended to be a superior administrative authority; this may, however, easily be the result if he deals with questions of an entirely discretionary nature, where the decision and the responsibility rest with administrative officials. We believe that public servants, who have a very difficult task especially in the exercise of administrative discretion, should be as self-reliant and independent as possible in their work.

It cannot be denied, however, that for the individual there exists a need for some authority outside the administration that can examine his case. This is especially so in cases regarding permissions, licences, grants, etc., which gradually have gained great importance in the administration. It therefore seems correct not to deny to the Ombudsman, in the statute, the right to deal with and express his opinion on the administration's exercise of discretionary power if he finds reason to do so. According to the broad wording [in our Draft Bill] the Ombudsman will have this right.

It goes without saying that the Ombudsman should exercise his power in this respect with great caution. He should not express any criticism unless he considers the decision so unreasonable that the administration in his opinion has committed an error. . . .[5]

The Government—depending on opinions expressed by several administrative agencies—did not agree with the Commission. To vest in the Ombudsman the power to examine the exercise of administrative discretion was thought to be rather precarious. He might thereby become a sort of superior administrative authority, which might prove harmful to the independence of the officials in their work. The Government went on to say:

If the Ombudsman were given power to review the administration's exercise of discretion with his own, he would only in a very few cases consider it possible to do this with the assurance and authority which he ought to possess in his work. What would be gained by extending the Ombudsman's power thus far, would, in the Government's opinion, be less valuable than the confusion and uncertainty that might arise within the state administration if a new reviewing authority were created on top of, or independent of, all established authorities.

[5] *Loc. cit.*, 8–9.

Disputes between the administration and the Ombudsman as to how discretionary power should be exercised would put the Ombudsman in a difficult position and might in the course of time undermine his authority. Nor is it necessary to give the Ombudsman such extensive power in order to enable the Ombudsman system to function adequately.

According to section 10 in the Government's draft, the Ombudsman's right to criticize the substance of decisions shall be limited to controlling their *legality* in the broader sense. Applied to the exercise of discretion this means that he—in the same manner as the courts—may criticize a decision only when it should be regarded as invalid because it is arbitrary or motivated by considerations falling beyond the scope of the governing Act. On the other hand, the Ombudsman may not express his point of view on the reasonableness and adequacy of the decision.

With regard to the right to criticize the procedure of the administration, of course, the Ombudsman should have great liberty. In addition to criticizing faults with regard to preparatory work on a decision, and stating whether or not the decision for this reason should be regarded as invalid, he should have the right to criticize any tardy dealing with the case, neglect of answering applications, the personal conduct of the officials and the like.[6]

The Government also pointed to the risk of creating among the public an expectation which the Ombudsman would not be able to fulfil if his competence were to include the discretionary element. Accordingly, the relevant provision in section 10 of the Government's Bill had been formulated as follows: 'If the Ombudsman comes to the conclusion that a decision must be regarded as unlawful, he may state this.'

As already mentioned, heavy criticism was launched against the Government's proposal on this point. Among other things, it was said that to limit the Ombudsman's importance in this way was to curtail the fundamental idea behind the institution, as his power would be no more extensive than that of the judiciary. The public discussion of this problem was still flourishing when the Bill came to the committee stage in the Storting, and the conflicting views prevailing among the representatives are plainly reflected in the following words in the report of the parliamentary committee:

The Committee realizes the necessity of proceeding cautiously in this important field, and concurs with the Government in its view that it would be injurious to the institution if the formulation of the Ombudsman's competence should create false impressions of his real task.

The Committee is, on the other hand, of the opinion that the Ombudsman's field of action should not be too strictly limited. Within

6 *Loc. cit.*, 10.

certain boundaries he ought to be empowered to review administrative discretion. In the opinion of the Committee this would be both in the public interest and in the interest of the administration as well.

In this connection regard has been taken of the experience in Denmark.

The Committee has therefore decided to give the Ombudsman an opportunity to take action against discretionary decisions to a further extent than proposed in the Bill, but agrees with the Government that the Ombudsman should not be granted a *general* authority to express his view on administrative discretion. He may review and give his opinion on discretionary decisions, but only those which are found to be clearly unreasonable or otherwise clearly in conflict with fair administrative practice.[7]

As mentioned, the provision in section 10 was consequently changed into this wording: 'If the Ombudsman comes to the conclusion that a decision must be regarded as unlawful or clearly unreasonable, he may state this.' And in this form the Bill was unanimously passed by the Storting.

Some months later the corresponding rule in the Instructions got a slightly different formulation: 'If the Ombudsman comes to the conclusion that a discretionary decision is clearly unreasonable *or otherwise clearly in conflict with fair administrative practice*, he may state this.'

The phrase in italics, the same as that used in the report of the Committee, was an addition compared with the Act. As the borderline here, of course, is set by the Act itself, this phrase can only be regarded as a construction or an elucidation of the expression 'clearly unreasonable'. It is a question, however, whether this well-intended supplement really has clarified and not confounded the important and disputed problem of competence regarding discretion.

VI. EVALUATION

It is rather difficult to make prophecies and—as it has been said— especially about the future. How the Ombudsman system will work in Norway is dependent on many uncertain factors. The nature of the institution will of course depend very much upon the actions of the first Ombudsman, Andreas Schei, who was elected by the Storting in December 1962. Mr Schei was a Judge of the Supreme Court, and is considered to be an excellent lawyer with many years of experience in the civil service and on the bench. There is no doubt that the Storting succeeded in obtaining a lawyer from the top of the list of desirable candidates.

[7] Innst. O.XV (1961–62), 5 [Committee for Foreign and Constitutional Affairs, *Report*, O.XV (1961–62), 5].

The Ombudsman started his work in January 1963, and issued his first report to the Storting in the spring of 1964. According to this report 1,257 complaints were registered at his office in 1963. In addition, 18 cases were raised on his own initiative. The number of complaints was unexpectedly high, even taking into account the special circumstances of the first year's existence of this new institution. Only 412 complaints were subject to further investigation, however, and 75 of these were still pending before the Ombudsman at the end of the year. Most of the complaints which were dismissed referred to matters outside the field of his competence—especially decisions by courts and municipal agencies.

Of the 327 cases decided, 250 resulted in no change or comment. In 39 cases the decision complained of was changed while the case was pending in the office, without any comments from the Ombudsman. There remained 48 cases which gave rise to criticisms or suggestions. In two of these, compensation was given where faults had inflicted damage upon the claimant.

The major groups of complaints are matters within the civil service (wages, working conditions, etc.) and the field of social insurance. In the cases taken up for consideration the complaints have usually been directed against the content of a decision. Only rarely has the administrative procedure been subject to attack, and then delay in answering applications has been the main issue.

The high number of complaints indicates that the Ombudsman has been met with confidence and high expectations, even though 'the man in the street' seems to be somewhat confused as to the Ombudsman's real competence and powers. It also appears from the report that his intervention has been useful and appropriate in quite a number of cases. However, he has not revealed any major defects in the administrative system or instances of corruption on the part of a civil servant. It is rather striking that so many complaints originate from civil servants themselves.

Even though it is generally admitted that the institution has come to stay, there is still some scepticism prevailing as to the necessity of this new institution. 'Is our public administration really so poor that we have to have such a special inspector?' is a question put forward from different quarters. The answer to this is obviously 'no'. There was, and is, no *compelling need* for an Ombudsman in our society. The experience so far gives a clear indication of that. The correct point of view is to regard this reform as an expansion of the existing safeguards in our legal system in order to improve even further the relationship between the public authorities and the individual citizen.

THE MILITARY OMBUDSMAN
AND HIS BOARD
by Arthur Ruud*

Norway established an Ombudsman scheme for the armed forces in 1952. Although the Swedish military Ombudsman was its prototype, this scheme diverges in certain essential respects from the Swedish system. The main reason for this is that the Norwegian scheme was adjusted to fit a previously existing system of representative committees in Norway's armed forces.

As early as 1912 there were provisions in the defence force's regulations to the effect that the rank and file could choose representatives who would be able to take up for discussion with superior officers the problems of the ordinary soldier. This system has in course of time been developed, especially since the last world war, so that today there is a representative committee for each military detachment of more than thirty-five men. The committee consists of the commander of the detachment and elected representatives of the rank and file. The development of the system in recent years is due particularly to the reports of two official committees, the Representatives Committee and the Service Term Committee, which reported in 1948 and 1950 respectively. The Committee of 1948 strongly recommended the further development of the system of representatives. It found that this would constitute a definitely democratic step, and would serve to create confidence, co-operation and solidarity among all categories of the defence forces.

In the formulation of the provisions for the representative committees, the view of the Representatives Committee, which was later supported by the Service Term Committee, was accepted that the committees should only be consultative and advisory bodies for the commanders. Thus they have no determinative authority. The right to make decisions and hence the responsibility still lie in the hands of individual commanders. In the committees both the commander and the representatives can take up for discussion any problems and difficulties which may arise for the rank and file during their term of military service.

On account of the authoritarian organization of defence forces, the representative committees could not, of course, be given determinative authority. Looked at from the point of view of the rank and file, however, this was a weakness in the system, for the representatives had no means of putting into effect any measure at all if the commander was opposed to it. The idea of a further development of the system therefore naturally emerged, and it is partly in this connection that the idea

* Ombudsman for the Armed Forces.

of a central representative, an Ombudsman for the defence forces, first came forward. The idea was that this central representative should be able to take up for consideration and carry further the matters that the representatives had had up for discussion in the committees without finding any satisfactory solution for them. The work in this sector has, in course of time, become an important part of the military Ombudsman's activity. An important feature of our scheme relative to that of Sweden or Western Germany is that with us the military Ombudsman forms the top point of the representative system, with all the tasks within this sector that this involves.

Another consideration which was determinative in setting up the Norwegian scheme was regard for the individual soldier and his feeling of legal security. It is true that the legal security of the rank and file is safeguarded in the defence laws and regulations, but under the conditions of obedience and subordination which exist and must exist in the armed services, it may sometimes appear to the individual that he has not the same legal protection as in civilian life. In order to remedy this the military Ombudsman was to be a functionary to whom the rank and file could apply, outside the regular service path, for advice and help. In this way the institution was to contribute to a stronger feeling of legal security.

The Service Term Committee, which proposed such a central representative, made the following statement:

In order to give conscripted men a stronger feeling of legal security the Committee proposes that there shall be created a Representative for the Armed Forces selected by the Storting [Parliament]. All members of the armed services will be able to apply directly to the Representative in order to get advice and help if they cannot obtain it in any other way. Also the representative committees ought to be able to go to the Representative if the questions concerned cannot be settled locally.

This central representative should have such a strong position that he can obtain information anywhere at all within the Defence Force in connection with the matters submitted to him.

Sweden has a *Riksdagens Militieombudsman* who has, however, a wider field of activity than what is suggested here for a similar Norwegian institution. According to his instructions the Militieombudsman shall exercise a general supervision to see that laws and instructions are observed by all service and civilian functionaries who are paid out of defence funds and shall take steps to prosecute any person who infringes them.

Our proposal does not, as stated, imply a system of such scope as the one in Sweden. The Representative for the Armed Forces shall primarily exercise control and intervene if the legal security and rights of officers or the conscripted rank and file are violated. Thus it is chiefly the juridical aspect of the work of the Militieombudsman we think should be assigned to the Representative for the Defence Forces.[1]

The Government reacted positively to this statement, and in its budget for 1951–52 the Ministry of Defence proposed an appropriation in order to get the system of a special representative, or Ombudsman as he was now called, put into effect. In this connection the Ministry stated:

The Ministry thinks that both the conscripted men and the Defence Force will be benefited by the creation of such a post as the Service Term Committee has proposed. No doubt the conscripts' legal security and legal position are satisfactorily protected by the law and regulations. Nevertheless an Ombudsman for the Armed Forces, to whom the conscripts and their representatives can apply outside the so-called regular service path, would acquire an important function in creating a feeling of legal security among the conscripted men and in fact contribute to the laws and regulations in force being observed in full. From the point of view of the Defence Force there is also ground for giving weight to the viewpoint of the Army Commander-in-Chief that it will be an advantage if criticism on the part of the rank and file is conducted to such an institution, instead of finding its way along other channels.

The Ministry agrees with the scope which the Committee has outlined for the work of the Ombudsman. If the Ombudsman is to be able to fulfil his functions, he ought, as the Committee suggests, to have such a strong position that he can obtain information in any part of the Defence Force in connection with the questions submitted to him. The Ministry thinks that it would serve the purpose best if the Ombudsman for the Armed Forces were appointed by the King and in administrative respects served under the Minister of Defence. The Ministry thinks that it would be wise to try the system in practice for a three-year period. Detailed instructions for the Ombudsman should be fixed by Royal Decree.[2]

The reports from the Service Term Committee and the Ministry, and the Ministry's Draft Bill, were subsequently considered by the Storting's Military Committee. The latter gave its support to the proposal, but stated:

The Committee would urge the Ministry to examine the question whether his field of activity ought not to be somewhat wider than

[1] Tjenestetidsutvalgets innst. (the Service Term Committee's report), 1950, side 34.
[2] St. prp. nr. 1, Forsvarsdepartementet (Ministry of Defence), 1951–52, KAP. 910, pkt. 6.

indicated by the Service Term Committee and in the Bill, and whether he ought not to have a relatively small committee to assist him.

The Committee thinks that the Ombudsman should be nominated by the Storting, in order to give him the most unfettered possible position and authority. The sphere of authority and responsibility of the Ombudsman and such a committee, in relation to the military and civil authorities, should be made clear in the Ministry's memorandum.[3]

The Ministry complied with the Storting's desire that the Ombudsman should be chosen by the Storting. It was proposed further that the Ombudsman should become chairman of a board with, besides himself, six members, and that their field of activity should be widened in conformity with the Storting's wishes. The matter was then debated in the Storting and the system was adopted. Instructions for the Ombudsman and the board were adopted at the same time.

Since the Instructions are brief, they are quoted here in full:

1. The Ombudsman Board shall assist in safeguarding the civic rights of personnel in the armed forces and also by means of its activities endeavour to increase the efficiency of the armed forces.

2. The Ombudsman Board shall consist of seven members elected by the Storting for a term of four years. One of the members shall be elected as chairman and shall be called the Ombudsman for the Armed Forces. The Ombudsman shall be paid a yearly salary. The salary shall be fixed by the Storting. The other members shall be remunerated in accordance with the scale for committees.

3. The functions of the Ombudsman Board are:
   a. to deal with matters submitted by the representative committees and individual conscripts regarding the period of service or service conditions such as the conscripts' economic and social rights, as well as matters concerning educational and welfare work, canteen service, pensions, equipment, clothing, food and accommodation;
   b. to deal with such applications from officers and NCOs in the armed forces as are not required by other regulations to go through service channels.

4. The representative committees, and individual conscripts, officers and NCOs may direct applications to the Ombudsman without going through the regular service channels, unless they are required by other regulations to do so.

5. Matters to be dealt with by the Board shall as a rule be prepared and submitted by the Ombudsman. Members may either individually or jointly submit matters or demand that they be submitted for discussion.

[3] Innst. S. nr. 68, 1951, fra Stortingets Militaerkomite (the Storting's Military Committee).

The Storting, the Storting's Military Committee, the Minister of Defence or the Central Committee of Service Commanders may submit matters to the Ombudsman Board for comment.

Applications to the Ombudsman in respect of matters mentioned in Section 3 may only be submitted to the Ombudsman Board if they are of a fundamental character or of public interest. The Ombudsman shall endeavour to settle matters submitted to him by direct contact with the authorities he considers to be the relevant ones.

The Ombudsman is empowered to demand information, in connection with matters submitted to him, from any source within the armed forces provided security considerations permit.

6. At the end of each year the Board shall send a report on its activities to the Storting. A copy of the report is to be sent to the Ministry of Defence.

When it finds it desirable the Board may send a report to the Storting on individual cases during the course of the year.

Where considered necessary the Ombudsman Board shall submit the results it has arrived at by means of inspection or study of a matter to the Head of the Ministry of Defence in the form of a report.

7. The Board shall hold meetings as often as necessary.

The main reason the Instructions are so brief is that the institution was new and there was no previous experience on which to base details. The intention was to reconsider the Instructions after seeing how the system worked. Thus it was a very scanty basis on which the Ombudsman started his duties. Yet no alteration has subsequently been made in the Instructions. The Storting has, however, given certain directions, and the Ombudsman himself has effected some adjustments and changes in practice which experience has shown to be necessary. Moreover, in 1956 the scope of the scheme was extended to include conscientious objectors.

The first person to be appointed to the office has been reappointed twice and is now serving his third term. Before 1952 he had been head of the Labour Party's sports movement, the Norwegian Sport Association, and Norway's Olympic delegation to Australia. Although neither he nor the members of his Board have legal training, this seems to present no particular problem, partly because his assistant and office manager are lawyers.

It will be noted in the Instructions that most of the powers of the institution have been given to the full Board. In practice, however, the Ombudsman takes the initiative in exercising these powers because the others are members of the Storting appointed from the different political parties and are only part-time members of the Board. The others do, however, travel with the Ombudsman on the most important inspection tours (for about three weeks each year). They also help him to decide the more important cases, and approve the recommendations made in the annual report.

The work of the Ombudsman can be divided into four main tasks:

1. As the summit of the system of representatives, to keep in close contact with the work of the representative committees.
2. To deal with applications from the individual private or officer.
3. To take up matters on his own initiative for consideration.
4. To act as an advisory organ for the chief military and civil authorities.

Regarding his work with the committees, the Storting has on several occasions expressed the view that it is a very important duty to make the work of the committees effective, and that the Ombudsman should be in a position at any time to handle the problems which cannot be solved by negotiation within a detachment's own representative committee. One of the methods adopted by the Ombudsman in his effort to follow the activities of the committees is to get copies of minutes taken during meetings of representative committees. When such minutes contain matters which the Ombudsman considers ought to be further investigated, these will be taken up as separate cases.

The Board's and the Ombudsman's visits to military establishments and the ensuing interviews and conferences with commanders and representatives constitute features likely to stimulate committee activities. If as a result it is decided that matters or circumstances ought to be investigated, these will be taken up with a higher military authority. Minutes taken as a result of visits by the Board to the establishments are forwarded to the respective military authorities and the Ministry of Defence. The Board's travels last about twenty days each year. In addition there are the travels undertaken by the Ombudsman alone. Other features aimed at stimulating such activities are lectures, the distribution of pamphlets and the holding of district meetings of representatives.

The committee work applies mainly to *general* questions raised by the rank and file. It is obvious, however, that during a sixteen-to-eighteen-months' term of military service under unaccustomed conditions, problems and difficulties arise which only concern the individual conscript. Such matters are not ordinarily handled in the detachment's committee of representatives. If the person concerned does not get any satisfactory solution by direct contact with his superiors he is entitled, independently of the regular service path and the system of representatives, to go direct to the Ombudsman. The wide scope of section 3 in the Instructions means that most problems which can arise in connection with the performance of military service can be dealt with by the Ombudsman.

Officers are also entitled to apply to the Ombudsman with their problems. According to the wording of the Instructions, however, this right is substantially restricted relative to that of the rank and file. It is provided in 3b that the Ombudsman shall deal with applications from officers where the matter is not required by some other provision to go along the regular service path. According to other provisions, the great majority of complaints raised by officers are handled via regular channels. This fact was borne in mind during the discussion on the Instructions in the Storting, and it was stated then that officers could take up matters for discussion with the Ombudsman after a case had been dealt with along the regular service path and a decision had been taken which the person in question was dissatisfied with.

Regarding the third main task of the Ombudsman, from the wording of the Instructions it might appear that the Ombudsman can only take action when a concrete complaint is presented. It was a presupposition, however, that the Ombudsman would be able to take up questions on his own initiative. This is implied in several sections of the Instructions.

Regarding the fourth task—to be an advisory organ for civil and military authorities—the Ombudsman and his Board have gradually acquired a knowledge of service conditions which the authorities are able to utilize by submitting cases for an opinion.

Little is specified in the Instructions about the actual handling of cases. In section 5 it is laid down that the Ombudsman shall prepare and submit matters to the Board. But since the Board is designed primarily as an advisory organ for the Ombudsman, he submits to it only cases of general interest or which involve questions of principle. In all other cases he is entitled to decide the matter himself. If after investigating a complaint he finds that there is nothing to criticize concerning either the handling of the case or the decision made, it is his duty to explain this to the complainant. In other cases he must try to settle the matter by direct contact with the authorities concerned, and in the course of his work on a case the Ombudsman can obtain information anywhere in the Defence Force, except where he is limited by security considerations.

Neither the Ombudsman nor the Board are authorized to issue any injunctions. The chief task of the Ombudsman in connection with the complaints he handles will therefore be to elucidate the circumstances, and if necessary, to induce the competent authorities either to deal with the matter or to take up for new examination a decision already made. If the competent authorities refuse to co-operate in reaching a settlement of a question which the Ombudsman and his Board think is reasonable and right, the Board can either include the case in its annual report or send a special report on the case to the Storting, although in practice it has never done the latter.

The importance of this right to report cases to the Storting lies particularly in its preventive character. A report to the Storting will signify a general publication of the matter. It goes without saying that the military authorities will be reluctant to risk this unless they are certain that the decision they have taken is correct. Although there are certain differences between the Ombudsman system in Norway and the Swedish and Danish systems, the preventive effect in the three countries is fairly similar. In all three countries the Ombudsman system gives to the individual a stronger feeling of legal security.

In the period that the Ombudsman institution has been operating so far, the following numbers of cases have been dealt with:

July 1, 1952, to December 31, 1953	227
1954	321
1955	394
1956	429
1957	383
1958	274
1959	321
1960	331
1961	346
1962	348
1963	367

The largest groups of cases are: (a) questions pertaining to call-up, exemption from and postponement of obligatory military service, (b) transfers and re-postings during the service period, and questions of demobilization, (c) billeting complaints, (d) diet, (e) leaves of absence, (f) disciplinary and punishable offences, (g) matters involving officers and privates, and (h) medical cases. Apart from this the cases are spread over a large number of fields.

All complaints are subject to thorough investigation by the Ombudsman, and the complainant is subsequently informed of the Ombudsman's findings irrespective of whether the result be positive or negative.

The office of the Ombudsman Board has, in addition to the Ombudsman himself, the following staff: an Office Manager (lawyer), a Secretary (lawyer), and two lady clerks.

Norway's experience of ten years with the Ombudsman Board for the Armed Forces indicates that it has worked successfully. It is natural that the system was met with scepticism by the officers, but this has in large measure been overcome. The general opinion today seems to be that this Ombudsman system has been of great value in helping to create a feeling of legal security for the personnel of the armed services and a relationship of trust and confidence between officers and the rank and file.

5

WEST GERMANY'S MILITARY OMBUDSMAN

by Egon Lohse★

Among the most significant provisions of the Basic Law (Constitution) for the Federal Republic of Germany dealing with the integration of the armed forces into the democratic state are those on the relationship between the Bundestag (House of Representatives) and the armed forces. They have led to a strengthening of parliamentary control in the military field such as never existed before in German constitutional history. In addition to the traditional means of parliamentary control— budget control, the obligation for the responsible Minister to be present in the Bundestag, the right to institute special or permanent investigating committees such as the Defence Committee, and the right of interpellation—the Constitution also created the office of Military Ombudsman or Parliamentary Commissioner for Military Affairs.

The Military Ombudsman (MO) is a new institution for German constitutional law. When the scheme was introduced, however, it was possible to have recourse to the experience of the Scandinavian countries. In particular to serve as a model was the Swedish *Militie-ombudsman*, the oldest institution of this kind, also created by constitutional law.

The idea to make parliamentary control over the armed forces more effective by a Military Ombudsman as the 'eye of Parliament' was first discussed in 1952 during the preparation of the legislation setting up the armed forces. The plan goes back to a suggestion made by Ernst Paul, a Social Democrat deputy of the Bundestag who had lived in exile in Sweden, and was very much furthered by the Chairman of the Committee for Defence and Vice-President of the Bundestag, Dr Richard Jaeger, a Christian Social deputy, and by the Deputy-Chairman of the Committee for Defence, Fritz Erler, a Social Democrat. Only four years later—with the unanimous support of both the Government and Parliament, and welcomed by the public—the idea was realized when article 45b was inserted as an amendment to the Constitution (in March 1956). Article 45b, however, only contains the obligation to appoint a Military Ombudsman and determines the scope of his functions: he is to be appointed to safeguard basic rights and to assist the Bundestag in exercising parliamentary control. Details as to

★ Head of Section, Ministry of Justice, Federal Republic of Germany.

his appointment, position, rights and obligations, were expressly left by the Constitution to interpretation by a 'carrying-out' law, which was passed in June 1957, as an Act on the Military Ombudsman of the Bundestag.

I. THE LEGAL POSITION OF THE MILITARY OMBUDSMAN

1. *Organic Position*

The question of the organic position of the MO within the system of the Basic Law can only be touched upon here. It is disputed in the literature. A widespread opinion deduces a double position for the MO from his double function under the Constitution and from his different rights of initiative in the fulfilment of his tasks. In so far as he acts as an 'auxiliary institution of the Bundestag in the exercise of parliamentary control' he is said to be a body of the Bundestag, but since he is also called upon 'for the protection of the basic rights', he is attributed the quality of an independent constitutional body which breaks the traditional system of separation and check of the executive, legislative and judicial powers. A contrary opinion, to which I would like to adhere, is based upon the position of Article 45b in the Basic Law. It has been placed in the section on the Bundestag, and the MO performs his function as a protector of the basic rights also as Military Ombudsman of the Bundestag. Despite his autonomous position, the MO is a subordinate organ (though not a mere executive organ) of the Bundestag, just as the military Ombudsmen of the Scandinavian countries are agents of Parliament. Therefore, in the entire field of his activity—including the protection of the basic rights—the MO cannot exercise wider powers than Parliament itself.

2. *Personal Status*

The MO is elected, without participation of other constitutional bodies, by the Bundestag in plenary session, by secret vote and without discussion, the vote requiring an absolute majority of the legal number of members of the Bundestag. Casual majorities of a thinly occupied House are thereby precluded. The right of proposal lies with the Bundestag's Committee for Defence and the parliamentary groups of the Bundestag. Eligible is every German who possesses the right to vote for the Bundestag, is 35 years old and—a condition fulfilled only by men—has served at least one year of military service so that he is familiar with military conditions from his own experience. Qualification for a judicial post or for high administrative service is not required. The person elected is appointed by the President of the Bundestag.

The MO's term of office lasts five years. Thus it is detached from the four-year election period of the Bundestag. Re-election, even repeated, is admissible. On the other hand, the MO may resign at any time, or he may be dismissed during his five-year term. This can be done by a motion of the Committee for Defence and a vote of the Bundestag with the same majority of its members as is prescribed for the election.

The Military Ombudsman holds office under public law. Unlike the members of his staff, he is not a civil servant. His personal legal status is more like that of federal Ministers. For instance, the provisions of the Act on Federal Ministers of 1953, regarding the oath and pensions, are applicable to the MO. He is not allowed to hold any other office for remuneration, or to engage in any trade or profession—not even that of a regular soldier. Nor may he belong to the management or the board of directors of a private enterprise, nor to any Government or legislative body of the federation or any of the states. He must not disclose secret matters which become known to him by virtue of his office, even after the termination of his office. He may make statements on such matters before or outside a court only with permission of the President of the Bundestag and the agreement of the Defence Committee. For the term of his office he is exempt from military service.

The MO's offices are attached to the Bundestag's administrative staff, and the budget for them is included in the budget for the Bundestag's administration. Under the law the MO is placed under the supervision of the President of the Bundestag. However, there exists no true relationship of superior and subordinate, since the MO is not bound to accept instructions from or give account to him.

The MO has no actual deputy. In case of a temporary prevention from exercising his official duties, if it extends over more than four weeks, the Defence Committee may charge the chairman of a military service division of the Federal Disciplinary Court with the performance of his functions.

II. THE DUTIES OF THE MILITARY OMBUDSMAN

As mentioned, article 45b of the Basic Law defines two main functions for the MO: he acts for the protection of the basic rights, and as an auxiliary body of the Bundestag in the exercise of parliamentary control. The carrying-out law added a third task: he has to take care that the officers observe proper principles of leadership and character guidance or moulding (*innere Führung*).

These tasks, however, may be fulfilled by the MO only to the following extent: he may deal only with the field of military defence, but not with such matters as civil air-raid precautions; and as an agency of the Bundestag he may act only within the scope of parliamentary control. He is thus limited to a supervisory or investigating activity and must abstain from direct interference with the domain of administration, military authorities included.

Despite the equal limitation of the MO's three main functions to the fields of defence and parliamentary control, these functions show certain differences concerning his right to initiative and his being bound to instructions. In his function as an auxiliary body of the Bundestag, the MO is more dependent; he acts upon instruction of the Bundestag or of the Defence Committee, unless the latter itself carries out the investigation. The instruction also includes the object of investigation. It may not be of a general nature, but must be directed to the examination of certain occurrences. In the performance of the more narrowly restricted tasks falling within the domain of individual legal protection (i.e. the protection of basic rights and the safeguarding of the principles of leadership and character guidance), the MO acts in his own discretion and without special order. Although the Bundestag and the Defence Committee may issue general directives for his activity in this field, none has been issued so far.

Complaints that basic rights or principles of leadership and character guidance have been violated are brought to the MO's attention either by members of Parliament, soldiers, his own troop inspections, or in other ways such as by the press. Since these are not instructions, he is not compelled to intervene. On the other hand, suspicion is a sufficient motive for intervention; he does not need proof of an illegality.

Included in the individual's fundamental rights—which remain unchanged during military service and the protection of which is confided to the MO—are human dignity, the right to life and to inviolability of person, free development of the personality, protection of family and marriage, secrecy of mail, and the right to petition as an individual. A number of other fundamental rights are necessarily limited in the case of soldiers, such as the right to freedom of movement and to assemble.

The principles of leadership and character guidance within the army involve an uncertain legal term not described more precisely by the legislator. They are to be understood as guiding principles for the correct behaviour of the superior towards his subordinate, as effects of the basic rights in the military domain. They are rules for modern personnel management, adapted to the changed post-war political and social conditions, which above all respect the individual personality of the soldier. They require from the superior the restriction of his commands to the limits of his legal mission, responsibility to mould the character of his men by his teaching and by his own example, justice and care for his subordinates, and at the same time from them the best possible performance of their duty and conscientious obedience.

III. THE RIGHTS OF THE MILITARY OMBUDSMAN

For the discharge of the duties entrusted to the MO, a number of rights are conceded to him. The most extensive of these is the right of information. The MO may ask the Federal Minister of Defence and all agencies and persons subordinate to him (i.e. any member of the armed forces) for oral or written information as well as for inspection of files, as far as cogent reasons of secrecy are not opposed. Only the Defence Minister himself or his permanent representative may refuse inspection of files. Also the MO can visit at any time without previous warning, with or without special reason, all troops, staffs, or administrative offices of the armed forces. This right to visit, which must be exercised by the MO personally, though he may be accompanied, is one of his most effective rights because it enables him at any time directly to look into the service and life of the forces, as well as to be in contact with them. He also has the right to request from the Ministry of Defence summary reports on the exercise of the disciplinary power in the armed forces, and from the federal and Land (state) Ministers of Justice statistical reports on the administration of penal justice as far as members of the armed forces or their dependants are concerned. Finally, the MO may attend court hearings in penal and disciplinary matters connected with his duties, even if they are held in secret. To the same extent as the public prosecutor, he has the right to inspect files. If the records have been transmitted to them by the MO, judicial and administrative authorities of the federation and of the Laender (states) are obliged to inform him of the institution of proceedings, the preferring of public charges, the nature of the investigation in disciplinary proceedings and the results of proceedings involving personnel of the armed services. In addition to this, the authorities of the federation and Laender generally have to assist him in carrying through the necessary inquiries.

Another right of the MO includes the power to give the competent authority in whose jurisdiction he has observed a violation of law, the opportunity to settle the matter. Besides, by forwarding a case record, he may enable the agency responsible for the institution of penal or disciplinary proceedings to call to order the guilty person by advice or disciplinary punishment. In all of these cases the MO has no right of instruction or other interference with the executive. Even if a violation of a basic right is involved, he may neither direct the preferring of public charges nor the institution of disciplinary proceedings; he may neither take action nor appeal nor make use of remedies provided by the military regulations on recourse or discipline. The important constitutional position of the MO in conjunction with his duty to report to Parliament guarantee, however, that his suggestions and indications are considered.

IV. THE SOLDIER AND THE MILITARY OMBUDSMAN

A direct relationship between the MO and the soldier exists by the fact that any soldier may directly address a request or complaint to the MO without observing official channels. This special right of petition co-exists with the ordinary channels for complaints under the military regulation on recourse, and with the right to address to Parliament a petition concerning the federal armed forces. The MO must within his own competence independently investigate and decide on a direct petition. It is permissible, even if its concern is not a violation of basic rights or principles of leadership and character guidance, provided that it is connected with military service. A soldier who has addressed a petition to the MO may not be reprimanded or discriminated against for having called upon the MO. Inadmissible, however, are petitions made by several soldiers jointly. Likewise, anonymous requests or complaints are disregarded. The MO decides at his own discretion whether or not to disclose the complaint or the name of the complainant, but he must refrain from disclosure if the complainant so desires and if no legal duties are opposed to compliance with that desire.

The right to petition the MO directly not only increases the soldier's legal protection, but is also an important source of understanding for the MO. Fears that a relationship of trust between soldier and superior might be disturbed by this right did not prove true.

V. THE MO'S PARLIAMENTARY REPORTS AND ACTIVITIES

Probably the most effective means by which the MO exerts his influence is his reporting to Parliament. This involves reports in an individual case or summary reports; for some of them there exists a duty to report, for others only a right to report. Mostly they are made in writing, but they may occasionally also be made orally. Upon request of the Bundestag, the MO has to make an individual report on an investigation which he has undertaken by order of the Bundestag; this report may also be given orally. Similarly, if he thinks fit, he may separately report on investigations made upon his own motion with regard to the violation of the soldier's basic rights or of the principles of leadership and character guidance.

A comprehensive survey and evaluation of the MO's activity is given by the annual reports submitted to the Bundestag. Since these are available as parliamentary printed matters, they give an account before the whole public as to how the MO exercised his functions. The first MO, Helmuth v. Grohlmann (former Secretary of State and retired Lieutenant General) took office in April 1959. The first annual report, therefore, covers only part of the year 1959. Since then four more reports have been made, the last three by the second MO, Helmuth Heye (retired Vice-Admiral), who held office from Nov. 1961 to Nov. 1964, when he resigned and was replaced by Matthias Hoogen, a lawyer and formerly chairman of the Bundestag's Legal Committee. Legal provisions as to the nature of the annual reports do not exist.

The first annual report contained an account of the history, organization and duties of the MO's office. The size of his staff was kept small on purpose. At the end of 1959, his total staff amounted to 19 persons.

Of these, only three belonged to the higher civil service: the head of the office, the officer concerned with matters of principle, and the officer dealing with petitions and complaints. In 1960 another officer for petitions and in 1964 an officer for discipline were appointed.

The first annual report also contained a chapter on the conditions of service in the federal armed forces, then only in the process of being set up. This probably exceeded in part the M O's duty to report. In 1960 the Defence Committee of the Bundestag stated that the M O should not give his opinion on political decisions taken by Parliament and the Government.

The last four annual reports, of 35–50 pages each, have followed an unchanged arrangement which will probably prevail in future: preliminary remarks, a main chapter on the M O's activity and its results, and concluding remarks. Included are statistics for the year under report.

The main chapter starts with a sub-section on troop inspections. Here, two kinds of inspection are distinguished: those made without a special reason, and those intended for investigation of alleged violations of basic rights or principles of character guidance. In most cases the M O visits the troops without previous warning. During the last three years, troop inspections have become more important. Interviews with commanding officers and unit leaders, conversations with soldiers without the presence of their superiors (who, however, are informed of the results of the talks), give a true picture of the conditions existing with the troops. In 1963 more than 95 units and offices were visited.

Important information on what is probably the most extensive activity of the M O is given in the next sub-section, 'Petitions and Complaints'. The report for 1963 shows that 5,938 petitions and complaints were received, among which 536 were inadmissible because they were anonymous or joint petitions, or fell outside the M O's powers. There were also 96 communications from members of Parliament. Of the admissible cases, 286 originated from officers, 1,653 from non-commissioned officers, and 3,463 from enlisted men. The vast majority of such petitions and complaints arose from simple grievances rather than violations of basic rights. They concerned such matters as abuse of authority, degrading treatment of subordinates, deficiencies in training, disregard in promotion, requests for release, objections to release, complaints concerning food, questions on pay and pensions, applications for bringing families together, schooling problems arising from transfer, assignment of an apartment, personal hardship by reason of call to arms, furtherance of ex-service training, violation of the state's obligation for care, unjustified blame of a soldier for addressing himself to the M O. Petitions are normally brought to the attention of the competent units and officers. The latter are invited to review and comment on them, or are requested to give information to the petitioner. The M O checks if the complaints raised have been properly investigated and settled. Serious cases in which the soldier's basic rights or the principles of character guidance have been violated are relatively rare.

The next two sub-sections of the annual report, 'Observation of the Exercise of Disciplinary Power' and 'Observation of the Administration of Penal Justice', are based upon the reports that the MO requests from the federal Ministry of Defence, as regards disciplinary law, and from the federal and Land Ministries of Justice, as regards penal law; other sources of information are the MO's right to attend court hearings and his right—exercised quite frequently—to inspect files and records on disciplinary punishments. Taking a brigade as an example, he reports the number, nature, frequency, and motive of the disciplinary punishments inflicted. In addition the MO reports five individual cases of general importance for handling the disciplinary power. He also describes developments in the administration of penal justice on the basis of penal proceedings instituted against soldiers within the district of a Court of Appeal (*Oberlandesgericht*). Then follow remarks on the co-operation between the prosecution authorities, the courts and the troops.

An important effect of the MO's reports is that they induce Parliament to take legislative measures or other appropriate steps toward exercising better parliamentary control over the armed services.

VI. THE MILITARY OMBUDSMAN AND THE PUBLIC

The new institution, from the first, has had the steady interest of the public. Our own and even foreign scholars and journalists have shown a great interest in the office. Press, radio and television have contributed to the understanding of its tasks. The MO's annual reports, especially have caught the attention of the press, in particular the one for 1963, which discussed the controversial question of character guidance. Almost at the same time as this report was distributed to the members of Parliament on June 12, 1964, MO Heye published in a popular magazine a series of articles entitled, 'In Anxiety About the Federal Armed Forces'. This caused quite a sensation because of the way the MO had chosen to publicize his views, the coincidence of publication with the annual report and, above all, the views he expressed. A central theme of the series was the claim that in the armed forces there was a trend towards a 'state within a state'. This, as the MO explained afterwards, was intended to mean the danger of self-isolation within society. The publication of the series not only exposed to the public the problem of an up-to-date guidance of soldiers, and the person and institution of the MO, but also caused the federal Government and the parliamentary party leaders to voice their opinions on these matters. In so doing, all parties reaffirmed their belief in the Military Ombudsman as an institution. So far, however, no plans have been considered to create an Ombudsman for civil affairs.

6

NEW ZEALAND'S PARLIAMENTARY COMMISSIONER

*by J. F. Northey**

The first Ombudsman appointed in a common law jurisdiction took up his office on October 1, 1962. Not only has the office been accepted in New Zealand but the word 'ombudsman' has also become part of our language. The decision to appoint an Ombudsman was presumably taken because the Government had become convinced that the means available to the citizen for ventilating his grievances against officials and gaining redress for administrative injuries were inadequate. The remedies available to a New Zealand citizen who wishes to challenge the validity or fairness of decisions taken by Ministers or state agencies should therefore be outlined.

Because political institutions cannot be understood or evaluated without some knowledge of their environment, a few comments on New Zealand's government organization should be made first. According to a recent official report there are in New Zealand forty-one departments of state or government agencies.[1] Like their counterparts in the United Kingdom all of them are subject to the control of a Minister who is answerable to Parliament for their administration. However, there is a significant difference between departmental administration in New Zealand and the United Kingdom. Most decisions in New Zealand are communicated in the name of the Permanent Head or senior local officer, not the Minister. New Zealand has not preserved the fiction that the Minister himself has taken the decision.

1. *Existing Remedies*

Apart from legal proceedings to challenge the validity of government decisions, the citizen may, and commonly does, seek relief from administrative injury by making a complaint to his local member of Parliament or direct to the Minister. Whichever course is followed, the action taken on his complaint is likely to be the same. The member, whether he be a supporter of the Government or in opposition, sends the complaint to the Minister in charge of the department concerned and invites his comments. The Minister will send the complaint to

* Professor of Public Law, University of Auckland.
[1] Royal Commission of Enquiry on the State Services in New Zealand, *Report* (Wellington, 1962), 18–19.

his department and ask for a reply to be drafted. Almost invariably the departmental reply will be adopted by the Minister, and the complainant or his member will be advised that the question has been investigated and that the Minister sees no reason to change the decision. Occasionally the Minister will not be satisfied with the explanation given by the department or he will be persuaded by the representations of the member that the decision should be varied. In a few cases the Minister will refuse to intervene on the ground that the exercise of the discretion complained of has been committed by statute to an independent agency over which he has no control (e.g. the Social Security Commission or one of the tribunals exercising judicial functions). A member could, if he wished, take the matter further by asking a question in Parliament or by seeking to have the issue debated there, but only important or patently indefensible decisions would be likely to lead to a debate.

Apart from making a complaint in the manner already discussed, in New Zealand a citizen may also present a formal petition for relief direct to Parliament. However, this form of complaint is not frequently used, is likely to be the citizen's last resort, and in any event is not likely to be any more successful than action through his local member. Particularly if he has other means available to test the validity of what has been done, his petition is not likely to receive a favourable recommendation from either of the Public Petitions Committees. For example, one of them, undoubtedly influenced by the knowledge that the company could challenge the decision in the courts,[2] refused to support a petition by suppliers to a co-operative dairy company.

Because of the bearing that this public petitions procedure has on the need for an Ombudsman, the New Zealand practice will be discussed in some detail. Professor de Smith has expressed the view that 'advocates of the Ombudsman might well take a look at the Public Petitions Committee of the New Zealand Parliament'; the apparent success of the work of the two Public Petitions Committees might, in his opinion, make an Ombudsman unnecessary.[3] An analysis of the outcome of recent petitions suggests, however, that this favourable comment is scarcely justified. In 1960, reports were made in respect of fourteen petitions, but only two earned from the House of Representatives a 'most favourable recommendation'—without which no further action is taken.[4] In only one of these two cases—a claim that arose in 1936—did the Government act on the recommendation. Of

[2] A remedy was granted by the Court of Appeal in subsequent proceedings; *Okitu Co-operative Dairy Co. Ltd.* v. *New Zealand Dairy Board*, [1953] N.Z.L.R., 366.
[3] See his review of J. E. Kersell's *Parliamentary Supervision of Delegated Legislation*, Int. and Comp. L.Q., 9 (1960), 740, 741.
[4] The reports are contained in *Appendices to Journals of House of Representatives* 1960, I 1 and 2.

the other twelve petitions, three were referred to the Government for consideration, eight received no recommendation for action and one was supported in part only.

The procedure is that petitions to Parliament are referred to one of the two Public Petitions Committees. The Committee gives the petitioner an opportunity to state his case and produce his evidence; the department or organization concerned is given a similar opportunity. The Committee then settles—usually immediately after the parties have withdrawn—the terms of its report to the House. Whenever possible, the Committee will support the petitioner, partly because this is seen as a form of solace for the petitioner. Because few of the members of these Committees have had administrative experience as Ministers, they tend to show more sympathy to the petitioner than to the department. The House does not usually devote much time to the Committees' reports, which are almost invariably adopted. It could be said that in doing this the House is being irresponsible, but in fact members are probably influenced by the knowledge that a further careful examination of recommended petitions will be undertaken by the Government. The Cabinet committee to which petitions and the parliamentary recommendations are referred makes a close study of only those petitions which have received a 'most favourable recommendation' from the House. It receives a detailed and frank report from the department concerned and may call for the attendance of a senior official. This investigation is probably more thorough than that undertaken by the Committee. In their representations the departments no doubt attach considerable importance to the awkward precedent that might be created by granting the petition, an argument to which Ministers are likely to be more sympathetic than a back-bench member. It could be argued that the public petitions procedure would be more effective if departments took the Committee more fully into their confidence, but departmental reluctance to do so in the presence of the petitioner and his counsel is understandable. About half of the petitions which receive a 'most favourable recommendation' from the House secure some kind of award, financial or otherwise, from the Government. This represents, on the 1960 figures, one petition out of fourteen presented to Parliament. On this basis, it is difficult to contend that the public petitions procedure is an adequate substitute for investigation by an Ombudsman.

As we have seen, a citizen who seeks redress by political means, either by parliamentary petition or complaint through the local member and the responsible Minister, has little prospect of having the decision changed. For obvious reasons the Minister will in most cases adhere to his own decision or stand behind his department's decision. Where the decision has been committed to an independent tribunal, it has been recognized that the Minister should not or cannot intervene; only legislation can effect a change. The other means available, a court action directed to having the decision declared invalid, is relatively expensive and, in order to succeed, a plaintiff must overcome the numerous advantages enjoyed by the state in litigation. The picture should not be overdrawn, however, as the *Law Reports*, especially for the last decade, contain many cases of successful actions impugning decisions taken by administrative tribunals. But in New Zealand there is a belief that there is room for a different sort of investigation—one that can be directed to an examination of the merits of a decision, and is so accessible and cheap that it is likely to be availed of by persons lacking the financial resources or the confidence to take court proceedings.

The large and more or less independent agencies that dominate the administrative scene in the United States have no counterpart in New Zealand. Relatively small areas of the economy have been committed to tribunals that function outside the normal departmental organization and are in no way controlled by a Minister or his department. New Zealand practice is to set out in the statute establishing the tribunal the basic procedural rules to be observed and to authorize each tribunal to establish its own regulations, consistent with the statute, governing the conduct of hearings and its other business. This permits each tribunal to adopt rules suited to its own special needs. Because of this and other differences in governmental organization, the solution to the problem of securing fair and efficient administration probably does not lie in subjecting government agencies to a uniform procedural statute as was done by the United States Administrative Procedure Act, 1946, and the various state codes that have since been enacted. It cannot be emphasized too strongly that practices successfully adopted in one country must be closely examined before being transplanted to another.

Much of the Report of the British Franks Committee[5] is concerned with the public inquiry as a prelude to a ministerial decision, but this device has not been copied in New Zealand. Here the practice has been to confer a power of decision on the person or persons who actually conduct the public hearing. The decision is not taken by an anonymous officer or group in a department to which the person conducting the inquiry makes a report. For this reason, those portions of the Franks Committee's Report dealing with public inquiries have no direct application in New Zealand.[6] But that part of the Franks Report devoted to the establishment of a Council on Tribunals and the functions it could perform is of more general application. The Council was established by the Tribunals and Inquiries Act of 1958, and since then has exercised a degree of supervision over the work of tribunals.[7] The

---

[5] Cmnd. 218, 1957.

[6] Professor J. Willis made a similar observation in respect of Canada; 'Administrative Decision and the Law: The Canadian Implications of the Franks Report', *U.T.L.J.* 13 (1959), 45, 46–7.

[7] H. W. R. Wade, 'The Council on Tribunals', *Public Law* (1960), 351.

Whyatt Report and other commentaries have pointed out that some, but not all, of the functions of an Ombudsman could be performed by the Council.[8]

2. Interest in the Ombudsman

No common law jurisdiction seems to have considered seriously the creation of a body similar to the French *Conseil d'État* with responsibility for supervising the work of the administration. The general conclusion appears to have been that the French institution is not likely to be transplanted successfully. Whether this is so or not, there is no great difference in principle between supervision by the judicial section of the *Conseil d'État* and control exercised by an administrative court with power to review the merits. The creation of administrative courts in common law countries has been suggested on a number of occasions, but the proposal has never received much support.[9] It is therefore surprising that there has been such interest in, if not enthusiasm for, the Scandinavian institution.

An explanation may lie in the proselytizing zeal of the Danish Ombudsman, Professor Stephan Hurwitz, whose radio and television appearances in the United Kingdom have popularized the office. Despite the relative youthfulness of the Danish office as compared with the much older institutions in Sweden and Finland, the Danish statute and the Danish incumbent are better known in the English-speaking world.

In a speech to the Canadian Bar Association in September 1964, the New Zealand Ombudsman made it clear that, even before the United Nations Seminar held in Ceylon in 1959, to which Professor Hurwitz delivered a paper entitled 'The Scandinavian Ombudsman', a few prominent New Zealand lawyers had advocated the appointment of an officer with power to review decisions made by the administration. At the New Zealand Legal Conference of 1960, R. B. Cooke delivered a paper in which he suggested that New Zealand might create an administrative court to which appeals would lie from administrative tribunals.[10] This proposal was not favoured by the Hon. J. R. Marshall, a former Attorney General and now the Deputy to the Prime Minister. In the discussion that followed Dr Cooke's paper Mr Marshall was reported as having stated (p. 137):

[8] *The Citizen and the Administration* (London, 1961) and articles thereon in *Public Law* (1962), 1–51.

[9] In Britain it has been suggested, for example, in W. A. Robson's *Justice and Administrative Law* (London, 1951), 453–65, but the Franks Report (Cmnd. 218, 1957, paras. 120–6) did not favour it any more than did the Committee on Ministers' Powers (Cmd. 4060, 1932, 110). The Hoover Commission's Task Force on Legal Services and Procedure (*Report*, 1955, 33–5, 239 ff.) favoured such a development in the United States.

[10] 'The Changing Face of Administrative Law.' The text of the paper and a note of the discussion that followed appears in *N.Z.L.J.* 36 (1960), 128.

While I would not favour an administrative court . . . I do feel that there is a case for the establishment of an administrative appeal authority—of an administrative, not of a judicial nature—to which any person affected by an administrative decision might appeal for a review of his case. Such an authority would have to be a very wise, a very mature, a very tolerant person—obviously a member of the legal profession! But he would also have to be independent of Government and responsible to Parliament, and he would have to have access to the files; he would have to have authority to call officers before him; and he would of course need to be able to get the facts, either in writing or by hearing the complaint. There would also, I must admit, have to be a filing fee to restrain such a rush of reviews as might follow if it were free. However, I seriously think there is a case for investigating the possibility of an administrative appeal authority. Whether I will ever have the opportunity of tackling that I do not know, but it is something to which the profession might give thought and possibly find a first step to restraint of the abuse of power in that way.

The next move was the inclusion in the National (Conservative) Party's manifesto at the general election in 1960 of a promise to consider the creation of a Parliamentary Commissioner to whom citizens might appeal against administrative decisions. After the election success of the National Party, the newly appointed Attorney General, the Hon. J. R. Hanan, made it clear that what was contemplated was something akin to the Scandinavian Ombudsman, but that his powers would be related to New Zealand's needs. It is significant that those countries which had established an Ombudsman or Parliamentary Commissioner —Sweden, Finland and Denmark—have relatively small populations; this suggested that the institution might be capable of being adapted to New Zealand's circumstances.

The success of the Scandinavian Ombudsman is generally conceded. The explanation is that the institution enjoys the confidence of the legislature, the administration and the general public. Early scepticism and suspicion have been replaced by support from those affected. It is natural that the public servants should come to respect an institution which indirectly protects them from unfair criticism. The relatively short term of office which might have made it difficult to secure the services of a properly qualified person has not in fact proved an obstacle. The explanation may lie in the remuneration and prestige conferred on the holder of the office. For example, the Danish Ombudsman receives, according to the Act establishing the office, 'remuneration at the same rate as a judge of the Supreme Court at the highest step in the salary scale'; and it would seem that politics have played little part in the appointment and reappointment of the Ombudsmen.

In 1961, about half way through the parliamentary session, the National Government introduced the Parliamentary Commissioner for

Investigations Bill, but it was given no more than a first reading and allowed to lapse at the end of the session. It is now clear that the Government's intention was to gauge public reaction to the proposal. Most published comments were favourable.[11] Further consideration was given to the Bill during the recess, and a different version, but with only minor amendments, was introduced and enacted the next year.

In proposing the office the initiative seems to have come from key persons like the Permanent Head of the Justice Department. Certainly there was no popular demand for its creation, and there had been no administrative blunder comparable to the Crichel Down affair which would have prompted Government action. The Bill was treated as non-controversial by the House and it was passed without substantial amendment. However, a change was made in the title of the office: by a substantial majority, the House decided to adopt the Scandinavian title, which is the one that has been used by the press since the first Bill was introduced; so the statute passed as the Parliamentary Commissioner (Ombudsman) Act 1962.

3. *Analysis of the Statute*

The Act contains twenty-nine sections and a schedule listing the government departments and other state organizations that are subject to the jurisdiction of the Commissioner.[12] The influence of the Scandinavian legislation, and in particular that of Denmark, is obvious. The Commissioner is to be appointed by the Governor-General on the recommendation not of the Government but of the House of Representatives (though he cannot be a member of the House or hold any other office without the approval of the Prime Minister). This method of appointment is unusual, indeed it may be unique, in that appointments to comparable offices are normally made on the advice of the Government. But in practice it will not involve a radical departure from what has been done in the past; only the Government can be expected to have approached suitable qualified persons and secured provisional acceptance of the post. Moreover, the Government, having a majority in the House, will normally be able to secure parliamentary approval of its candidate. The method of appointment does emphasize, however, the special responsibilities of the officer to Parliament, not the Government. His main function, after all, is to act as a watchdog over departmental administration. In this respect, the Commissioner will occupy a position comparable to that of the Controller and Auditor General, who frequently finds himself obliged to criticize decisions of

[11] But see the editorial in *N.Z.L.J.* 37 (1961), 225, criticizing the modest powers to be conferred on the Commissioner.

[12] Though s. 2(1) provides that there shall be a 'Commissioner for investigations, to be called the Ombudsman', the other sections speak of the Commissioner, the title which will be used in the remainder of this chapter. Much of what appears below was included in an article contributed by the author to *Public Law* (1962), 43–51.

the Government, including those taken at a high level, in his annual report to Parliament.

Although the Controller and Auditor General is appointed by the Governor-General on the advice of the Government, he holds office during good behaviour, and is removable by the Governor-General only on an address from the House of Representatives. The term of office of the Commissioner, on the other hand, is related to the life of Parliament. The recommendation for appointment is to be made in the first or second session of every Parliament. This means that the Commissioner will have a three- or four-year term unless the office is vacated earlier by reason of resignation, removal or suspension, or death. He may be removed or suspended by the Governor-General upon an address from the House for disability, bankruptcy, neglect of duty or misconduct. This is similar to the provision protecting judicial tenure. During a recess, the Governor-General in Council may suspend the Commissioner. If a Commissioner dies while the House is in recess the Governor-General in Council may fill the vacancy. Such an appointment must be confirmed by the House on its resumption; otherwise the appointment will lapse.

The Commissioner is eligible for reappointment, and it is to be hoped that the reappointment of a person who has efficiently performed his duties and is still able to do so will become the rule. Whether a person will be reappointed will depend more on his personal qualities than his political affiliations. If the appointee has comparable experience (though of course in a different field) to those appointed to the higher judicial offices, into which appointments political considerations rarely enter, it is likely that the appointment would be renewed even after a change of Government. This factor is extremely important because few persons of the required competence would accept an appointment under conditions which necessitated their being politically acceptable to the government of the day. The Attorney General, however, cast some doubt upon the conditions of appointment when he stated:

His position comes up for review every three years, so that in effect it is easier to get rid of him than it would be to get rid of the Controller and Auditor General or a Judge. He will be in a very powerful position to criticize Government administration, and our Government might appoint a man who was not the concept of what an Ombudsman should be for, say, a Socialist Government, which might want a quite different type of individual.[13]

The removal provision is not likely to be exercised; failure to reappoint is much more likely.

The Commissioner's salary (£4,100 p.a.), though payable without annual appropriation, unlike that of the Danish Ombudsman is sub-

[13] N.Z. *Hansard*, August 29, 1961, 1806.

stantially lower than that of a Supreme Court judge. The relatively low salary and the provisions as to tenure make it almost certain that a retired civil servant or one approaching retiring age (between the ages of 55 and 65) will be appointed. It is unlikely that any other person with the necessary qualifications would be ready to accept the appointment, at least in the early years of the institution. Although there is a provision for the payment of a retirement allowance to the Commissioner, the age of retirement is not specified. A provision for retirement at the age of 72—the retiring age for judges—was deleted from the Bill on its third reading. Retirement at an earlier age than 72 is probably contemplated.

The first appointee to the new post is Sir Guy Powles, formerly New Zealand High Commissioner to India. Sir Guy, who is 58, has had wide experience, first as a lawyer, then as a soldier and more recently as Administrator of Western Samoa while under United Nations Trusteeship and as a senior diplomat. If any fault can be found in his qualifications, it is on the administrative side. His lengthy service abroad denied him an up-to-date knowledge of New Zealand's public administration and upon appointment he was virtually unknown to many of the senior officials with whom he must deal.

The Commissioner is empowered to appoint his own staff, but the number and class of staff must be approved by the Prime Minister, and the Minister of Finance must approve their salaries and conditions of appointment. Though some government control over staffing must be conceded, these provisions appear to be unduly restrictive and may impair the Commissioner's independence of the executive.

The Commissioner's jurisdiction has been very carefully defined. It has not been possible to adhere strictly to the principle advocated by K. W. B. Middleton that 'he should not be concerned with questions of legality [which is the sphere of the courts] on one hand, nor of policy, which is a matter for Parliament, on the other hand'.[14] Inevitably, the Commissioner will be drawn into considerations of legality and policy. His jurisdiction is confined to the acts or omissions of the departments of state and other organizations listed in the Schedule. None of the 'sensitive' departments, such as External Affairs, Prime Minister's, Defence or Inland Revenue, is omitted from the Schedule. Few of the statutory administrative tribunals, however, are within the Commissioner's jurisdiction, and local authorities are outside his powers, though it is now being suggested that they be included. Under the Act (sec. 11), his principal function is to investigate, on complaint or of his own motion:

. . . any decision or recommendation made (including any recommendation made to a Minister of the Crown), or any act done or omitted, relating to a matter of administration and affecting any person

[14] *Juridical Review* (1960), 305.

or body of persons in his or its personal capacity, in or by any of the Departments or organizations named in the Schedule to this Act, or by any officer, employee, or member thereof in the exercise of any power or function conferred on him by any enactment.

His powers are exercisable despite any privative clause purporting to limit review. However, he is to have no jurisdiction over, *inter alia*:

(1) Any decision, recommendation, act or omission of any person acting as legal adviser to the Crown pursuant to the rules for the time being approved for the conduct of Crown legal business, or acting as counsel for the Crown in relation to any proceedings;

(2) Any decision, recommendation, act, or omission in respect of which there is, under the provisions of any enactment, a right of appeal or objection, or a right to apply for a review, on the merits of the case, to any Court, or to any tribunal constituted by or under any enactment, whether or not that right of appeal or objection or application has been exercised in the particular case, and whether or not any time prescribed for the exercise of that right has expired.

Although the first exclusion seems to be a reasonable protection of the Crown's litigation, the second is likely to be most troublesome. In the first place, does it mean that a person with a grievance must first exhaust his other remedies before petitioning the Commissioner for review of the appellate body's determination, or does the existence of a right of review or appeal debar the Commissioner from making an investigation even after the right has been exercised? Secondly, the phrase 'on the merits of the case' is ambiguous and conceals one of the most debatable issues in administrative law. It apparently means that the Commissioner can investigate cases where there is review by means of the writs because these do not involve review on the merits. But though theoretically the courts have no power to review an administrative decision on its merits, there are cases which show that this self-denying ordinance imposed by the courts is not always observed by them.[15] It will therefore be difficult to determine in a given case whether review on the merits is available and, in consequence, whether the Commissioner has competence. However, he has been given the right to apply for a declaratory judgment as to his jurisdiction.

In order to preserve the important constitutional principle of ministerial responsibility to Parliament,[16] the Commissioner is limited

---

[15] E.g. *Roberts v. Hopwood*, [1925] A.C. 578; *Prescott v. Birmingham Corporation*, [1955] Ch. 210; [1954] 3 All E.R. 698.

[16] This principle was emphasized by the Attorney General (N.Z. *Hansard*, August 29, 1961, 1804). Many writers regard it as overrated, however; see H. Street, *Jl. Soc. Public Teachers of Law*, 6 (1961), 63. K. W. B. Middleton in *Juridical Review* (1960), 304, refers to the 'dogma of Ministerial responsibility to Parliament' and to the tendency for the Government to support the official view, thereby reducing the effectiveness of an appeal to Parliament by a citizen. See also F. H. Lawson, *Public Law* (1957), 89.

to work done within departments and he has no direct power over Ministers. But this limitation may not be as significant as it appears at first sight, for the Commissioner has power to investigate a recommendation made to the Minister. If the recommendation is accepted by the Minister, any criticism by the Commissioner is inferentially a criticism of the Minister; yet failure to act on a departmental recommendation has been and presumably will be rare. It is natural that Ministers should be reluctant to concede to a relatively new officer the power to examine and criticize their decisions. On the other hand, the Controller and Auditor General already has the power to comment on the financial operations of the Government and individual Ministers. A decision to extend the Commissioner's jurisdiction to include Ministerial decisions might well be taken once the novelty of the institution has worn off. The Commissioner has, after all, only a power of recommendation and if a Minister acts upon it the decision is his and the principle of ministerial responsibility is preserved.

Even if the Commissioner believes that an administrative decision is wrong, he may not alter it. His function is limited in the first instance to making a report or recommendation to the department or organization and to the Minister concerned. He may fix a time within which he must be notified of the action taken on his report. If his advice is not accepted and acted on by the department, he may bring the issue to the attention of the Prime Minister and thereafter to Parliament. Only if the decision is unchanged will the House be likely to hear of the action taken by the Commissioner. It was said of the Bill introduced in 1961 that if the Commissioner were authorized to make only one report to Parliament each year, he would be unable in the period between reports, and especially while Parliament is in recess, to have his criticisms ventilated in the press. But a new provision was incorporated in the second Bill enabling the House of Representatives to authorize the publication of reports of the Commissioner's investigations, even though they had not yet been presented to Parliament; and under rules adopted by the House in 1962 the Commissioner was given this authorization. His reports are expected to state the grounds for his conclusions unless these would prejudice security, defence, international relations or the investigation or detection of crime.

It has been said by way of criticism that these modest powers will render the Commissioner impotent,[17] but the Scandinavian experience does not bear this out. Provided the Commissioner possesses the necessary qualities of judgment and tact, it will almost certainly be found that the wide administrative experience gained in his office will result in his advice being accepted. It must also be remembered that few officials are likely to relish the task of defending before their Minister—or he before Parliament—decisions which appear to be unfair or arbitrary. To give the Commissioner more than advisory

[17] In an editorial in *N.Z.L.J.* 37 (1961), 225.

powers would be inconsistent with and tend to diminish departmental and ministerial responsibility. Protection against the Commissioner's abuse of his powers is afforded by the provisions requiring him to give the department or officer concerned an opportunity of being heard before reporting adversely on what has been done. Such a direction should have been unnecessary because observance of this elementary rule of good administration is precisely what it is the responsibility of the Commissioner to encourage in departmental officers.

Petitioners will pay a modest fee of £1 ($3) when they appeal to the Commissioner. This amount will, it is expected, be sufficient to discourage the frivolous and the crank, but not be so high that genuine complaints will be inhibited. If there had been no provision excluding the Commissioner where there is a right of appeal, the smallness of the fee involved would have encouraged persons to appeal to the Commissioner rather than exhaust their statutory or common law remedies. Complaints may be made by persons in custody on a charge or after conviction, and by inmates of mental institutions. Their letters must be sent to the Commissioner unopened by supervisors.

The Commissioner is empowered to drop an investigation if existing remedies, other than a petition to Parliament, are thought to be adequate under the law or 'existing administrative practice' (sec. 14). The words presumably mean that if the Commissioner is satisfied that the complainant is likely to have had or to secure fair treatment from the department concerned, he need not intervene. But it is difficult to see how he can be satisfied about a practice which may not be adopted in the particular case. He may also drop an investigation if, *inter alia*, the complaint has been unduly delayed or is trivial, frivolous, or lacking in good faith, or if the complainant lacks a sufficient personal interest in it. If this introduces, in relation to the Commissioner's functions, a requirement of *locus standi*[18]—that the applicant show that he has a sufficient interest in the proceedings—the scope of the new administrative remedy will be much diminished. If the Commissioner decides to investigate, however, he must inform the petitioner of the result.

Except to the extent that the Act or the rules adopted by the House of Representatives provide otherwise, the Commissioner may adopt such procedure as he thinks fit in conducting an investigation. The Act does provide certain requirements, however. Before he begins an investigation, he must inform the department concerned of his intentions. His proceedings will be private and he need not hold a hearing unless he proposes to make a report adversely affecting a department or officer. He may consult the Minister concerned during an investigation and if requested by a Minister must do so. He has the power, subject to certain exceptions, to require any person, whether an officer of the relevant department or not, to furnish information and produce

---

[18] The plaintiff in *Collins* v. *Lower Hutt City Corporation*, [1961] N.Z.L.R. 250, was denied redress on this ground.

documents relating to an investigation. He also has the power to summon and examine on oath officials and complainants, and may examine other persons with the approval of the Attorney General. Witnesses' expenses are payable. It is an offence to obstruct, mislead, or refuse to assist the Commissioner, and the secrecy provisions of the Public Service Act, 1912, and the Official Secrets Act, 1951, are waived in an investigation. However, where the Attorney General certifies that the information sought might prejudice security, defence, New Zealand's international relations or the investigation or detection of crimes, or involve disclosure of the deliberations of Cabinet or a Cabinet committee, the Commissioner cannot require disclosure. The Commissioner and his staff will be required to take an oath of secrecy regarding information disclosed to them, but will be protected (though not absolutely) from legal proceedings in respect of what is said or done in the course of their official duties.

The grounds on which the Commissioner may make a recommendation or report in relation to administrative action or inaction are extremely wide. Under the Act (sec. 19) he may take action with respect to any decision, recommendation, act or omission if he is satisfied that it:

(*a*) appears to have been contrary to law; or

(*b*) was unreasonable, unjust, oppressive, or improperly discriminatory, or was in accordance with a rule of law or a provision of any enactment or a practice that is or may be unreasonable, unjust, oppressive, or improperly discriminatory; or

(*c*) was based wholly or partly on a mistake of law or fact; or

(*d*) was wrong; or

(*e*) involved the exercise of a discretionary power for an improper purpose, on irrelevant grounds, through taking irrelevant considerations into account, or where reasons should have been given for the decision.

The action that may be taken by the Commissioner includes reference to the appropriate authority for further consideration and a recommendation that an omission be rectified, a decision cancelled or varied, or a practice changed; the Commissioner may also recommend amending the law or giving reasons for a decision. These powers, especially those in relation to altering administrative practices, amending the law and giving reasons for decisions, should enable the Commissioner to use his powers of persuasion effectively and should result in necessary modifications of law and practice.

It has already been mentioned that the Act expressly empowers the Commissioner to exercise his duties despite the existence of any privative clause purporting to exclude review. At the same time, the Act contains a privative clause of its own, protecting the proceedings of the Commissioner from being called in question in a court, except on the ground of lack of jurisdiction. It is natural that this exception should be included: the courts, as they have frequently asserted, are the proper bodies for determining the quite involved question of jurisdiction; and in the early years of the institution the Act will very likely need interpretation of its provisions as to jurisdiction.

Among the incidental powers conferred on the Commissioner is a power of entry on premises occupied by any of the scheduled departments. However, this may be exercised only after notification to the Permanent Head of the department concerned, and the Attorney General may exclude the premises of certain departments or organizations if he is satisfied that security, defence or international relations might be prejudiced by entry and search. With the consent of the Prime Minister, the Commissioner may delegate any of his powers to his employees. This requirement of consent, along with the earlier-mentioned provisions requiring executive approval for staff, could lead to the stultification of the work of the Commissioner by an unsympathetic Government.

The existence and powers of the Parliamentary Commissioner are not intended as a substitute for existing remedies—petitions to Parliament and applications to the courts or tribunals for review of decisions. These are preserved, and in particular 'the citizen's ancient right to petition Parliament', to use the Attorney General's phrase. The Act provides that a Public Petitions Committee may refer a petition to the Commissioner for investigation and report to the Committee. This is a useful power in that the Commissioner can be expected to make a more detailed and possibly more intelligent investigation of the complaint, but it may, if it were to be used extensively, weaken parliamentary supervision of the administration and the member's sense of responsibility to the citizen. The power to send complaints or petitions on to the Commissioner might be treated by some members as an easy method of disposing of an awkward problem. Yet investigation by the Commissioner would save the time of the members and enable them to carry out their parliamentary duties more effectively.

4. New Zealand's Experience

The Ombudsman has not relied solely on his annual reports to Parliament to inform the public of the manner in which his office works and the disposition of the complaints he has received. Very properly, he has decided that he should give the widest publicity to the achievements of the new institution; he has therefore accepted invitations to speak to interested groups both in New Zealand and abroad, including a speech to the Canadian Bar Association in the fall of 1964. In a recent public address, he reviewed his first eighteen months in office. He said that he had received during that period 1100 complaints, 334 in the first six months and 760 in the following year.[19] As might have been

[19] See statistical tables in Appendix.

expected, the revenue departments, Customs and Inland Revenue, and the Social Security Department have attracted a large share of complaints. The intake, he reports, has been fairly constant, averaging about fifteen per week. He has fully investigated about half of the complaints. Of the remaining 50 per cent, only 80 are still under action and the balance of 515 have been declined for want of jurisdiction, or withdrawn by the complainant, or not proceeded with for one reason or another.

Of those fully investigated, 505, the Ombudsman has found that 107, or more than 20 per cent, were justified. They led to remedial action, either satisfying the particular complainant or changing the procedure or policy adopted or both. In slightly more than half of the justified complaints, the departments concerned rectified the matter promptly, in many cases before the investigation had progressed very far. The largest number of complaints concerned the exercise of discretion by the departments. In some cases, the complaint showed that the officials were not fully informed, or that wrong principles had been applied, or that rulings and procedures were too inflexible. Another frequent source of complaint was failure to notify the public of their rights and obligations in unambiguous language. Citizens claimed that they had been misled in many of these cases. The intervention of the Ombudsman has led to publicity materials being changed or withdrawn. A fairly common complaint alleges unreasonable delays on the part of officials or incorrect application of the relevant legislation. A small class, recognized by the Ombudsman as important nonetheless, relates to unauthorized or improper activities by departments, for example the espousal by a department of a point of view, and the circulation of material in support of it, on an issue, such as fluoridation of water supplies, which by Government decision was to be determined by local polls.

In one of his public addresses the Ombudsman stated his view of the office:

The Office of Ombudsman is new and unique among the political systems of the Commonwealth, and cannot be adequately described in the orthodox terms of British constitutional practice. It would not be correct to say that the Ombudsman is a part of the judicial system, and it is also incorrect to assume that it is part of the Administration. The Ombudsman is an officer of Parliament. He has responsibilities of a kind that have not before been fixed on any individual under the British parliamentary system. On the other hand, the office as established in New Zealand does resemble the longer established institutions in Scandinavia.

If the Office developed the formality, trappings and traditions of a Court, it would, I think, fail in its object. On the other hand, if it came to be regarded by the people as another arm of Government administration, it would also fail in its object. It seems to me that the Ombudsman must carve and tread his own path, being careful to maintain his independence both of the executive and the judiciary so as to be able to build a tradition of strong and impartial criticism of Government administration on the one hand and of helpfulness to citizens in their dealings with the administration on the other. If this is achieved justice will be better served, and efficient and humane administration will be promoted.

In his second report to Parliament[20] the Commissioner stated that he has found a need for the kind of supervision he exercises and that his powers are adequate. He also reported that the procedure of recommendation has been almost 100 per cent successful. He has received full co-operation from the departments whose actions have been investigated and has been able to attend to the volume of complaints on a personal basis. He has a staff of only four, including one legal officer, and intends to keep the staff at this level even if it does result in some delays. He also mentioned that he had found cases where in his opinion the departments showed a 'too close-fisted approach' towards minor claims and a disposition to apply a predetermined rule or practice rather than exercise their discretion on the merits of each case; in another case, the Minister's decision was based on an incorrect statement of fact. The variety of complaints, the proved need for the investigation and correction of mistakes, and the relatively small staff involved in running the office—all indicate that for a modest cost a substantial contribution is being made to better and fairer administration by the Ombudsman system in New Zealand.

It may be argued that the adoption of an Ombudsman system will result in a loss of efficiency and a diminished sense of responsibility to the Minister. This has not been the Scandinavian experience so far, and has not been the reaction of public servants in New Zealand. Instead, they take greater pains to discharge their duties in such a way as not to attract the attention of the Ombudsman. Hence his very existence results in improved administration. Moreover, his advice, based on a broad understanding of government administration, is bound to be useful, for even senior officials charged with policy-making functions are often unaware of administrative practices outside their own departments.

Even in the United Kingdom, which has a highly skilled and efficient civil service, there have been instances of abuse of power by civil servants. The Crichel Down affair, which inspired the appointment of the Franks Committee, is the best known example because it was the subject of a special investigation. How many other cases there have been where persons have suffered injustice in silence, is not known. But it is likely that many over-enthusiastic officials have exceeded or abused

[20] *Appendices to Journals of House of Representatives*, 1963, A.6.

their powers (with the best of motives of course) and that their actions have passed unnoticed by the Government or the press. The improvements recently made in the United Kingdom to secure the proper exercise of administrative power fall far short of the Scandinavian-inspired New Zealand innovation. For the payment of only a small fee citizens are now able to secure an impartial review of administrative decisions which appear to them to be unfair. Other countries will undoubtedly watch the New Zealand experiment with interest; if it can succeed in a relatively small common-law country, it may be capable of being adapted to the needs of larger ones.

II

RELATED INSTITUTIONS

7

THE INSPECTOR GENERAL
IN THE U.S. ARMY
*by William M. Evan**

Constitutionalism, like justice, is an evolving conception of law. It encompasses such doctrines as the 'rule of law', the limited power of the sovereign ruler, and procedural due process of law. Among the values that constitutionalism seeks to preserve are the liberties of citizens against the arbitrary and capricious authority of the state with its monopoly of force. As states increase their scope of power over their citizens, the problems of constitutionalism become more urgent and more complex.

The various Ombudsman systems—as the essays in this book make plain—attempt to implement the values underlying the American constitutional doctrine of procedural due process of law (i.e. preservation of basic rights in legal or administrative procedure). One institutional sphere of application of the Ombudsman system is the armed services. The United States has a very close approximation to an Ombudsman system in the Office of the Inspector General of the Army.

The right of the American soldier to lodge complaints apparently dates back as far as the Continental Army of the United States during the Revolution. Until 1813 these complaints were reviewed by the Judge Advocate General. After this date they became the responsibility of the newly formed Inspector General's Department.[1] The Inspector General (IG) system of complaints is one of the less well-known institutions of the US Army. It is but one of several functions of the Office of the Inspector General—a staff organization—to receive complaints of any kind from any person in the Army.

All US Army personnel, enlisted men and officers alike (and even civilian employees), have a right to register complaints directly with an Inspector General officer instead of taking them up with their immediate superiors.[2] After inquiring about a complaint—defined in Army regulations as 'an allegation of wrong or injustice suffered by the complainant, or inconvenience, grievance, or injury incurred'[3]—the IG

---

* Associate Professor of Sociology and Industrial Management, School of Industrial Management, Massachusetts Institute of Technology.
[1] Personal communication from the United States Military Academy at West Point.
[2] Department of the Army, *Army Regulations*, 20–1 (Washington, DC: US Government Printing Office, July 16, 1958), 18, para. 24b.
[3] *Army Regulations*, 20–20 (May 16, 1951), 1, para. 1a.

recommends action to the relevant commanding officer. If the complainant is not satisfied, he may appeal to an IG officer at a higher echelon or to the Office of the Inspector General at the Headquarters of the Department of the Army in Washington.[4] This established right of army personnel to communicate grievances orally or in writing with the IG may be interpreted as involving a right of 'procedural due process of law'.

I am not suggesting that the IG complaint procedure is the only provision for procedural due process of law in the Army. The Uniform Code of Military Justice incorporates this set of norms and values as well.[5] But whereas the Uniform Code applies to courts-martial in which the complainant is always the Army—or rather the United States, since they are criminal proceedings—in the case of the IG procedure the complainant is invariably an individual. As a type of constitutional guarantee against arbitrary authority, procedural due process as it relates to the IG complaint procedure has not received the attention that court-martial proceedings have in recent years.[6]

The IG complaint procedure may seem to involve an organizational anomaly in granting all army personnel a legal right to lodge complaints directly with IG officers, for it thus sanctions the circumventing of the chain of command. In an organization such as the Army few organizational principles are as fundamental as the chain of command. This involves the ordering of virtually all the positions of the Army in a strict hierarchy and specifies that all communications, upward and downward, shall be through channels. Except for one's immediate superior and subordinate, *indirect* communication is the rule in this type of organization. Thus, if X wishes to communicate with Y who is neither his immediate subordinate nor his immediate superior, officially he may not communicate directly but rather through his superior, who in turn contacts Y's superior until finally Y is reached. In granting all personnel the right to communicate *directly* with an IG officer, the Army has developed an institution which is incompatible with the principle of the chain of command. We may characterize this conflict of organizational principles as that between a *vertical* and a *horizontal* (or lateral) principle of communication. This conflict of principles has created obstacles to the full implementation of the IG complaint system. Since the military Ombudsman systems in other countries—and even to some extent those for civil administration—likewise involve this conflict, it may help to contribute to a more

---

[4] *Army Regulations*, 20–1 (July 16, 1958), 21, para. 32a.

[5] *United States Code*, 1958 ed., Title 10 (Washington, 1959), 997–1036.

[6] See, for example, Frederick Bernays Winer, 'Courts-Martial and the Bill of Rights: The Original Practice', I, II, *Harvard Law Review* 72 (November and December, 1958), 1–49; 266–304; Joseph W. Bishop, Jr., 'Civilian Judges and Military Justice: Collateral Review of Court-Martial Convictions', *Columbia Law Review* 61 (January 1961), 40–71.

effective working of these systems if we examine these obstacles more closely.

The sources of the obstacles are threefold. First, the recruitment of IG personnel involves a status sequence for them which in some respects is inherently dysfunctional for the IG complaint system. The personnel of the IG are not career staff specialists, but line officers recruited to the IG for a relatively brief tour of duty, after which they return to their duties as line officers. As a line officer, the IG officer has been socialized in accordance with the values and norms of the principle of the chain of command. Upon transfer to the IG, he learns of the opposing principle of direct and horizontal communication. Since he is destined soon to return to his duties as a line officer, he is not likely to repudiate the principle of the chain of command, much less become committed to the function of the IG complaint system. Moreover, he probably perceives his being 'detailed' to the IG office as a down-grading, which in itself obstructs acceptance of the values and norms of his new status. Accordingly, he may be inclined to uphold the prevailing norm of 'going through channels'; and may prefer that army personnel take up complaints with their immediate superiors rather than come to him, even though it is the complainant's acknowledged right to do so. He may also have a hypercritical attitude toward complaints submitted to him, and a tendency to view them as being largely unjustified. Thus the decision to recruit IG officers from the line organization for a brief tour of duty may well be a major structural obstacle to the implementation of the basic principle inspiring the IG complaint procedure—the right of procedural due process of law.

A second obstacle to the implementation of the IG complaint system is the attitude of line officers in general toward it. Committed to the principle of the chain of command, they are likely to resent the complaint system as incompatible with this principle. Resentment would be realistically based on the belief that any complaint involving an officer casts an aspersion on his leadership ability and is interpreted by higher echelons as 'a strike against him'. Furthermore, line officers are likely to view all complaints lodged with an IG officer, regardless of whether they themselves are the objects of the complaint, as evidence of a lack of confidence in them by their subordinates. In fact, line officers, although aware that it is everyone's right to submit a complaint to the IG, may be inclined to view such action by subordinates as virtually disloyal conduct; otherwise the complainant would have submitted the complaint to his immediate officer. It is not surprising then to find that commanding officers tend to urge their personnel to communicate their complaints to their immediate officers first before taking them up with an IG officer.

A third impediment to the complaint system stems from the general orientation of army personnel toward superior authority. On the one hand, army personnel, whether enlisted men or officers, may fear that if they register a complaint with the IG they will be the object of reprisals by their officers; the fact that they can also register a complaint regarding victimization—if it should occur—will not necessarily diminish this fear. On the other hand, registering any complaint with a superior in the Army, even if the complaint does not directly involve the superior's judgment or ability, probably arouses feelings of anxiety or guilt on the part of the subordinate. As an organization with a rigid and formal system of controls, the Army instils a keen sense of obligation to obey one's superiors. Moreover, the elaborate system of grading enlisted men and officers with different increments of authority, prestige, and other forms of rewards generates a sense of awe, respect, and fear of superior office. The prevalence of this 'office charisma', together with the orientation toward submission to authority indoctrinated by the Army, probably inhibits personnel from registering complaints with an immediate superior or even with an IG officer, who is generally a major or higher in rank.

The analysis of the IG complaint system set forth above was supported by the observations of four IG colonels whom I interviewed in 1960. Three of these informants were infantry officers prior to their assignment to the IG, and one was an artillery officer. All four evidenced little commitment to the function of the IG, presumably because of their continuing loyalty to their previous status as line officers. Thus two of the colonels repeatedly expressed surprise that enlisted men did not first discuss their problems with their commanding officers instead of with an IG officer.

Perhaps because of the obstacles to the free operation of the IG complaint system, the office of the chaplain has unofficially acquired a function in handling complaints. Personnel who lack confidence in the IG complaint system can bring their grievances to the chaplain, who provides a type of counselling not unlike that of the counsellors frequently employed in American industry.[7] Informally the chaplain may make representations on behalf of the complainant rather than process complaints in a judicial or adjudicative manner. Another staff organization which is unofficially performing a similar function is the Mental Hygiene Consultation Service established after the second world war in the Surgeon General's Office.

In spite of the serious barriers to the implementation of the IG complaint system, it probably contributes significantly to the resolution of conflicts. The mere existence of this mechanism probably restrains officers from acting arbitrarily against one another and against enlisted men, for even if an officer or enlisted man should not be permitted to submit a complaint to the local IG officer—which occasionally happens

---

[7] See, for example, The President's Committee on Religion and Welfare in the Armed Forces, The Military Chaplaincy (Washington, 1950), 15; also, Department of the Army, The Chaplain as a Counsellor, Pam. 16–60 (Washington, April 22, 1958), 6.

—there is always the possibility that he will write a letter to the Office of the Inspector General in Washington.

The IG complaint system is probably more useful in preventing the occurrence of serious rather than routine grievances, for at least two reasons. First, notwithstanding the structurally induced reluctance of subordinates to avail themselves of the IG system, substitute channels for grievances, such as the Office of the Chaplain or the Mental Hygiene Consultation Service, serve to some extent to apprise higher echelons of the existence of inter-status conflicts, particularly those involving flagrant violations of the rights of subordinates. The fact that some grievances do funnel up, whether via the IG system or the ancillary and informal system, probably serves to discourage superiors from engaging in arbitrary behaviour. Second, it is well known among all commissioned officers that the rate of IG grievances is one of the criteria employed by higher echelons in appraising the performance of officers. Thus, the existence of the IG system probably serves as an incentive to officers to conform to uniform standards in their relations with subordinates and to avoid any obvious infringement of their rights.

Given the obstacles to the full implementation of the IG complaints system discussed above, at least two classes of factors are significant in the registering of complaints with the Inspector General: (a) the social-historical situation in which the Army functions; and (b) the status attributes and orientations of personnel.

In the peacetime Army, such as that before the second world war, enlisted men as well as officers served voluntarily. Accordingly, we would expect such personnel to have a different orientation toward the Army from those who serve involuntarily, as was the case during the war and post-war period. In particular, regular army personnel, who are 'professional soldiers', are likely to be more identified with the Army's goals and norms than are drafted personnel. Hence, professional soldiers are more likely to internalize norms pertaining to duties than norms pertaining to rights, whereas the reverse is probably true of amateur soldiers.

If these hypotheses are true, it follows that Army personnel in the period before the second world war were probably less sensitive to injustice than their counterparts during the war, and hence were less disposed to register complaints with the IG. These expectations were confirmed—in the absence of more systematic data—by the observations, based on personal experience, of my four IG informants.

In addition, the status attributes and orientations of personnel probably affect the registering of complaints with the IG. We would anticipate, on the basis of findings by the authors of *The American Soldier*,[8] that personnel whose civilian status is higher than their Army status are more likely to experience relative deprivation and hence more

[8] Samuel A. Stouffer *et al*, *The American Soldier* (Princeton, N.J.: Princeton University, 1949), I, 326–8.

F *

likely to lodge complaints than those with the reverse attributes. Similarly, the higher the level of education, the greater the knowledge of legal rights and the greater the sensitivity to these rights. We may further predict that Army personnel who are more oriented to their civilian than to their Army careers are more likely to take the risk of victimization in submitting complaints to the IG.

Fortunately, some data bearing on these questions are available in a survey conducted in 1945 by the Research Branch of the War Department.[9] Of a sample of 2,908 enlisted men, representing a cross section of soldiers stationed in the United States, 20 per cent answered 'Yes' to the question: 'Have you ever taken a problem or complaint to the Inspector General ?' On the other hand, 40 per cent answered 'Yes' to the question: 'Have you ever felt like taking a problem or complaint to the IG *but then decided not to do so*?' This suggests that there were indeed obstacles in 1945 to the free operation of the IG complaint procedure. The reasons given for not registering a complaint when one felt like doing so were classified by the authors of *The American Soldier* as follows: difficulty in getting to see the IG, uselessness of seeing the IG, and fear of reprisal.[10] The Doolittle Board's report in 1946 recognized some of these weaknesses in the Office of the Inspector General.[11] Whether its recommended structural changes have since strengthened this institution is a question for further inquiry.

The weaknesses of the IG system are by no means unique to this particular type of Ombudsman scheme. Obviously, all Ombudsman schemes require suitable structural provisions to make them effective instruments for protecting the rights of a particular group of people. In addition, they presuppose that the group in question has internalized the norms and values underlying the Ombudsman system. We may therefore predict that the IG system will function more effectively if the Ombudsman idea is extended to other governmental spheres on a federal, state and city level in the United States. For this will help all citizens, including soldiers, to internalize the values of constitutionalism. Moreover, if this extension occurs, we may then witness a greater interest in the further extension of constitutionalism to the realm of private organizations, which exercise enormous power over the lives of citizens in democratic, industrial societies.[12]

---

[9] *Ibid*, 398-401.

[10] *Ibid.*, 399.

[11] US War Department, *The Report of the Secretary of War's Board on Officer–Enlisted Man Relationships* (Washington, DC: Infantry Journal Press, 1946), 19–20, 29.

[12] See my 'Due Process of Law in Military and Industrial Organizations' *Admin. Science Quar.* 7 (September 1962), 187–207.

8

THE PRESIDENTIAL COMPLAINTS AND ACTION COMMITTEE IN THE PHILIPPINES

by Leandro A. Viloria*

The existence and availability of means and processes for the peaceful correction of governmental defects in general and of bureaucratic sins in particular is one of the fundamental features of the Philippine political and administrative system. These measures have been firmly established since the beginnings of American colonial administration of the Philippines.[1] They may be availed of *outside* and *inside* the governmental structure. At the broadest level the Constitution guarantees outside recourse in the following sections of the 'Bill of Rights' (article III):

(8) No law shall be passed abridging the freedom of speech, or of the press, or the right of the people peaceably to assemble and petition the Government for redress of grievances.

(21) Free access to the courts shall not be denied to any person by reason of poverty.

The right of individual redress through the courts for specific sins of a civil servant is further guaranteed in the Civil Code in this wise (article 27):

Any person suffering material or moral loss because a public servant or employee refuses or neglects without just cause to perform his official duty, may file an action for damages and other relief against the latter without prejudice to any disciplinary action that may be taken.

Moreover, the rule and practice that the conduct of government employees and officers is a legitimate subject of public inquiry and comment has been long established in the Philippines. Among the acts

* Associate Professor and Executive Director, Graduate School of Public Administration, University of the Philippines. The kind assistance of Manuel Sadiua III in the preparation of this paper is hereby gratefully acknowledged. Mr Sadiua was vice-chairman of the P C A C and is now a student of the Graduate School of Public Administration, University of the Philippines.

[1] Onofre D. Corpuz, *The Bureaucracy in the Philippines* (Manila, 1957), 242 ff.

of civil servants that are prohibited, and therefore within the public's right to be informed, are the following:

6. Discourtesy to private individuals or to government officers or employees, drunkenness, gambling, dishonesty, notoriously disgraceful or immoral conduct, physical incapacity due to immoral or vicious habits, . . . lending money at exorbitant rates of interest, wilful or dishonest conduct committed prior to entering the service.[2]

However, the effectiveness of these outside measures must necessarily be related to the degree of political consciousness and civic-mindedness of the people in general. At best, the press could evolve as the public watch-dog of bureaucratic sins. But even the effectiveness of press criticism and publicity is circumscribed by press circulation.

If outside recourse is not generally effective and the results are merely diffuse, the inside processes tend to be better in the Philippine setting. As it has developed in the Philippines, the institution for inside recourse against bureaucratic errors revolves around the Chief Executive. As early as 1907 the Philippine Commission authorized the Governor-General to appoint commissioners to conduct official investigations of any action or conduct of any officer or employee in all branches of the Insular Government.[3] This authority has been incorporated in the Administrative Code and now reads:

SEC. 64. *Particular powers and duties of President of the Philippines*. . . .
(c) To order, when in his opinion the good of the public service so requires, an investigation of any action or the conduct of any person in the Government service, and in connection therewith to designate the official, committee, or person by whom such investigation shall be conducted. . . .

SEC. 71. *Power of investigating officer to take testimony*.
Any officer, committee, or person designated by the President of the Philippines to conduct any investigation which may be lawfully prosecuted upon his order may, in the execution of such duty, summon witnesses, administer oaths, and take testimony relevant to the investigation in question.

Filipino political architects have vested in the Presidency extraordinary powers, including control of the bureaucracy. Thus the Constitution

[2] Rule XII, 'Civil Service Rules', *Philippine Commission Report, 1905*, Part I, 692; now Rule XVIII, Section 18 of the 'Civil Service Rules', approved September 19, 1962.
[3] *Act No. 1697*, August 23, 1907.

vests in the Presidency 'executive power'. The President is sworn to 'execute its laws' and must take care 'that the laws be faithfully executed'. He has 'control of all the executive departments, bureaus, or offices' and he exercises 'general supervision over all local governments'. Further, he has the prerogative to appoint and remove executive officials. Moreover, the President possesses not only the foregoing powers but also those necessarily implied and included in the powers expressly granted to him by the Constitution and by existing laws.[4] The rationale and implications of such extraordinary presidential powers have been succinctly stated by a leading Filipino constitutional lawyer in these terms:

The power of control vested on him by the Constitution makes for a strongly centralized administrative system. It reinforces further his position as the executive of the government, enabling him to comply more effectively with his constitutional duty to enforce the laws. It enables him to fix a uniform standard of administrative efficiency and to check the official conduct of his agents. The decisions of all officers within his department are subject to his power of revision, either on his own motion or on the appeal of some individual who might deem himself aggrieved by the action of an administrative official. In cases of serious dereliction of duty, he may suspend or remove the official concerned.[5]

Until the time of President Elpidio Quirino (1950), however, no Filipino Chief Executive had attempted to create a regular and formalized procedure for executive direction and control of the bureaucracy. Even Quirino's efforts were unsuccessful, for the Integrity Board which he created lasted only for six months. The five-man Board was established in May, 1950, in response to vitriolic attacks in the Philippine and US press against the seeming indifference and apathy of President Quirino to rampant graft and corruption in his administration. It was empowered to receive and pass upon all complaints against the conduct of any officer of the Government pertaining to graft, corruption, dereliction of duty, or any other irregularity in office. Further, the Board was charged to investigate specific complaints and to recommend to the President the course of action to be taken in each case. Although the Board was granted ample legal powers, it operated with extreme difficulty. The Chairman bewailed the lack of civic spirit of citizens for failure to substantiate their complaints after a preliminary investigation had been conducted by the Board.[6] Moreover, as pointed out by Vice-

---

[4] *Planas* v. *Gil*, 1939, 67 Phil. 62; *Myers* v. *U.S.*, 1926, 272 US 52.

[5] Vicente G. Sinco, *Philippine Political Law: Principles and Concepts* (Manila, 1954), 243.

[6] Remedios C. Felizmeña 'The Presidential Committee on Administration Performance Efficiency: A Study of Executive Direction and Control of the Bureaucracy' (M.A. thesis, University of the Philippines, Manila, 1961), 131.

President Fernando Lopez who had been groomed earlier to head the Integrity Board, no funds had been·appropriated for its operation.[7] But worst, six months after its creation, all the members of the Board resigned *en masse* in virtual protest against President Quirino's action in not following the recommendation of the Board in the case of a provincial governor.[8] This particular case evoked an indignation rally which was held in one of the public plazas in the city of Manila.

The presidential election in 1953 provided the vehicle for the articulation of a novel idea. In his campaign, presidential candidate Ramon Magsaysay promised the electorate repeatedly that if elected he would establish in Malacañang a complaints and action department. He would assign to it dutiful, honest and hardworking men with the common touch who would serve the citizens, attend to their complaints against the government or any of its officials, listen to their problems, and bring them to his attention for action. Magsaysay's experience as defence secretary had fortified his belief in the efficacy of a complaints office. When he took over the defence portfolio in 1950, the morale of the army was in such a low state that its campaign against the dissidents and the Communist elements was almost wholly ineffective. It was imperative that order and discipline be restored in the ranks. More important, it was necessary to win back the confidence of the people in the military. Magsaysay therefore created a complaints section in the defence department. He urged aggrieved citizens to file complaints against erring and undesirable military personnel and used the press, the radio, and the civil affairs units of the army to disseminate his message throughout the country. He saw to it that all complaints filed with the defence department were compiled, evaluated and acted upon with dispatch. He thought that if the plan worked for the defence department, an expanded version with a wider clientele should also work under the President. The office would serve as a tool for rendering service both to the President and the public—for helping the President control the bureaucracy and for bringing the government closer to the people.

Magsaysay was elected President with a majority still unsurpassed in Philippine history. Upon assumption of office, his first official act was the promulgation of an executive order creating the Presidential Complaints and Action Commission.[9]

1. *Powers and Procedure of the PCAC*

The primary purposes of the PCAC were twofold: to expedite action on complaints received by the Office of the President against the

[7] *Manila Daily Bulletin*, May 30, 1950, 1, 5.

[8] 'Integrity Board Members Quit', *Philippines Free Press*, XLII, 47 (November 24, 1950), 14.

[9] *Executive Order No. 1*, December 30, 1953. This was later superseded by *Executive Order No. 19*, March 17, 1954, which changed the name from 'commission' to 'committee'.

manner in which the officials of the executive departments and offices were performing the duties entrusted to them by law, or against their acts, conduct or behavior; and to encourage public participation in making government service more responsive to the needs of the people.

In specific terms, the PCAC was authorized to receive, process and evaluate complaints; to conduct by itself or cause other appropriate agencies to conduct preliminary fact-finding investigations of such complaints; to refer for action and/or recommend to the government agency concerned proper action on any complaint so that justice, economy and efficiency, and a high standard of morality may be observed and effected in the government. Further, it was the duty of the PCAC to keep the President informed on the implementation of government measures designed to improve the public service and the efficiency of government personnel, and to make studies and recommendations for the improvement of the administration of the government and its essential services and operations.

Personnel of the PCAC were empowered to summon witnesses by *subpoena* and *subpoena duces tecum*, to administer oaths, and to take testimony relevant to investigations conducted by them. All officers and agencies under the executive branch of the government were, by presidential order, enjoined to extend full assistance and co-operation to PCAC personnel, and the heads of these agencies were required to designate an official whose services were to be made available to the PCAC whenever such services were needed. The PCAC was directly under and responsible solely to the President. Headed by a technical assistant appointed by the President alone, the PCAC had only a few regular personnel of its own but was authorized to draw personnel from other instrumentalities of the government.

Anyone anywhere in the Philippines could file a complaint against an official or government agency. Qualified complainants included persons in distress or in need or who had problems to take up with the government, and employees who had complaints against their superiors but could not obtain satisfactory action. At a nominal cost of ten centavos (five US cents) per telegram not exceeding fifty words, any citizen could file his complaint by telegram with the President or with the PCAC directly. Outgoing telegrams and incoming telegrams containing reports from agencies to which complaints had been referred for action were free of charge. Complaints could also be presented by letter, telephone, or orally. In many instances, they were brought to the attention of the PCAC through radio broadcasts, the newspapers (in the form of news items, open letters, or letters to the editors), or the personnel of the PCAC in the field.

In general, action on complaints began with an acknowledgment in which the complainant was informed that his complaint had been received and was being processed and evaluated. The complaints were then distributed to a panel of evaluators, composed mostly of lawyers and social workers, who determined the merit of each complaint, briefed it and suggested action to be taken. In this process, urgent and special cases were segregated from routine cases for priority action. Unmeritorious cases were dropped outright and the complainants informed why no further action need be taken.

Anonymous complaints if carrying a semblance of merit were routed to a research and investigation staff for discreet investigation or surveillance. Cases found to be lacking in merit after discreet inquiry were filed away. Where the investigation led to the finding that the case was meritorious, the case was then built up until sufficient evidence was obtained to warrant overt and formal investigation.

Routine cases were referred to the government agency concerned for necessary action and report. Most of these cases were followed up by a liaison service staff until action had been completed, and a report on them was then made to the PCAC. Complaints against the acts, conduct or behavior of government officials or employees were first required to be placed under oath before action was taken. Urgent and special cases were in the main acted upon directly by or though the intervention of the PCAC. In all cases referred to other agencies for action, the agencies were encouraged to inform the complainants directly of the action taken but to furnish the PCAC with a copy of their reply.

During the first two years of its operation, the PCAC received 79,840 letter-complaints, 33,671 telegram-complaints, and 14,510 oral or verbal complaints—or a total of 128,021 complaints presented by citizens in various parts of the country. Of this number, 127,698 complaints had been acted upon at the end of the second year; only 305 were pending evaluation and referral to other agencies; 472 were pending investigation and/or completion by direction of the PCAC. The number of cases considered closed or satisfied with proper action reached 92,605; out of this number 2,771 were found to be lacking in merit. Cases directly and speedily acted upon by the PCAC with the assistance of other government agencies reached 4,712 in number. At the PCAC's request and/or through its intercession, 85,122 complaints were expeditiously acted upon by other government agencies and by private individuals.

To the PCAC was also assigned the task of clearing proposed appointees whose appointments were to be approved by the Office of the President. In 1955 alone, it passed upon 17,071 appointments.

During its heyday, the image of the PCAC was such that even in the most obscure 'barrios', the rural folks could be heard to say to a government official who was likely to abuse his power or turn in a sub-standard performance: 'Ipapi-PCAC ko kayo!' (meaning, 'I will have the PCAC check on you!'). In his second annual state-

of-the-nation address, President Magsaysay commended highly the PCAC:
It has helped to make the government truly a government of the people . . . under this Administration, the people in their simple faith have not hesitated to come forward for redress. What cannot be expressed by these or other statistics is the service this agency has performed in demonstrating to our people that this is a Government truly responsible to their will and their needs.[10]

2. The Fate of the PCAC

Despite the fact that Magsaysay was elected together with an over-whelming majority of members of the Congress who supported him, the PCAC even during its early days invited suspicion and fear among members of the legislative body. Even as early as January 10, 1954, a few days after the executive order creating the PCAC was implemented, a non-partisan group in the House of Representatives urged the aboli-tion of the PCAC.[11] It was proposed that the appropriations committee conduct a probe of the activities of the PCAC with a view to curbing alleged usurpation of powers and other irregularities. It was alleged that its methods of investigation encroached on the civil liberties of the citizen.

In time, other government offices such as the National Bureau of Investigation, the Philippine Constabulary and the courts joined Congress in openly questioning the legality of the PCAC's activities. Two reasons may be cited for this phenomenon in the Philippine setting. One was the historical experience on the use of the presidential prerogative to conduct investigations into any action of a government agency or official. Up to that period, this primarily administrative tool had been used to further political ends. The second was the personal-ized attachment of the PCAC to President Magsaysay. Thus, barely two months after the ill-fated plane crash snuffing the life of President Magsaysay, the Chairman of the PCAC tendered his resignation on the grounds that "the PCAC, an office which heretofore had been free from political machinations, has finally been submitted to political pressure . . ."[12] Retorted President Carlos P. Garcia, successor of Magsaysay, 'The trouble with the Chairman is that he has become a politician'. In July 1958, the PCAC was abolished.

With the demise of the PCAC, President Garcia created his own Presidential Committee on Administration, Performance and Efficiency (PCAPE). This committee served as the instrumentality to 'render the necessary services . . . to the end that administration of government may thereby attain higher proficiency, keep itself informed of actual

[10] The Manila Times, January 1955, 14.
[11] Felizmeña, op. cit., 145–7.
[12] Manila Chronicle, May 8, 1957, 1, 8.

conditions of the Republic, and prove more efficaciously responsive to the needs of the people'.[13] As expected, the PCAPE was manned with personnel who were personally close to President Garcia. Unlike the PCAC, however, the PCAPE not only handled complaints and investigations but also engaged in performance efficiency surveys and assistance to the public. In time, the latter functions overshadowed the complaints function.

It seems that Magsaysay's PCAC, at the least the concept, is here to stay. Even President Diosdado Macapagal, who campaigned against 'the graft and corruption' of the Garcia administration, has deemed it fit to retain the PCAPE.[14]

As was true during President Garcia's time, only trusted lieutenants of President Macapagal now grace the top echelons of the PCAPE. Future Philippine Presidents will find utility in a complaints office although its nature will probably change to bear the personal imprint of the creator, so long as the present attitude of most Filipinos to the government and the Chief Executive remains. This attitude has been aptly described by a foreign student of the Philippine Presidency as follows:

Government, in sharp contrast to fundamental American ideology, is not something to be feared or looked upon as a necessary evil. Rather, it is an institution from which one seeks benefits and receives assistance in the solution of any and all problems. . . . The President, as head of the government, is the personification of this institution. As national leader he is expected to solve all problems, and to him are addressed petitions for every kind of aid and assistance. . . . [There are] long-established agencies that have, in many instances, field offices to which the people could turn more easily for help. Yet the average Filipino will go directly to the Presi!ent, if he can, for the chief executive is considered to be *the government*.[15]

The distinct advantages and disadvantages of a presidential complaints office in the Philippines may now be summarized. By placing the office directly under the Chief Executive there is focused in his own person a responsibility and authority consistent with earlier Filipino tradition. This arrangement may or may not be consistent with democratic traditions, however. Perhaps one important gain here is that presidential actions usually are given more widespread publicity; the effects of this in keeping administrators in line cannot be gainsaid. On the other hand, dramatic and politically valuable as this approach may be, because of the political nature of the President's office it does not meet

---

[13] *Executive Order No. 306*, July 15, 1958.
[14] *Executive Order No. 1*, December 30, 1961.
[15] John H. Romani, *The Philippine Presidency* (Manila, 1956), 205.

the need for a rationalization of government power and structure. Nevertheless, the existence and availability of such an instrument for self-criticism and self-correction in the political and administrative system ensures peaceful means of arresting and controlling the errors of bureaucracy. This is vital in a democracy.

9

THE EUROPEAN COMMISSION
OF HUMAN RIGHTS

by John F. Smyth*

The preamble to the Convention for the Protection of Human Rights and Fundamental Freedoms, signed at Rome in November 1950, recites that the signatory governments were resolved to take the first steps for the collective enforcement of certain of the rights stated in the Universal Declaration of Human Rights. Article 1 of the Convention provides that 'the High Contracting Parties shall secure to everyone within their jurisdiction the rights and freedoms defined in Section I of the Convention'. Section I of the Convention and articles 1 to 3 of the First Protocol contain the rights and freedoms to be protected. Section II provides for the setting up of the European Commission of Human Rights and the European Court of Human Rights.

The functions of the Commission are laid down in articles 24 to 31 of the Convention. In brief, it is provided that any contracting state may refer to the Commission any alleged breach of the provisions of the Convention by another contracting state;[1] and that the Commission may receive petitions from any person, non-governmental organization or group of individuals claiming to be the victim of a violation by one of the contracting states of the rights set forth in the Convention, but only when the state concerned has made an optional declaration that it recognizes the competence of the Commission in this respect. Of the fifteen states that had ratified the Convention by the end of 1963, the following ten had made such declarations: Austria, Belgium, Denmark, Federal Republic of Germany, Iceland, Ireland, Luxembourg, Netherlands, Norway and Sweden. The first members of the Commission were elected in 1954.

The Commission must first examine the inter-state or private petition as to its admissibility. If it decides to accept the petition it proceeds

---

* Barrister-at-Law (King's Inns, Dublin) and Assistant Secretary at the Council of Europe. The views expressed are those of the author and are not to be understood as representing the opinion of the Council of Europe.

[1] By December 31, 1963, the following member states of the Council of Europe had ratified the Convention and the First Protocol: Austria, Belgium, Cyprus, Denmark, Federal Republic of Germany, Greece, Iceland, Ireland, Italy, Luxembourg, Netherlands, Norway, Sweden, Turkey and the United Kingdom of Great Britain and Northern Ireland. France has signed the Convention but has not ratified it and so is not a Contracting Party. Switzerland became a member of the Council of Europe in 1963.

to ascertain the facts and to attempt to reach a friendly settlement. In the event of no friendly settlement being effected, the Commission must draw up a report containing the facts and its opinion as to whether they disclose a breach by the state concerned of its obligations under the Convention. The adoption of the report concludes the principal task of the Commission. The report is then transmitted to the Committee of Ministers of the Council of Europe which takes the final decision on the petition unless the case is referred to the Court.

As at December 31, 1963, three inter-state applications had been made to the Commission and all three had been declared in whole or in part admissible. At the same date the Commission had received 2,090 non-governmental petitions; of these, 1,600 were declared inadmissible and 27 were accepted in whole or in part for further examination. Two of the inter-state applications had been withdrawn by the complainant states when they were pending before the Committee of Ministers and in the third, *Austria v. Italy*, the Ministers decided, in October 1963, that there had been no violation of the Convention. Five non-governmental petitions had been considered by the Committee of Ministers; in three of these cases the Ministers found that there had been no violation of the Convention and in the other two the Ministers took note of the report of the Commission and after expressing their satisfaction with the legislative measures introduced, *pendente lite*, by the respondent state to ensure the full application of the Convention, decided that no further action was required. Also, the Court had given judgment in two cases. In the first case, *Lawless v. the Government of Ireland*, the Court held that the facts found did not disclose a breach by the Irish Government of their obligations under the Convention; in the second case, *De Becker v. the Government of Belgium*, the Court decided to strike the case out of its list.[2] For the purpose of this essay, however, the activities of the Committee of Ministers and of the Court are not relevant as they are only concerned with taking the final decision on a petition, which in all cases must be examined by the Commission first.

1. *The Work of the Commission*

The contracting states imposed upon themselves an obligation to observe the rights and freedoms set forth in the Convention in respect of everyone within their jurisdiction without discrimination. In some countries the substantive provisions of the Convention have been incorporated into national law and made applicable before the domestic

[2] Publications of the European Court of Human Rights, Series A: *Judgments and Decisions 1960–61, and 1962*, respectively (Strasbourg). The basic texts relating to the European Convention on Human Rights, decisions of the Court and of the Committee of Ministers, the principal decisions of the Commission on admissibility, and other information are found in *Yearbook of the European Convention on Human Rights* (Hague), of which five volumes have appeared to date covering the years 1955–62.

courts; in others the Constitution does not give a treaty, such as the Convention, the force of law and so a litigant cannot rely on these rights as defined in the Convention in the course of proceedings before a domestic court. This distinction in the application of the Convention is not important when a petition is lodged with the Commission, for then it is only the Convention that matters.

The first duty of the Commission is to see whether a petition is admissible. At this stage the ordinary position of litigating parties is reversed in that the petition is looked at to see if it falls under one or more of the headings which would render it inadmissible; this happens if the applicant has failed to exhaust all domestic remedies, according to the generally recognized rules of international law, or to lodge the petition within a period of six months from the date on which the final decision was taken in the respondent state; or if the petition is substantially the same as a matter already examined, or incompatible with the provisions of the Convention, or manifestly ill-founded or an abuse of the right of petition. During the preliminary examination the Commission may communicate the petition to the Government of the respondent state to have the issue of admissibility argued in writing or orally by the parties. Furthermore, the Commission is entitled—and even has a duty—to raise *ex officio* any alternative allegations of a breach of the Convention which the applicant may have omitted to include in his complaint. Unlike that in most national legal systems, the procedure is quite informal as regards the evidence and arguments and no fees are payable to the Commission by either party.

At the conclusion of this procedure, which sometimes requires several exchanges of written pleadings and one or more oral hearings, the Commission takes a decision on the question of admissibility. If it decides to reject the petition the proceedings are at an end and the applicant is sent a copy of the decision which sets out fully the reasons why his petition could not be received. If it finds the petition admissible it notifies the parties accordingly and proceeds, by means of a sub-commission, to establish the facts and to attempt to secure a friendly settlement.

In cases declared admissible the decision so stating sets forth the issues which are to be retained for further examination. On this basis the parties are asked to submit further written observations to the sub-commission and the examination may require oral hearings of the parties, with or without the examination of witnesses. On occasion, the sub-commission may carry out an investigation on the territory of the respondent state.

The negotiation of a friendly settlement is a most important task and is obviously a very delicate one. A Government may be reluctant to settle a case for fear of a political upset in Parliament or at an election, or of a flood of similar petitions being lodged on the same grounds. Furthermore, the petition itself may well be one having political ramifications or motives which render it almost impossible for the Government to make a conciliatory gesture. These considerations probably explain why to date no formal friendly settlement has been effected and published under article 30 of the Convention.

It should be noted that article 33 of the Convention provides that 'the Commission shall meet in camera'. It follows that all the proceedings of the Commission are secret. Except for publication of the text of decisions on admissibility (after deletion of references capable of identifying individuals) and press communiqués about the state of proceedings in cases which have already received publicity, not much is known by the general public of the actual work done by the Commission or its influence on governments of the contracting states. For example, it could happen that, in a case involving hardship on an individual, even where it might be found that there was no breach of the Convention if the proceedings ran their full course, a Government might take steps to remove the grievance on receiving either a formal notice of the petition lodged with the Commission or an informal inquiry requesting information. A concrete example of a change in the circumstances of a case was the new legislation introduced by the Belgian Government while the case of De Becker was pending before the Court, concerning certain statutory penalties to be automatically imposed on persons convicted of collaboration with the enemy during the second world war.

The veil of secrecy may be lifted later when a case is finally decided and the report of the Commission is published by authorization of the Court or the Committee of Ministers as one of the documents in the case.

Thus, in the cases of *Pataki* and *Dunshirn v. Austria*, the Commission, in its report, expressed the opinion that the proceedings against the applicants in the Austrian courts had not been in conformity with the Convention and then considered that a new procedure introduced in Austria by amending legislation while these petitions were at hearing before the Commission, would not give rise to any objections. By the enactment of this amending legislation a new remedy was made available to the applicants in the Austrian courts and the Commission proposed that the Committee of Ministers should decide that no further action should be taken. In its decision the Committee of Ministers accepted the proposal.[3]

In the inter-state case of *Austria v. Italy*, it was alleged that several breaches of articles 6 and 14 of the Convention had occurred during the proceedings taken in the Italian courts against six young men accused of having committed a murder and as a result of which they had been sentenced to terms of imprisonment. The Commission, after expressing a majority opinion that there had been no violation of the Convention, added that it considered it desirable for humanitarian reasons, among which might be counted the youth of the prisoners,

[3] Publication of the Council of Europe, 1963.

that measures of clemency be taken in their favour. The Committee of Ministers decided that there had been no violation of the Convention and at the same meeting took note of the fact that the Commission considered it desirable that measures of clemency be taken in favour of the six young persons.[4]

2. *Comparison of the Commission with an Ombudsman*

While the office of the Ombudsman either has been established or is being seriously considered in several countries to resist a modern tendency for private interests to be submerged by administrative machinery, the Commission was set up for an entirely different purpose. It has the duty of being the 'watch-dog' of the rights and freedoms set forth in the Convention and can even question the compatibility of national laws with the provisions of the Convention. The Ombudsman, on the other hand, is concerned with the ways in which laws and regulations are being administered, and is not expected to dispute their validity. The Ombudsman, however, may reprimand officials for minor errors of conduct, or may report that a particular measure is working unfairly and propose amendments, but the Commission may not. It is concerned with the examination of complaints in the light of the Convention. If it finds that the subject matter of a petition falls outside the scope of the Convention it must reject such a petition; if it holds a petition to be admissible it later states its opinion as to whether or not there has been a violation of the Convention and with this opinion may make such proposals as it thinks fit.

Notwithstanding these primary differences between the purposes for which they were established and the limits of their respective jurisdictions, there are some remarkable similarities between the functions of the Ombudsman and those of the Commission. One of the most important is that they both provide a private person with a chance of having a genuine, well-founded grievance thrashed out on its merits before an independent and impartial organ. Moreover, before launching on a thorough investigation of a case, both bodies employ a somewhat similar method of screening complaints. Certain time-limits are laid down within which a complaint must be lodged and neither the Commission nor usually the Ombudsman will receive a petition which is capable of being dealt with by an administrative tribunal or a court of justice within the normal framework of the law of the land. Also, the investigations by both bodies are characterized by their informal approach and lack of hard and fast rules of procedure. The maintenance of an informal and flexible procedure is of the greatest importance in order to prevent any calcification which would cause both institutions to suffer from the very defects of the authorities whose actions are called into question before them.

Another and most valuable aspect of both the Commission and the

[4] *Ibid.*

Ombudsman is the right of access to them which individuals possess. The Commission has always insisted that in countries where the Government has recognized the right of individuals to petition the Commission under article 25 of the Convention, such right should be freely exercisable. As pointed out by Sir Humphrey Waldock, then President of the European Commission of Human Rights, on occasions the Commission

found that the authorities of prisons or mental homes were refraining from forwarding the complaints of inmates, with the best intention of keeping the Commission from being troubled with a futile case. The Commission held that the defenceless position of persons in prison or in a mental home makes it essential for the Commission to retain in its own hands the decision as to whether any notice is to be taken of a complaint from such sources. Representations were promptly made to the Governments requesting that general instructions in this sense be sent to the relevant authorities and these representations met with the fullest co-operation.[5]

In countries where the office of the Ombudsman has been established it is generally provided that any person may communicate with the Ombudsman and this even by correspondence which the authorities are not permitted to see beforehand. The Commission has had occasion to consider complaints of censorship of correspondence addressed to it by prisoners, and also allegations that persons have been punished for having complained to the Commission of conditions in prisons or reformatories. In so far as censorship of correspondence is concerned the Commission held that

in the view of the Commission, the consequence of recognition by a Contracting Party of the right of the individual to appeal is that any applicant, even if imprisoned, has the right freely to correspond with the Commission; . . . this right does not, however, necessarily imply that the correspondence between a detained applicant and the Commission shall not be subject to any control by prison authorities, so long as any censorship imposed by the latter does not in itself or through any undue, arbitrary or abusive effect on the fate of the person concerned, hinder the effective exercise of the right of individual application.[6]

The Commission further found that

punishment inflicted . . . raises a serious problem when it is considered that the exercise by an applicant of his right to correspond with the

[5] Address delivered in 1958 at Brussels, on the occasion of the fifth anniversary of the coming into force of the European Convention on Human Rights.

[6] Decision of the Commission on the admissibility of application No. 833/60, *Yearbook of the European Convention on Human Rights*, vol. 3, 1960, p. 328 et seq.

Commission has led to such serious repercussions as his punishment by decision of the prison authorities.[7]

The fact that the Commission is fully prepared to insist that the Governments enable it to investigate petitions gives its work a positive value in that national authorities must become more and more aware of this international organ which may one day call their actions to account.

Other important similarities between the functions of the Ombudsman and those of the Commission may be mentioned briefly. Both may investigate complaints made against any part of the administration in its widest meaning, but their competence is restricted in that they will not receive petitions directed against private persons or bodies for whose actions no government could be responsible. Subject to the rule regarding the exhaustion of other remedies, both may investigate the activities of any organ for whose activities a Government must accept responsibility. This could conceivably be an administrative officer or body at a very low level from whose decision there is no means of appeal in accordance with the law of the land. From this it is not to be understood that the Commission or the Ombudsman will review the decision of such a body to see if it took the right or wrong decision, but they might review the procedure and standards applied by this body in the conduct of a matter before it and in arriving at its decision. The Commission cannot look into the merits of a decision unless some right or freedom protected by the Convention is involved, and the Ombudsman will not do so unless the decision was clearly unreasonable.

It may be noted with regard to decisions of domestic courts that errors of law or fact committed by such courts concern the Commission, during the examination of the admissibility of applications, only in so far as they may appear to have resulted in the violation of one of the rights and freedoms limitatively listed in the Convention, particularly in article 6 which provides generally that 'everyone is entitled to a fair . . . hearing' and also lays down more detailed requirements.

Perhaps the greatest similarity between the Commission and the Ombudsman is the fact that neither takes a final decision. They are both investigating agents and accomplish their duties by submitting a report to another body or organ for decision and action. Yet both are influential and effective. In those cases which have run their full course through the Commission, the decisions eventually taken have followed the opinion expressed by the Commission in its report, and in the case of De Becker against the Government of Belgium the Commission saw no objection to the case being struck off the list in

[7] *Ibid.*

the light of events which had followed the adoption of the Commission's report.

3. *Conclusion*

In comparing the functions of an Ombudsman with those of the Commission one cannot take into account the differences between the offices of the Ombudsman from one country to another. It may be seen from our over-all picture, however, that what the Ombudsman does on the national level is somewhat similar to the work of the Commission on the international level in regard to states which have ratified the Convention and recognized the right of private persons to lodge petitions against governments. Moreover, it does not suffice to create such a body unless it is also given wide powers of investigation and thereafter by its own conduct inspires the confidence not only of persons who may have recourse to it but also of the government or governments that put it in being. The direct and obvious results of the Commission's work are not many but this is only natural as regards states which accept for all persons within their jurisdiction the rights and freedoms guaranteed by the Convention. It is to be noted that three of these—Denmark, Norway and Sweden—already have an Ombudsman for civil affairs and allow individual complaints to the Commission. Although the business of the Commission is conducted in camera and so the general public is not well informed of its work and opinions, like the office of Ombudsman its very existence is in itself a check on administrative abuse and provides a guarantee against despotic behaviour.

III

PROPOSED SCHEMES

THE UNITED KINGDOM
by Geoffrey Marshall★

1. *Background to the Ombudsman Proposals*

The relatively recent onset in Great Britain of what might be dubbed (strictly without prejudice to the issue) 'ombudsmania' seems to need an explanation. After all, discretionary powers, administrative misdemeanours and public resentment of the insolence of office are not particularly novel. It may be guessed that the answer is to be found in a mixture of two things—first, the obviously strong tradition which insists that even a twentieth-century House of Commons is still the Grand Inquest of the Nation, and second, the immense social respectability of the British civil service. Administrators in Britain may be criticized but they are not actively disliked. A good deal can be deduced from the jokes which are made about them. One of the better known specimens is Sir William Harcourt's remark that if politicians did not exist the country could be extremely well governed by the permanent officials, for a period of from twelve to eighteen months, at the end of which time the public would hang all the heads of the civil service to the nearest lamp-posts. That of course would be one way of containing bureaucracy. Indeed we are told that something not unlike it was attempted in nineteenth-century Russia.[1] But Englishmen have usually believed, rightly or wrongly, that officials are to be trusted. After all they are servants of the Queen and at the higher levels have attended the universities of Oxford and Cambridge. In any event it is to Ministers that we look, as Harcourt added, to tell the civil servants what the public will not stand.

Dissatisfaction with administration and proposals for its reform have therefore tended to focus upon parliamentary remedies. Between the wars complaints were certainly heard about 'the New Despotism' of the departments but they generally led their authors to suppose that an alteration in legislative organization—to provide, for example, specialist subject committees which might be attached to and debate departmental business[2]—was the appropriate remedy. The Committee

---

★ Fellow of the Queen's College and Lecturer in Politics, University of Oxford.

[1] 'An intelligent Russian once remarked to us, "Every country has its own constitution; ours is absolutism moderated by assassination" ' (Count Münster, *Political Sketches of the States of Europe 1814–1857*, London, 1868, 19).

[2] Such proposals have continued to be made. They were rejected by the Select Committee on Procedure (House of Commons, *Paper No. 92*, 1959).

on Ministers' Powers, which reported in 1932 (Cmd. 4060), recommended the institution of a parliamentary scrutiny committee to examine
ministerial rules and orders (and in 1944, after a decent interval for
reflection, such a committee was set up). The Committee of 1932 dealt
both with the rule-making powers of Ministers and with the appeals
from departmental decisions which are handled in certain cases by
administrative tribunals. Between 1955 and 1957 the Franks Committee
re-examined the tribunal system and also made a number of proposals
for the improvement of the procedure at public inquiries.[3] The essence
of public inquiry procedure in the United Kingdom is that it is a
statutory opportunity for the public to make known their objections to
a government department or a local authority before the authority
carries out a scheme (usually one for the compulsory acquisition or
development of land). In the context of the Ombudsman discussion it
is perhaps important to emphasize that over a large part of the administrative field in which official decisions affect the property or financial
rights of individual citizens there is in Britain—possibly to a greater
extent than in some other European countries—either recourse to an
administrative tribunal or the opportunity to state objections at a public
local inquiry. As a result of the Franks Committee report there has
been set up an additional forum for the ventilation of general grievances
about tribunal and inquiry procedure, namely the Council on Tribunals
(though this is an advisory and in no sense an appeals body).[4]

There remain, as the Franks Committee pointed out, many things
about which the citizen can complain only through political or parliamentary channels. That Committee did not regard it as within its
terms of reference to consider whether this was a desirable state of affairs
and whether there ought to be more facilities for appeal or formal
complaint. It was this question which was taken up in 1960 by a
committee created by 'Justice', the British section of the International
Commission of Jurists, with Sir John Whyatt as director of research.

Unfortunately, the question raises a problem of principle and of
definition. Plainly there cannot be opportunities for formal appeal
against every official decision. In the foreword and preface to the
report of the 'Justice' Committee, Sir Oliver Franks and Lord Shawcross refer to the fact that no complaints machinery exists in respect
of a large part of 'the relationships between the citizen and the state'
and reference is made to the 'interventions of central and local govern-

---

[3] *Report of the Committee on Administrative Tribunals and Enquiries* (Cmnd.
218, 1957).

[4] The Council has now produced three annual reports. Complaints which
in the Council's opinion raise points of principle about the working of tribunals
or inquiries are drawn to the attention of the Lord Chancellor or of the appropriate Minister. The duties and composition of the Council are set out in the
Tribunals and Inquiries Act of 1958 (6 and 7 Eliz. 2 c. 55). For a general de-
scription see H. W. R. Wade, *Administrative Law* (London, 1961), Chaps. 6
and 7.

ment into the lives and affairs of the ordinary citizen'.[5] But the difficulty is that phrases such as 'the citizen-state relationship' or 'governmental intervention' do not define the area under debate at all clearly. Almost everything the government does constitutes an intervention in the life of the citizen. A change in economic policy or an alteration of the Bank Rate affects the lives and properties of individual citizens and is a part of the relationship between the citizen and the state. What most people have in mind in using these phrases is a dispute between individual and governmental interest in which a discretionary decision affects the interests of a particular person or a group as distinct from a policy decision which alters the rights of citizens generally. But this distinction is only one of degree. A decision not to release certain categories of men from the army or a decision to place a new town or highway at place X rather than place Y both affect some citizens and not others, but we should probably think of the first as administrative policy and the second as a dispute between state and private interests. Merely to use the word 'dispute' at all is partly to beg the question. Which decisions taken by civil servants or Ministers should and which should not be treated as giving rise to a 'dispute' and the right to an impartial adjudication? Nobody has so far elucidated a general principle that clearly distinguishes such cases. The statute setting up an Ombudsman for New Zealand (No. 10 of 1962) merely defines his jurisdiction as 'any decision or recommendation made (including any recommendation made to a Minister of the Crown) or any act done or omitted relating to a matter of administration and affecting any body of persons in his or its personal capacity'. But what is 'a matter of administration' and 'a body of persons'? The British Government's decision to make the railways pay their way affects a body of persons, namely railway travellers. The decision to defend Britain by means of submarine-fired missiles rather than air-launched ones adversely affects the jobs of a number of aircraft manufacturers and their employees. Would these decisions qualify for examination if the New Zealand definition were adopted?

2. The Whyatt Report, 1961

The 'Justice' Committee (Whyatt) report begins by indicating two facts. There are, it is pointed out, a number of statutes which provide for payments to be made or resources to be allocated by official decision without providing for appeals tribunals. Some of these decisions do not differ in principle from others which may be disputed before tribunals whose decisions are binding on the relevant department. The reasons for the discrepancy may be accidental or historical. The refusal of an application for a telephone by the Post Office, for example, gives rise to no right of appeal. Other examples follow. No statutory right of appeal

[5] *The Citizen and the Administration: the Redress of Grievances* (London, 1961), XI, XIII.

G

was provided for farmers against the amount allotted to individuals by way of agricultural subsidies or against orders to destroy diseased animals—though in each case informal opportunities for registering objections have been provided. There are no tribunals to handle refusal by local education authorities to allot pupils to a particular school, or against the Ministry of Education's refusal of a grant or scholarship. Though there is machinery for hearing of patients' complaints about general practitioners in the National Health Service, there are no corresponding bodies for complaints against hospital treatment or refusal by the Ministry of certain medical preparations or of special equipment provided free under the service. The powers of the Home Office to deport aliens and to refuse admission to immigrants are exercised at its own discretion, and in practice through the discretion of immigration officials at ports of entry without the possibility of an independent appeal.[6]

The Whyatt Committee's view was that the principle of impartial adjudication should be applied as far as possible to these areas unless overriding considerations make it necessary in the public interest for decisions to remain entirely discretionary and subject to review only in Parliament. In Britain this is an unfinished debate. The powers of the Home Office are probably the ones that excite most disagreement as to whether considerations of public policy should override the principle of impartial appeal. Departments that exercise the royal prerogative are particularly inclined to adopt a prerogative viewpoint and see overriding considerations of public policy surrounding them on all sides. The Whyatt report proposes the setting up of more tribunals where this is thought possible, with perhaps a general or miscellaneous tribunal to consider appeals from discretionary decisions not sufficiently numerous to merit specialized tribunals. It then proceeds to the question of the Ombudsman.

At this point it is necessary to mention the distinction made by the report between a 'complaint about maladministration' and a desire to complain about (in the sense of 'appeal from') a discretionary decision. Obviously both of these desires can be satisfied in those cases where tribunals or statutory inquiries exist; here the courts are adequate to deal with allegations of malpractice, and the appeals procedure with reconsideration of the merits, and the Ombudsman is not required. If the Whyatt recommendations about a general tribunal were to be accepted, therefore, there would be fewer discretionary decisions lying outside the jurisdiction of the tribunal and court system and correspondingly less for the Ombudsman to do. The Ombudsman's field of operations covers those decisions which are likely to remain outside the purview of any further special or generalized tribunals, particularly

---

[6] The position of Commonwealth citizens is governed by the Commonwealth Immigrants Act (10 and 11 Eliz. 2, ch. 21). See also *Instructions to Immigration Officers* (Cmnd. 1716, 1962).

decisions taken at the discretion of officials in the Home Office, the Foreign Office, the Ministry of Defence, the Ministry of Health, and the Ministry of Housing and Local Government. But here the distinction between maladministration and incorrect decision is difficult to draw.

It is characteristic of these fields (as distinct from say Pensions, Labour or National Insurance) that decisions are not taken in accordance with a fixed and detailed body of statutory rules. The distinction, therefore, between, on the one hand, acting wrongly yet not improperly (i.e. misapplying the rules), and on the other hand acting in a way which is in some sense improper or an abuse of the rules, becomes far from clear. The Whyatt report tries bravely to maintain the distinction (which is at least notionally valid) between complaints that an administrative act is 'wrong policy' or 'unwelcome to the complainant' and complaints that a decision fails to observe 'proper standards' or is 'oppressive' or is a 'misuse of power'. Only the second type of complaint it suggests should concern the Ombudsman. But in areas where Parliament has conferred wide discretionary powers, neither complainants nor the Ombudsman could be expected to make consistent use of this distinction. In fact if one sets out the facts of any of the celebrated administrative fiascos of the past, it is difficult to decide which aspects of them were proper but unwise, imprudent or unwelcome, and which were improper, unjust or oppressive. Could the complaints of Commander Marten about Sir Thomas Dugdale and his men have been parcelled out according to this formula in the Crichel Down inquiry of 1954? The New Zealand draftsmen at any rate have not puzzled their heads over it. Nor does the Ombudsman have to. For the New Zealand Parliamentary Commissioner is (by section 19 of the Act) to be unleashed upon decisions which are 'unreasonable, unjust, oppressive or improperly discriminatory' or 'wrong', and even upon decisions taken in accordance with *a rule of law* which is unreasonable, unjust, oppressive or discriminatory. In an interview with *The Times*, Sir Guy Powles, the first appointee to the post, is reported as saying that 'happy results can often be obtained without in any way calling in question the probity of departments or officials'.[7]

Clearly, therefore, there may be differences of opinion about the extent of an Ombudsman's operations. Should he exist only as a check upon *improper* administration, or should he work more widely as in effect an informal appeal agency for securing a reconsideration of official action? The New Zealand Parliamentary Commissioner appears to act as a general straightener of difficulties and in a certain sense, therefore, in an appeal capacity, though one which can only be effective by persuasion and with the co-operation of departments. The Whyatt report fully concedes that complaints may be of 'infinite variety' and that they cannot be precisely defined. A good deal will

[7] *The Times*, December 4, 1962.

simply have to be left to an Ombudsman's own instincts and sense of justice.

The proposed machinery is outlined in chapter 14 of the report. It is emphasized that this would be supplementary to existing avenues for complaint—particularly the parliamentary question, the adjournment debate and the *ad hoc* inquiry set up by a particular department or under the provisions of the 1921 Tribunals of Inquiry (Evidence) Act.[8] The office should be known as that of the Parliamentary Commissioner, or some other suitable name.[9] He should have the same status as the Comptroller and Auditor-General and be removable only on an address by both Houses of Parliament. In the beginning he should receive complaints only from members of either House of Parliament but consideration should be given after a trial period to receiving complaints direct from the public. The Commissioner should notify the appropriate Minister before beginning an investigation of a complaint against his department and the Minister should have the right to veto any proposed investigation. It is hoped, however, that a convention would develop that he would not do so save in exceptional circumstances. The Committee believes that there would be no serious interference with the ordinary working of departments if the Commissioner's investigations were conducted informally. Except that the inquiries would be conducted by an outside person independent of the department, the inquires would not be substantially different from those which occur when the answer to a parliamentary question is being prepared or a complaint against a junior officer is being investigated by the senior officials. As in Denmark it is hoped that a spirit of mutual confidence might develop between the Commissioner and the civil servants, who would see in the Commissioner's office a protector of their interests against ill-informed criticism and not merely a potential source of publicity for their mistakes. (A psychological parallel might be seen in the general approval often expressed by officials in the nationalized industries of the investigations of the Select Committee on Nationalized Industries.)

The question of access to files is a delicate one since one of the prime articles of belief in the British civil service is that freedom and candour of communication within the service can only be preserved with the aid of a guarantee of absolute privacy for internal minutes. Crown privilege to refuse the production of documents in the courts rests upon this proposition and is defended by the argument that Ministers must be in a position to receive frank, anonymous advice.[10] It is supposed

8 The procedure under this Act is very fully described in G. W. Keeton, *Trial by Tribunal* (London, 1960).

9 'Ombudsman' really will not do, if only because of a difficulty over the plural. Ombudsmen would be neither English nor anything else.

10 It is noteworthy that in the New Zealand scheme the rule of crown privilege which applies in the courts is declared not to apply to proceedings before

that advice would not be frank or full if there were the possibility of subsequent disclosure. The 'Justice' Committee concedes that the administrative process might well be slowed up if it were necessary to draft minutes with an eye to defending them later against public criticism and cross-examination. But it should be noted that *public* criticism is not suggested. Defending one's minuting of papers in private to a person with first-hand knowledge of the public service seems a risk which is more supportable. In any event, the proposed scheme treats the departments with extreme tenderness on this point. What is proposed is that the Commissioner—assuming that he is not warned off by a ministerial veto—shall have access in investigating a complaint to outward and inward correspondence of a department (including correspondence with other departments) but not to the internal departmental minutes.

This internal/external distinction possibly needs to be gone into in greater detail. Where the Minister gets his advice from in a particular case may be largely accidental. What has become known as the 'Chalk-pit case' in Britain provides a good example of expert advice being furnished to a Minister from various sources and of the difficulty of distinguishing between factual information, expert evaluation of facts and advice on policy.[11] Very often the appropriate experts or affected interests may be in another department and the kind of 'internal' consideration which hitherto civil servants have been anxious to protect from outside scrutiny is not different in kind because inter-departmental. Whether any of it should be immune from the scrutiny of the Commissioner is a question which deserves to be debated. As a result of the Franks Report the advice given to Ministers by the inspectors who preside at public inquiries is now revealed—a development which marks a significant step in the direction of what the Report called 'openness, fairness and impartiality'. The 'Justice' Committee plainly felt however that some compromise had, at the moment, to be made between complete disclosure to the Ombudsman and no inspection of files at all if its report were to have any chance of success. It would be open for the Commissioner to make a request to the permanent head of a department or to the Minister for further facilities to see internal minutes if he felt that his investigation could not otherwise be carried out, and it would be his duty to report to Parliament any dissatisfaction he might feel about the Minister's attitude or the facilities offered him.

There should be, it is suggested, a select committee of Parliament to

the Commissioner. The Attorney General may certify that information or documents need not be supplied if they might by being produced endanger security, defence or international relations or if they might reveal Cabinet proceedings or confidential proceedings of a Cabinet committee. (S. 17 of the Act.)

[11] See *Third Report of the Council on Tribunals*, 1962.

which annual or special reports should be given. (This in a way would provide for departmental administration a similar watchdog to the Select Committee on Statutory Instruments which informs Parliament about departmental rule-making.) Civil servants should not be mentioned by name in these reports, and disciplinary action should be left to the appropriate departmental authorities.

3. *Reactions to the Whyatt Report*

In a curious way blame has fallen on the Whyatt report because of its moderation. One serious academic critic, Professor J. D. B. Mitchell, is opposed to the general enthusiasm for the Ombudsman solution since he fears that it will stand in the way of a much more radical rethinking of the role played by the courts in the supervision of administration.[12] This is a dangerous line of conservative-liberal opposition to adopt since it bears recognizable affinities to a well-known form of reactionary argument. Professor Mitchell's thoroughgoing reform is rather unlikely to take place and the acceptance of the Whyatt proposals will not affect the probabilities very much either way. It is true that at some future date government spokesmen might cite acceptance of the Whyatt report as a reason for not undertaking further inquiries, just as the Franks report has been cited as evidence that no further thought need be given to maladministration (though that report was not about maladministration). But the causes of political and administrative change bear little relation to what ministerial spokesmen say. It could be argued in any event that royal commissions, however composed, are less likely to bring about changes in the scope of judicial review than changes in judicial outlook. Perhaps the bench should be prodded on at the stickier stages by piecemeal statutes such as the Tribunals and Inquiries Act of 1958 (though Professor Mitchell would be entitled to reply that this argument carries an even more conservative odour than his own).

Criticism by those who favour the Whyatt conclusions on the Ombudsman question falls on those parts of it—restricted access to files and indirect access of complainants to the Commissioner—which the Committee may well have felt were necessary to avoid collision with as many current prejudices as possible. One such set of prejudices are those of members of Parliament who might feel that their functions as controllers of the administration and grievance investigators were being diluted or in part removed. No member who has given his attention to the scheme as outlined could emerge with any such belief. He would

---

[12] See his essay in this volume and 'The Ombudsman Fallacy', *Public Law* (1962), 24. The spring issue of this journal is a special number devoted to the Ombudsman question. For other comments on the Whyatt report see *Political Quarterly* (January–March 1962), 9; *The Lawyer* 4, 29; *Journal of the International Commission of Jurists* IV, 150; *Modern Law Review* 25, 220; *Public Administration* 40, 125; *The Economist*, November 4, 1961.

still be able at his discretion to make his own investigations or to refer expensive or technical inquiries to the Commissioner. The existence of the Commissioner's office moreover would give the back-bench member an additional (and possibly more potent) formula for use at question time or when an adjournment debate fails to yield concessions or clarity. 'In view of the unsatisfactory nature of the Minister's reply', he might say, 'I shall refer the correspondence in this matter to the Parliamentary Commissioner's Office'.

Some points of parliamentary procedure would perhaps need to be clarified. It would for example be undesirable that reference of complaints to the Commissioner should give opportunities for the invocation of the *sub-judice* rule so as to curtail parliamentary freedom of discussion. There could be questions which Ministers might be glad to shelve temporarily by a reference to the Commissioner followed by a refusal to answer further questions in the House. A brake on such tactics would lie, one would hope, in the eventual publication and debate of the Commissioner's report. But it would be unfair to the House and to those members who might prefer not to invoke the Ombudsman procedure if it were possible for one or a few members (or Government back-benchers by arrangement) to frustrate the desire of a majority of Opposition members to attack the Government in the House. The answer is surely that the *sub-judice* rule is too wide anyway, and that the reasons for adopting it in relation to the courts do not apply to the Parliamentary Commissioner. There is no reason why parliamentary debate, questions, private investigations by members and consideration by the Commissioner should not go on simultaneously.[13]

It is the role of the Ombudsman in relation to Ministers that is the biggest stumbling block in Britain. It was reported in April 1962 that the Danish Ombudsman had disagreed with the Minister of Public Works and two permanent heads of other departments in a controversy about the duties of government representatives on the board of the Scandinavian Airline System. This kind of news item causes the imaginations of many Englishmen to boggle and fail. When Professor Hurwitz, the Danish Ombudsman, gave a number of lectures in the United Kingdom several years ago, academics were eager to ask him how he managed his relations with Ministers. They were not easily able to understand his answer, namely that he managed them without difficulty. No one has suggested, and the Whyatt report certainly does not, that a British Parliamentary Commissioner should have any

[13] A select committee was appointed in December 1961 to consider the working of the *sub-judice* rule in relation to proceedings in the House (see 651 *H.C. Deb.*, 45–7). Its report (H.C. 156 of 1962–63) relates the rule to civil and criminal courts and to 'any *judicial* body to which the House has referred a specific matter for decision and report'. Presumably a Parliamentary Commissioner would not for this purpose be classed as performing judicial functions though he might be so classified for *certiorari* purposes.

executive power to make decisions or to give rulings on matters of governmental organization. Nevertheless, in pursuing his inquiries it would be essential to get agreement upon procedure. If a Minister has permitted an inquiry to go forward, will he be subject to cross-examination by the Commissioner? Will he permit senior civil servants to be questioned about the advice which they gave to him or allow the Commissioner to solicit their views about an alternative course of action which may have been rejected at the ministerial level? In the Select Committee on Statutory Instruments, Ministers do not submit themselves to examination and officials consequently answer questions of an explanatory, factual and procedural kind and are not asked to defend policy. But this restriction would make the investigation of administrative discretionary activities pointless. The whole question presents a challenge to ingenuity which it was easy for Mr MacMillan's Government to decline under cover of the slogan 'no derogation from ministerial responsibility to Parliament'—a phrase which completely misrepresents the essence of the proposed reforms.

Several discussions of the Ombudsman scheme have taken place in the House of Commons and in the Lords.[14] At first the Government were unenthusiastic. Then they were eager to await the deliberations of the 'Justice' Committee. Finally they were unenthusiastic again and satisfied that adequate means already exist 'for the redress of any genuine complaint about maladministration'. Two other points perhaps deserve mention. Proposals for Ombudsman machinery for investigating allegations about police misbehaviour were put forward by several members of the recent Royal Commission on the Police which reported in 1962 (Cmnd. 1728). Similar suggestions[15] followed controversy about ministerial and civil service behaviour in security matters, promoted by several spectacular espionage trials and a number of committees of inquiry. Lord Denning's appointment in the autumn of 1963 to inquire into the Profumo scandal and its related security risks provided the British public with a temporary demonstration of how it might feel to have an Ombudsman. Earlier, 'Justice' had circulated to members of Parliament a memorandum replying to criticisms of its proposals (see Note below). A change of Government was a necessary, though possibly not a sufficient condition, for their adoption. The Liberals are already believers (*ex officio*, so to speak). Mr. Wilson, a recent convert, is electorally pledged to supply the United Kingdom with an Ombudsman, but is taking his time.

---

[14] In the Lords on July 12 and May 7, 1961, and in the Commons, May 19, 1961.
[15] See Sir Hartley Shawcross in *The Times*, December 17, 1962.

NOTE

Extract from a Memorandum Issued in 1962 by 'Justice' (British Section of the International Commission of Jurists) on the Whyatt Report.

. . . The more serious [criticisms], and our answers to them, are:

1. *The office of Parliamentary Commissioner will conflict with the doctrine of ministerial responsibility*

It already appears that this will be the main argument relied upon by opponents of the institution of a Parliamentary Commissioner. It invokes a hallowed constitutional doctrine (though one which is often overworked) and has an emotive appeal. But we do not think that in this context it will bear examination.

No-one suggests that the functions of the Comptroller and Auditor-General conflict with ministerial responsibility. The C. & A.-G. has a far wider network of agents in the departments than the Commissioner would ever have. Their function is to supply factual information for the use of Parliament. The Commissioner's functions would essentially be similar, the only difference being that they would extend to administrative standards generally and not merely to expenditure.

Similarly no-one suggested that the Crichel Down inquiry of 1954 was inconsistent with ministerial responsibility. It led, in fact, to an extreme example of the working of the doctrine: the resignation of the Minister of Agriculture on account of administrative failings by various officials for which he was personally in no way to blame. The purpose of the proposed Commissioner is to provide regular machinery for investigating grievances against administration in a discreet and informal way by contrast with the formality and publicity of ad hoc inquiries such as the Crichel Down inquiry. But so far as ministerial responsibility is affected, the essence of both procedures is the same.

The truth is, we think, that the Commissioner would help to make ministerial responsibility more effective. He would penetrate the screen which ministers interpose between members of Parliament and government departments, and he would keep Parliament informed about administrative practices which were open to criticism. Ministers would then be called to account in Parliament in the usual way. The Commissioner would *not* be concerned with policy, and in any case it is proposed (in paras. 146 and 155 of the Whyatt Report) that the minister should be entitled to veto investigations if he wished to take full responsibility on himself.

There is an important distinction between the deliberate carrying out of policy, for which of course ministers must be solely responsible, and administrative aberrations which are not required by the department's policy and for which ministers have a qualified responsibility. In the latter class of case the minister is responsible in the sense that he must acknowledge that something has gone wrong in his department. But he has no obligation to take responsibility for some particular action which is reprehensible or of which he disapproves. This was explained by the then Home Secretary (the present Lord Kilmuir) in the Crichel Down debate (Hansard vol. 530, pp. 1286–7). The Commissioner would be concerned with maladministration, i.e. with exactly the class of acts for which the full rigour of the doctrine of ministerial responsibility is relaxed. The only possibility of conflict would be if the Commissioner criticized something which the Minister wanted to defend. In that case the Minister could perfectly well make his defence in Parliament in the ordinary way. It would be quite wrong to suggest that the responsibility of the minister for what is done in his department would be reduced if a Commissioner investigated complaints. The responsibility would remain the same as at present, neither more nor less.

It is difficult to see what is in the minds of those who make an objection out of ministerial responsibility. If they feel that a minister must have *exclusive* responsibility for investigating errors in his department, the answer is that the doctrine has never required this, as the Comptroller and Auditor-General and the Crichel Down inquiry show. (See para. 155.)

2. *The office of Parliamentary Commissioner would diminish the rights and functions of Members of Parliament in the taking up of grievances on behalf of their constituents.*

We take the view that a Parliamentary Commissioner [who received complaints only through members of Parliament] would reinforce the rights and effectiveness of members of Parliament rather than diminish them. They would still receive and deal with the complaints and would, as at present, settle most of them satisfactorily with the Minister. But there is a residue of complaints, some of them important, where the Member and/or his complainant is not satisfied that justice has been done. Sometimes, for reasons which in no way reflect on him, it may be embarrassing for the Member to attack the Minister or to try to probe the matter further. Sometimes a matter which should be discussed objectively is made into a political issue in which the Government cannot afford to give way.

The ability to refer such cases to the Parliamentary Commissioner would be an additional weapon in the hands of Members of Parliament, and a means of ensuring that the matter was dealt with fairly and to the satisfaction of the complainant.

Parliamentary questions and adjournment debates can deal only with a small number of cases, and are most effective where the case has political appeal. One of the main arguments for the Commissioner is that he will be able to handle the flow of complaints for which Parliamentary procedure is less suitable, and so strengthen the present system at its weak point.

We would further point out that the Parliamentary Commissioner would be the servant of Parliament and answerable only to Parliament. (See paras. 156 and 157.)

3. *A Parliamentary Commissioner may be all right for a small country like Denmark, but he would be swamped with complaints in a country of the size of Britain.*

This objection has been foreseen and provided for by the channelling of all complaints, for an experimental period, through Members of Parliament. It is difficult to estimate the number of complaints which would require serious attention, but the Parliamentary Commissioner should not require a large staff during this period. (See paras. 158–161.)

4. *The real value of a Parliamentary Commissioner, from the point of view of members of the public, is that they should have direct access to him.*

We agree that this would be the ideal arrangement, and it is this which has gained for the office the public confidence it enjoys in Scandinavian countries. The Whyatt Report looks forward to the same thing in this country after a transitional period. Meanwhile the criticism is met to some extent by the proposal that the Parliamentary Commissioner or a member of his staff should give the complainant a personal interview if he thought that this was needed. (See paras. 146, 156 and 157.)

5. *A far better solution of the problem would be to make provision for all serious complaints against the administration to be dealt with by the courts.*

It is certainly desirable to extend and complete the courts' control over excess and abuse of power, and to preserve their control over points of law. But the courts dislike passing judgment on the *merits* of administrative action and on questions of administrative technique. A formal legal process is the wrong method for dealing with most complaints, and of course it is also open to serious objection on grounds of expense. There is also the difficulty, when investigating action in a government department, that the Minister is prone to claim Crown privilege and refuse disclosure of documents. The courts have an important part to play, but they cannot carry out informal investigations as the Commissioner could do. The fundamental point is that the courts can deal only with illegalities—they could have said nothing, for example, in the Crichel Down case.

Further, the majority of complainants do not want to bring legal actions, or to claim damages or to win victories. They merely want a fair and impartial adjudication of the complaint, to feel that their point of view has been properly explained to them. (See paras. 13 and 14.)

6. *Civil servants will not be able to do their work properly with the threat of an outside investigation always hanging over them—they will be even more frightened of making decisions.*

These same fears were expressed by civil servants in Denmark when the appointment of a Parliamentary Commissioner was being discussed. In the outcome they have not been realized. On the contrary, the Danish Ombudsman has come to be regarded by civil servants as a valuable and impartial defence against unjustified attacks to which the individual civil servant cannot himself respond. He has brought about a new relation of confidence between the civil service and members of the public. The Parliamentary Commissioner is not simply a watchdog for the public, or an apologist for the administration, but the independent upholder of the highest standards of efficient and fair administration.

One of his powers and duties has an important bearing on this point. If he receives a series of similar complaints and finds that they are due to stupid or unjust regulations which civil servants have to administer perhaps against their will, he can call the attention of Parliament to these regulations and ask for their amendment. (See paras. 162 and 120.)

CANADA

*by D. C. Rowat and Henry J. Llambias**

Canada shares the general characteristics of the parliamentary system that exists in the Commonwealth countries. Among its main features are: a union of executive and legislative powers in a politically dominant Cabinet, a single-member, single-vote electoral system that often throws up a huge parliamentary majority which gives obedient support to that Cabinet, a tradition of secrecy that permeates the whole administrative structure, and severely limited opportunities for the appeal or judicial review of administrative decisions. All of these lend support to the proposition that the citizens and Parliament need the help of an Ombudsman in any attempt to get at the facts regarding a complaint of maladministration or arbitrary administrative action.

In fact, there are good grounds for believing that the need for the Ombudsman institution in Canada is more pressing than in many other Commonwealth countries. As in the United Kingdom, the liberties of the subject are not entrenched in a written constitution. But Canada has fewer administrative tribunals, where decisions can be made in a judicial manner, and no Council on Administrative Tribunals. Also, she has inadequate legislative prescription of administrative procedure; many regulatory boards and commissions with power to decide cases but no provision for appeal to the courts; antiquated laws on Crown privilege, expropriation and liability; weak arrangements for free legal aid to needy citizens; and no formal procedures in either Parliament or the provincial legislatures for settling the grievances of individuals. In addition to all this, the federal division of powers means that the provisions protecting the citizen's rights against administrative action are worse in some provinces than in others, and that the administration of justice varies because it is divided between the federal government, which appoints and pays the judges, and the provinces, which appoint all magistrates and control the organization and civil procedure of provincial and lower courts.

Throughout the Commonwealth countries there seems to be a general attitude of complacency about the protection of the citizen's rights, perhaps engendered by the strength of the tradition of 'the rule of law'. People do not realize that due to the modern growth of administrative powers the meaning of this tradition has lost much of its content. In Canada, one of the most frequently voiced objections to the Ombuds-

* Graduate Student, School of Public Administration, Carleton University.

man proposal is that it is not needed: citizen's rights seem to be adequately protected already, and one doesn't 'hear about' very many cases of persons who have been dealt with unfairly by the administration. The objectors do not appreciate that, since administrative action is secret, the great majority of such cases do not come to light. Only some of the most serious ones are revealed and, since they concern isolated individuals, often they are not widely publicized by the press and are soon forgotten by the public.

To meet this objection, the authors of this essay have made it their business to collect cases of maladministration, arbitrariness and outright injustice which have been publicly reported within the past few years and which were not adequately handled by existing machinery. These reveal a bewildering variety of examples of bureaucratic bungling at all three levels of government—federal, provincial and local; they range from simple (but none the less serious) cases of red tape such as failure to answer an inquiry or make a decision, to heart-rending stories of sane persons incarcerated for years in the cockroach-ridden mental wing of Montreal's Bordeaux jail.[1] We have collected about 60 such cases, most of which have occurred in the past three years. In all of them an Ombudsman could have improved the situation for the complainant, usually by finding out the true facts at a much earlier date, by obtaining either redress or a change in the decision, and by doing so with far less injurious publicity. In several, he would no doubt have secured administrative and perhaps even legislative reforms.

These cases, however, are ones that, by good fortune or the strenuous efforts of the complainant, happen to have been revealed. There are countless others that are never brought to light and in which the aggrieved persons may suffer years of heart-breaking frustration. This was demonstrated by the numerous letters that Professor Rowat received from aggrieved citizens when he wrote a magazine article and spoke on radio and television about the Ombudsman idea. Their cases are of much the same type that the Ombudsmen receive and investigate. (Aggrieved citizens in Britain similarly sent cases to Ombudsman Hurwitz in Denmark after he returned home from speaking about his office on television in Britain.) Another indication of the volume of unsatisfied complainants is the number of cases handled by a voluntary organization called Underdog, recently organized in Toronto to help mistreated persons. In Underdog's first eighteen months of operation there were 173 cases involving government officials. Of these, 69 had to do with the federal government, 84 were provincial and 20 were municipal.[2]

---

[1] Llambias, 'Wanted—An Ombudsman', *Edge* 2 (Spring, 1964), 81–91; Rowat, 'We Need a New Defense Against So-Called Justice', *MacLean's* 74, 7 (Jan. 7, 1961), 10, 82–3.

[2] Robert McKeown, 'Why Canada Needs an Ombudsman', *Weekend Magazine* 14, 2 (Jan. 11, 1964), 24.

On the basis of the Scandinavian experience, one can estimate that the total case-load for Ombudsmen at all levels of government in Canada might be about 7,000 per year, with perhaps 3,000 at the federal level alone. Even using the low Danish figure of about 10 per cent that require some kind of corrective action, this would mean that the number of cases of uncompensated administrative injustice in Canada must be at least 700 per years. However, these figures may be far too low because of the earlier-mentioned inadequacy of Canada's protections against arbitrary administration. Also, the federal division of the country into two levels of government causes administrative conflict and delay, and creates confusion for the citizens, who are likely to complain to the wrong level of government at first, thus increasing the total case load at both levels. Another significant difference from the Scandinavian countries is Canada's higher level of post-war immigration and the accompanying administrative problems of eligibility for admission and citizenship.

While opponents may admit that most of an Ombudsman's cases could not be handled by the courts in Canada, they frequently object that with the single-member district it is the job of the member of Parliament to handle such cases for his district. In effect, they say, Canada already has 265 Ombudsmen at the federal level of government, to say nothing of those at the lower levels. To investigate this argument —to find out how many and what kinds of complaints MPs receive, how they handle them and whether they think an Ombudsman would help—Mr Llambias sent a questionnaire to all members of the House of Commons in the spring of 1964, and received 80 replies. Nine of these were refusals of information, of which two were from Ministers who declined to express any opinion for fear that this might be interpreted as Government policy. Although the remainder is probably a biased sample, in the sense that only the most interested and sympathetic MPs replied, it does reveal some interesting facts.

The MPs were asked to estimate 'how many complaints about some aspect of governmental administration in relation to individuals' they received per month from constituents, and there was a surprising scatter in the replies. Thirty-six MPs estimated they had fewer than 10 complaints per month while twelve said they received more than 30, and two indicated that they were burdened with as many as 65. The difference in the number of complaints seems to depend mainly on the rural or urban character of the constituencies and their total populations, which at present vary tremendously. The average number of complaints received by the forty-four MPs who replied to this question was about 15. Extending this average to all MPs would mean that in total they receive an estimated 4,000 per month, or nearly 50,000 per year. Even if we assume that it was mainly the overburdened MPs that replied, and that an average for all MPs would be closer to 10 per month, this would still mean a total of 32,000 complaints per year. The replies indicated that a surprising number of complaints concern provincial or local government and even non-governmental bodies. Only about 70 per cent relate to federal departments or agencies, so that complaints of the latter type may total about 22,000 per year.

To a question on whether the complaints concern the personality of officials, the manner of proceeding or the substance of the action taken, there was considerable variation in the replies. However, most of the MPs thought that about 10 per cent concern personalities, 35 per cent the manner of proceeding, and that a majority are directed to the substance of the action. It is likely that many of the latter deal with the reasonableness of a decision or the effect of a law or policy. These matters an Ombudsman would not ordinarily investigate. MPs would continue to handle such cases, as well as requests for help and information and demands for change in the laws or regulations.

When the MPs were asked to identify the areas of governmental activity into which complaints mainly fell, they named 41 different areas, departments and agencies. However, there was a heavy concentration on certain areas. Decisions regarding pensions seemed to cause the most trouble, appearing in 20 questionnaires. The next most common areas of complaint were citizenship and immigration, income tax, health and welfare, unemployment insurance, and veterans' affairs.

Questions were also asked on the efficacy of the existing procedure for handling complaints. It is interesting that there was considerable disagreement about whether being on the Government or Opposition side of the House made a difference to the success of a complaint, although a majority of the MPs felt that it made no difference. Perhaps the reason for this disagreement, as one stated, is that being on either the Government or Opposition side has advantages and disadvantages. While access to information is easier for Government MPs, they are reluctant to ask the Minister a question in the House for fear of embarrassing the Government. As one MP wrote, 'No questions to the Minister, as I am on the Government side!' An Opposition MP, on the other hand, is free to publicize a case and to press an attack on the floor of the House.

A crucial question was: 'Do you ever handle complaints which are settled in a manner unsatisfactory to you and/or the complainant?' To this the great majority (55 out of 63) answered yes, and many said that half or more of their complaints were settled unsatisfactorily. Various reasons were given for the shortcomings of the existing system. One stated bluntly, 'Insufficient time and secretarial assistance to deal with each complaint'. Another felt that a basic inadequacy of the system was the 'weakness of individual MPs who are unwilling to intercede on behalf of constituents'. A third believed that not all MPs had the 'experience or training to deal with some of the issues which arise', while two MPs pointed out that in most cases they could only obtain information at second-hand from the Minister or civil servant, since they lacked access to the files.

The M Ps were then requested to describe one or more typical cases, or cases in which they felt that the Minister's explanation and/or the department's action was unsatisfactory. Although many MPs felt that they could not take the time to do this, the others went to the trouble of presenting a great variety of interesting and sometimes shocking cases. While space does not permit an analysis of these cases here, it is clear that many of them would fall within the competence of an Ombudsman.[3]

To the final question, whether they thought that a Parliamentary Complaints Commissioner (Ombudsman) would be of help, 53 MP s answered yes, 13 said no, and 2 were doubtful. Of this sample of 68, then, the proportion in favour of the Ombudsman exceeded three to one.

Because of the large number of unsatisfied grievances against administrative action in Canada, and the inability of members of Parliament to deal with them adequately as revealed by the questionnaire, interest in the Ombudsman proposal has been rising—especially since New Zealand's adoption of the scheme in 1962. As early as December of that year, Arthur Smith, a member of the majority Conservative party, presented to the House of Commons a private member's Bill for a Parliamentary Commissioner. As often happens with such Bills, it was not debated or voted on. Much the same Bill was introduced again in 1963, this time by R. N. Thompson, leader of the Social Credit Party, but its second reading was disallowed by the Speaker because a private member's Bill may not propose the expenditure of public funds. He introduced it again as Bill C-7 in February 1964, with provision for the Commissioner to be financed by private benefactions—a change obviously designed to circumvent the Speaker's previous ruling. This time it was successfully debated.[4] By then a royal commission had reported favourably on the idea[5] and a Liberal Government was in power. Being more sympathetic to the proposal, the new Government agreed to refer the Bill to a standing committee, which will probably support it in principle.

Bill C-7 is based on the New Zealand Act of 1962, but is a much simplified and condensed version. Because it is reproduced at the back of this book, only some of its main features need to be mentioned here. As in the New Zealand Act, the Parliamentary Commissioner's grounds for criticizing an administrative action are to be very broad. For example, he may make recommendations where he adjudges that an authority

---

[3] Mr Llambias has analyzed and outlined some of these cases in his M A thesis, 'The Need for an Ombudsman System in Canada' (Carleton University, Ottawa, 1964).

[4] Canada, *House of Commons Debates* 109, 21 (March 17, 1964), 1167–73.

[5] Canada, Royal Commission on Government Organization, *Report* (Ottawa, 1963), V. 5, 94–5.

or officer is administering a law 'unreasonably, wrongly . . . or by using a discretionary power for an improper purpose, or on irrelevant grounds'. The scope of his jurisdiction is to be even broader than that in New Zealand. The judiciary and the Governor General acting on the advice of the whole Cabinet are exempt from his purview, as in New Zealand, but any other 'power or authority or officer', apparently including individual Ministers, can be investigated and criticized if need be. The authors of the Bill were obviously unimpressed by the fears expressed in Britain that an Ombudsman might interfere with ministerial responsibility, for they included neither the proposal of the 'Justice' report that a Minister should have power to stop an investigation or refuse to release departmental minutes, nor even the stipulation in New Zealand's Act that, where an investigation relates to a recommendation made to a Minister, the Commissioner must consult the Minister at his request. Unlike the provisions in New Zealand, his powers of inquiry, rather than being spelled out in great detail, are simply said to be those of a commissioner under the Inquiries Act, and his investigations are not required to be private; no fee is required to make a complaint, no limits are placed on his power to investigate the armed services, and his scope is not limited to only those departments and agencies named in a schedule.

It is important to recall, however, that the jurisdiction of an Ombudsman created under federal law in Canada could not extend to the provinces or municipalities. For this purpose each province would need to provide its own Ombudsman. Realizing this, a number of provincial bar associations and legislative representatives have become interested in the idea, and several provincial Governments are considering it. In the early spring of 1964, for example, the Governments of Saskatchewan, Nova Scotia and New Brunswick announced that the idea would be investigated. And in May the Government of Ontario appointed a royal commission on human rights and civil liberties. This inquiry arose out of a controversy stirred up by that Government's ill-fated police bill, which would have given the Ontario Police Commission power to question any suspect in secret and to hold him in custody indefinitely if he refused to answer questions. One of the royal commission's objectives is to explore the office of Ombudsman.

Indeed, it is very likely that an Ombudsman will be established in one of the provinces of Canada before it is adopted at the federal level. But this is perhaps as it should be. One of the great advantages of a federal system is that an experiment with a new idea or institutional form can be tried on a small scale in one of the states or provinces first. If it is successful there, it will then spread to the others and can safely be adopted by the central government.

The needs at the provincial level, however, are different, and therefore the provincial and federal offices should not be mere carbon copies of one another. Because the provincial governments are smaller, an

Ombudsman would get to know the senior officials personally so that he would be less likely to criticize them. The Cabinet's control over the administration is more direct, party patronage exerts a greater influence, and provincial Governments frequently have very large majorities in the legislatures for long periods of time. For these reasons, stronger provisions will be needed to ensure the Ombudsman's independence from the executive. Moreover, while there may be grounds for exempting the higher courts from an Ombudsman's supervision, the situation regarding the lower courts, which the provinces control completely, is different. The Chief Justice of the Supreme Court has some disciplinary control over the judges of the higher courts but any disciplining of magistrates must be initiated by a provincial Government. Because of the tradition that the executive should not interfere with judicial independence, provincial Governments rarely undertake to do this. Yet magistrates are often inadequately trained and inexperienced, and, because of the large volume of cases they must consider, frequently make decisions involving civil liberties that are too hasty, or delay making decisions so long that the delay amounts to a denial of justice. Theoretically, the appeal system should take care of such faults, but it is in the lower courts that the real 'underdog' most frequently appears—with no education, no money, no counsel, and no thought of appeal. The case for including the lower courts in a provincial Ombudsman scheme is therefore strong.

Another difference between the federal and provincial governments is that the latter control the local governments. Hence a provincial Ombudsman would need to have jurisdiction over decisions made by municipal officials. Indeed, it may be that the largest city corporations, such as Montreal, Toronto, and Vancouver, should each have an Ombudsman of its own, such as has already been proposed for Philadelphia.[6] On the other hand, the federal government controls the armed services. There is plenty of evidence that cases arise within them which need the aid of an Ombudsman. But perhaps the nature of military organization and the laws governing service personnel are sufficiently different to justify a separate office for military cases, as in Sweden, Norway and Western Germany. Although in most provinces a single Ombudsman may be adequate to handle the volume of work, one wonders whether this would be true at the federal level. The countries in which the Ombudsman system now exists all have small populations, and it may be that Bill C-7 copied New Zealand's scheme too directly in this respect. A plural Ombudsman, in the form of a Complaints Commission, would probably meet the need more adequately in larger countries like Canada.[7] Sweden, the biggest of the

---

[6] See H. J. Abraham's essay.

[7] For further comments on the adjustments needed to fit Canadian conditions, see Rowat, 'An Ombudsman Scheme for Canada', *Canadian Journal of Economics and Political Science*, 28, 4 (November 1962), 554–6.

Scandinavian countries, is itself seriously considering this idea, now that the work of the Ombudsman and his Deputy is growing so rapidly.

Whatever adjustments may be required to make the institution coincide more neatly with conditions at the federal and provincial levels, there is no doubt of the need in Canada for an institution like the Ombudsman. Yet it is important to realize that such an institution cannot cure all administrative ills. It will work successfully only in a country, province or state that is already reasonably well administered. Where an administration is riddled with political patronage or corruption, the problem is too big for an Ombudsman, and a reform of the whole system is required. Even where this is not the case, the need for additional protections against arbitrary administrative action is now so great in most Commonwealth countries that other reforms will be needed if the institution is not to become overloaded. Canada, like other Commonwealth countries, is now living on its past reputation for 'the rule of law'. We are like the dog in the anonymous rhyme:

> There was a dachshund, one so long
> He hadn't any notion
> How long it took to notify
> His tail of his emotion;
> And so it was that, though his eyes
> Were filled with tears and sadness,
> His little tail went wagging on
> Because of previous gladness.

Faced with our failure to solve the problem of protecting the rights of the citizen in the modern administrative state, and with the progress made in solving this problem by other democratic countries, our eyes are 'filled with tears of sadness'. But our tails go wagging smugly on, because of previous gladness.

THE UNITED STATES
by *Henry S. Reuss and Everard Munsey**

In the years since the Great Depression, the United States government has assumed unprecedented social and economic responsibilities. Since the end of World War II, it has had to administer the affairs of a vastly increased number of veterans and operate a huge 'peacetime' defense establishment. The American economy has become more complex.

A result of these events has been an expansion of the federal bureaucracy and a great increase in the contact between the average citizen and the federal government. For the United States, as for other Western nations, this has emphasized the old problem of how to give the administrators the power and discretion they require to act effectively and, at the same time, to provide avenues for checking abuses and excesses and means of correcting errors and misjudgments.

One American solution to this problem has been the evolution of the member of Congress as a mediator between citizens and the bureaucracy. Congressmen receive and look into citizens' complaints about social security matters or veterans' benefits, about alleged discrimination in the granting of government contracts, mistreatment in the military, and countless other subjects. The public image of the Congressman as the citizens' advocate against governmental abuse is so widespread that members of Congress continually receive pleas for assistance in state and local matters that are beyond their power. On the other hand, the Congressman also has the role of explaining the bureaucracy to the citizen in many cases where the bureaucracy has been too wrapped up in jargon or technicalities to explain itself. Foreign parliamentarians are continually amazed to see members of the US House of Representatives equipped with three-room suites and up to ten aides, and members of the Senate with an even more lavish allocation of human and material resources. This paraphernalia is in no small measure due to the Congressman's role as mediator.

It is sometimes argued that the American Congressman has no business in such a role and should be remodeled after the example of his British counterpart. Whether this is correct or not—and we do not believe it is—the role of Congressman as mediator is a well-entrenched and virtually unalterable part of the American system of government. It is a principal means of resolving the conflicts between administrative

* Mr Reuss is a member of the US House of Representatives (5th District, Wisconsin), and Mr Munsey is his Legislative Assistant.

power and efficiency on one hand and civil liberties and individual rights on the other. It is a way of humanizing the bureaucracy and making it responsible.

The real political problem is to assure a reasonable balance between this function as mediator and other vital Congressional duties. Unfortunately, the balance in recent years has swung to a disproportionate emphasis on mediation, on activities that Congressmen call their 'casework'. The volume of casework has mounted steadily—perhaps more than proportionately—as the role of the federal government has expanded. In response, Congressional staffs were increased, the Legislative Reorganization Act of 1946 banned several types of private bills to redress citizens' complaints that formerly consumed much time and effort, quasi-judicial review boards were established in some exectuve agencies, and the General Accounting Office, an arm of Congress, was created to audit the legality of government expenditures. Yet, almost every Congressman finds himself spending more time on casework and, inevitably, less on his other duties. This development has coincided with an increase in the complexity of legislation before the Congress. Although bills are demanding more and more attention, less and less time for this is available.

The Congressman does not needlessly divert time from legislation to casework. Even if a Congressman should prefer to be rid of his mediating function, neglect of casework can have a political repercussion that will rid him of all the burdens of office. One astute reporter of Congressional affairs hardly exaggerated when he wrote recently that:

The plain fact is that a man's legislative work is commonly a matter of indifference—if not outright suspicion—for his constituents. What can hurt politically is the charge that he has failed to look after his district. Neglect of correspondence, of constituent services or of vital local needs lies behind the defeat of a vast majority of those few in Congress who fail of re-election.[1]

Under existing circumstances Congress is doubly hampered. The impediment of an excessive casework burden is added to the impediment resulting from unrepresentative districting and intolerable rules. Both impediments must be removed to make Congress really effective. Lightening the casework burden is not a cure-all but it is one of several positive steps that need to be taken.

1. Proposal for an Administrative Counsel

The need is clear, then, for a new device to aid the Congressman in helping his constituents so that he can continue to be a protector of their rights and still have time to be a thoughtful legislator. A further

[1] David S. Broder, 'Portrait of a Typical Congressman', *New York Times Magazine*, October 7, 1962, 31.

expansion of the Congressman's staff might be one answer. But, for reasons to be presented later, we do not believe it would be the best solution. Instead, we have proposed (in HR 7593, introduced on July 16, 1963) the creation of an Administrative Counsel of the Congress. The proposal represents an attempt to adapt to the American governmental system the institution of Ombudsman. Naturally, substantial changes have been necessary because of constitutional and political realities.

The Administrative Counsel would be appointed by the Speaker of the House of Representatives and the President *pro tempore* of the Senate 'without reference to political affiliation and solely on the basis of his fitness to perform the duties of his office.' His term of office would normally expire at the beginning of the Congress following the Congress in which he was appointed except that, if the two appointing officers could not agree, an Administrative Counsel could continue in office until the end of the Congress following that in which he was appointed. In the absence of a prolonged deadlock between the Speaker and the President *pro tempore*, this provision would avoid any period in which there would be no Administrative Counsel in office.

Constituents' complaints against the administrative departments and agencies would continue to come to members of Congress. Congressmen would, in turn, be able to refer such complaints to the Administrative Counsel who 'shall review the case of any person who alleges that he is being subjected to any improper penalty, or that he has been denied any right or benefit to which he is entitled, under the laws of the United States, or that the determination or award of any such right or benefit has been . . . unreasonably delayed as a result of any action or failure to act on the part of any officer or employee of the United States'.

The Administrative Counsel, who will be assisted by an adequate staff, would look into the claim on the basis of material submitted by the complainant and through inquiries to government officials, investigations of records, or any other necessary fact-finding procedures. He is given powers of inquiry comparable to those of Congressional committees, which exceed the investigatory authority of a single Congressman. His inquiry could extend to all aspects of good administrative practice as well as to the correctness of the administrative decision. All governmental officers and employees are required to co-operate with him and to give him full information and access to any books or records.

The right of Congress to obtain information from the executive branch is well established. One cloud on this right, however, has been the claim of 'executive privilege' as a basis of withholding information from Congress. The House Government Operations Committee has consistently maintained that claims of 'executive privilege' are without foundation in law, but such claims have been made from time to time, occasionally by minor officials. Although the question will remain in doubt until a Supreme Court decision is obtained, President Kennedy at least declared that 'executive privilege' can be invoked only by the President himself. Access to information should not prove a serious problem to the Administrative Counsel.

The Counsel's area of activity would include departments, agencies or instrumentalities of the United States. Specifically excluded from his jurisdiction, however, are the President, the Congress and its employees, the federal judiciary, the government of the District of Columbia, and of course state and local governments. In addition, he would be empowered to exclude 'any . . . officer or employee of the United States whose activities are of such a nature that . . . the application of this Act thereto would be contrary to the public interest'. One instance of the application of this provision almost certainly would be a determination by him that he should stay out of matters involving the intelligence agencies. Undoubtedly, there will be other areas he should stay out of, but it seems better not to try to foresee and specify them.

After completing his investigation, the Administrative Counsel would report his findings and his recommendation, if any, to the Congressman concerned. If his recommendation were in favor of the constituent, in many instances the erring administrative agency would have rectified the matter in the course of the investigation. If the error had not been rectified, the member would undoubtedly wish to transmit the Counsel's recommendation to the agency concerned, with his own request for remedial action. An administrative agency would be more likely to respond to a member's request for relief if it were accompanied by the Counsel's recommendation; a member's request by itself can sometimes be laughed off as 'political pressure'. However, if the member preferred, he would not need to refer a matter to the Administrative Counsel at all, but could handle it himself as at present. Moreover, if he did refer a matter and the Counsel upheld the administrative agency rather than the constituent, the member could always, if he wished, pursue the matter further on his own.

In addition to the reports on specific cases, the Administrative Counsel is directed to make an annual report to the House and Senate and may make specific reports to either body at any time. These provisions should be of great value because the Counsel will be able to obtain an unprecedented insight into administrative practices, the lack of sufficient or competent staff, and the laws and regulations that are the sources of numerous, recurring problems between the bureaucracy and the citizenry. At present, with the casework divided among 535 congressional offices, the breeding grounds of citizens' problems are not readily spotted. In his general report to Congress, the Counsel should be able to recommend action to eliminate the roots of much friction between the bureaucracy and the citizenry.

In many cases, legislative action by Congress will not be needed. If the Administrative Counsel is a person of high qualification and unquestioned standing, as the Nordic Ombudsmen have been, his criticisms in reports to the Congress should acquire the same capacity as theirs to bring prompt remedial action by the administration. Indeed, he will be able to make the remedy fit the administrative crime: a report to the referring Congressman, with or without recommendations, in individual cases; a public report criticizing poor administrative practices or a recommendation for legislative action, where that seems desirable. He will be able to investigate, recommend, criticize and publicize. He is given complete discretion in making special reports to Congress, and they may deal with individual cases as well as groups of cases. Although his reports to individual Congressmen will not be published, his annual and special reports to Congress will be printed as House or Senate documents and will undoubtedly receive widespread press coverage. The sanction of public opinion could become a powerful force for the improvement of administration.

2. *Advantages of the Scheme*

Two major advantages to be obtained from establishment of the Administrative Counsel have already been set forth: (1) Congressmen would be relieved of some of the burden of casework and allowed to spend more time on legislation, and (2) problems between the bureaucracy and citizens could be more readily spotted and eliminated. In addition, such an office would make the Congressman's mediation between citizens and the bureaucracy more effective. It would provide centralized, expert handling of casework. At present no one congressional office can afford to maintain true experts in even the most common type of cases. Much time is wasted by staff members of an individual Congressman who lack adequate knowledge in the subject of a constituent's complaint and thus cannot discuss the matter with the administrative technician concerned on anything like an equal basis. Centralizing the operation in the Office of the Administrative Counsel would permit specialization, just as has been done for the supervision of financial transactions by creating the Office of Comptroller General in the General Accounting Office. The handling of citizens' problems by the new office should promote efficiency and reduce the need for continual, costly increases in congressional staff and office space.

An Administrative Counsel of the Congress would be in harmony with the system of separation of powers and of checks and balances that characterizes the American government. For he would represent Congress in exercising a check upon the executive branch. Yet he would neither act with respect to nor in any way supplant the function of the judiciary.

The congressional-constituent relationship, it should be emphasized, would not be impaired by the work of such an officer. The Congressman would still retain control of the beginning and end of each case. He would have the option of referring the case to the Administrative Counsel or not. He could pursue the matter further after receiving the

Counsel's report. And the benefits of specialization in the Counsel's staff should result in better service to constituents.

The Counsel's effectiveness will largely depend upon the confidence that Congressmen repose in him. To gain and maintain this confidence, he will of course have to operate so that Congressmen do not have to 'follow up' cases referred to him in the same manner as inquiries they send directly to agencies of the executive branch.

The success of this new office will also depend in large measure upon its holder being, as the Swedish statute requires of the Ombudsman, of 'conspicuous integrity'. That he should also have extraordinary ability and judgment is of first importance. The proposed legislation provides that he be paid a salary of $22,500, equal to members of Congress, in order to give him the status and prestige that he needs to operate effectively.

3. *Possible Objections*

What may be said in objection to the proposals? It will no doubt be said that the Administrative Counsel will require such a large staff that this will merely mean the creation of another bureaucracy. But because of the efficiency that can be obtained through specialization, this staff should be considerably smaller than the total of congressional staff members saved from handling casework.

It may be objected that the Administrative Counsel will become a 'fixer', a powerful favor-seeker, a leader of contract-seeking Chamber of Commerce delegations. Congressmen, it may be said, will try to use his power to bludgeon unjustified concessions from the administration. But, in virtually all cases handled by Congressmen, they attempt nothing more than to assure that the constituent obtains his due, after full and fair consideration. Congressmen who wish to 'pressure' the administration will be able to do so whether the new office exists or not. Moreover, the Counsel will have a legal right to refuse to be used in such a way. The statutory language limiting the Counsel's power to review of cases in which citizens allege that they have been subjected to improper penalties or deprived of rights or benefits should help prevent his office from degenerating into a general information bureau. The provision allowing him, at his discretion, to exclude from his jurisdiction any official 'whose activities are of such a nature that ... the application of this Act would be contrary to the public interest' will allow the Counsel to stay out of areas where policy considerations are dominant and where political pressure is most likely.

It may be asked whether the Counsel should make recommendations directly to administrators. However, under the separation of powers system, it seems better that he make his reports to Congress formally. The Legislative Counsel believes that the legality of direct recommendations to officers of the executive branch by an appointed agent of the legislative branch is questionable. But in practice the legal distinctions are not likely to be important. The Administrative Counsel will be able to make informal recommendations to administrators, and his formal reports to individual Congressmen and to Congress will be sent to the administrators concerned. Often when the Counsel makes a recommendation in favor of a citizen, his recommendation by itself will bring corrective action. Less frequently in such cases officials will not respond promptly to the Counsel's recommendation, and action by the individual Congressman concerned will be necessary and effective. Action by Congress as a whole will usually occur only when citizens would be subjected to severe inequities or injustice, or where a need for general remedial action has been revealed.

Finally, it may be complained that the Counsel deviates most markedly from the other Ombudsmen in that citizens may not approach him directly but only through a member of Congress. A Congressman could, of course, refuse to submit a complaint to the Counsel, even as he may now ignore a constituent's problem. But a desire to be returned to office may be depended upon to make such behavior a rarity. Besides, each citizen has three Congressmen—one representative and two Senators—each of whom has a particular interest in being of service to him. In addition, a citizen can write to any of the other 532 members of Congress, who may refer the matter to the Administrative Counsel. Practically, it would seem that any citizen wishing to bring a matter before the Counsel would be able to do so, with little difficulty.

The requirement that citizens approach the Counsel through a member of Congress results from the decision to use an Ombudsman-like official to strengthen an existing American means of harmonizing relations between the citizenry and the bureaucracy—Congressional mediation. Any arrangement providing for direct access to the Counsel would inevitably have the effect of weakening the Congressman's role as mediator. Of course, the Counsel could be in direct communication with the complainant *after* the case is referred, just as Congressional staff members now telephone or interview complainants on occasion. In any case, it is doubtful whether Congressmen would support any proposal to remove them from their role as champions of citizens' rights against the federal bureaucracy. For, although this role is burdensome, it is a source of great strength at the polls. The scheme proposed, then, can make a valuable contribution to democratic government in the United States without a radical alteration of our institutions and traditions of government.

IRELAND*
by Max W. Abrahamson†

1. The Problem

In Ireland a convicted criminal has a right of appeal against sentence, generally to a Supreme Court judge and two High Court judges, sitting as the imposing Court of Criminal Appeal. The case is heard in public and the convict may argue in person or by a lawyer and the Court gives reasons for its decision. But after all that the sentence as settled by the Court may be mitigated by the Minister for Justice. The Minister acts in private on the advice of anonymous officials, so that the convict has no right to see that his case is fairly presented to the person deciding it. And we have been told by the Minister that 'it is not the practice to disclose the grounds on which the Minister has acted in the exercise of his statutory powers and it would not be in the public interest to do so'.[1]

Could anything be more out of balance than this, which is a microcosm of the whole system in Ireland, as elsewhere? Administrative action now matters more than private action—the relations, for example of an industrialist with administrators may be far more important to him than his relations with private individuals, particularly in Ireland where the Government is carrying out a policy of industrial expansion by licensing, discretionary grants, tax reliefs, prohibitions, and permissions.[2] But private action is regulated at length by the traditional law of contract, property, etc., and the exercise of administrative discretion is not subject to independent regulation at all. Yet it is generally, if not universally, admitted that politicians and officials are flesh and blood, and we have enormous evidence from many fields that it follows from this alone that a proportion of their decisions will be unreasonable, negligent, biased, even dishonest.

* The author and editor wish to thank the editor of *Administration* for permission to reprint portions of the author's article, 'The Grievance Man in Ireland?', Vol. 8, No. 3, pp. 238–42.

† Solicitor, Dublin.

[1] Dail Eireann (House of Representatives), *Official Reports*, Vol. 182 (June 10, 1960), 1128.

[2] By way e.g. of the state-sponsored Industrial Credit Co. Limited, Industrial Development Authority, Agricultural Credit Corporation Limited, Shannon Free Airport Development Co. Limited. There are more than fifty state-sponsored bodies in all employing 35 per cent of the total of approximately 140,000 state workers. See Garrett Fitzgerald, *State-Sponsored Bodies in Ireland* (Dublin, 1961).

Three examples only need to be added here to the many given in this book:

1. In 1898 official information reached the British Home Office that, if properly understood, proved conclusively the innocence of Adolf Beck, who had been convicted of a crime committed by Smith. The relevant official, who did not understand the information, dealt with it unsympathetically and passed it on inaccurately, and Beck was left to complete his prison sentence three years later. In 1904 he was re-arrested and again went through the whole agonizing process of being convicted of another crime committed by Smith, and he was eventually set free only as a result of private inquiries. To prevent the sort of miscarriage of justice which had occurred at the first trial the Court of Criminal Appeal was created, but strangely no real step was taken to prevent similar errors by the Home Office.[3]

2. In a British case forty years ago a faulty Post Office line damaged a nearby gas pipe, and as a result the gas pipe leaked back and injured the line.[4] Not only did the Postmaster-General's Department refuse to pay for the damage to the pipe, but sued the owner of the pipe for the damage caused to its line. The case (involving £40) was brought by the Department—with the aid of three King's Counsel and two junior counsel—through four courts to the House of Lords. In each court the Department lost and the whole business was described in the House of Lords as 'monstrous, tyrannical and unjustifiable'.[5]

The case has been cited by Sir Carleton Allen with great indignation, as reaching heights of despotism not reached before and not likely to occur again.[6] Yet I have recently had to approve on behalf of a private individual a printed form of licence put forward by an Irish state-sponsored board (which shall be nameless), which provides that 'the Licensee shall be liable for all loss of or damage to any property of the Board sustained or caused . . . (whether by negligence or breach of statutory duty on the part of the Board, its servants or agents or not) which may in any way arise by reason or on account of the granting of this Licence . . .'. And I was informed that no amendment whatsoever would be countenanced.

3. Moreover, I feel bound to say that in my own experience in this country I know of a far more than prima facie case of over £100,000 of public money lost and a private individual very seriously injured in the process, because a government department repeatedly refused to admit a mistake which it had made.

---

[3] *Report of Committee of Inquiry into the Case of Mr Adolf Beck* (1905, Cmd. 2315); an English case, but the Irish and English legal and administrative systems were of course joined at this time.

[4] *Postmaster General v. Liverpool Corporation* (1923) A.C. 587.

[5] Per Lord Shaw, *Ibid.*, 601.

[6] *Law and Orders* (London, 1st Ed., 1945), 269–70.

Of course there is no reason to suppose that administrators are more sinful than doctors or lawyers or businessmen as a class. For example, unreasonable terms are giving trouble in the standard form contracts of big business concerns generally—private as well as state-sponsored. But administrators wield enormous powers, and it seems to many in Ireland to be a particular perversion that those who tell us what to do in the interest of public justice should create injustice. Someone has quoted in this context the caption to a cartoon of the famous Thurber couple—'But Martha, what do you want to be inscrutable *for* ?' I would ask that question of administrators if I did not know the attraction of not forcing oneself to reason out a decision, and of not revealing one's reasons because they may be wrong although the decision is felt to be certainly right. On the other hand, there is no human characteristic so strong as that of believing the worst of others, and any delay or decision not explained will be presumed to be a result of the worst possible motives. This, quite apart from any question of fault on the part of the administration, is the basic justification of the Ombudsman, particularly in Ireland where cynicism is perhaps a national characteristic. Scandinavian experience suggests that an Ombudsman would reveal conclusively that the public attitude and attacks on administrators of the Hewart ('The New Despotism') and Allen ('Bureaucracy Triumphant') school exaggerate the position substantially.

As to the only other remedies of a frustrated citizen: in cases where a major abuse has been rectified as a result of questions in the Oireachtas (Parliament) or similar activities of an elected representative, our reaction has been not to inquire why more injured subjects do not make use of the procedure, but rather to marvel at the extraordinary tenacity of the party who has done it successfully. Moreover, in Ireland as in many other democracies, public opinion is by no means in a position to force a remedy for every abuse that sees the light of day; and recent developments in Britain have underlined the dangers there are in leaving to the press alone the right and duty to act for public opinion.

The Irish legal system is of course based on English law and, with the exception of their powers under the written constitution which are discussed below, the Irish courts have powers similar to their counterparts in England—principally to set aside an official decision made without legal authority or contrary to the rules of natural justice. For their emphasis on the necessity to strive for the independent judicial decision, which is the great prize they have given us, we must thank the common law judges. But the argument of some lawyers that if any change is made it must be by increasing the jurisdiction of the courts merely helps to prevent anything being done, since for good reasons there is no possibility that this very limited jurisdiction will be extended to give the courts full control over administrative action. These reasons will become clear by contrasting our court system with the Ombudsman institution.

2. Virtues of the Ombudsman

To say nothing of the lack of sympathy, at the least, of the judiciary to administrative policy,[7] the contrast is between the court system giving a formal, expensive, slow speculation by an amateur as opposed to the Ombudsman providing an informal, cheap, speedy investigation by an expert. This is not the place to deal with the question of formality and expense,[8] save to stress that informality and flexibility are essential if administrative vitality is not to be sapped; it is in the other two elements—speed and expert investigation—that the essential superiority of the Ombudsman lies. The Scandinavian legal systems as a whole place great emphasis on an investigation of the facts. In criminal cases, for example, the accused is entitled to make use of the services of an investigator provided by the state. In keeping with this, the Ombudsman is essentially an investigator with the fullest powers and scope to dig for the facts, and with the most far-reaching right to see public papers. And although he is a lawyer the Ombudsman must be or become also an expert on administration and can make full use of expert advice and discussion in particular fields to get the feel of any particular problem. In contrast the common law judge, an amateur at everything except law, has no power to investigate, not even to call a witness. The stress is on verbal argument about rather than investigation of the facts; a peculiar emphasis on speculation pervades the administration of justice.

In short, the ordinary courts do deal with difficult and technical matters but they do not deal with them well—note for example the law of patents, the interpretation of some sections of the Public Health Acts, and the flight from the courts to arbitration by businessmen and technicians.[9] The courts cannot do justice in bulk or where the main problem is to get at the facts or where one adversary can, indeed feels bound to, make use of every aid that money can buy to fight a case. But it seems that the Ombudsman can.

There is in Ireland no legislation equivalent to the English Tribunals and Inquiries Act, 1958.[10] There are, however, a number of appeal tribunals within the administration for dealing with specific administrative disputes, such as the Appeals Officers under the Social Welfare

---

[7] See e.g. W. A. Robson, *Justice and Administrative Law* (London, 3rd Ed., 1951), 534–45.

[8] See Robson, *loc. cit.*

[9] W. I. Jennings, 'The Judicial Process at its Worst', *Mod. Law Rev.* I (1937–38), 111. 'For 46 years administrative authorities have had to deal with a pressing social problem without knowing what the law was or, what is worse, knowing what it was and realizing that it was ridiculous and futile.' See also the lamentation in Hudson's *Building and Engineering Contracts* (London, 8th Ed., by Rimmer, 1959), V, VI.

[10] 6 and 7 Eliz. 2, c. 66; see Geoffrey Marshall's essay. And we still have no full equivalent of the Crown Proceedings Act, 1947 (10 and 11 Geo. 6, 3. 40).

Act, which are themselves part of the administration. At the moment a committee of the Institute of Public Administration is sitting under the chairmanship of the Chief Justice of Ireland to consider the development of appeal tribunals of this kind. Many unfortunately believe that support for this development necessarily involves opposition to the introduction of an Ombudsman. It has of course been pointed out that this is not so and that in the Scandinavian countries the two controls are complementary.[11] But while there is therefore need for an Ombudsman despite the existence of some appeal to tribunals, there is a danger, in common-law countries especially, that any general system of appeal tribunals would tend to move toward the ordinary courts and become lawyer dominated—that 'the doctrine of precedent would be introduced, the law of evidence would hamper [them] and [their] procedure become cumbersome, slow and costly'.[12] Those who advocate that we set up tribunals to deal with all problems of control apparently do so in the belief that we would then be modelling ourselves on the French *Conseil d'État* (the unbiased examination of which, postponed for so long by Dicey, has produced a complete reversal of the previous opposition). But in fact the *Conseil* is nearer to, and its success in the field of administrative abuse an argument for, the Ombudsman rather than a system of tribunals akin to the ordinary courts. The *Conseil* is not a court in our sense but an investigating body:

There is not in the *Conseil d'État* procedure any equivalent to our notion of trial . . . once the applicant has brought his complaint before the *Conseil* the *Conseil d'État* may itself move to action. It is not merely a passive spectator . . . [it] itself participates in the preparation of the case.[13]

The absence in the Ombudsman procedure of a day in court—superficially the startling innovation for traditionalists—is no essential loss where there must be written records of the transaction being examined. The move from speculation to investigation is the mark of maturity in a science. An Ombudsman would appear to represent that move in its fullest and most decisive form in the field of adjudicating on administrative abuse.

3. *The Future of the Ombudsman in Ireland*

The Constitution of Ireland (1937) provides for a separation of judicial powers:

[11] Report by 'Justice', *The Citizen and the Administration* (London, 1962), Ch. 8.
[12] R. S. W. Pollard, *Administrative Tribunals at Work* (London, 1950), XX.
[13] C. J. Hamson, *Executive Discretion and Judicial Control* (Cambridge, 1962), 32.

Art. 34. Justice shall be administered in courts established by law by judges appointed in the manner provided by this Constitution.

Art. 37. Nothing in this Constitution shall operate to invalidate the exercise of limited functions and powers of a judicial nature . . . by any person duly authorized by law to exercise such functions and powers, nothwithstanding that such person is not a judge or a court appointed . . . as such under this Constitution.

Legislation inconsistent with these articles is invalid. But it is clear that an Ombudsman with power to report to Parliament only and no power to prosecute—as in Denmark, Norway and New Zealand—would fall within article 37 and no constitutional change would be necessary to introduce the office to Ireland. And a recent decision suggests that the right to prosecute also would be unobjectionable.[14] Indeed, there is an interesting constitutional precedent in the office of Comptroller and Auditor General—who reports directly to the legislature on the accounts of Government expenditure, is appointed by the House of Representatives, and may be removed from office only for stated misbehaviour or incapacity (art. 33).[15]

On many grounds, then, it seems that we in Ireland must not approach the institution of Ombudsman only on the basis that we have here an interesting foreign institution which we may consider for our abstract enlightenment. We have a problem which is very large at least in intensity, which must become worse in the future, and which threatens the practical execution of our whole social philosophy. Because it can without doubt give us some assistance in solving this problem, we must grasp at the idea of the Ombudsman.

And there is a very real practical possibility that the Ombudsman may be brought to Ireland, adapted as may be necessary. Whilst the introduction of the office has not yet been officially considered, the Department of Justice has embarked in the last two years on an ambitious scheme of law reform. When completed it will put Ireland in the forefront of the common law countries in the modern development of the legal system; and we have been given notice that institutions and principles from the legal systems of other, even non-common-law,

[14] In Ireland a District Justice decides on a preliminary hearing whether the state has made out a prima facie case on which to send an accused forward for trial on indictment. But if the Justice decides that a prima facie case has not been made out, the Attorney-General has a statutory right in effect to overrule the decision and to order that the accused should be sent forward for trial despite it. This right was considered in *The State at the Prosecution of Diana Shanahan v. His Honour Judge Conroy and Anor* (1961, not yet reported). In the High Court Davitt P. held the right of the Attorney-General to be unconstitutional as an 'unwarranted interference with the operation of the courts in a purely judicial domain', but his decision was overruled by the Supreme Court.

[15] But as to the distinctions between the two offices see 'Justice', *loc. cit.*, Ch. 13.

countries may be adopted. Most important, many lawyer-politicians of the major opposition party have already expressed very great interest in the office. As early as February, 1960, an editorial in the *National Observer*—a journal published by leading members of the party—summarized the position to be that 'the introduction [of the Ombudsman] to Ireland would do more than any other single step to convert public suspicion and hostility into public confidence'. This interest has been reiterated since in private communications with the author. Ireland may therefore certainly be classified as one of the many countries keeping a deeply interested and hopeful eye on the travels and development of the institution.

H

14

THE NETHERLANDS

by René Crince Le Roy[*]

An Ombudsman system for the Netherlands has been considered several times during the last few years. Moreover, under the auspices of the Society for Administrative Law a study of the Scandinavian systems was completed in 1963.[1] Since this study concentrates on the Scandinavian countries and does not deal with the question of whether an Ombudsman would be suitable for the Netherlands, the following essay is an attempt to answer this question.

As in all countries that recognize the principle of the rule of law, in the Netherlands the relation between the executive and the citizens is built on norms that limit free discretion; in other words, the executive is bound to the citizens by objective standards, laid down by the legislator. But it has not been possible to regulate these norms in such a way that arbitrary action will be absolutely excluded beforehand. It is the executive that applies and interprets these norms, and the norms often leave to the executive a rather large margin of freedom. This may be regrettable, but it is inevitable. If the executive is to cope with its largely expanded task, it must have this margin. The more complicated the structure of society, the greater the need for such a margin.

In a country that recognizes the rule of law it is essential that the citizen who feels that he has been injured by the executive should have a legal remedy. This is all the more necessary when the norms of the legislator are not very strictly formulated and leave a considerable degree of freedom to the administration. The larger this freedom the greater the need for a guarantee of rights.

Dutch law has a variety of protections against unjust and unlawful decisions of the administration. Following Professor Donner,[2] one can distinguish three types. First, there is administrative appeal. In some cases one can appeal against acts of the administration to a higher level, for instance to a council of provincial deputies (*Gedeputeerde Staten*), a Cabinet Minister (sometimes with the advice of a commission), or

[*] Research Lecturer (Administrative Law), University of Utrecht; staff member, Institute of Public Administration, Utrecht.
[1] J. G. Steenbeek, *De Parlementaire Ombudsman in Zweden, Denemarken en Noorwegen* (*The Parliamentary Ombudsman in Sweden, Denmark and Norway*) (Haarlem, 1963).
[2] A. M. Donner, *Nederlands Bestuursrecht* (The Executive in the Netherlands) (Alphen aan den Rijn, 1962), Part I, 339.

the Crown. In 1963 Parliament passed a Bill, which has now come into force, to provide more generally for appeals against administrative action. The acts of local authorities, however, are excluded from this legislation. Appeal will be to the Crown. The Netherlands also has a Council of State (*Raad van State*). But this Council is not a Supreme Administrative Court, and its competence in the field of administrative appeal is different from the French *Conseil d'État*. The Dutch Council of State has an advisory task and does not decide by itself: it must be heard before the Crown makes a decision in an administrative conflict.

In addition to appeals within the administration are decisions in conflicts between the administration and the citizen by special administrative courts which have, broadly speaking, the same status of independence as ordinary courts. These special courts are founded by law and possess general competence in a particular field. Thus, for administrative justice in disputes regarding the application of laws relating to social security, we have boards of appeal (*Raden van Beroep*), and as a second instance the Central Board of Appeal (*Centrale Raad van Beroep*). Similarly for all disputes between civil servants and the administration regarding the official regulations as to legal status, we have the civil servants' courts (*Ambtenarengerechten*), with the second instance also the Central Board of Appeal. Furthermore, the Court of Appeal for Industry (*College van Beroep voor het Bedrijfsleven*) handles conflicts between interested parties and the bodies concerned with regulating industrial organization.

Third, there is the indirect settlement of administrative conflicts by the ordinary courts. This settlement is indirect because the judge is not concerned about the conflict as such, but is only involved in the case because a civic right has been injured or menaced, or because a claim exists or may exist. The jurisdiction of the ordinary courts has been greatly extended in the last twenty-five years by judicial interpretation. Moreover, by certain laws the ordinary courts have been instructed to deal with the administrative conflicts mentioned in those laws.

In common law countries there are some remedies available such as mandamus, prohibition and certiorari, to compel a quasi-judicial administrative authority to perform a duty, or to question the legality of its actions. These remedies are unknown in the Netherlands. In our country, which follows the European civil law tradition, administrative authorities cannot be directly compelled by the courts to carry out their duties. In fact they do obey the courts. If, however, the administration does not carry out a decision of a court, it cannot be forced to do so unless the obligation relates to a payment in money. The administration can then be ordered to make good the damage.

Besides these judicial or quasi-judicial remedies, the Dutch citizen has other means to get redress from arbitrary acts of the administration. In the first place, the Constitution contains a right of petition. Article 8 gives a right to everybody to put forward written petitions to the proper authorities. Though this right does not have much practical meaning as far as the guarantee of rights is concerned, one cannot deny it a certain importance. Further, in a parliamentary democracy such as the Netherlands, Parliament exercises a fairly extensive control over the actions of the executive. In principle each Cabinet Minister can be called to account for his department's decisions or refusals to decide, for decisions made by his officials, and for his policy in general.

1. *The Desirability of an Ombudsman*

It will be seen that in the Netherlands we have a fairly ample system of constitutional, judicial and parliamentary control of the administration. Furthermore our administration, with competent civil servants, bears comparison with any other. All the same, the introduction of a parliamentary Ombudsman seems desirable.

As a rule public opinion is a good indicator. Stephan Hurwitz wrote that the Danish Ombudsman owes his origin to the fact that public opinion in Denmark considered the existing safeguards—'consisting in the criminal and disciplinary liability of civil servants and in the citizens' access to the courts or right to administrative appeal'—to be insufficient.[3] As for the Netherlands, the problem of protecting the citizens' rights certainly is not purely academic. This appears from the daily press and other publications, and also from the foundation, in the autumn of 1960, of the Society Against the Arbitrary Conduct of the Executive. Also, the proposal for an Ombudsman has been made in Parliament. These are all signs of a process of fermentation, which lead one to think that an Ombudsman scheme will be introduced sooner or later.

Why this desire for an extension of safeguards, for a resort to which the citizen can have refuge in case of complaints? To my mind, the main reasons for this are the following:

1. Not from every administrative act of the executive can one appeal to an ordinary court, an administrative board or tribunal, or within the administration. Sometimes it is impossible to find any good reason for this inviolability of certain administrative acts. This incompleteness of jurisdiction is a serious gap.

2. The government goes about its work with an almost painful formalism, and often it works very slowly, owing to which the interests of citizens are menaced. Every big organization suffers more or less from the evil of bureaucracy. In general this is also true of government. This may be understood and even excused: government is expected to produce sound and fair decisions, which means that as a rule they must go through many hands. Even taking all this into consideration, one often has the impression that they take a longer time than is necessary

[3] 'Control of the Administration in Denmark', *Journal of the International Commission of Jurists* (Spring–Summer, 1958), 224.

or reasonable. Here, then, is a task for an authority to which the citizen can appeal when he is injured through the delay of decision.

3. Though in a democratic state such as the Netherlands the citizen is 'ruling and being ruled', it is undeniable that he feels as though he is only being ruled. When he comes into contact with the administration he feels displeased: as an insignificant individual he finds himself opposite the all-embracing and supreme administration. This, however, is a matter outside the field of the guarantee of rights, being more a general aspect of the relations between the ruler and the ruled. Yet there is no doubt that the relations between government and citizen in this country might be improved. To the solution of this problem the Ombudsman institution might make a positive contribution. In our society of today, bureaucratic and technical as it is, the individual has a need to submit his problems to an absolutely independent person, who is willing to listen to him and who might be able to do something about his problems. The participants from Finland and Denmark in the United Nations seminar held in 1962 at Saltsjöbaden, Sweden, felt that the Ombudsman institution helps to change the often too passive attitude of the citizen towards public affairs and stimulates the responsibility of the individual citizen as well as the civil servant.

Besides an Ombudsman for civil affairs, there should be a military Ombudsman as in Sweden, Norway and West Germany. The Dutch military force, of which an important part is manned by compulsory service, is a strictly hierarchical community with a coercive character, and is almost isolated from civil society. The soldier is not only barracked and uniformed—which are strong means of isolation—but also radically withdrawn from civil society as far as labour, recreation, jurisdiction, and medical and religious care are concerned. This isolated position, and the fact that in military society norms and standards are in force which are not applied or are applied in an enfeebled form outside of it, plead for a separate military Ombudsman, who would be an expert in relations within the military apparatus. He must have an eye open for the interests of the service as well as for those of the soldier. His task, of course, would be to help military personnel, primarily the ordinary soldiers, and to deal with grievances and complaints regarding military service.

Also, the civil defence service in this country gets an important part of its manpower by means of compulsory service. For the civil defence personnel there are penal and disciplinary regulations which find their origin in the military regulations. The remarks made about the character of the military apparatus are therefore applicable in a more moderate form to the civil defence service. For this reason it seems desirable that the military Ombudsman should act also as a complaints commissioner for civil defence.

2. *The Proposed Dutch System*

My suggestion for a Dutch Parliamentary Commissioner follows the same lines as the Ombudsman institutions in Denmark and Norway (except, of course, that there would be a separate military Commissioner as in Norway and Sweden). The task of the Commissioner for Civil Affairs, to be appointed by the Second Chamber of Parliament (comparable to the British House of Commons), would be a general supervision of the whole administration. My suggestion deviates here a little from the Danish and Norwegian systems, which at the outset confined the activities of the Ombudsman to the central government (although Denmark in April 1962 extended his supervision to the municipal administration). As for the Netherlands, my opinion is that a limitation in this respect is arbitrary and therefore to be rejected. Here, it is not always clear whether a certain matter is to be considered as regarding the central government or the lower public corporations. For instance, there are state schools and municipal schools. If the activities of the Commissioner were confined to the state administration, then there would be the awkward situation that a complaint against personnel of one school could be submitted to the Commissioner, while a complaint against personnel of another school could not. Similarly, police service is provided in municipalities with more than 25,000 inhabitants (and in some smaller municipalities) by a municipal police force; in the other municipalities it is carried out by the national police force. In this field, too, it would be wrong to distinguish between central and local administration. The man in the street would not understand such a distinction, because to him every policeman simply is 'the police'.

The Parliamentary Commissioner must therefore be empowered to operate in the whole field of public administration. Injury of the citizens' interest by unjust or arbitrary conduct of the administration can be brought about by any part of the public service and a limitation of the Commissioner's competence on this point will lead to an ill-balanced system that will satisfy no one. Every citizen that feels himself injured, either by delay of a decision, unsatisfactory grounds for a decision, wrong application of the law, excess of competence, or by an unjust or unreasonable decision, must be given access to the Parliamentary Commissioner. In the interest of the independence of the ordinary courts, however, judges should be kept outside the Commissioner's domain. The same is true for the members of the above-mentioned administrative courts. These members are, by their position of independence from the administration and their appointment for life, comparable to the judges of the ordinary courts.

To perform his task the Parliamentary Commissioner must have a number of far-reaching powers. If demanded by the investigation of a complaint, he must have the competence to hear civil servants and to inspect documents, and in general he must have all powers necessary for the settlement of a complaint. Also, civil servants must be obliged to give information and to allow inspection of documents.

An important question is what the Commissioner should be enabled to do if he judges that a citizen has sent in a legitimate complaint. It would not be right to give him the competence to alter an administrative act. His task should be to supervise, not to correct. If the administration appears to have acted wrongly, the Commissioner should give his opinion to the agency (or official) concerned and at the same time indicate how it should have acted. Whether it would then follow the suggestions of the Commissioner would be a matter for it to decide, but one may expect that the Commissioner's opinions would not be lightly put aside. In this connection the Commissioner should have the obligation to report every year to Parliament about the cases dealt with. Persuasion and publicity must be the weapons for giving force to the institution of the Parliamentary Commissioner.

In a short essay I have been able to outline an Ombudsman scheme for the Netherlands only very briefly. Some important aspects—such as the relation between Parliament and the Commissioner, and the procedure for dealing with complaints—could not be dealt with. However, the provisions would be much the same as for the Scandinavian institution. I have aimed at giving some main thoughts, which will of course have to be elaborated at several points. Minor adjustments to fit Dutch conditions would have to be worked out later.

In conclusion, I should make it clear that I do not see the Ombudsman institution as a panacea for all the evils of bureaucracy. But I am convinced that as part of the control system for public administration it can be of much value. This is why I think it very important that the Netherlands follow the example of the Scandinavian countries.

IV

APPLICABILITY ELSEWHERE

15

COUNTRIES WITH A SYSTEM OF ADMINISTRATIVE COURTS

HOW ADMINISTRATIVE COURTS MEET THE NEED

*by Mme Nicole Questiaux** *

It has been stressed in preceding chapters how much the need for protection against administrative arbitrariness has grown, parallel with the activities of the welfare state, in modern democratic societies. The Ombudsman scheme specially meets this need. But there are other ways of insuring a democratic control over the administration, and among these, the French system of administrative courts under the supervision of the *Conseil d'État* or more precisely its *Section du Contentieux* (section for conflicts, as opposed to its advisory sections), shares with most Ombudsman schemes at least one major advantage: the organization has been in place for many years, and it has progressively risen to its present state of eminence as public opinion became more and more conscious of the right of the private citizen to appeal against administrative decisions, and more determined to use it.

If French law has recognized the menace to individual rights contained in the evolution of the modern state, it has done so in a pragmatic way, more frequently associated with common law countries. The *Conseil d'État* and the subordinate administrative courts stand out now as an original institution in France, and the way they have tried to give the ordinary citizen redress against arbitrariness, without impeding administrative action, is generally considered as successful by French public opinion.

However, to compare the French administrative courts with the Nordic defenders of the law can only be misleading. The two experiences have developed in fundamentally different settings, and the French example can hardly be referred to as an argument for or against the extension of the Ombudsman scheme to other countries. Moreover, no thought has ever been given to such a method of parliamentary control for France. It is not only through ignorance of the Nordic experience. The essential functions of the Nordic office are assumed by the administrative courts; if it were to be instituted in this country it would unnecessarily compete with them. But even if this were not so,

* Member of the French Council of State.

constitutional, judicial and administrative organization in France leaves no place for an Ombudsman. For this reason, which is quite unrelated to the office itself, or to the way the administrative courts have fulfilled its objective in France, it is hard to imagine the office ever being discussed in France in any way other than as an academic point of comparative law. The purpose of the present essay will be to explain the above points.

1. *Administrative Courts Provide Efficient Protection*

The French system of administrative courts can be described in a few words, even if the reader is not familiar with details of French administration. Its centrepiece is the *Conseil d'État* which also plays the part of general adviser to the Government. In the *Conseil d'État*, the *Section du Contentieux* works as the highest administrative court; originally it had a general competence over all administrative decisions, but since 1953 the local administrative courts (*Tribunaux Administratifs*) have become the courts of first instance and the *Section du Contentieux* is now essentially a court of appeal.

The private citizen's case against the administration is thus in the hands of professional administrative judges. This requires further explanation. Young members of the *Conseil d'État* and the *Tribunaux Administratifs* are recruited among students of the civil service school (*École Nationale d'Administration*); but a limited number are also chosen by the Government among civil servants of a high professional record. Thus, through their origin, as well as through the advisory function of the *Conseil d'État*, members of the courts are in every way familiar with the problems of administrative action. But a strong tradition of independence and the respect shown by successive Governments towards a body which plays an essential part in French public life, give the members of the *Conseil d'État* the outlook of the professional magistrate. Their job is to protect the private citizen's rights, and the history of the *Conseil d'État* since the days when it used to be part of Napoleon's administration shows how a growing consciousness of this fact has become the foundation of the administrative court's authority.

This protection is insured in the following ways, which will be discussed in turn:

1. The ordinary citizen has an easy access to the courts;
2. The proceedings are juridical and associate wide powers of investigation with the rule of contradictory defence;
3. Appeal either results in quashing an administrative decision, or provides financial compensation for the damage received through illegal or arbitrary action

1. The administrative courts cannot take the initiative in proceedings against the administration; it is not in their power to investigate cases at their own discretion, or to prosecute the Government or the administration. As courts, they are only entitled to try the cases brought before them by the citizens or the administrative bodies. However, the administration has no way of evading such proceedings. If the private citizen wants to appeal to the courts, he must state which administrative decision has caused his grievance. But he can always provoke such a decision, as the rule is such that refusal to answer a petition after four months is considered as a decision. This is very important, because the administration cannot take refuge in silence or dilatory answers. Any administrative decision, whether its author may be the most lowly official or a Minister, or the Prime Minister, or even the President of the Republic, can be carried before the courts. One is only requested to submit a written complaint, and to do this within two months after the decision has been published or brought to the notice of the interested party. Proceedings are as informal as possible and a lawyer's assistance is not compulsory in many cases, in particular for the all-important 'recourse for excess of power' (*recours pour excès de pouvoir*).

This form of appeal, however, has some of the inconveniences of any lawsuit. Two major difficulties await the complainant; he must make sure his grievance really concerns an administrative decision, and he must bring it before the proper local court. An administrative decision under French law is to be opposed to several other types of decisions which to the ordinary citizen may well seem to be of the same nature as those usually examined by the administrative courts. Their competence only covers acts of the executive; any matter concerning relations between the Government and Parliament, such as the initiative in drafting law or the relations between the Government and a foreign power, is out of bounds for them. Second, quite a number of cases involving administrative actions come before the ordinary law courts under the supervision of the Court of Cassation, either because the ordinary courts are by tradition the sole protectors of individual freedom and private property in France, or because some public services of a commercial nature are allowed to function more or less as private enterprises.

Even if the complainant is sure his is a case for the administrative courts he has to bring it before the right one. This secondary difficulty has arisen as a consequence of the administrative courts' success; the *Conseil d'État* was so encumbered with cases, and delay in judgment had been prolonged to such an extent, that decentralization was necessary in 1953. Practice is slowly clearing up the confusion which resulted from such a major change in proceedings.

The Ombudsman scheme provides, as we shall see later, an answer to such difficulties, but whether the solution can be seriously advocated in France is another question. As things are, however, the problem of getting a case before the courts is not really as complex as this brief analysis seems to make out. On the contrary, it is fair to say that the ordinary citizen in France has the benefit of a reasonably easy way to gain redress.

2. Appeal before administrative courts may seem complicated and overly technical when the complaint is to be formulated. But their technique becomes an advantage once the case is actually examined. Not only do the administrative courts have extensive powers of investigation; they also provide the essential guarantees of juridical procedure.

Too much stress cannot be laid on the way the courts investigate cases brought before them. In the literal translation, the administrative judge is said to be 'master of the instruction of the case'. This means that he does not allow the parties to build up their case alone; he communicates with the administration concerned, asks for any further information he may need, and may refer to expert advisers. The administration is under the obligation to answer; if no answer is given to a complaint, the administration can be said to have admitted the facts of the case. As an example, a public body suspected of having refused entrance into the civil service on illegal grounds was requested to produce all documents in its possession concerning the candidates; refusal to do so was interpreted as an admission of the illegal motives stated in the complaint.[1]

The juridical procedure gives the complainant two securities: he can discuss every document submitted to the judge (that is to say, contradiction is possible at every stage in the proceedings); and secondly he is entitled to know the detailed reasons for the court's decision. Every case results in a written decision, which must contain an answer to all the complainant's arguments.

The collective examination of each case by the subordinate courts, and in appeal by the *Conseil d'État*, involves a high degree of technicality. It is not surprising that the members of the courts consider it requires extensive training, first in the civil service school, then in years of day-to-day experience. The jurisprudence of these courts has progressively shaped what the French call the 'droit administratif', which is a series of rules to ensure the protection of private citizens against administrative action, whatever form this action is taking or may take in the future.

3. Last but not least, appeal before the courts leads to effective results. They are obtained in two different ways. By the 'recourse for excess of power', an administrative decision can be quashed, is reputed never to have been in force. By the 'recours de plein contentieux', the complainant can ask for adequate financial compensation against illegal or arbitrary action.

[1] *Conseil d'État, Barel Case*, May 28, 1954, published in the *Recueil Lebon* (official record of cases), 1956, p. 308, where the details of the case are explained in the conclusions of M. Letourneur as *Commissaire du Gouvernement*.

The recourse for excess of power is the simplest and easiest form of complaint. It can be introduced against any decision which is reputed to be contrary to the terms of the law. Its effect is limited to the quashing of that decision. Illegality is given a wide interpretation by the administrative jurisprudence: a decision can originate from the wrong authority, or carry irregularities in form or procedure. The purpose of the law may not have been fulfilled, so the nature of control on administrative decisions depends very much on the way each particular law is drafted. If special conditions for administrative action are provided, control over the facts of the case goes very far indeed; the court does not, of course, examine the reasonableness or the wisdom of the decision, but this does not exclude a very thorough control of discretionary administrative action. For example, in cases of disciplinary action against civil servants it is not for the judge to decide whether or not punishment is adequate in relation to the offence; but it is for him to say whether, in the facts of the case, there is an offence liable to disciplinary action. Furthermore, observance of some general principles particularly suited to a democratic society, what the jurisprudence calls 'les principes generaux du droit', is insured even if they are not expressly stated by law. One of these is the principle that no infringement on individual liberties can be ordered except by the law; another, that no administrative punishment of misdemeanours can be undertaken before the person involved has been allowed to defend his case; and there are many other such rules. Finally, the courts can act in cases where officials have made use of their powers for biased or personal reasons unrelated to the avowed purpose of their decision. All this leads up to one conclusion: the administrative decision is quashed, is reputed to be of no effect. The court does not go any further in its ruling, does not in particular tell the administration what to do next. But even so, the 'recourse for excess of power' provides the citizen with a most effective means of redress; no administrative action can be taken in the same case in contradiction with the court's decision.

In the 'recours de plein contentieux' the contender finds a more general mode of appeal. He can ask in particular for compensation for the damage caused through any fault of the administration. The administration may be obliged to take material action—to pay a pension, evacuate a property, correct irregular local elections, etc. It is regarded to be at fault not only when illegal action has been taken; tardiness, inefficiency or negligence can cause sufficient harm for compensation as allowed. This is the way of appeal open to the civil servant who has unduly lost his office, to the patient who has suffered from mismanagement in the public hospitals, to the citizen who has suffered an accident or damage from any public construction, etc. It would be impossible to make out an exhaustive list of the situations in which such compensation might be allowed. The administrative courts were for a time criticized as being too strictly economical of public funds in dealing with these complaints; but this tendency has been completely reversed in the last five years or so, and very large sums are paid out to provide adequate compensation for the most varied damages.

On the whole the public in France seems to be satisfied with the protection afforded by the administrative courts. More often than not, attacks and criticism against the system come from the administration— which itself tends to prove that in a pragmatic way the courts have taken to heart their mission as 'public defenders'. This does not necessarily mean, however, that such a system can be suggested for other countries as an alternative to any scheme of the Ombudsman type. The fundamental differences to be noted between the two systems of administrative control are not only significant; they are the reflection of a completely different outlook on constitutional and political issues.

2. *Administrative Courts and the Ombudsman are not Alternatives*

When it comes to arguing the case for an Ombudsman as compared with the French system, no definite conclusion can be reached. In theory some weighty arguments are in favour of the Ombudsman scheme. But these would be the scheme's undoing if it were ever to be tried out in French law; however, this is no argument in favour of the supremacy of one or the other method, and it is wise not to expect too much from their confrontation.

Two main factors justify the interest shown in many countries for the Ombudsman type of control as compared with any other and in particular the French administrative courts. First, the Ombudsman copes with any complaint, irrespective of form or content. No more general, simple way of redress can be conceived in modern societies. His scope of action ranges both lower and higher than that of the administrative courts. Very often all the bewildered citizen wants is an explanation; he can ask for it from the Ombudsman, who acts then as a general information office. But under some schemes the Ombudsman can go as far as supervising the courts, as he does in Sweden and Finland. Also, more variety appears in the solutions given to different types of complaint: he can call upon government agencies for explanations, obtain correction from the department concerned, report critically and publicly to Parliament, in some systems such as in Sweden or Finland even prosecute officials before the courts. From the citizen's viewpoint, nothing could be more simple. The system does away with all difficulties in drafting the complaint or carrying it before the proper authority. There is one door to knock at, and the complainant will always get an answer, which might be sufficient in itself or help him in introducing a further lawsuit. And if the individual does not know his own rights, the Ombudsman can himself initiate investigations.

Second, informality is associated with authority in the person of the

Ombudsman. His authority derives directly from Parliament and, by the publicity given to his actions, leans firmly on the support of public opinion. This gives a very modern touch to the office, in the days when democracy lies in a proper contact between the individual and the state, through Parliament and through the mass media of expression.

Progress towards wider openings for appeal against arbitrariness, towards increased authority and independence for the institution whose job it is to control administration does not, however, run along the same lines in France. Many commentators have regretted the complexity of the French system. But it is practically inevitable. The administrative courts cannot look forward to monopolizing all forms of complaint against administration. Access to their elaborate proceedings cannot be opened to the mere consultant, someone who cannot precisely state which administrative decision has caused his grievance, who requires only information. If the courts were to deal with such cases, it could hardly be as courts; but then would differences in procedure be justified? And who would decide what guarantees each complainant is entitled to? Also, the risk for the courts of being overwhelmed with complaints is not to be underrated. After all, the overflow of cases, all proper lawsuits, brought before the *Conseil d'État* has already justified the decentralization measures of 1953.

In a country like France the tendency to discuss any action of the administration is very common. One man could hardly deal adequately with the complaints of all kinds actually received by administrative courts. The Ombudsman in France could not be simply a respected public figure, ready to examine personally each grievance. He would become the head of an office, the chief of a number of bureaucrats who would spend a lot of time asserting their authority over other bureaucrats.

Moreover, separation between the executive and the judicial powers has been for generations a fundamental principle of French law. It infers that no judge shall interfere with administration. If public services are to be inspected, criticized and asked to mend their ways it cannot be by a court; control of administration by the administrative courts has only grown to be accepted by the executive on that understanding. This principle has a most important counterpart: neither the administration nor the administrative courts, regarded as too closely related to the administration, are allowed to infringe in any way on the ordinary law courts. Not only would it be a heresy to suggest in France that these should be supervised by the *Conseil d'État*; because of the ordinary courts' strong tradition of independence, an overlapping unity of jurisdiction could only mean the disappearance of the administrative courts. And no opinion has so far been expressed to suggest that to transfer their function to the ordinary courts would be a progressive step in the control of the administration.

Whether the Ombudsman is thought of as an extension of or separate from the administrative courts, there is not much to be gained through favouring his appointment by Parliament as opposed to the recruitment of the members of the administrative courts from the civil service. Certainly Parliament has never in France held any powers of nomination, and it would be surprising to advocate such measures under the Constitution of 1958, drafted intentionally to temper the supremacy of Parliament. However, it is not a matter of constitutional law, but of authority and independence. In each case independence from political influences lies not in the institution itself, but in the tradition supporting it.

What is true of both systems is that an efficient control of administration in a modern democracy can only work if it has the support of public opinion and of its lawful representatives in Parliament. We in France think that such support has been acquired by the administrative courts through their tradition of independence and the quality of their protection; it does not seem necessary to give Parliament such exceptional powers of nomination to achieve the same object. But the matter is certainly open for discussion since it is difficult for an author like myself who holds office in an institution to be sure he is expressing an objective opinion on the independence of that institution.

The French administrative courts, then, cannot be expected to take on the characteristics of an Ombudsman system. And as long as the control of the administration is in their hands, there can hardly be room for a separate office under French law. If the Ombudsman were to be instituted in France only to fill the gaps in administrative control, he would not have a general mission and would not in fact be an Ombudsman, maybe only a general information bureau. He could not on the other hand receive the full powers connected with the office in the Nordic countries without delaying and confusing appeal before the courts. In particular, such an institution would not in any way provide a solution to the problems created by the coexistence of the two court systems, one of which specializes in the control of administration; indeed, it would only add to the confusion.

No proper conclusion can be drawn from this, however, about the relative excellence of the two systems. It seems only that in the search for a proper balance between individual rights and sufficient freedom of action for the administration, no country ought to claim pre-eminence for its own solution. If a French commentator finds it difficult to imagine the Ombudsman functioning in his country, he certainly has no reason to suggest that the French administrative courts could be successfully transplanted elsewhere. Their experience shows, however, that special courts, closely related to the administration, can efficiently protect the individual against arbitrariness; if they have been able to do so, it is because the two fundamental principles of justice in a democratic society—pre-eminence of the rule of law and independence of the judge—are strongly backed by public opinion in the French

Republic. The Nordic Ombudsmen meet the same need with the same backing; under great differences in technique lies a common spirit of action.

THE NEED FOR AN OMBUDSMAN TOO
by Kurt Holmgren*

In the last half-century few subjects have been as lively discussed among those interested in the problems of administration as the question of how to protect the citizens against the misuse of administrative power. It is important to point out that the question of a review of the authorities' exercise of their powers is not the primary problem with regard to the protection of the citizen. More important than legal checks and the possibilities of appeal is naturally the character of the administration itself—the existence of a secure tradition of justice, a properly recruited corps of civil servants, at least some of whom should be legally trained, and a sense of consistency, impartiality and independence. The importance of these things is clearly shown if one considers that, of necessity, there are so few administrative decisions for which an appeal is practically possible or for which a subsequent checking can lead to any real restitution for a mistake. Moreover, the difference between form and content, between the outer organization and the living reality, is often considerable. On paper a country may have the best imaginable organization and the most complete possibilities of appeal from administrative decisions, and yet in practice the administration may suffer from inherent serious deficiencies, such as a lack of care in the handling of business, defective training of civil servants or even a sensitivity amongst them to corrupting pressures.

With regard to arrangements for challenging administrative decisions or taking steps in the case of mistakes made by the authorities, Western Europe may generally be divided into two groups of countries, one including Great Britain, Denmark and Norway, and the other comprised of most of the other countries. In the first group the principal rule is that administrative decisions may be challenged by instituting proceedings in the regular courts. In addition there are varying possibilities of appealing to councils and commissions, which are sometimes called 'administrative tribunals' but do not have the character of real law courts; although this way of challenging an administrative decision may be much used and quite efficient, the general and basic method is to institute proceedings in the regular courts. In the other group of countries—of which France and Germany are especially representative but to which the original Ombudsman countries, Sweden and Finland,

* Judge, Supreme Administrative Court, Sweden.

also on the whole belong—the basic idea is that administrative decisions of a legal character are challenged in special administrative law courts.

Because Sweden has both an Ombudsman and administrative courts, it may be of interest to say a few words about Sweden's appeal system as it relates to the administrative courts. The basic rule (with very few exceptions) is that any administrative decision of a subordinate agency may be challenged by an appeal to a superior agency. If the appeal concerns entirely matters of expediency, it is decided by purely administrative agencies, but where the legal element is supposed to dominate, the appeal in the last instance is handled by the Supreme Administrative Court (*Regeringsrätten*), created in 1909. Taxation cases and some other kinds of cases are handled first on a lower level by an administrative law court (*Kammarrätten*), which has been in existence more or less in its present form since the end of the eighteenth century. There are also two specialized administrative courts for insurance matters. In Swedish legal discussions it has been suggested that most or all administrative appeals, where the legal element dominates, should go first to an administrative court of appeal, with only final appeals going to the Supreme Administrative Court; this would probably mean establishing a system of regional administrative courts, more or less in conformity with the French reform of 1953. Finally, it should be noted that a characteristic feature of the Swedish system is that questions of expediency fall inside the competence of the administrative courts to a larger extent than in other countries.

Before discussing the pros and cons of the Ombudsman as an international model, it would be worth while to mention that its success in Sweden, the only country where the institution has been tested for a long time, is dependent to a certain extent on historical conditions. The office gained strength during a period when royal power was fairly strong and when the administration was controlled almost entirely by Ministers appointed by the King. In the legislature (*Riksdag*), on the other hand, in addition to a 'King's party', there were considerable opposition groups; and the Ombudsman, as chosen by the legislature, came under these conditions to have a more independent position in relation to the administration than he would have under a parliamentary regime where (in reality) both the Ministers and the Ombudsman base their authority on the confidence of a political majority. Aside from such historical conditions, it is proper to ask whether, once a system of administrative courts has been established, as in Sweden or Finland, there is reason to maintain an Ombudsman. It may even more pertinently be asked whether it is justified to introduce the Ombudsman in countries in which a system of administrative courts has been in existence for a long time, such as France and Germany. The aim of this essay is to give some reasons why an Ombudsman may be desirable even in countries where administrative law courts exist.

1. *Advantages of an Ombudsman*

1. The important argument for not leaving the institution untried even in countries with well-developed administrative courts is, in my opinion, quite simply the constant growth of the administration and its concomitantly increased power over many human affairs. Within a country's administration, every day many thousands of decisions of a more or less legal character are made, and no doubt some of these will be erroneous. It is not practical or possible, even for someone well oriented in the mazes of the administration, to turn to an administrative court to get redress, however effective the appeal system may be. The procedure of the administrative courts is, as a rule, simpler and less costly than that of the regular courts, but even so it is always a ticklish business for a private person to appeal a decision which he believes to be incorrect. This is especially true of people who cannot afford the services of a lawyer, who have no administrative experience, or who have no connections with persons knowledgeable about administrative matters. In addition, it must be remembered that the administrative courts have by no means been able to avoid the inherent shortcoming of all tribunals, slowness in handling matters. Even that model institution in the field of administrative courts, the French *Conseil d'État*, had, as late as the middle of the 1950's, a frightening backlog going back several years. Furthermore, in most countries administrative law courts normally cover only juridical wrongs and mistakes; but often it is the decisions involving both law and expediency that cause most trouble for the private individual; in such cases there is a need of an independent authority to which the citizen may turn without strict formality.

2. It may be worth while to be able to have a complaint tried by some official independent of the administration, who does not represent the bureaucratic 'establishment' but who instead has received his authority from Parliament. In discussions on this subject in Scandinavia, the administrative law courts have sometimes been indicted for what has been called 'friendliness toward the administration'. One ironic observer has spoken of 'the community of interests which always arises, however veiled, between the Government (regardless of its political colour) and the bureaucracy'; to a certain extent the administrative courts have been included in this latter category. In my opinion this criticism is without foundation—in European countries with administrative courts these courts are as independent as the older courts—but as a psychological tendency amongst observers outside the administration it should not be ignored.

On the other hand, as already mentioned, in a parliamentary regime even the Ombudsman's independence of the Government may to a certain extent become a fiction, since of course the Ombudsman gets his authority from the same centre of power as does the Government—

the majority in the legislature. However, the Scandinavian legislatures have shown noticeable objectivity in choosing an Ombudsman out of the possible candidates. There have been few cases of political recruitment to this job, although on some occasions a jurist, known to be of a political colour other than that of the parliamentary majority, may have been handicapped in the competition. Of course the position of the Ombudsman is strengthened if he is elected for a longer period (in Sweden four years).

3. A typical feature of court procedure, in both regular and administrative courts, is that the initiative must normally be taken by one of the parties to the case. But those affected by administrative decisions are not always conscious that an error has been made and at any rate are often faced by a *fait accompli* which they are not in a position to do anything about themselves. The requisite correction in such cases may be obtained through the activities of an Ombudsman. In Sweden, an especially important source of information for the Ombudsman is the inspections he makes of regional, or county, authorities; through thus checking at random he is able to observe and criticize sins of commission and omission, which would have remained undiscovered if he had had to rely only on individual complaints. It should also be noted that the intervention of the Ombudsman in a considerable number of cases has occurred as a result of newspaper articles about administrative anomalies.

4. Another point of importance is that the Ombudsman may bring about a more informal correction of wrongs in a way hardly possible in a court procedure. The Ombudsman in Sweden nowadays seldom uses what was originally his principal weapon, prosecution of an erring civil servant. Though sometimes he makes the payment of a suggested reasonable indemnity a condition for abstaining from prosecuting, in most cases he is content to express his criticism or, through a clarifying statement, to answer the question at hand. Neither criticisms nor informative statements are formally binding on the administration; yet they are generally followed and have great significance for administrative procedure. Very often the Ombudsman tries to clarify not only the single question involved but also the general practice in that field in a way which is not so easily done in the administrative law courts.

It cannot be denied that a risk of confusion exists between the checking and criticizing activity of the Ombudsman and the trial of complaints in administrative courts. Great care and tact is obviously demanded here on the part of the Ombudsman; as long as a case is *sub judice* (or still can be appealed to a law court) the Ombudsman—except only for evident violations in the discharge of official functions—abstains from interfering. Beyond this it would carry us too far to give a detailed report of how the relations between the Ombudsman and the courts have developed in Sweden and Finland, but at least during recent years there has been no threat of conflict of competence. Hence the statement seems justified that the risk of confusion is not especially great.

5. An objection to the proposal for an Ombudsman likely to be raised in countries with a well developed system of administrative courts is that since these courts already occupy the field of legal appeal, an Ombudsman would, in some unfortunate way, be forced into encroaching upon the traditional rights of the members of the legislature to act for constituents and to criticize and inquire about the administration. On the contrary, I should like to suggest that an Ombudsman provides a happy supplement to administrative courts as well as to the citizen's right to turn to his elected representative with his troubles. It is obvious that in the modern welfare state it is quite impossible for a representative, no matter how zealous he may be, to look after the administrative troubles in a constituency, which includes many thousands of inhabitants. The right of inquiry in the legislature cannot possibly suffice to get redress for wrongs and mistakes committed in the administration yet not suitable to be challenged in the administrative courts. Taking up an administrative decision in the sensational form of a question in the legislature is not often psychologically the best method of bringing about correction. Obviously both the Minister in question and the officials involved in the matter may, when faced with political publicity, be forced into a defensive position, which is not favourable for the person who wants a wrong to be admitted and rectified.

6. In the discussion as to whether the institution of the Ombudsman is suitable for transplanting to other countries, the objection is sometimes heard that an Ombudsman might officiously meddle in both large and small matters within the administration and thus damage its prestige and muffle the authorities' power to act. This might seem especially to apply to countries with administrative courts, where the citizens already have an avenue of redress for wrongs of a legal nature, because the Ombudsman might have little else to do. But this has not been the case in Sweden, where citizens may seek redress through the administrative courts sometimes even on matters concerning expediency. The number of matters covered by modern administration hardly favour a tendency to meddle; any tolerably sound Ombudsman must reserve his zeal for a limited number of the more important things. Indeed, according to the experience of countries in which the Ombudsman institution has existed for some time, it has been a support for the administration. The Ombudsman's investigations in many cases—not least in matters of a sensational nature—have resulted in sweeping aside unjustified criticism and unfounded suspicion in a way which is not to the same extent possible within the procedure of administrative courts. For he can act on the basis of a single complaint or even on his own initiative; he can investigate a question quickly and informally yet thoroughly; and he can give a well-balanced report on the pros and cons, designed if necessary to quieten an irritated public opinion.

The continuous activity of the Scandinavian Ombudsmen as a defence against unjustified criticism may be demonstrated statistically from their annual reports. Those of the Swedish *Justitieombudsman*, for example, show that more than 90 per cent of the complaints are found to be groundless. Especially in recent years he has been at great pains to give extensive reports as to the reasons for his opinions, even in cases where the complaints were dismissed. The work of the Ombudsman in such cases has no doubt served a double purpose: on the one side, to vindicate the action of the accused official and, on the other, to make clear to the complainant that his suspicions were unfounded.

2. *Problems of Transplantation*

It would be unrealistic to deny that a transplanation of the Ombudsman institution to foreign countries would meet with difficulties. The largest of the Scandinavian countries, Sweden, has only eight million inhabitants. Naturally, in a country with many times that population the multitude of questions arising may create organizational difficulties. These might be surmounted, to be sure, but it may be difficult to meet the demands for unity and consistency in the Ombudsman's activities in a larger country with many thousands of matters to decide, no matter whether the choice be to have different Ombudsmen for different regions or kinds of questions, or a college or commission of Ombudsmen.

The Swedish institution was created and became rooted in an epoch when party politics in the modern sense did not exist. The introduction of an Ombudsman in a modern parliamentary state, where the political atmosphere is heated, may not be as easy. Very important, of course, is that the legislature from the beginning should give its representative a free and independent position; the Ombudsman must not appear to be a party man, and the members of the legislature as his principals must not succumb to the temptation to attempt to interfere in his work. In the Scandinavian countries—even those where the Ombudsman is a recent innovation—difficulties of this kind seem to have been avoided. Of course a contributory factor has been that most cases brought before an Ombudsman are of a decidedly non-political nature.

For the institution to succeed, the personal factor is of great significance; it is necessary to get for the task people with a high reputation, both as jurists and for their personal integrity. It is important that the job be made attractive in various respects; its delicacy as well as the exposed position of its holder dictate this. In the Scandinavian countries the Ombudsmen have usually been selected from among judges, but in some cases also professors from the schools of law have been chosen. On the whole, we seem to have succeeded in achieving a suitable alternation between active reformers and sound experts in administrative and juridical practices.

THE OMBUDSMAN AND ADMINISTRATIVE COURTS
by Miss I. M. Pedersen

No country ought, as Madame Questiaux says, to claim pre-eminence for its own solution to the problem of control over the administration. The methods of control must be considered in their relationship to the complete legal system of the country and especially its constitutional and administrative law. The historical and political background of a country is also of immense importance in this connection and may well be a quite decisive factor when a choice has to be made between different methods of supervising the executive. On the other hand, a comparative study of the different systems of control may provide important material for lawyers and politicians when they discuss how existing systems ought to be amended. Facts are always important, but they are especially important in this field, where opinions are frequently influenced by emotional, political or national bias.

I emphasize these points because the purpose of my comments on the essays of Madame Questiaux and Judge Holmgren is not to advocate the setting up of Ombudsmen on the Scandinavian model all over the world, but only to draw attention to some of the technical aspects of the Ombudsman's control as opposed to control by courts.

It is quite deliberately that I use the word 'courts' without distinguishing between administrative courts and ordinary courts, because in principle there is not—at least not in Europe—a great deal of difference between the sort of control exercised by these two types of courts. Except for the Swedish Supreme Administrative Court, which is entitled to decide questions of pure discretion in the cases within its jurisdiction, both systems have a common function: to try only issues of *fact and law* in the disputes put before them and to make orders that are binding upon the parties. Law is in Denmark, as in the jurisprudence of the *Conseil d'État*, taken in a fairly broad sense: it includes not only rules laid down in acts or statutory instruments, but also unwritten law, including flexible standards like the important French doctrine of *détournement de pouvoir*.

This is, by the way, no coincidence. The attitude of the Danish courts towards a number of fundamental principles of administrative law have, over the last forty years, indirectly been influenced by the ideas underlying the jurisprudence of the *Conseil d'État*.[1]

There is good reason to stress this point, because both in countries with and without administrative courts the belief is widespread, although often somewhat vague, that there is of necessity a fundamental

---

[1] The history of this development is given in an essay by J. L. Frost in *Festskrift til Professor dr. juris Poul Andersen* (Copenhagen, 1958), 7-32.

difference between the type of control exercised by the two sorts of courts. But there is no inherent need for such a difference. The French and Danish examples show that ordinary and administrative courts may develop a jurisprudence along similar lines and offer the citizens efficient and independent protection of the same type in cases where individual legal rights have been violated by public authorities.

A detailed comparative analysis of the jurisprudence within the field of administrative law in other countries would in all probability show that this state of affairs is not unique, but on the contrary that the main rule is that the *fundamental* legal principles underlying control over the administration are shared by all countries whatever their system of control.

For this reason it is dangerous to argue that the mere fact that a country has a system of administrative courts is in itself a proof that an Ombudsman would be superfluous, although it is true that such courts offer applicants procedural advantages, especially the right to institute proceedings in an easy and informal way. This, of course, means that an Ombudsman has a *special* mission in countries where ordinary courts control the administration: he gives the citizens a general right to a cheap and easy method of putting their grievances before an impartial authority with wide powers to investigate their complaints. Even in a country like Denmark where it is comparatively easy to obtain free legal aid in lawsuits against public authorities, this has been felt to be an advantage.

But the Ombudsman system offers other advantages than this. It has created methods of dealing with the problem of control that are usually not open to courts, *ordinary or administrative*. My analysis of the Danish Ombudsman's work in chapter 3 has shown that the fact that his powers are different from those of the courts has made it possible for him to *supplement* their influence upon administrative matters. To give an important example: he may give his opinion not only on the dispute in issue, but on the principles that ought to guide the authorities in the future, and he has often done so. He may even recommend legislative amendments.

It is also necessary to emphasize another point: the Ombudsman has dealt with a considerable number of questions that normally are outside the jurisdiction of any court. As noted in the above-mentioned chapter, these questions may be classified into two main groups. Let us review each of them.

1. Minor Errors of Procedure and Conduct, and Similar Questions of Organization and Efficiency

If officials fail to return documents put before them as evidence, if they are rude and arrogant, if they delay a case by collecting unnecessary evidence, if they have failed to give notice of a right of appeal where there is no statutory duty to do so, if the general investigation of a problem has caused undue hardship to a citizen, if officials persist in writing unreadable signatures—in most if not in all these cases the citizen will have no remedy in law unless he can prove that the error has caused him an economic loss. Many of them are characterized by the fact that the importance of the issue is out of proportion to the annoyance felt by the citizen. And there are many borderline cases where the courts may be competent, but where even a very angry citizen may feel that it is too much to bring his case before a court, although he lives in a country where there is easy access to an administrative court. A case in point is the one mentioned in chapter 3 in which a postman was informed orally about the final decision in a disciplinary case against him, but was refused a written notification.

2. The Purely Discretionary Element in Administrative Decisions

If A and B apply for a taxi-driver's licence, and the chief of police awards it to B, the courts may quash the chief's decision if they are of opinion that he made the decision for a political or personal reason. But if he awards it to B because he honestly thinks that B is the better driver, the courts cannot do anything about it, even when they are definitely convinced that A is the better driver. As shown more fully in chapter 3, the Danish Ombudsman exercises a somewhat wider control than the courts in these matters.

In both these fields, in my opinion, the Ombudsman's work has been useful and has fulfilled a mission that is of growing importance in a world where public authorities take over more and more functions. There are, admittedly, more vital problems in public law and administration than these. On the other hand they are by no means of so little significance that they ought to be dismissed without a thorough discussion of how they might be handled. This is especially the case now that the Danish experience has shown that it is possible to fit an institution for dealing with these problems into the traditional system of controls, and moreover to do it without creating an enormous and overstaffed organization, without weakening the influence of control by independent judicial bodies and without disturbing the balance of power between Parliament and the executive.

This is in itself no argument for introducing Ombudsmen in other countries, but it is very decidedly an argument against the point of view that the Ombudsman problem is only a question of academic interest in countries with administrative courts.

16

THE CONGRESSIONAL SYSTEM OF GOVERNMENT

THE NEED FOR OMBUDSMEN IN THE UNITED STATES

*by Henry J. Abraham**

Both professional and lay analysts of the administrative and political process in the United States point to supposed inadequacies of our often exasperatingly vexatious, often duplicative, occasionally confused and confusing, and always maligned federal system of government. Omnipresent—some would contend omnipotent—the vast American bureaucracy, with its approximately 2,500,000 employees throughout the land (not counting state and municipal employees), is thus consistently in proverbial 'hot water' and a steady butt of not only criticisms and complaints but also a peculiar type of less-than-original native humor. There may well be little justification for such criticisms, but there are inevitably *reasons* therefor. Some of these are readily apparent, finding their roots in the expansion of government since the turn of the century, and especially during the past 35 years (teasingly bringing to mind the historic admonition of Thomas Jefferson that it would be best to rewrite our Constitution every 34 years!).

The government of the United States has undergone tremendous growth both in the areas in which it operates and in the machinery deemed necessary for purposes of administration. America, in undertaking the role of an active, 'positive' state, has thus witnessed increasing governmental regulation of every facet of public life, of commerce and industry and agriculture, of health and labor and morals—to name but a few. And while brought into the world by Congress, the sundry programs and plans were almost always conceived by the Executive. This fact of governmental life has brought with it an aggrandizement of the executive branch that has posed many crucial challenges to the operation of our representative democracy. Sheer bigness has at times undermined both efficiency and procedural fairness, and has imposed ever-growing problems of control and responsibility upon institutions and processes which have not always been readily adaptable. Moreover, the mounting need for the delegation of legislative power by Congress to the Executive, coupled with the need for administrative expertise

* Professor of Political Science, University of Pennsylvania.

and for lightening the already-too-heavy burden of the Judiciary, has witnessed the rise of administrative agencies and bureaus that perform quasi-legislative and quasi-judicial functions without being directly responsible to either Congress or the President.

A further and in some ways more serious problem has arisen from the fact that while these various agencies of government are very much involved in procedures which directly affect individual citizens, the redress of grievances is both limited and cumbersome. Recourse through the bureaus themselves against unreasonable delays or errors raises the question of strict impartiality and, in the absence of a system of administrative courts like that in France, judicial action involves delays and expenses that are as frustrating as they are galling to the ordinary citizen. Moreover, although the Anglo-Saxon principle that the government (the sovereign) cannot be sued without its consent has been somewhat abridged by such adoptions as the United States Court of Claims (1855) and the Tort Claims Act of 1946, their effect has not remedied the larger problem at issue. Hence the average citizen, rightly or wrongly, often views himself as being at the mercy of a seemingly ever-growing and inaccessible bureaucracy which, if permitted to continue unchecked, might well get out of control. This view is normally directed to the administration at the national level of government, but it is readily applied also to the state and municipal levels.

Yet—though perhaps not diametrically opposite—other views obtain. There are those who contend seriously that, far from failing to provide legal safeguards, the American administrative process is 'over-legalized', and indeed legalized to a greater extent than in most countries. Others believe that it is precisely the allegedly 'informal' nature of the administrative regulatory process that permits it to function effectively. They decry the complaints of individuals, though understandable and perfectly human, as wildly exaggerated and typical of the 'citizen-on-a-lark', and view those of professionals and academicians as unrealistic 'do-gooding'. For reasons given later, however, I cannot fully agree with these views.

Nor can I agree with those who argue that all problems have been solved by our long string of reports designed to improve the administrative process on all levels of government—from the Attorney General's Committee on Administrative Procedure and its report of 1941, to President Kennedy's Administrative Conference of the United States, whose final report was submitted late in 1962. Between these two landmarks a host of proposals, notable among them those of the two 'Hoover Commissions' (on the Organization of the Executive Branch of the Government) in 1949 and 1955, and some drastic ones in 1960 by former Dean Landis of the Harvard Law School, were submitted to the President and Congress—and, in part, adopted. This is not the place to enumerate the specifics of these various reports and recommendations. Suffice it to note that none specifically dealt with the need for the institution of the Ombudsman. Yet it is precisely the Ombudsman (and more specifically the Danish-Norwegian model, which excludes supervision of the courts and direct prosecutions) that *could* provide an answer—*the* answer—to a very real need. Although there are considerable doubts that the Ombudsman is feasible at the national level in the United States, the institution would appear to be quite readily adaptable at the state and, particularly, the municipal levels of government. It richly merits a try.

1. *Why the Institution is Needed*

A viable solution to the mass of administrative problems that exist must accomplish at least two things: First, it should provide protection and redress to the individual citizen against abuses by an increasingly remote yet omnipresent administrative process. Second, it should provide an institution capable of demanding certain standards of conduct and perhaps even of suggesting reorganization and delineation of responsibility of and among the various bureaus and agencies. As Professor Kenneth Kulp Davis has suggested, there are at least three essential lines of defense against improper use of governmental power: able and conscientious personnel who strive for quality performance; procedural safeguards; and the principle of the outside 'check'.[1] With the obvious exception of the human limitations of the first of these, America's record has been quite respectable. Certainly our procedural safeguards are as plentiful as they are extensive—and, as suggested above, may even lend themselves to some 'overlegalization'. We do have judicial review of administrative action and—at times perhaps even more meaningful, if unpredictable and uncertain—congressional committee review and oversight.

Respectable though our record has been, it is precisely at the level of the 'check' that an Ombudsman could provide that blend of expertise, speed and political independence that is so essential to the principle of effective oversight. Even when the judiciary is politically independent as it is at the national level of government, it often lacks authority to provide the desired redress in the field of administrative action. For its power of judicial review of administration is far more circumscribed than the power it enjoys in other fields. Nor can it act expeditiously, because of its omnipresent excess work-load. By its very nature the legislature is laced with political considerations; it is, after all, the political branch of the government *par excellence*. But an Ombudsman, patterned upon the Danish model and readily accessible to the people, could stand above the strife and winds of politics. By continuing, well-publicized (where warranted) criticism of administrative action, he could not only bring about redress of grievances but could also focus attention on lack of efficiency; and he could make recommendations

[1] 'Ombudsmen in America', *University of Pennsylvania Law Review* 109 (June, 1961), 1057.

to the legislative body. Although he would be presumably appointed by the latter, he would be in that rare position of independence or 'splendid isolation' that has made the Comptroller General, for one, such an effective figure in government. Still, the question arises at once whether the institution is feasible at all levels of government.

2. A National Ombudsman?

The difficulties in establishing an Ombudsman at the national level center around those of size and power. In contemplating the adaption of the institution to an area of government as large and diverse as the United States, it becomes painfully obvious that one man and a small staff (one of the most engaging and delightful aspects of the Ombudsman system) could hardly hope to cope with the unquestionably large volume and diverse nature of the complaints that would reach the institution once its function were properly understood by the populace. Nonetheless, in February 1963, Representative Henry Reuss, a Democrat from Wisconsin, spoke at length on the need for a national Ombudsman, whose staff he saw as 'a corps of agents to help members [of Congress] deal with their government agencies on behalf of their constituents'.[2] If it should be found that such a central office would be unmanageable, regional boards of Ombudsmen might handle the load. But then the so-important and symbolic concept of a single 'people's tribune' or 'public watchdog' would be seriously impaired and diminished. The effectiveness of the Ombudsman rests upon certain highly significant intangibles: his personality; the image he creates among the people; full support by the press; and upon the ability of the people to understand and support the institution.

Moreover, there arises the problem of the crucial distinction between the parliamentary form of government, where the Ombudsman has thrived to date, and the congressional form. Would Congress be willing to bestow upon the Ombudsman the kind of authority over administrative actions he needs if he is to perform the functions he does in Scandinavia? Under the fusion of powers of the parliamentary form, where the executive is directly responsible to the legislature, the Ombudsman, as the agent of Parliament, is in an excellent position to press for adoption of both corrective and prophylactic measures. But under the American form, even if the Ombudsman were—as he would have to be—similarly the agent of Congress, the separation of powers would provide further complications. These, however, would not be insurmountable. It is essentially the overriding problems of America's size, both in terms of geography and population, the awesome heterogeneity, and the traditional disinclination to experiment with 'foreign' or 'unknown' governmental institutions that militate against its adoption at the national level. America is not blessed with Scandinavia's

[2] *The Philadelphia Inquirer*, February 11, 1963. On the final form of his proposal, contained in a bill which he introduced in July, see Chapter 12.

absence of pronounced class distinctions; with its homogeneous, well-informed, and almost invariably alert electorate; with the same degree of consensus.

3. Proposals for State and Local Ombudsmen

Although, at first blush, many of the same negative considerations might seem to govern vis-a-vis the adoption of the institution at the state or local level, they are much less valid and persuasive there for several, more or less self-evident, reasons. While the basic needs for an Ombudsman are similar, in some ways they are considerably more acute, given the frequently lower quality of governmental performance —especially in terms of personnel and of defense against unduly selfish interests. Moreover, the problem factors of size, population, diversity, etc., appear on an infinitely less grandiose and complicated scale.

For these reasons, no doubt, proposals for Ombudsmen at the state and local levels appeared even before Congressman Reuss's bill in July 1963. The first state bill, known as the 'State Ombudsman Bill,' was introduced in Connecticut by Representative Nicholas B. Eddy, the Assistant Leader of that State's General Assembly, in March 1963. It is patterned closely upon the Danish model.[3] Indeed, the Danish model would need comparatively little modification to become effective at either state or local levels. This is especially true of certain municipal areas, where an alert and sympathetic press and a well-informed public could readily both comprehend and support the institution. Thus it was the Danish model that was officially recommended for Philadelphia, Pennsylvania, by a special three-man 'watch-dog' committee established by Mayor Richardson Dilworth in 1961, and headed by Dean Jefferson B. Fordham of the University of Pennsylvania Law School.

The Fordham Committee's report, released in March 1962, acknowledged the existence of certain administrative 'watchdogs' and means of redress on the American scene—e.g., 'financial watchdogs', 'legislative oversight committees', 'bureaus of information and complaint', the 'right of petition to elected representatives for the redress of grievances'. But it contended that none of these was clothed with the kind of sanctions, means and influence required for the redress and prevention of administrative abuses. Hence, the Committee called for the adoption by the City of Philadelphia of the Danish Ombudsman, to be known as Commissioner of Public Affairs, at a salary of $26,500 per annum (to give him and his office 'an aura of respect in the general community').

The Commissioner, said the Committee, should be a professional man of outstanding quality and above partisan politics, like Denmark's

[3] See Ralph Nader, 'An Ombudsman for the U.S.?', *The Christian Science Monitor*, April 1, 1963.

Ombudsman, Professor Stephan Hurwitz. He would provide a forum and then an impartial investigation for any complaint from the body politic—be it from a public official or a private citizen. The Commissioner's sanctions against any city official deemed to be guilty of misconduct or conflict of interest would be practically the same as in Denmark: public disclosure of any irregularity; recommendation of criminal or disciplinary action in appropriate cases; and the power to make recommendations to the City Council (the City's legislature) and to any 'office, agency or department of the city'. The Committee also suggested that the Commissioner be appointed by City Council from a panel of two or three individuals selected by a distinguished nominating committee of civic leaders, composed of, for example, the president of one of the local universities, the chancellor of the Philadelphia Bar Association, and the president of the Chamber of Commerce of Philadelphia.

The Fordham Committee's call for a Philadelphia Ombudsman was met with a veritable barrage of frank hostility and intemperate criticism on the part of the segments of the community that comprise the seat of power, led by the three daily newspapers, the incumbent political leadership in City Council, and the Democratic City Committee, headed by Congressman William Green. The most surprising and discouraging reaction was that of the press: without even giving Dean Fordham or other members of his Committee so much as a chance to explain and support the plan in print, the press not only rejected the proposed Commissioner of Public Affairs as an unwarranted expense and just another 'politician on top of a bunch of politicians', but also ridiculed the entire idea as an 'ivory tower lark'. City Council, undoubtedly responsive to Congressman Green, saw it as an 'unnecessary' and unknown quantity of conceivably awkward if not 'dangerous' potential. And presumably silently backed by the City Council's ex-President, James H. J. Tate, who had become Acting Mayor of Philadelphia upon Richard Dilworth's resignation, it chose a less vociferous, if more effective, avenue of approach: it simply bottled up consideration of the proposal in a Council committee. Unfortunately, most of the responsible centers of influence in the city, such as the Bar, the Committee of Seventy, and the Greater Philadelphia Movement, took no action to further the recommendation—in part because it received so little publicity, and in part because the Ombudsman does not, at first glance, lend itself either to easy interpretation or to colorful analysis. Its future in Philadelphia seems bleak.

It is true that Mr Tate did establish in January 1963, by executive decree, the office of 'Director of Citizens' Relations', to which he appointed an old Philadelphia 'mugwump', Harry K. Butcher (who for years had served as Executive Secretary of the Committee of Seventy, an influential, privately-financed group of 'good government watchdogs'). But this officer is no Ombudsman: he is an executive not a

I

legislative appointee, who reports to his appointer; he is not guided by a statute or statutes; the office is more of a complaints bureau and its incumbent more of a peripatetic trouble-shooter and general 'sniffer' than a tribune of the people.

Withal, the need for an Ombudsman, especially at the state and municipal levels, remains persuasive. The institution's underlying concept—that the citizens of a community should have rapid, inexpensive and reliable access to an impartial 'public watchdog', who is not involved in the governmental decision-making process, and who is clothed with powers of public criticism and the initiation of requests for remedial action—is as fundamentally sound as it is intriguing. And the institution *is* workable, given a sympathetic hearing, an initial willingness by the public to understand it, and a fair trial. As it has amply demonstrated where it has been adopted, it has more than proved its mettle and, indeed, has almost invariably become enormously popular.

OMBUDSMEN FOR STATE GOVERNMENTS
by Ralph Nader*

Under the American federal system the fifty states encompass a broad variety of governing processes within similar constitutional frameworks. Also, sizable differences in their population, geography, economy and political traditions pattern different results from comparable structures. While it is well to recognize such heterogeneity, there is sufficient, common ground for generalizing about the governmental context at this level for Ombudsman institutions.

For a generation, observers and practioners alike have been bemoaning the loss of power and prestige of the states to the federal government. The reality of this loss notwithstanding, no other governmental unit pervades the lives of more citizens more regularly than does the state. All states have undergone in recent decades an enormous growth of regulatory, service and fiscal operations which have increased sharply the interactions of citizen and administration. At the same time this growth is posing serious obstacles to practical remedies for the citizen against administrative abuses. The bureaucratic apparatus of all state governments share similar traits which do violence to equal protection for citizens in their variety of dealings with the administration.

State constitutions, with their neat separation of government into legislative, executive and judicial branches allegedly balancing and checking one another, make no provision for the rise of a vast state

* Attorney and Counselor at Law, Winsted, Connecticut.

bureaucracy now employing over a million and a half people and having expenditures exceeding $30 billion in 1963. The operating realities of this bureaucracy have forged above and beyond the formal structures and assumptions of state governments to create a towering imbalance between the executive and legislative branches of government.

The vast administrative framework necessary to perform state functions can be shown by taking a representative state such as Kentucky. This state has 33 constitutional and statutory departments. Within these departments there are some 150 subordinate boards, divisions and bureaus. There are approximately 80 independent agencies and 9 inter-state agencies. All 272 of these administrative units have the express or implied authority to promulgate rules and regulations. The output of new regulations annually in Kentucky is proceeding at an approximate rate of four times the volume of 15 years ago.[1] Along with this prolific exercise of basically legislative power, many state agencies adjudicate cases and thus combine all three of the 'separate powers' under single administrative units. This truly stupendous upsurge in state administrative activity has come about primarily in the last three decades. Sizable federal grants, totalling $8 billion in 1963, have helped expand several of these activities.

The development of the administrative state has undermined deeply the effectiveness of the old institutions of check embodied in the principle of separate powers. The legislatures, in creating new agencies and expanding existing ones, have delegated broad policy making powers affecting intimately the lives of most citizens. These agencies have acquired vested interests in ways of doing things that have long gone unchallenged. State legislative oversight of the administrative agencies is non-existent in many cases, highly sporadic and superficial in others.

In sharp departure from the period up to about 1915 when the legislature reigned supreme, the executive is now by far the most active branch in the government; it is the chief proposing power in legislative formulation and it has strong powers of persuasion stemming from party discipline, expertise with the subject matter of legislation, and association with pressure groups having similar objectives. Conflicts of interest within the legislature, such as that affecting subtly or overtly many lawyer legislators having an active practice before state regulatory agencies, tend to compromise the independence of the legislature further.

Moreover, constitutional restrictions seriously impede legislatures from asserting a stronger role in the initiation of legislative policy and the process of representing the electorate generally. Only 18 state

---

[1] Commonwealth of Kentucky, Legislative Research Commission, *Administrative Procedures Law in Kentucky* (Frankfort, Kentucky, Research Report No. 12, 1962), 5–6.

legislatures meet annually and often are constitutionally limited to 60 or 90 day sessions. The remaining 32 states have biennial sessions many of whose length is similarly curtailed. Legislators work under great time pressure and are grossly underpaid in most states, compelling many of them to consider their legislative duties as part time employment subsidiary to their regular job. This offers increased opportunities for representatives of special interests, who descend upon the legislature and, together with seasoned spokesmen of state agencies, are largely responsible for rendering perfunctory most hearings and formal debates on pending legislation.

Lack of an assertive role in law making and in oversight of administrative agencies by legislatures has profound significance for the quality of justice which many citizens receive from these agencies. Vague policy standards in the delegating acts and inadequate procedural safeguards pave the way for uncontrolled discretionary authority by the agencies to enforce, adjudicate and promulgate rules. Discretionary authority too often turns into partiality, which sees some infractions and overlooks others. When coupled with detailed but little enforced regulations, such as sanitary rules for barbershops, such authority can be used arbitrarily to intimidate any barber who does not give unqualified assent to the mandates of the barber licensing and supervisory commission, which is controlled by the barber association. The proliferation of such licensing boards for occupations ranging from architects to undertakers and from cosmeticians to tree surgeons, largely through the efforts of the occupational associations themselves, is part of the widespread process of legislating group privileges under the guise of regulation. They are 'little governments' characterized by many of the trappings of tyranny.

This differential treatment of organized interests and individual claimants extends throughout state administration. Teachers, organized labor, utilities, insurance companies, agriculture, shipping, motor transport and mining interests are all part of a functional or group representation via a large number of agencies. Administrators are likely to come to their position from a former position in the industry or group they are to regulate. Many take well placed jobs in the industry after finishing their term of office. Advisory bodies composed of members representing the regulated group maintain close consultation, familiarity and understanding with the particular agency which they are appointed by law to advise. The few administrators who try to resist forfeiture of the 'public interest' in this environment find that the statutory independence of their agency within the executive branch actually increases the likelihood of capitulation to group demands. This overwhelming dominance of group government in a polity dedicated to the safeguarding and respect of individual rights has obvious strains for the lone claimant.

The decentralization of power and responsibility in the executive is so widespread as to amount to a particular kind of administrative lawlessness without adequate sanctions. In many instances, Governors do not have control or co-ordinated responsibility over departments and agencies. In many states, a number of the principal administrative officers are directly elected. Heads of other important state departments may be appointed to a term exceeding that of the Governor who appointed them. As a consequence, in state after state, Governors have been able to stand aloof and emerge unscathed from the exposure and prosecution of major scandals affecting the agencies.

The corruption or laxity uncovered when a scandal breaks usually reveals that hundreds or even thousands of people in or close to the agency involved knew about the situation but the facts remained effectively insulated from the larger public audience. Such revelations spotlight how large and important a part of the governmental process is hidden from public scrutiny.

The public information policies of agencies border on the disgraceful. Less than a third of the states have adopted explicit administrative procedures governing their agencies. Attorneys for claimants regularly find themselves unable to locate the rules of state agencies, prevented from seeing the factual basis for agency determination, and thwarted by influences channelled through ex parte communications by agency administrators and hearing examiners. In cases possessing little monetary value, these difficulties easily discourage citizens from retaining counsel and counsel from accepting such cases. The fact that the system is flexible enough to allow redress for important personages through personal contacts, favors and the like from counsel or a local politico, only encourages the perpetuation of the evils of the system.

The difficulty in obtaining information about how the agencies are carrying on their responsibilities—a kind of access that is basic to democratic politics—is seriously impeding the most elemental type of scholarly analysis of state administration. William J. Pierce, Professor of Law at Michigan, phrased the problem well:

At the present time it is extremely difficult in many situations to uncover any information concerning the policies, objectives, and procedures of administrative agencies even when it is obvious that their operations have a tremendous impact upon a substantial segment of the populace. . . . The mere availability of the knowledge will make it possible for society's leaders to come to grips with some of the basic policy problems that will inevitably demand re-evaluation. This in turn will lead to improvements in the law and public confidence in our democratic institutions and the rule of law.[1]

The courts, as presently constituted and under the well-established judicial acceptance of a limited reviewing function over administrative

[1] 'The Act as Viewed by an Academician' in 'Symposium on the Model State Administrative Procedure Act', *Administrative Law Review* 16 (Fall 1963), 53.

behavior, cannot be considered as a practical source of remedies for complainants except in the more egregiously abusive acts. Moreover, many of the controversies between citizen and agency are not justiciable in nature and are heavily larded with political considerations avoided by a court of law. Judicial delays and appeals contribute to the rarity of recourse to the courts.

Awareness of the need to establish channels for publicly exposing misconduct by public officials goes back many years. For neither the ballot nor the press—the two traditional checks on governmental malfeasance toward citizens—were considered adequate even in the last century and they are even less so today if for no other reason than the exponential growth and complexity of state activity. Many states long have allowed their grand juries to make investigations and present-ments about inefficient, incompetent public officials or agencies, along with the power to indict for criminal behavior. But the grand jury does not often show an initiative greater than the public prosecutor who guides it. Its probing into bureaucratic abuses is mostly reserved for the most serious aberrations from proper administrative conduct.

More recently, particularly since 1945, many states have established Legislative Councils which, besides researching on legislative proposals, are often commissioned by statute to examine the effects of previously enacted laws, recommend amendments, search out waste and engage in other administrative oversight. However, this function has rarely been pursued vigorously and has never been backed up with sufficient authority even if the will was present. The Council staff has been fully occupied with being the research arm of the legislature. Those legis-lators who make up the Council's bi-partisan membership are careful to minimize the investigative role lest they arouse the enmity of other legislators over trying to create a 'little legislature' under their domina-tion.

The growing number of state laws on conflicts of interest will often empower the Attorney General to make periodic inspection of state agencies and investigate situations which come to his attention relating to suspected conflict of interest situations. Political complexions which inevitably attach to the Attorney General's Office are not conducive to thorough pursuance of such duties except for flagrant situations teetering on the brink of public exposure. More often than not, the Attorney General will take his cue to investigate from his Governor, rather than act on his own initiative in an area having possibly severe political consequences for the incumbent party.

Another check on administrative waywardness has been attempted by a few incoming Governors usually flush from victory at the polls. This has taken the form of opening their office a few hours a week or month to any citizen who wants to come in and express a complaint, want or suggestion. These 'citizen sessions' rarely last more than a few months. One reason is that the agencies resent them and furthermore the possibility of a Pandora's box of abuses being inadvertently uncovered by an innocent gubernatorial probe for a complainant is not relished by the Governor himself as his incumbency matures.

Finally, professional politicians holding public positions through patronage make representations informally to agencies whose acts may have aggrieved a party faithful or even an ordinary citizen, as a significant method of solidifying party loyalty or their political image.

From the foregoing, it can be seen that an Ombudsman attached to the legislature and empowered to directly receive and investigate citizens' complaints against the administration as well as to initiate inquiries and make inspections unilaterally, would start his work in a considerably hostile and suspicious political environment dominated by party professionals, state administrators and representatives of organized pressure groups. Quite expectedly, the Ombudsman institution would be viewed as a threat to these groups. For any intrusions into the informal pattern of relationships between them will incur their opposition. Connecticut's brief experience with an Ombudsman proposal introduced into the General Assembly in 1963 revealed this opposition.

Thus both the authority of the Ombudsman and his initial effectiveness will depend to a large extent on three factors: (1) the kind of support for and the circumstances preceding enactment of an Ombudsman bill, (2) the level of administrative and political integrity and competence of the particular state, and (3) the stature and skill of the person holding the new office. These factors will vary with each state.

While a model Ombudsman Act may give the officeholder authority to present the case of a complainant in court under certain conditions, limit the requests to investigate that are made by legislators in order to maintain his non-political position, eliminate any filing fee for complaints, eliminate the requirement for a complainant to have 'standing' (a sufficient personal interest in the subject matter of the complaint)—all these may have to be omitted or compromised, as they were in the Connecticut Bill, to increase the chance of being enacted. In every state, advocates of such legislation may have to decide whether no Ombudsman is preferable to one shackled by severe restrictions on his authority.

However, while the Ombudsman will have to be given certain minimum authority, such as the subpena power, as the *sine qua non* of his mission, his power and influence should increase out of the judicious handling of his duties at a measured pace. The zeal he must express to draw the confidence and support of the public and legislature must be tempered by restraint in his investigations of administrative terrain long accustomed to little external scrutiny and having considerable political strength. Such seems to be the experience of the Danish Ombudsman now in his tenth year of office.

The sensitivity of the areas to be probed can be illustrated by a sample of abuses which would be the concern of the proposed Connecticut Ombudsman: preferential treatment and influence peddling, inadequate or unpublished regulations, wrongful detention, state police overzealousness or laxity, unjust procedures in agency hearings, arbitrary censorship or secrecy, agency reluctance or refusal to give explicit reasons for decisions, patronage excesses, inefficiencies and delays by state personnel, undesirable conditions in prisons and mental institutions, payoffs and kickbacks in state contracts, and discriminatory enforcement or flagrant non-enforcement of state laws.

Perhaps the best way to conceive of the role of an Ombudsman on the state governmental level is to compare the office to a continuous, nonpartisan linchpin for initiatives working toward administrative justice. As an example, the press may not dig out abuses on its own accord, but it is quite likely to report and possibly follow up an Ombudsman's findings of such abuses. The legislatures may have neither the time, skill nor inclination to oversee administrative methods, standards, manners and corruption, but the findings by its Ombudsman, flush before the public, together with his reasoned recommendations, may prod it into action. The head of an agency may be lax in supervising his subordinates, but knowing that an Ombudsman having the confidence of the legislature is nearby may stimulate him to greater attentiveness. For the Ombudsman would be obtaining, from the feedback of citizens, information on administrative behavior in specific cases which is now mostly unknown outside the agency concerned. In addition, if it is of little avail to complain, or if to do so might incur retaliations by agency personnel, complaints will very often not be made. Affording an outlet for complaints will result in data of very considerable importance, under a skilled Ombudsman, for varied improvements of the public administration.

Thus a chief impact of the office would be preventive, as has been the case in Sweden and Denmark. Here the existence of power is more important than its exercise. Although too much can be expected of an Ombudsman, to underestimate the catalytic impact of a wisely operated office, quite apart from the direct handling of complaints, would be to err in the other direction.

A RESTRAINED VIEW
by Samuel Krislov*

It was inevitable that interest in the Scandinavian Ombudsman would radiate out to the United States. Attention here has not reached the level it has in Britain, where, as H. W. R. Wade has observed, 'the

* Associate Professor of Political Science, University of Minnesota.

British public knows more about the Danish Ombudsman than it knows about our own Council on Tribunals'.[1] On the other hand, any administrative remedy that has the support of names such as those of Kenneth Culp Davis and Walter Gellhorn cannot be properly described as neglected.[2]

The notion of inevitable attraction is not entirely *post hoc*. For the Ombudsman proposal is a peculiarly apt response to current dissatisfactions and flounderings in American administrative law. Geoffrey Marshall piquantly wrote of British suggestions along these lines that 'the cut of the proposals fits the cloth of the Liberals'.[3] (It is apropos that the Scandinavian institution itself reflects the heritage of Radical parties.) In the United States the suggestions have yet to become party matters, but they do fit the mood and longings of an increasing number of scholars and observers who are troubled by inequities in administrative tribunals but unwilling to re-enact the conflicts of the thirties. A growing body of opinion in the United States concludes there is a need for regularized procedure in the regulatory agencies but is unwilling to entrust the regular courts with extensive powers to develop such a body of legal restraints. Oddly, the trend is rather the other way; commentators conclude that there is excessive legalization and insufficient political control of tribunals. At the same time they doubt that political control has led or would lead to justice in the treatment of citizens.

Since this body of opinion rejects both judicial control (i.e. the application of judicial procedures) and political control (i.e. accountability through party processes) it is—at least on the surface—a utopian longing for a frictionless administrative system. The Ombudsman proposal comes, therefore, as a godsend—a modern Scandinavian gift to administrative folklore comparable to that other distinguished contribution from the north, Kris Kringle. It seems to provide some hope for greater remedies without the interference of the judiciary and the cumbersome machinery of legal precedent; it promises political retribution without the unpredictable vagaries of politics.

Since Americans have been tinkerers with their political institutions as much as with other segments of their environment, such a proposal —all gain and no loss—has peculiar attractions. What is most remarkable about the proposal is that it comes from a segment of opinion that does not—in the main—quarrel with the present trend toward regulatory agencies, but is dissatisfied only in peripheral matters of justice and

---

[1] Kenneth Culp Davis, 'Ombudsmen in America', *University of Pennsylvania Law Review* 109 (June 1961), 1058n.

[2] Davis, *idem*; Walter Gellhorn, *Federal Administrative Procedure* (Committee on the Judiciary, US Senate, November–December, 1960); Gellhorn, 'Administrative Procedure Reform: Hardy Perennial,' *American Bar Association Journal* 48 (March 1962), 243.

[3] 'Comment', *Public Law*, Spring 1962, 1.

I *

equity. This, then, represents a third wave of reactions to administrative agencies in recent American history. The first reaction was to call for their eradication, root and branch, as lacking in the 'rule of law', as being a 'new feudalism', a needless 'wonderland of bureaucracy'. The second wave aimed toward moving the agencies under more stringent court control, a development symbolized by the Administrative Procedure Act of 1946. The current proposals seek neither eradication nor external control but, rather, amelioration within an accepted system of regulatory agencies.

Surely this is a modest goal with which all observers must have essential sympathy. The sole question must be the appropriateness and utility of the particular proposal for reform.

1. The Appropriateness of the Ombudsman Proposal

As a matter of history and logic any decision-making system must create inequities as a by-product of its processes. 'He who acts', Goethe observes, 'is always unjust.' Remedial systems may or may not be created to review the original decision process. This depends upon societal notions of the tolerable limits of injustice as against the social need to have decisions expeditiously made. Involved in this complicated calculation are the social costs of the remedial system itself—the setting up of the system, the slowing down of the original decision process, the accumulating of complex files and records for possible review. Weighed against this must be the cost of any loss by the citizens of identification and contentment with the total system. Their alienation is likely whenever the decision system allows felt injustice, and alienation is itself an expensive social cost. Such costs also apply to the non-governmental sphere but are harder to reduce. As J. D. B. Mitchell points out, while governmental tribunals are inclined toward reversal of decisions when criticized, 'the unchallenged discretion of tailors, furniture removers and plumbers has never yielded so satisfactorily to blandishments'.[4]

These are complex calculations. It is, for example, not at all clear that the court system of any country is 'economically sound'—that is, the total costs of operating the courts and paying lawyers' fees may very well exceed the total amount of resources that shift hands as a result of cases. Certainly it seems extremely likely that at least some aspects of any court system will not meet such an economic test. The simple fact that no one ever thinks in such terms or makes such evaluations is in part a consequence of inertia and in part a recognition of the overweening importance of the intangible benefits of the judicial process. Only when new review agencies are suggested are such considerations ever raised.

It is revealing that critics of current tendencies in the administrative process are not really willing to pay the price of legal control. This

[4] J. D. B. Mitchell, 'The Ombudsman Fallacy', *Public Law*, Spring 1962, 24.

recognizes the worth of the traditional apparatus and the need for speedy day-to-day decisions. It also indicates that the regular courts have had their day. Further, the unwillingness to pay the price of legal control must be regarded as, at least to some extent, an index of the intensity of the demand for reform. Kenneth Davis has compiled an imposing list of proposals for review agencies.[5] The significant fact is that to date none of them has been adopted.

It is important here, also, to distinguish among these many proposals, particularly between the two types often discussed in connection with the Ombudsman. The first is the notion of a personalistic, non-legalistic reviewer of administrative decisions who, relying almost solely upon the influence of public opinion, will call attention to injustices—a sort of government-sponsored American Civil Liberties Union. A second set of proposals relates to the establishment of some sort of board of review that will have rather more legal authority. There is a tendency for the two to be discussed as if they were identical, but intelligent discussion cannot take place when the two are confounded. Indeed, a sort of game can be played by the various advocates of the Ombudsman idea—if one criticizes the voluntaristic plan, one can be referred to proposals with more teeth in them. If there is criticism of legal restraints, supporters can revert to the less formal scheme, arguing that administrators come to accept non-compulsory restraints.

Above all, there is a tendency to confuse the Ombudsman proposal with the general goal of further limiting administrative discretion. There seems to be a universal feeling that the trend of modern administration is toward rather more discretionary powers than the average citizen would like to see. But it is not clear that society is willing to pay the price that machinery for review would entail. It is not sufficient to talk generally about the need for 'due process of law'. When one is considering this or any other administrative proposal, one has to evaluate the advantages and disadvantages of a particular plan.

2. *Problems of Size and Diversity*

The scope of the 'American empire' clearly presents particular problems for adopting the Ombudsman proposal. There are a variety of built-in sources of pluralism in our society which would render difficult personalistic operation of, say, the Danish variety. As Bent Christensen has pointed out, Denmark is only twice the size of Massachusetts and has a relatively homogeneous population, both with regard to ethnic background and social distinctions; it also has a highly centralized government and a civil service with a strongly professional orientation. The editor of this volume has suggested that 'the arguments against transplanting the Ombudsman scheme may be effectively demolished'.[6]

---

[5] Davis, *loc. cit.*

[6] Rowat, 'An Ombudsman S cheme for Canada', *Canadian Journal of Economics and Political Science* 28 November 1962), 550.

But in the light of these considerations, this is perhaps more easily written than agreed to.

Nor will it do to embrace uncritically the observations of the *Economist* on this matter. One of the objections raised against the introduction of the scheme in Great Britain was that a commissioner would not, in fact, be able to handle the volume of complaints in so large a country. The London *Times* suggested that such a flood of complaints would, in turn, cause the failure of the system. In response the *Economist* argued that this was to reverse logic, that the very need for the remedy was being urged as the basis for not seeking a remedy.[7] At first sight this reasoning seems compelling. But this is to misunderstand the basic nature of life and politics. Again the question is not whether remedies should be sought, but whether this particular remedy would be better than no remedy at all. If in fact the flood of complaints would exceed the resources of a personalized system, this alone might be a sufficient argument against its adoption. The inability to handle the complaints might well create a growing disrespect for a system of remedies that provides no remedy at all, that brought the disadvantages of review without any of the advantages.

The Scandinavian Ombudsmen usually review personally every complaint made. Indeed, it is basic to the nature of the personalistic system that there be some such review. This does not mean that a thorough fact-finding takes place in unwarranted cases, but the citizens feel that the Ombudsman is an accessible, dependable, regular, not a sporadic source of relief from bureaucratic excesses. It is therefore instructive to note the number of complaints handled by the Danish Ombudsman, and the large proportion of these that were formally investigated further, particularly in the early years:[8]

	1955	1956	1957	1958	1959	1960	1961	1962
Total cases	565	869	1,029	1,101	873	1,100	1,065	1,080
Formally investigated	315	430	384	292	181	209	174	152

The volume of complaints in the United States would be unimaginably greater than this. The fact that an American Ombudsman—to say nothing of a more cumbersome board or commission—could personally deal with only a tiny fraction of these, compared with the personal involvement in nearly all investigated cases by the Nordic Ombudsmen, militates against the effectiveness of an imported personalistic scheme.

At the same time federalism and the diversity and range of American society work against a scheme whose success is founded on publicity and moral authority. Denmark's heaviest population density centers around a metropolitan region containing 25 per cent of the total population of the country. The existence and effectiveness of a national press

[7] Rowat, *op. cit.*, 549.

[8] These figures are from Bent Christensen, 'The Danish Ombudsman', *U. of Penn. Law Rev.*, 109 (June 1961), 1105, and Miss Pedersen's essay, Ch. 3.

under these conditions and a national audience for the announcements of the Ombudsman are therefore assured. The feeling of the British that they will have severe problems in attracting the citizens' attention and in developing moral authority through the press has implications for the U S, since they at least have newspapers with genuine nation-wide audiences. The competition facing an American Ombudsman for publicity in our diffuse news system may well prove to be an overwhelming disadvantage. The delicate balance between overt publicity-seeking and complete inability to gain the attention of the public may prove to be much more difficult to achieve in our country.

Thus size and diversity militate against the personalistic scheme. But, as we shall see, moving to a more formal and legalistic scheme, such as an empowered board of review, would compound problems arising from the separation of powers in our constitutional structure. The arguments assayed here would apply against the more legalistic scheme as well, though hardly to the same degree. Similarly, the separation of powers creates problems for a personalistic Ombudsman, though not in aggravated form.

3. *Problems Created by the Separation of Powers*

A characteristic of the Scandinavian system is that the Ombudsman can operate within a context of multi-party coalition governments. Shifts of power often occur within as well as between parties. Continuity thus develops both because of the limited changes within coalition patterns and because of the need for regularity in the civil service. Cabinet control and ministerial responsibility are regarded as assured. The ideal of neutrality among the civil servants is historically inculcated and characteristically internalized. By contrast, the American system features a two-party arrangement in a separation-of-powers pattern. It is already criticized for diffusion of responsibility. Numerous isolated pockets of administrative resistance to presidential authority continuously create severe problems. Neustadt is characteristic of those emphasizing the already serious debilitation of the presidency, speaking of the President as 'chief clerk'.[9]

The establishment of the Ombudsman would aggravate this trend toward weakening of the presidency and diffusion of control. Current thinking among students of the regulatory process suggests that congressional control of the commissions—particularly the setting up of overlapping terms of office, to prevent presidential control—which are independent of executive responsibility, has on the whole been deleterious. Proposals have been advanced, for example, that the President have power to remove commissioners over differences in policy. The Ombudsman proposal goes against the tenor of such thought.

It is not at all clear how a distinction will be made between questions of due process and problems of administrative policy. In Sweden, where

[9] Richard Neustadt, *Presidential Power* (New York 1960), esp. Ch. 1

the Ombudsman reviews actions only of the civil servants, whose activities are largely autonomous, rather than policies of the Government, there is a relatively precise line of differentiation. By contrast, in the American administrative structure questions of procedure shade into the penumbra of policy. The success of a reviewing institution would depend upon a delicate walking of the line, dependent in turn upon the attitudes of the formulators of the policy and the members of the affected administrative agency.

Should the Ombudsman be instituted as a creature of Congress, antagonism with the executive would be intensified. Should the institution develop a partisan attitude, with each new administration there would be a crisis of confidence. One cannot predict with certainty that these will be severe problems, but it would be naïve to assume that they will be avoided. While it would be a worthwhile challenge to our party system to attempt the creation of bodies or institutions with a tradition above party strife, we have not yet achieved such a pattern to any appreciable degree. Even in the relatively remote area of fact-finding and investigation, the partisan aspects of such activities have tended to come to the fore. Thus the report of the first Hoover commission, which was universally highly regarded, was succeeded by the more ideological second commission report; and the changeover in administration between the Eisenhower and the Kennedy régimes resulted in a re-structuring of the Civil Rights Commission staff.

In considering the Ombudsman the British have already expressed misgivings over the problem of 'internal minutes'—i.e. the internal communications of a ministry. Here again, some of the Scandinavian countries have relatively simple situations; in Sweden such materials are public documents, and therefore the Ombudsman is merely exercising an extension of the prerogative of the average citizen.[10] Even in a normal cabinet government, this will be something of a bone of contention; it will be a much graver problem in a presidential system where the officials are regarded as subordinates of the President and responsible primarily to him rather than to the Congress. A principle of our constitutional law is that matters of executive consultation are privileged, even against congressional investigation. The British, with all their misgivings, can resolve this problem politically—Parliament can decide whether or not it wishes to have such material made available on any terms it chooses. But in the United States, the question would eventually come under adjudication if Congress itself should draw the line and the executive were to in any way resist it.

There is a similar threat of extended constitutional litigation over other questions. One delicate and complicated question, for example, is the extent of the Ombudsman's control over purely executive as opposed to 'quasi-legislative, quasi-judicial' agencies. At least two

[10] L. J. Blom-Cooper, 'An Ombudsman in Britain', *Public Law*, Summer 1960, 147.

somewhat analogous bodies in recent years have had histories of serious litigation over this matter. The Civil Rights Commission found it necessary to engage in a series of tests of its powers to obtain materials and to deal with witnesses.[11] So, too, the Loyalty Review Board was, years after its abolition, found by the courts to have exceeded its powers in reviewing decisions by departments on the loyalty of their employees.

The history of the Loyalty Review Board (though created by Executive Order) presents interesting and conflicting evidence of the fate of such an agency as the Ombudsman. On the one hand, in only one public instance was a recommendation of the Board, legally merely advisory, ignored. This supports the view that legal control may not be necessary. On the other hand, the sharp changeovers in administrative policy that resulted from a party change in the presidency does not argue well for the notion of non-partisan continuity. Furthermore, the earlier radical shift in policy that occurred when Seth Richardson was replaced as chairman by Senator Bingham also suggests that the twists and turns of American politics will predominate over notions of due-process regularity.[12]

Another sample of the problems that the proposed agency might raise in our constitutional system is to be found in the activities of the Comptroller General. The Comptroller has never acted as the 'independent watchdog' which the proponents of the office envisaged. This has resulted in large part from the terms of the statutes establishing the office, as well as from the inclination of the people occupying the position. In spite of many calls for changes in the pattern of the Comptroller, he persists in preferring pre-audit control of expenditure to post-audit oversight. Executive pressures have not significantly improved the situation.

Even more discouraging for those who have hopes for such 'watchdog agencies' is the attitude of the Comptroller toward another such agency, the Court of Claims. While he accepts the verdict of the Court in any particular case, he refuses to recognize its decisions as precedents in similar cases and thus narrowly restricts the effects of verdicts of the court. Oddly this 'watchdog of Congress' has operated to limit the effectiveness of an agency intended to mitigate the rigors of the same administrative process.

Such bodies as President Truman's Civil Rights Committee or the Temporary National Economic Committee have provided more scholarly material than action. Thus, the historical experience of the United States with committees and boards established without powers, operating only with moral authority, does not lend support to an

[11] *Hannah v. Larche, Hannah v. Slawson*, 363 US 420 (1960). The case contains a useful 31-page appendix to the opinion of the Court summarizing investigative powers and procedures of various agencies—indicating the complexity of the structure the Ombudsman would have to deal with.

[12] Ralph S. Brown, Jr., *Loyalty and Security* (New Haven, 1958), 246–8.

expectation of compliance with their findings. On the other hand, formalization by Congress creates conflict with the President. And participation by the President, as Packer has clearly pointed out, carries with it changeovers of administration and the possibility of political antagonism.[13]

The more formalized the remedy becomes, the more likely is conflict with the executive agencies. The more legalistically defined the scope of the agency, the more likely the need for litigation. Further, not the least significant deterrent to the development of moral confidence in the Ombudsman will be the difficulty of obtaining favorable adjudication to legitimize the function. In this regard, the experience with the Loyalty Review Board of having its actions declared illegal long after it had ceased to exist is instructive.

Thus, while federalism and the vast size of the American nation are the chief deterrents to the development of a personalistic Ombudsman, the separation of powers is the major objection to a more formalized authority. Any proposal must not only steer a middle course between political and judicial controls, but also between the problems engendered by federalism and presidential responsibility.

4. Conclusion

The real potentialities of the Ombudsman proposal seem to me to lie in another direction. It is likely that the proposed agency would be more useful to local and state governments. Here the scope of activity, the span of attention of the public, and the magnitude of the task would seem peculiarly commensurate with the situations and traditions in the Scandinavian countries. The size, population and ecological setting, all more nearly approximate the home countries of the institution.[14]

There are strong indications, too, that the need is at its maximum at the community and the state level. Studies of the Civil Rights Commission have found indications of great abuse of discretion at the local level. Comparison has shown that city and state police are much more prone to abuse of legal rights than federal authorities. The morale, the training, and the recruitment of officials are often less than ideal at that level, and the potential value of such a review institution is correspondingly greater.[15] Indeed, some cities have already created a

[13] Herbert S. Packer, *Ex-Communist Witnesses* (Palo Alto, 1962), 235–47. The discussion on pp. 221 ff. of the utility of various types of inquiries—trials, legislative committees, executive agencies—in seeking out truth and in the protection of individuals is quite germane to the whole question of the Ombudsman.

[14] Davis, *Public Law*, Spring 1962, 39–40, seems to be in agreement with this point; cf. also Henry Abraham's essay and his 'A People's Watchdog Against the Abuse of Power', *Public Administration Review* 20 (Summer 1960), 157.

[15] See United States Commission on Civil Rights, *Report on Civil Rights*, Book 5, *Justice* (1961), part 7, 'Equal Justice Under Law', 79–87.

Board of Public Review with regard to police action. The extension of the institution to other agencies as well seems appropriate.

There are other informal precedents for its application on the local level. Cities have experimented with complaint bureaus or individual officials in the correction of bureaucratic faults. The Ombudsman proposal may be the vehicle for the restoration of local interest, the bringing of local government back to intimate contact with the people. As such, it deserves support and consideration.

Nor will its adoption at the local level preclude its application on a national level as well. Indeed, as experience develops and more evidence accrues, this may very well be found to be feasible. Objections to the proposal are not ones of principle, but a simple recognition of pragmatic problems inherent in accepting the scheme in its present form. In recent years, the Swedish and Danish governments have extended the application of the Ombudsman from the national to the local level. Logic and experience suggest that in the United States the reverse application might be more desirable.

The current dreams for more due process in the national administrative sphere should not be discredited by too hastily embracing a solution that will take on more than it can really solve. If this should happen, it would be too easy to group such demands with the irrational and shrilly ideological complaints of the 1930's. An Ombudsman that failed would be worse than no corrective at all. The corrective to administrative ills should develop as slowly and as adaptively as have the regulatory agencies themselves.

THE IMPORTATION OF FOREIGN INSTITUTIONS

by Fritz Morstein Marx*

Faced with the overwhelming requirements of public management that are typical of industrial society, a considerable number of countries have come to suffer from a nervous itch to do something about the seeming imbalance between administrative powers and individual rights. As these countries look around to see what might be learned from the experience of other nations, we should endeavor to evolve a rating pattern or a strategy for a conceivable importation of foreign institutions. A hit-or-miss gamble is the opposite pole to the working methods of scientific analysis.

This sort of strategy begins logically with an assessment of need. Clear understanding of established need offers a frame of reference for

* Professor of Comparative Administrative Science and Public Law, Academy of Administrative Sciences, Speyer.

ascertaining the kind of redress that holds greatest promise of meeting the need. In the existing institutional context, certain things may fruitfully be done, while others may yield no benefit, without being inferior on abstract grounds. Actions proposed should be appraised in terms of likely effects, not merely in terms of noble intentions.

When it comes to consideration of attractive designs and devices found elsewhere, an equally cautious bent of mind is called for. What is the domestic judgment? Who are the Crown witnesses? Are they interested parties? Is there a reliable foundation to what they say? What is the state of research on the subject? Only by working the matter through such a series of sieves can we assure ourselves that we do not fall prey to the conspiracy of excellent ideas that insinuate themselves as obvious solutions.

What is necessary, in short, is a reasonably complete diagnosis. Such a diagnosis, for instance, was never offered in the United States by the intellectual fathers of the Administrative Procedure Act, unless it consisted in failing to reflect adequately on the extensive empirical groundwork provided by the Attorney General's Committee on Administrative Procedure. In addition, however, it is no less obvious that an equally conscientious prognosticating job must be done. Amelioration is rarely accomplished in one quick turn. Successive steps or at least continuing efforts are usually required to effect a significant change. One must be willing to think about the chain of related moves.

This may sound like making speed slowly. There is no doubt that careful examination is the foe of haste. But dispatch, in comparison with effectiveness, is one of the least important factors in finding solutions to the basic problems inherent in the administrative state. These problems have been creeping up on us for half a century. They are not likely to yield in a hurry.

A strategy such as the one outlined above does, however, guard us against desperate yet inconsequential ventures toward 'doing something'. Moreover, the significance of what is being proposed should not be shrouded in pleasant vagueness. It should also be more than one small thing, put forth as an appeasement to our impatience. In the adjustment of institutional patterns one does not get very far with the old bromide that every little bit helps. On the contrary, although the little bit may be far too feeble to help in any form or shape, it may prove unexpectedly a source of dislocation to existing arrangements, political or administrative, an evil chip of rock to grind into the turbines.

1. Nature of the Ombudsman Institution

As part of the widespread itch mentioned earlier, a warm reception is currently given a magic word. That word is Ombudsman, signifying an officer who undertakes, as a parliamentary agent, to defend the law against official abuses affecting the interests of individuals.

Historically, the institution is the gift of Sweden. Its beginnings go back more than 150 years. For most of this period it would have caused astonishment among Swedes to learn that one day the Ombudsman was to be regarded as an importable commodity by other nations.

For a student of comparative administration drawing on Swedish prototypes, three distinctive features appear worth stressing about the position of Sweden's citizen in his relations with public offices. In the first place, government agencies in Sweden possess a relatively high degree of independence from the political level of decision-making. They are significantly less subject to day-by-day parliamentary influences than is true of most other administrative systems. In a sense, the Ombudsman is therefore a compensatory device. Secondly, in pursuit of his own interests the individual has a powerful weapon at his disposal. That is his right to examine governmental files and other official papers, with certain exceptions designed to safeguard state secrets and comparable public interests. In cases of friction between the citizen and a department, the genesis of the administrative decision in question is thus a matter of record. As a result, an individual complaint can be pressed upon the public agency a good deal harder than would be possible in a setting where the private party has no direct access to the hidden anatomy of the case. And thirdly, as Professor Nils Herlitz has pointed out on various occasions, there is not quite as much ease in Sweden in bringing cases to judicial review as obtains in certain other Continental European countries, where administrative courts have long exercised extensive jurisdiction.

I am not aware of any study made in Sweden to determine how closely these three factors are intermeshed. Have they come to form a 'balance of nature' in the national context? Are there other factors equally relevant to such a balance? In particular, could it be that the presence of the Ombudsman has weakened the case, argued repeatedly in Sweden, for a more inclusive application of judicial review? If it came to a choice between these alternatives, it might well be that enlargement of legal remedies would have the greater public appeal. To conjecture about these matters is, of course, a poor substitute for adequate analysis.

One thing, however, stands out in bold relief. Legal redress through formal court procedure will never absorb but a fraction, perhaps only a very small fraction, of all cases where the affected individual believes he is entitled to an administrative decision different from that confronting him. In countless instances, it is true, his quarrel will simply be with a negative response. He wants an accommodation of his interests, never mind whether the law or any other compelling public consideration stands in the way. That may be the sum total of his grievance. Nothing can be done about it, except on the slippery and forbidden path of favors. But the affected party may darkly suspect that, for one reason or another, his interests were not properly considered in accordance with applicable legal provisions or standards; that an error of judgment occurred in the office; possibly even that he was made the victim of foul play. He wants a full review, not simply a juridical unravelling of the threads of law if he can afford the price.

Review by the Ombudsman is poor man's justice, and rich man's as well. It is obtainable virtually at the cost of a postage stamp. This is a tremendous fringe benefit for the common citizen and an equal gain for the general cause of justice. But how are both accomplished? Through inexpensive as well as independent examination of the pertinent facts. In this perspective the Ombudsman, as a defender of everybody's right, is a cousin, however distant, of other agencies of ready review. One may think of the French *Conseil d'État* and of the system of independent administrative courts traditional in Central Europe. Although to free societies he may seem to make a strange companion, the Soviet procurator has official duties that include the review functions of the Ombudsman.

2. *Suitability for the United States*

How would a parliamentary review officer fit into a political system as basically different from the Swedish as is the scheme of coequal powers in the United States?

On one point it should not be too hard among Americans to achieve agreement. Independent review of administrative determinations, extending beyond the strictly legal aspects, is not formally provided. Even legal reconsideration is not now sufficiently widely available to anyone who would be deterred by substantial costs and undue delay. That is especially true of the little man, standing by himself. In this respect, the Administrative Procedure Act has not materially changed the general picture on the federal level. Face to face with a welter of additional authorities on the levels of state and local government, the untutored individual confronts a situation even less secure. A complaint officer might look like the knight of the Holy Grail to the citizen who feels choked by 'red tape'.

This pleasing prospect is marred, however, by a jurisdictional consideration. In a country of continental width like the United States, an Ombudsman would have to support a sizable machine to cope with the business flowing to him as a result of federal operations alone. With fifty states and, if fashion spreads, perhaps ten times as many of the larger local governments in the market for an Ombudsman, we are bound soon to greet a new professional association, holding annual meetings like the others, and finding a hospitable roof perhaps as part of the '1313' cluster of similar bodies in Chicago. Conceivably, one of the first roundtables of the American association might deal with the attainment of economy and efficiency by the Nordic Ombudsmen.

This embarrassment of riches would be a small matter compared with the organizational task, in the American pattern of legislative-executive dichotomy, of setting up the new office and defining its powers and responsibilities. Past experience in the federal realm is not particularly inviting. It may be remembered that the establishment of the General Accounting Office headed by a Comptroller General was accompanied by considerable friction between Congress and the President. Although generally in favor of the first comprehensive bill providing for budgetary control and independent audit, Woodrow Wilson vetoed it in 1920 on constitutional grounds. He took the view that the legal formula specifying the role of the Comptroller General infringed upon the constitutional status of the executive. This meant that the legislation had to be passed again, with what was hoped to be acceptable as a suitable modification. It did prove acceptable to President Harding, who saw matters somewhat differently, partly as a Republican, partly because his knowledge of business practices induced him to think of the Comptroller General more as a company officer than as an antagonist to the Chief Executive. Subsequent developments proved Harding wrong, at least for troublesome periods. History therefore does not hold the door open for a federal Ombudsman functioning as an officer of the legislative branch.

But even if the episode of 1919–21 were completely struck from public memory, a moderately alert President is likely to recoil with agitation from the idea of a legislative agent independently delving into executive operations. Moreover, the constitutional domain of the executive is not one open in every respect to legislative examination. Presidents have refused to deliver privileged information. An Ombudsman, when succumbing to the institutional solidarity of the legislative branch, would not be above organizing a 'fishing expedition'. Observation in Washington allows the inference that at times the Comptroller General has been moved by an understandable desire to be politically helpful to one or another standing committee of Congress. When considering the advisability of a veto of proposed legislation to create an Ombudsman, the President would certainly have to ask himself some important questions. Not the least of these would be whether the benefits expected of such an office would significantly outweigh the added imposition of another legislative agent with a general hunting license for the area of the executive branch.

The constitutional juxtaposition of the legislative and the executive branches has rendered Congress far more inquisitive and critical in its surveillance of administrative activities than holds true for most legislatures. Hours on end are spent each session by department chiefs and their immediate aides before legislative committees eager for executive views on pending legislation and for detailed accounts of operational performance. During the months in which the subcommittees of the Appropriations Committee of each House conduct hearings on the budgetary requests of the departments, the interrogatory process comes to a peak. The flow of information to Congress is massive.

The printed record of committee hearings runs every session to thousands and thousands of pages of which not a small share is caused by questions reflecting the close relationship between lawmakers and constituents.

Considering the generous recognition Congressmen by and large give to any manifestation of personal interest from their constituency, including Rippy Miller's high school term paper on foreign aid, American legislators may be thought of as Ombudsmen *en masse*. This leaves room for the argument that a single Ombudsman might succeed better in channeling and reviewing the total flow of grievances. But it would be utopian to assume that an American lawmaker would permit a formally established agency, however attractive its designation and even its record, to stand between him and those whose votes he hopes to get for his re-election. Hence a federal Ombudsman may not do a great deal more than occupy half a page of official prose in the *United States Government Organization Manual*. Or he may come to discover and cultivate a particular clientele, as some observers believe is done by the German counterpart for military affairs in extending his special care to the professional military personnel. After all, any office must make its job, at least to some extent.

For reasons already given, it is understandable that an unusually high degree of transparency is ascribed to American administration. The tactics of the informational leak to the outside are merely one aspect. The lateral connections among administrative offices, legislative committees, and organized interests represent another aspect. Lacking integration by a unified corps of higher civil servants, the executive machinery still resembles in many particulars a conglomeration of going concerns rather than a structure suitable for general direction and central accountability. To give due weight to this tendency, it should be borne in mind that the reform movement of the first three decades of our century exerted itself strenuously in the opposite direction. The markers on the way toward a reinforced system of public responsibility pointed to a strengthened executive as the first stage. The executive staff units typical of modern American administration were justified in good part as a necessary central support. Staff organization was to enable the Chief Executive to achieve broadly conceived plans of operation and to bring forth a counter pressure to the centrifugal drives active in the departmental system.

An Ombudsman would be likely to encourage these separatistic urges precisely by his independence. By calling on particular agencies and offices to justify their conduct in individual instances, he might weaken correspondingly the hold of the Chief Executive on the machinery of administration. An Ombudsman might supply these agencies and offices with an opportunity for excusing themselves with alleged requirements of centrally defined rules and regulations, thus inviting him to serve as arbitrator in the vertical as well as horizontal conflicts of an executive branch which the Constitution expects to function as one. Observers of the new Danish Ombudsman, an upstart barely ten years old, have suggested that subordinate officials soon discovered the possibilities of bringing the Ombudsman into their quarrels with superiors. Under congressional-presidential government, such implications are bound to stimulate considerable hesitation, unless they can be removed by thorough study.

3. *Experiments, Precedents and Alternatives*

Appropriate caution, it was urged earlier, is desirable when it is proposed to transplant a foreign institution in the hope of its taking root firmly in quite a different soil. But such reserve should not become the unimaginative counsel of inertia. The best test, of course, is a practical trial, preferably as a limited and reversible experiment.

From the point of view of gaining some receptivity for the supposed blessings of an Ombudsman in the United States, nothing would be more welcome than venturesome adoption of such a scheme in, say, Canada, either on the federal or on the provincial level. Ten years of practical experience with the new institution in a neighbor country familiar with the peculiarities of the federal plan would furnish good evidence. It might have considerable impact on the underdeveloped imitative trait of the American mind in governmental matters. Moreover, because of the high estate of political science in Canada it could be expected that the progress of the experiment would be followed more closely and more searchingly by empirical analysis than has been deemed warranted in Sweden. Of course, even then it might give pause that Canada does not display the sharp legislative-executive dualism that puts the United States into a political category by itself.

One aspect that might be expected to attract particular attention in any such experiment would be the concrete record of accomplishment. An assessment could not be complete if confined to measuring the volume of business carried by the complaint unit. More important, though at the same time more difficult, would be a reasonably dependable judgment of the actual ease obtained by the common citizen in gaining a fuller consideration of his interests by administrative agencies. If a complaint unit cannot show convincingly what it adds in this direction, one might well question whether the unit deserves to be added to the existing machinery. Indeed, if it deserves to be added, it is proper to ask what other piece of machinery could possibly be taken out of service. Nothing is gained by piling various devices one upon the other. The common itch mentioned earlier encourages this tendency. The outcome might be an all-round deterioration of conditions admittedly less than satisfactory in the first instance.

Even if Canada should not feel stirred to take the lead and thus serve incidentally as a tactical sandbox for the United States, some useful studies could be undertaken by American scholars in their own back yard to see what an Ombudsman might be like. The mayor of New York City, for example, has been maintaining something like an Ombudsman in the form of what is known as Post Office Box 100. This is the address to write to for anybody aroused over improper treatment by municipal agencies or situations that invite suggestions for improvement. One of the mayor's legal aides serves as the manager of this correspondence. He may ask the head of the agency concerned to have the matter looked into, to send the writer an appropriate reply, and to mail a copy to City Hall for information and reference. Or, in more serious complaints, he may direct the agency to report the pertinent circumstances to him, as a basis for further action, perhaps even to have the Commissioner of Investigations take over. Exactly how this arrangement works in all respects is not known to political science. Here is a pertinent scheme that warrants objective scrutiny.

Nor is this the only related institution that comes to mind. In not a few of the American cities that benefit from the council-manager plan, similar improvisations can be observed. How do they work out? What can be done to make them more effective? How frequently do they include provision for an oral explanation to the applicant of the reasons for a negative decision? There is room for more extensive research on these propositions, although we are not entirely without empirical data.

As for the possibility in the United States of a controlled experiment with the Ombudsman scheme, especially in one of the cities or one of the states, the history of American local government offers some encouragement. We recall Galveston's initiation of the commission plan, though that form of municipal government eventually proved a dead alley. A happier instance is Staunton, Virginia, Woodrow Wilson's birthplace, where nearly sixty years ago the first stumbling steps were taken that ended with the success story of the modern city manager. If there is something to be said for a trial balloon, let it be small. One shudders to think what a seven-league place like Chicago could do to as unorthodox a thing as a municipal Ombudsman.

One last point. Anyone presenting a coherent argument for an Ombudsman scheme inadvertently develops a persuasive case for related approaches. Is the Anglo-American tradition still in bonds to the hallucinations of Professor Dicey? What about the concept of administrative courts in the Continental European manner? If this is still too sticky a proposition, how about designing a more meticulous yet uncluttered complaint procedure, functional rather than legalistic, as part of the normal operation of each administrative agency? How about entrusting to a special staff unit in each agency the continuing task of evaluating the agency's institutional product, particularly as it affects the citizen? How about giving fuller consideration to the obvious fact that more attention to the needs of the general customer of public administration requires strengthened budgetary support, adequate to the efforts to be made? And finally, let us not forget that administrative actions are shaped in good part by professional attitudes, concepts of personal responsibility, and the play of ethical judgment. Well understood, the civil servant's role includes the function of Ombudsman. He does not live up to that role when he sits through the hours of his working day; or when the pressure of things to be done keeps him running all the time; or when he is abused by the public as the whipping boy of mass society.

17

THE COMMONWEALTH
PARLIAMENTARY SYSTEM

THE CASE FOR AN OMBUDSMAN
by Louis Blom-Cooper*

Two English journalists were recently committed to prison (for three and six months, respectively) for contempt of court; they had both refused to divulge their sources of information to the Radcliffe Tribunal set up to investigate the case of John Vassall, an Admiralty clerk, who had been convicted, in October 1962, of handing over secret information to the Soviet Union; the inquiry was aimed primarily at testing newspaper rumours that there had been laxity in the Admiralty in recruiting Vassall. The upshot was an almost frenzied debate among the British public about the claim of the press to journalistic privilege, a privilege, incidentally, which thirteen years ago had been denied to journalists by another Commonwealth court, the High Court of Australia.[1]

It is not necessary to argue in favour of the journalists' claim—to use the words of Carlyle and Macauley—that the press is in fact the fourth estate of the realm. It is enough to demonstrate that this socially cathartic issue on the British scene is symptomatic of an ill-formed system of administrative law throughout the Commonwealth, demanding either some radical overhaul or some buttressing by an institution like the Scandinavian Ombudsman.

Why was it that these two journalists resorted to obtaining information about the security risk of an Admiralty clerk in a highly confidential way, the source of which their consciences ultimately forbade them to reveal? This was not a *Der Spiegel* affair, where the information supplied touched the nerve centre of the state's authority. The information at

---

* Barrister-at-Law, and Visiting Lecturer in Sociology of Law, U. of London.
[1] The English journalists' case is *Attorney-General v. Foster* [1963] 2 W.L.R. 658; see also *Attorney-General v. Clough* [1963] 2 W.L.R. 343. In the Australian case, *McGuiness v. Attorney-General of Victoria* (1940) 63 C.L.R. 73, a Royal Commission had been appointed to inquire into a question whether there had been bribery of members of the Victorian Parliament. A journalist who was asked what his source of information was, declined to give it. He was found guilty of contempt and fined £15. For a study of the claims to journalistic privilege in a variety of countries, see the International Press Institute's survey published by the Institute in Zürich, 1961.

most concerned knowledge about a person who might, by virtue of that knowledge, have been revealed more clearly as a security risk. But such knowledge was of a highly personalized character, and did not bear upon any matter of state secrets.

There are two fundamental reasons for masking the informant's identity. The first, more cogent and compelling, is the existence of the Official Secrets Act, which applies to any person holding office under the Crown, including a civil servant. If the informant commits, however technical, a breach of the Act he will require to be ensured against disclosure of the source of such information.[2] An Act of Parliament with such a title would, one might presume, be concerned with state secrets. In fact, any information emanating from a government source is caught by the Act, and a divulging of it without lawful authority constitutes an offence.

The second reason is the corollary of the first. Even if the divulging of the confidential information is not likely to be subject to any real risk of criminal proceedings, there is still need for masking the informer's identity, since leakage of government information may be considered sufficiently a breach of civil service etiquette to merit some form of internal disciplining. But should a civil servant be subjected to such threats? After all, it is generally accepted that the democratic process depends upon leakages from government sources to the press. But the members of a Government of this or of any other day like to feel they have control of the situation, and if things get out of hand the whip can be cracked or—more suitably—the story, when publicized, can be officially denied. The Government then sits back under both a barrage of verbal abuse from the press and parliamentary harassment, with the hope—not always pious—that the storm will be weathered, and that the much-maligned Tribunals of Inquiry (Evidence) Act, 1921 (under which the Radcliffe Tribunal was appointed) may not have to be invoked. One has only to recall the Burgess-Maclean case to be aware of a *cause célèbre* in which the British public still does not know the extent to which there was laxity in the security arrangements, in giving two Soviet sympathizers in the British Foreign Office the opportunity of defecting to Moscow.

Compare that affair with the way the Danes dealt with a similar case. Einar Blechingberg, aged 63, was a career diplomat who, while serving in his country's Bonn embassy, delivered secret documents to an Eastern European embassy. Blechingberg was returned to Denmark, tried and sentenced to eight years' imprisonment. A rumpus took place in the Danish Parliament which finally resolved to refer the case to the Ombudsman, although he had the power to initiate his own inquiry. The inquiry led to the revelation that Blechingberg had mounted gambling debts while serving in Denmark's Mexican embassy. This fact was known to the

[2] See *R. v. Fell* (1963), The *Guardian* Law Report and *The Times* Law Report, January 22, 1963.

Danish Foreign Office, which transferred Blechingberg to Bonn where, since it was the most important ambassadorial post in the Danish foreign service, he could earn more money. The Ombudsman criticized the Foreign Secretary for continuing to employ a security risk; this blow at Danish officialdom was somewhat softened by the humanitarian motives imputed to those who posted Blechingberg to Bonn. The public disquiet was stilled.

In Britain government by secrecy still prevails. The British Constitution, unwritten as it may be, is clear about the demarcation of the powers of the Administration. There is a large area of administrative action which is subject to neither public scrutiny nor even independent inquiry through the courts or other quasi-judicial forum. And this traditional principle of government has been inherited by most of the other Commonwealth countries. No such principle persists in Sweden. There, ever since 1766, it has been a fundamental right that every citizen is entitled to gain access to the records of public authorities, subject only to certain specific exceptions connected with state secrets in their very restricted meaning. What could be more natural therefore than that the Swedes should appoint a single man to exercise the collective right of all Swedes ? It is not surprising that the Ombudsman has existed in Sweden since 1809.

Because of this deep-rooted constitutional precept, which is wholly absent in the Commonwealth, Sweden does not present us with a good example of the workings of the Ombudsman—in Sweden he is merely exercising a collective right of all Swedes. He has no greater rights than any citizen has. Denmark, on the other hand, does not have this precept. Nor is the freedom of the press specifically guaranteed in her constitution as in Sweden. It is not remarkable, therefore, that the Ombudsman came to Copenhagen only in 1954. Even though Sweden provided the model, the predicament of the Danes resembled much more clearly the problem facing every twentieth-century democracy, in which the administrative organs of government, in an increasingly complex society, appear only too often to have triumphed over parliamentary control. Some of the more perfervid supporters of the Ombudsman have visions of a dark conspiracy by the executive to usurp every function of Parliament—an attitude redolent of that outrageous polemic of the 1930's from the pen of Lord Hewart, a former Lord Chief Justice of England. If *The New Despotism* was nowhere near the bull's eye, it did at least focus attention on the growing tentacles of administrative power. It was not, however, the wickedness of delegated legislation that was gnawing away at our liberties but the sheer weight of bureaucratic government.

The highlight of the reaction of the public came with the Crichel Down affair, where it was discovered that Commander Marten's land was ordered to be compulsorily acquired by the Ministry of Agriculture and Fisheries for bad reasons, namely that civil servants found the

Commander a tiresome citizen to deal with. Dr Brian Chapman is right in suggesting that its investigator, Sir Andrew Clark, Q.C., in his report (to which widespread credence was given) used an extravagance of language that blurred the public's vision to the reality that there had been error in administration but no wickedness.[3] Dr Chapman rather spoilt his case by adding that any provincial solicitor could quote almost daily instances of far worse cases of partiality and prejudice in magistrates' courts without this involving more than a shrug from those most furious in their denunciation of civil servants. This sally at the bench is misplaced; magistrates at least conduct their activities under the spotlight of the utmost publicity. 'Justice must not only be done but seen to be done' is, of course, a hackneyed maxim—strangely enough coined by Lord Hewart.[4] It is the threat of injustice—however remote—done behind closed doors in Whitehall that ferments distrust and breeds suspicion of unfairness. It may not be possible, even under the Ombudsman system, always to bring the administrative dispute into the open; but the public should at least have a remedy against secret administrative action by being allowed a means of probing the correctness of a decision. And the Ombudsman is recognized as one of 'us' rather than 'them'.

There is no better example of British and Commonwealth insistence to govern by secrecy than the maintenance of the doctrine of Crown privilege.[5] Can it really be said that the production of state documents in civil or criminal litigation would imperil the state and so outweigh the interests in properly administering justice? Of course, one could not expect the production of those documents which fall into the category of military or naval secrets; but most others record merely the trivia of government action.[6] Only political and diplomatic embarrassment would have been experienced had the British Government in the Soblen case responded to the subpoena to produce any communications between President Kennedy and the British Prime Minister.

It was conceded by the Lord Chancellor a few years ago that of the many documents in the Crown's possession for which privilege might be claimed, there were many of which it could not plausibly be said that their production would imperil the state more than it would serve the administration of justice. Yet if the Government was, as a result, prepared to relax the claim to Crown privilege there has been in practice little sign of it. The suggestions made by Sir Jocelyn Simon in

---

[3] 'The Ombudsman', *Public Administration*, 1960, 303.

[4] *R. v. Sussex Justices; ex parte McCarthy* [1924] 1 K.B. 256 at p. 259.

[5] Although the doctrine applies in most Commonwealth countries, there is a restlessness in at least Australia and New Zealand at its unrestricted application; see [1963] 79 L.Q.R. 37 and 153.

[6] *Ellis v. Home Office* [1953] 2 Q.B. 135; *Broome v. Broome* [1955] p. 190; *Gain v. Gain* [1961] 3 W.L.R. 1469, and *R. v. Governor of Brixton Prison; ex parte Soblen* [1962] 3 W.L.R. 1154 at p. 1163; that point was not challenged on appeal.

1955, that the issue of Crown privilege could be dealt with in closed court and a Minister's claim upheld only where full disclosure would be prejudicial to national security, have not been heeded, despite the fact that he was a member of the former Government for some years.

1. *The Inadequacy of Existing Machinery*

Administration of government in countries modelled on the British system has traditionally been conducted in secret partly because constitutional lawyers have never seriously questioned Gladstone's advice to the House of Commons that 'your business is not to govern the country, but it is, if you think fit, to call to account those who govern it'. Britain has, subject to parliamentary action, accepted a degree of authoritarianism and a breadth of executive discretion that should not now be tolerated. The question is: can, and do, members of Parliament effectively call the Government to account for its actions ?

So long as the state was largely concerned with the wider issues of foreign and colonial affairs and of defence policy the British attitude of forbearance to probe Government action was tolerable. But when the state became a planner, on a large scale, of the country's everyday activities and impinged more and more upon the rights of the individual citizen, this tolerance became, if not positively harmful to the citizen's rights, certainly irksome and productive of a sense of injustice which *is* harmful to the relations between authority and the individual.

Ever since the last war there has been increasing evidence that the public has chafed under the inability of the courts and other quasi-judicial bodies to deal effectively with the growing problem of complaints against administrative action. While Crichel Down was given undue prominence, it did serve to demonstrate the deep-seated unrest over the way in which civil servants could—and sometimes did—ride roughshod over the ordinary citizen's rights. The Franks Committee was ostensibly set up to review the unwholesome picture presented by the report on Crichel Down, but its terms of reference precluded it from discussing problems of administration other than those arising out of the powers exercised by administrative tribunals.[7] The Franks Committee recognized that it was asked to review only one side of the coin: it specifically stated that its inquiry was 'only part of the relationship between authority and the individual'.[8] The Government appeared—in a suspiciously deliberate way—to avoid facing the real problem: namely, the whole field of English administrative law. It was therefore left to the organization 'Justice' to undertake a task which the Government abdicated. The Government's (almost out of hand)

---

[7] This was the second limb of the work begun by the Donoughmore Committee of 1932, whose prime function was to review the increasing use of delegated legislation. The Franks Committee took over where the Donoughmore Committee left off in its review of the nascent administrative tribunals.

[8] *Report* (Cmnd. 218, 1957), 4, para. 19.

dismissal of the 'Justice' proposals in 1962 was both predictable and shabby.

All this indicates that there is much wrong in the administrative law of Anglo-Saxon countries. The effectiveness of the parliamentary question and of the adjournment debate is diminishing as the field of administrative action broadens. The use of tribunals of inquiry throughout the countries of the Commonwealth is reserved for major scandals of a public kind, and is in any event discredited as a method for probing the truth. In the British Parliament, men like Lord Poole—the person upon whose head a pile of innuendoes was heaped in the Bank rate inquiry of 1958—have made a restrained plea for curtailment of the inquiry tribunals' powers as they affect innocent witnesses. Mr Richard Crossman, the British Labour member of Parliament, echoed the sentiments of many other public figures when he flayed the inquiry procedure, both in and out of Parliament. There are also the *ad hoc* inquiries, which are set up only when the Government feels the need. Very often they lack the impartiality which should be inherent in any judicial or quasi-judicial body. The setting up recently of an inquiry body, consisting of the visiting magistrates, into the allegations of beating and lack of medical treatment at Durham Prison is an example.[9] For the magistrates to find any allegation proved would be to pass judgment on themselves for failing to perform their duties as visitors to the prison. There were also mutterings against the *ad hoc* inquiry held by Lord Denning into the Profumo affair, where the investigation was conducted privately without any powers of a judicial character being conferred on Lord Denning, unlike a tribunal under the 1921 Act.

2. The 'Justice' Proposals

There remain for consideration the proliferating administrative tribunals, supervised since 1958 by the Council on Tribunals. In an attempt to remedy some of the defects of the present situation, the 'Justice' (Whyatt) report recommended an extension of the tribunal system; it pointed out that in many cases of discretionary decisions by a Minister there is no—and ought to be a—right of appeal. If this recommendation were accepted—the Government gave it the coldest of douches—the Council on Tribunals would have to have its hand considerably strengthened. When the Council bravely tackled the Government over the Essex Chalkpit case in 1961, its was ultimately silenced by the Lord Chancellor and the Minister of Housing and Local Government, who in unison denied any remedy for the aggrieved person in that case.

A defect in the Whyatt report was the supposition that tribunals are necessarily a worthwhile palliative in the present difficulties of administrative law. The administrative tribunal, according to the report, was

[9] *The Times* (London), June 20, 1963.

dignified by the epithet 'impartial', while the Minister's discretionary decision was not accorded the distinction of being 'responsible'. The tribunal was never characterized as 'irresponsible' though the Minister's action was always dubbed as 'partial'. This was unfair; but what, in the face of the Government's intractable opposition to an institution like the Ombudsman, was the 'Justice' Committee to do ? If tribunal adjudication is not necessarily to be preferred to Ministerial decision, at least some check upon the wrong exercise of discretionary powers as well as maladministration by government departments must be provided.

The 'Justice' report did recommend the setting up of a Parliamentary Commissioner to investigate cases of alleged maladministration, but its recommendations were somewhat lacking in boldness. The Parliamentary Commissioner would not deserve even to be considered as an Anglicized Ombudsman. For instance, a Minister could veto any inquiry. Although it was hoped that the power would be exercised sparingly, this would provide an unnecessary loophole for Ministers who are prone to protectiveness towards their civil servants. The power of a Minister to exclude inter-departmental and departmental files from the information available to the Commissioner would be unnecessarily inhibiting upon the quest for the truth. Finally, the recommendation that for an initial period of five years he should be approached only through members of Parliament is regrettable. It is not that MPs are necessarily less conscientious than anyone else in pursuing complaints. But one of the distinctive features of the Ombudsman is the direct contact individuals have with this single, outstanding man, who by nature of his office promises relentlessly to investigate their grievances.

There is one thing in the Government's statement on the 'Justice' report with which most reformers would agree. Any extension of the system of reference to special tribunals for ministerial inquiry would lead to inflexibility and delay in administration. The field of town and country planning in Britain has demonstrated how the inquiries under that legislation have nearly caused havoc in good town planning. But recognition of these facts makes it more, not less, incumbent that the citizen should have some means of testing impartially the good faith and correctness of a ministerial decision.

The Government made two substantive objections to the 'Justice' recommendation for a Parliamentary Commissioner. One of them is almost naïve; the other laughable. It said that there is already adequate provision under our constitutional and parliamentary practice for the redress of any genuine complaint of maladministration—in particular by means of the citizen's right of access to MPs. But *access* is a long way from possessing any satisfactory investigation and redress of the complaint. This kind of official statement reveals a state of mind which is precisely what all the fuss is about. I can do no better than quote the editorial opinion of *Public Law* (Winter 1962):

If the need for a break-through of the official façade were ever doubted, this document will dispel the doubts. Here, in its simplest and purest form, is revealed the attitude of mind which is at once so self-sufficient that it thinks a reasoned statement superfluous, so limited that it cannot free itself from the restraints of its private mythology, and so obtuse that it will not see the effect of its own arrogance. It is this attitude which caused the whole inquiry; and which shows how far we are from impressing on our masters even the notion that a problem exists.

These are strong and heady words, but they reflect an irritation at the British Government's attitude in failing to deal with the reasoned argument put forward. They reflect also a common government failing in according too much credence to well-informed opinion which is based, however, on no social data.

The Government's second objection, which it said applied to both proposals (for a Commissioner and an extension of administrative tribunals), is that they would be irreconcilable with the principle of ministerial responsibility to Parliament. This kind of claim brings forth only a hollow laugh, since the doctrine of ministerial responsibility seems to be most in disrepute in the very place where it is supposed to apply most rigorously—the British Parliament. Suez, Hola and Vassall, in which Parliament was unable to deal with the consequences of irresponsible action, spring instantly to mind. The resignation of the Minister of Agriculture over Crichel Down now seems almost an excess of zeal for public spiritedness. New Zealanders, moreover, no less zealous in guarding valuable constitutional safeguards, found no difficulty in reconciling the doctrine with the setting up of an Ombudsman.

There are, in any event, answers to the Government's plea. Any Parliamentary Commissioner would be the servant of Parliament, and Parliament would decree what should be done on receipt of any report. The Parliamentary Commissioner's function would be performed privately—much as MPs now conduct their inquiries with ministries without the power to see documents. And no one suggests that the financial functions of the Comptroller and Auditor-General, who is an officer of Parliament, conflict with ministerial responsibility. Indeed, there are grounds for thinking that the doctrine of ministerial responsibility would be more effectively complied with if there were a Parliamentary Commissioner.

3. Concluding Comments

Two important points must be clarified, however, before there can be wholehearted acceptance of the Ombudsman in countries with a parliamentary system patterned on the British model. There are, first, some issues—such as the Vassall case or the Burgess-Maclean affair—that touch the heart of the political life of a country so closely that no government can abdicate to a single investigator, however impartial and trusted, its ultimate power to decide on political action. Parliament is the repository of governmental power and, so long as it commands a majority in Parliament, the Government must have the final say in major political issues. Part of the answer to this problem is that the Government would always retain the right to reject an Ombudsman's report, though of course it would have to surrender its secrets to him in the course of the inquiry. But the dilemma can best be resolved by leaving a discretion with the Ombudsman: it would be understood that on profound political issues he would investigate only at the instance of Parliament—after all he is removable by Parliament and therefore must, to some extent, do its bidding in taking up or declining to investigate a case. In any event, the number of cases which transcend the plane of individual grievance and provide an issue on which Governments can fall are likely to form a minimal part of the Ombudsman's work.

Secondly, if the Ombudsman is allowed to enter the most secret corners of government activity, his inquiries will always have to be conducted wholly in private, thereby depriving the citizen of one of democracy's great safeguards. But the secrecy then involved is not exclusively the Government's. It is shared with the public's watchdog. And he is the arbiter of how much 'secret' material is revealed in his reports. The Ombudsman would be in a position of access to the source material and would not be dependent on judging issues simply on what the disputants put before him. The recent inquiry by Lord Denning into the Profumo affair was a classic example of how an Ombudsman would work in practice. When Bentham declared that publicity is the very soul of justice he had in mind judicial proceedings, and could not have envisaged the kind of dispute which present administrative action throws up. Even now this safeguard of publicity is available only when a court or tribunal is hearing a dispute, or when a Government is prepared to set up a tribunal of inquiry. Those who want an Ombudsman—and, despite a certain disenchantment of late born out of over-familiarity with the institution, I am one of them—must be prepared to admit that this valuable safeguard has to operate within reasonable limits. But this restriction on publicity during the conduct of the inquiry is certainly worth while if through it we can obtain a perpetual public watchdog over the whole range of public administration.

THE IRRELEVANCE OF THE OMBUDSMAN PROPOSALS

by J. D. B. Mitchell*

Few would dispute that the expanded field of state activity has produced problems of control which have not yet found an adequate solution. Few would readily accept the implication in the Lord Chancellor's statement[1] (in which he announced the rejection by the British Government of the proposal for a Parliamentary Commissioner) that, with the addition of an appeal here or there in relation to discretionary decisions by Ministers, the United Kingdom would, administratively speaking, enjoy the best of possible worlds. On the other hand, few would deny that the Ombudsman institution has in its various forms achieved much good in those countries where it exists. It is also probable that some institution on those lines might, if it took root, do a certain amount of good in other countries such as the United Kingdom, though the qualification is important. Any argument is not therefore about the merits of a particular Ombudsman in a particular jurisdiction where he exists already, nor is it based upon a hypothesis that nothing is needed in the United Kingdom. The argument is about the problem to be attacked in each particular country, and whether the Ombudsman technique is the right method of attack in each country. The present essay is particularly concerned with the United Kingdom.

An element of particularity in the argument is at once apparent. The argument which follows therefore will not, essentially, be concerned with whether any other country would be right, or has been right, to adopt an Ombudsman or Parliamentary Commissioner. It will only be concerned with whether the United Kingdom would be right in so doing at this point of time, and without other substantial changes. This element of particularity is necessary for two reasons. First, the importance of the size of a country in relation to its constitutional arrangements is often under-emphasized. Denmark has a population of four and a half million and New Zealand about two and a quarter million, while Great Britain has close to fifty million. If with these figures are considered those of the density of population (and it is remembered that England has the highest density of population in Europe and that many of the problems of a modern state spring from industrialization and urbanization), it becomes clear that like is not being compared with like. In no other form of organization would these factors be overlooked. Organization is to a large extent a function of size and density of population. Even within the United Kingdom this is apparent; rules and institutions which work effectively in Scotland (a unit comparable in size to those where the Ombudsman

---

* Professor of Constitutional Law, University of Edinburgh.
[1] November 8, 1962, 503 *H.L. Deb.*, 384.

had his origin) could not work in England. The significance of the adoption of a Parliamentary Commissioner by New Zealand must be assessed against this background. New Zealand like Denmark is a community for which one such official (together with his necessary staff) will suffice. The United Kingdom is not, and the institution is to a high degree personal.

The second reason for insistence on particularity is similar. There may be universal ideals which underlie constitutions, but there have never yet been discovered methods of achieving or approximating to those ideals which are universally effective. Governmental machinery is the product of, and adjusts itself to, local circumstances. This consideration does not make the transplantation of governmental institutions an absolute impossibility, but it does make that process an uncertain one. The more an institution owes to the conditions and history of a certain country the less are the chances of successful transplantation. Even within Scandinavia transplantation has been accompanied by changes in the institution. What has to be considered is not merely the plant that is to be moved, but also the soil into which it is to be placed. The fact that there are peculiarly dominant institutions of a certain character in a country makes it especially difficult to introduce new and specialized institutions, which will, or may, conflict with the old. This difficulty is not so great if the institution is of a generalized type having its own strength. The Ombudsman is not of that latter category. Ministerial responsibility is of thefor mer, dominant and resistant, type.

This element of particularity in the argument must be insisted upon, for it would be presumptuous to write without many reservations about the remedies to be adopted to cure even a general malaise in systems with which one is not intimately familiar. Nevertheless it seems likely that much of what follows may be capable of adaptation to parliamentary systems of government which have been patterned after, and have substantial elements in common with, the system in the United Kingdom.

These introductory generalities are important. What is being sought is a solution for the problems of the modern state as they exist in eacn particular society. The problems in the United Kingdom go deeper than is suggested by concentration on the fact that individuals have grievances against the administration and feel hard done-by. Such a feeling of grievance will always exist so long as men are individualists yet live within a complex organization, with whose immediate and detailed aims they will inevitably be in conflict from time to time, and so long as that organization must itself be worked by fallible human beings. It is probably true that this feeling is increased by the human desire to have the best of all worlds. We desire a national health service, but not the regulations which must go with so complex an undertaking. We approve, in principle, of planning, though disapproving of plans which come too close to our doorsteps or our interest. A close reading of the relevant *certiorari* and similar cases emphasizes this. Even when allowance is made for the fact that the forms of action tend to emphasize procedure, it is clear that it is only in rare cases that the authority has erred in substance or in principle; it has erred in procedure, and the procedural error is seized upon. The substantive grievance which is felt by the individual is the fact of a compulsory purchase or demolition order, and that is met by a side wind, though had the substantive grievance itself been at issue the result might well have been different.

1. *Inadequacy of the Existing System*

These cases not only emphasize the point that the general acceptance of the welfare state is accompanied by a natural dislike of it, and all its works, when it impedes or adversely affects an individual; they also emphasize another. Procedural due process has its importance, but with us the fact that it is almost the whole of due process has warped our ideas of public law, and has obscured the real issue. The feeling of grievance, so far as it ever will be remediable, is largely due to the fact that we have not achieved the development of a proper system of public law. That failure has many causes. Among the immediate ones is this concentration by the courts on procedural matters. It enables courts to stay safely on the surface, avoiding issues of substance and policy. While procedural rectitude may be controlled, that control may be empty. Too much turns upon phraseology; granted the use of the right wording a decision may be unchallengeable.

It is by the modern rules extremely difficult and sometimes impossible to go behind the words and look at realities. Courts are left in the dark, and cannot themselves seek light.[2] These limitations are in part the result of procedural rules, and in part the result of a deference which courts, as at present composed, pay to representative bodies, whether local councils or Parliament. The doctrine of ministerial responsibility has played its part in limiting the control exercised by the courts. At its furthest extreme this deference can lead to questions of the definition of discretionary powers being exclusively left to Ministers subject to the control of Parliament.[3] Short of that extreme it is, from time to time, asserted that the Minister is answerable only to Parliament. Yet outside the courts it is a commonplace that this answerability is somewhat episodic in its incidence, and, when operative, is substantially affected by party discipline.[4] Thus, the effectiveness of judicial

[2] Consider *Iveagh v. Minister of Housing* [1961] 3 All E.R. 98 at 106–7.

[3] *Pollok School v. Glasgow Town Clerk* 1946 S.C. 373 at 386, and compare *R. v. Chandler* [1962] 2 All E.R. 314 at 320 with the more cautious words of Lord Reid in the same case *sub nom. Chandler* D.P.P. 1962 3 All E.R. 142 at 147. The line of argument in *Liversidge v. Anderson* [1942] A.C. 206 is familiar in this context.

[4] For a clear example see G. Marshall and Moodie, *Some Problems of the Constitution* (London, 1959), 104–5; and see Mitchell, 'The Flexible Constitution', *Public Law*, 1960, 332.

review is substantially limited by the particular operation of rules and by other more generalized concepts which are not always fully examined.

Outside the field of judicial review the state of public law is in no better state, and probably in a worse one. It is possible for a person to enter the public service under regulations which to a judge, at first sight, 'seem to . . . purport to lay down mutually binding terms of employment between the Crown and the employee, to which the assent of the employee has to be obtained'. Yet the employee finds that this apparently binding force is entirely illusory, though he, being less skilled than the judge, may well be forgiven for accepting them at their face value.[5] Again, acting on the assurance of an appropriate office that a particular piece of land had 'an existing use right as a builder's yard, and no planning permission is therefore necessary', an innocent citizen went ahead with his purchase and used the land as a builder's yard, for which alone he wanted it. When the local authority later decided that the existing use right did not exist and refused permission for such a use, the builder, reasonably, felt aggrieved, yet was entirely without remedy.[6] Clearly the defence of the planning mechanism required the authority to be able to act even against the earlier assertions of officials, but that necessity need not necessarily mean that the individual should be denied compensation. That denial entirely neglects the moral responsibilities which public authorities have. These moral responsibilities can never be translated into legal responsibilities without a specific system of public law.

2. Need for a Proper Administrative Court

Examples of this type could be multiplied. The law relating to the responsibility for the acts of the police is entirely obscure, and indeed is in a somewhat worse state than the law relating to Crown servants before the Crown Proceedings Act, 1947. The law in relation to employment in such bodies as the National Health Service takes no account of the service or *corps* element in such employment, nor of the near monopolistic position of the employer in many aspects of possible employment in such fields. We have neglected to notice that, just as the modern state stretches out into many more branches of life, so also it stretches out in ways which affect many more people. Clearly, for example, many more will find themselves in service or contractual relationships with public authorities. If those relationships are governed by existing rules developed from cases between private individuals, injustice is likely to result to one or other party, because the public service and other special characteristics of one side are neglected. Rules which are appropriate to the child who plays in my garden are not necessarily the appropriate ones to govern the situation of the child

---

[5] *Riordan v. The War Office* [1959] 3 All E.R. 552.

[6] *Southend-on-Sea Corporation v. Hodgson (Wickford) Ltd.* [1961] 2 All E.R. 46.

who plays in the public park provided by the community as a public service amenity. It is not only individuals who may suffer, it is also the community in the guise of the government. The American practice of re-negotiation of contracts was a public necessity to protect the government, and yet had itself to be regulated in order to afford a continuing protection to the individual against the abuse of necessary governmental rights. To the extent that the relationships here in question are governed by rules having a specific public law character, those rules tend to have been formulated in the light of the prerogatives regarding defence and the like, and to be too blunt instruments to do justice in other circumstances. The lingering life in England of the rules finally determined in *Duncan v. Cammell Laird*[7] makes that point with sufficient clarity. The rules admittedly work injustice, but they are modified not by law but by administrative declaration lacking binding force.

It must be emphasized that these matters are potentially even more serious than those commonly talked about in the context of grievances. They indicate a fundamental imbalance in the constitutional machinery. They involve injustices which cannot be properly redressed without the payment of compensation. Circumstances commonly arise, as has been indicated, in which the mere rectification of an administrative blunder is an entirely inadequate remedy. Meanwhile the citizen has suffered a loss which can only be remedied by a judgment. In effect therefore within the field where it now operates the law at present lacks effective means of doing all that it should. It must, because of the techniques and attitudes of the courts, stop at the threshold of the administration. Unless the techniques are altered, that must remain the position. At the present time the ordinary courts cannot, it seems, of their own motion adopt new techniques, particularly procedural ones. Nor can the courts evolve the necessary rules of law to contend with the increasing number of situations in which the individual is through contract or delict involved with public authorities in ways which are marked by the public character of these bodies.[8]

These things cannot be touched by an Ombudsman, at least by one of the Danish pattern. They can be done by a court properly composed. Such a court can, as has been abundantly emphasized by the *Conseil d'État* in France, create and enforce what M. Waline has called '*une moralité administrative*',[9] a morality which can go beyond the obligations of literal compliance with the law; such a court can, in effect, be a court of administrative equity, marked by suppleness which can achieve at the same time both the protection of the interests of the individual and

---

[7] [1942] A.C. 624. These rules do not apply in the same way in Scotland, yet government appears to survive north of the border.

[8] See *Western Heritable Investment Co. v. Glasgow Corporation*, 1956 S.C. (H.L.) 64.

[9] See his note to *Legros* C.E. 20 June 1952 in *R.D.P.*, 1953, p. 727.

those of the state. The state as such can act unhampered, but when its actions injuriously affect those with whom it has particular relationships it can no longer stand immune like the Gaulish warrior crying '*Vae Victis*'. Such a court can therefore do (and do cheaply) not merely all that an Ombudsman could do, it can do more. It can attack the essential problems of public law which are of growing importance but which the Ombudsman scheme, from its nature, is incapable of attacking. It must be noted that this alternative of a court akin to the *Conseil d'État* was in no way adequately considered in the report of 'Justice'.[10] It is an alternative which has other substantial advantages. In the first place the methods of the *Conseil d'État* are close to those of a common law court in its use of the system of precedent, though fortunately lacking undue rigidity. Where it gains is from the intimate knowledge its members have of the processes of administration, a knowledge not acquired as advocates for the administration. The lack of that knowledge is probably one of the matters which most hampers our own courts in their dealings with the administration. It gains too from procedural techniques, the absence of which impedes our courts even more. These considerations suggest that the creation of such a court, as distinct from the mere addition of jurisdiction to the ordinary courts, is required. Not merely must recruitment differ, but to establish new methods a break is needed, lest the weight of past tradition prove too heavy. The temptation is always to resort to the old even when the old is not appropriate.

What is required to attack the real problems of the modern administrative state, then, is the institution of a proper administrative jurisdiction analogous to the *Conseil d'État*. It is possible to avoid many of the jurisdictional conflicts with the ordinary courts that arise in France, though in the first instance it may be necessary for such a court to have a degree of separation. It is only in such circumstances that it is at all likely that the distinct rules both of procedure and of substance which are necessary are likely to emerge. The short history of the Restrictive Practices Court shows that there is a real possibility of that emergence granted the necessary separation. Such a court would have to be carefully composed, and some break with tradition may be required. Probably it would need, in the first instance, to be a multi-judge court, with some of its members drawn from the civil service, for an expertise in the working of the administrative machine would certainly be required if the mystique of that expertise is not to dominate, as it now does. Conceivably, too, an adaptation and expansion of the office of the Registrar of Restrictive Trading Agreements would also be desirable so that the office would approach that of *avocat-général*. Above all, such a court must have the standing of a superior court. It would not be an

---

[10] What was rejected by the Franks Committee was a general administrative appeal tribunal and not anything in truth akin to the *Conseil*. Therefore the foundation for sec. 13 of the 'Justice' report is lacking.

administrative tribunal in the current British sense of the term. In its operation it is probable that a considerable extension of the legal aid principle would be desirable. The long purse of the administration remains perhaps too significant a factor since, unlike so many litigants, the administration may not be so much interested in a decision as in the establishment of a principle, regardless of cost.

3. *Ineffectiveness of an Ombudsman*

Other considerations also urge such a court as a solution. One thing made clear by the Lord Chancellor's statement on the 'Justice' report, had it not already been made abundantly clear in all debates following the Franks report, is the near overwhelming weight of the belief in the efficiency of the doctrine of ministerial responsibility. Even the 'Justice' proposals were modified out of respect for that doctrine. Probably the only constitutional institution which can relieve the present situation is one which can stand against the pressures of that doctrine. These pressures can be overcome by a court, as the history of the Restrictive Practices Court demonstrates. It is unlikely that an Ombudsman could so overcome them. Analogies with the Comptroller and Auditor General are inexact. He does not deal with material of such current political significance as would an Ombudsman. He maintains moreover the careful air of being the servant of the Public Accounts Committee and, in form at least, it is their report which emerges. Since the public result of his activities comes so long after the occurrence of the events involved, even the simple element of time distinguishes his action from any possible actions of the Ombudsman.

The difficulty goes deeper. Suppose a complaint of maladministration arises, and the Ombudsman makes a recommendation. In such circumstances, if for reasons which seem good to the Minister he rejects the recommendation, the dice are loaded against the Minister. Yet the rejection may be as reasonable as the recommendation; the decision may simply turn upon the weight to be given to certain factors. Such a conflict of view is particularly likely if the Ombudsman is to work within the limits considered appropriate in the report of 'Justice'. If the Minister accepts the recommendation, there is in substance a transfer of responsibility which is inconsistent with the doctrine of ministerial responsibility. It must moreover be remembered that this doctrine is the necessary foundation for the essential party conflict. Thus the Ombudsman either forestalls and prevents parliamentary criticism or else provides the ammunition for political battles. There is already sufficient complaint in relation to the *sub judice* rule or in relation to the fact that the establishment of a Tribunal of Inquiry silences continued parliamentary probing of a suspected grievance, to indicate that an extension of such rules would be unwelcome to members. An Ombudsman would probably cause such an extension and might often rob an Opposition of the opportunity of pressing home its attacks at the

K *

critical moment. Again it must be noted that the circumstances in which the Comptroller and Auditor General operates are so different as to afford no precedent.

Thus the institution of an Ombudsman appears to fit so uneasily with the British doctrine of ministerial responsibility as to be irreconcilable with it; and since that doctrine is so deep rooted and dominant, over the years it would be the Ombudsman who would suffer.

There is, however, a deeper reason why the Ombudsman in the guise of a Parliamentary Commissioner is an inappropriate innovation. Complaint is constantly made of the pressures on parliamentary time. Such complaints certainly have substance. Yet it is proposed to add still one more official reporting to Parliament. By adopting proposals for such a court as has been suggested above, that difficulty is avoided, and something much more gained. As has already been suggested the distinction between a political and a justiciable issue has become blurred. The former is increasingly absorbing the latter, because methods of dealing with possible justiciable issues in the field of public law are lacking.[11] Yet what is required, if Parliament is to be saved from itself, is that the real issues of politics should be fought there without the interruption of matters which could best be dealt with elsewhere. No more than the report of an Ombudsman, can the answer to a parliamentary question give redress in the full sense discussed above. Such redress can only be found in a court. Moreover, the operation of the party system in Parliament at the moment may well create either a storm in a teacup (of which there have been examples in the last few years), or else the impression that something has been covered up. Neither is good for the general political life of the community, and neither helps to produce a sound administrative system. By reviving the place of the courts Parliament will be helped, not hindered, and benefits will flow to the citizens.

Without that revival, and with the institution of an Ombudsman, Parliament will in the long run be hindered by the reinforcement of the present over-insistence on parliamentary controls. Indeed, parliamentary methods make the successful institution of such an office uncertain. No party will be happy at being robbed at a critical stage of good political material through an investigation by a Parliamentary Commissioner. It may be no more pleased at the intervention of a court, but experience shows that the prestige of courts can enable them to survive this critical stage. It is only a court, which is a generalized institution with sufficient strength in itself, that can contend successfully with dominant local institutions and ideas. Thus it is a court, and not an Ombudsman, that has a reasonable chance of taking root.

[11] This can lead to a general restriction of the field of legality in public law. See the First Report of the Air Transport Licensing Board (1961), which discloses a disregard, with ministerial encouragement, of a statutory injunction to the Board.

Accepting then that all is not now well, and that complacent acceptance of existing institutions is unjustified, the choice appears to lie between an institution the successful establishment of which is hedged about with uncertainties, and which if established could not undertake the full tasks which are now required, and the establishment of a court which could do all that is required and which might the more easily and certainly be established. What is required is that the basic problems should be examined and that the possibilities of this reasonable alternative should be properly examined. Indeed, perhaps what is really required is that those who are concerned with the rule of law should look less at administrative palliatives and more at the traditional means by which the rule of law is established and is customarily enforced.

COMMONWEALTH CONSTITUTIONAL COMPLICATIONS
by *Albert S. Abel**

Like the Commonwealth itself, the constitutional foundations of the Commonwealth countries have an identity as incontrovertible as it is undefinable. At least that is true of the senior members and seems to be so generally, although the recent burgeoning necessitates a disclaimer of competence to speak for the whole lot. The pessimist may see both Commonwealth and constitutional premises going the way of the Cheshire cat. But certainly the political landscape will for a long time to come be dominated by the pervasive smile.

Just what constitutional assumptions characterize the governments of Commonwealth countries ? And how far are those assumptions congenial to the office of the Ombudsman ? These questions, it is submitted, are as relevant as any about the attractiveness of that office in the abstract. It is otiose to observe that the action of the bureaucracy falls short of perfection and the ways of improvement are to be commended when they are found. Of what human conduct is that not true ? It is pointless to examine the relative merits of Ombudsman and *Conseil d'État* if the political organism would reject either graft regardless of intrinsic soundness. A predilection for the *Conseil d'État* has not been able to stifle my grave doubt whether the alien career patterns of its members that really explain its success can catch on with us. Similarly, despite a genuine if slighter admiration for the Ombudsman on his native fiord, I think I see environmental differences such that transplantation of the office to the Commonwealth would require alterations either in it or in our basic constitutional notions.

Various lists of the distinctive elements common to the constitutions

* Professor of Law, University of Toronto.

of the Commonwealth can be plausibly urged. Making no pretence to be exhaustive or definitive, it is submitted that three grand concepts or catchphrases that would regularly appear are 'parliamentary supremacy', 'ministerial responsibility', and 'the rule of law'. Whatever their content, all three have a formal popular appeal which no innovation, however attractive, can successfully challenge. Yet it is hard to see how the Ombudsman can occasionally avoid challenging some and quite probably all of them, if he is to preserve the sturdy independence which has been his Scandinavian strength. His essential function, a roving commission to articulate authoritative judgments about frictions between the operating mechanisms of the state and individuals, runs afoul of basic pre-suppositions implicit in each of these constitutional axioms.

1. *Parliamentary Supremacy*

Once a directive is attributed to Parliament, the doctrine that emerged in Great Britain and which has been taken over in other Commonwealth countries (subject in federal systems to being *intra vires* whatever legislature, central or constituent, is involved) is that its command prevails and nothing else matters. Were the body politic a true body with every nerve end twitching in immediate sensitive response to the great legislative ganglion, Ombudsman and parliamentary supremacy might exist in perfect harmony, for by definition they could never work at cross purposes. But equally the bureaucracy would always be doing just what Parliament would have it do and there would be no occasion for the public to supervise it, except indirectly by supervising Parliament. The difficulty is in identifying Parliament's directive. No doubt a formal reconciliation of the Ombudsman and parliamentary supremacy could, and would, be formulated by making the Ombudsman's judgments yield to explicit parliamentary disavowal but, when they are not so disavowed, by supposing them to manifest and implement the legislative will. Although by such a process courts callous to consequences have insisted on an artificial construction and have thus ignobly foisted on the legislature the blame for particularly wooden decisions, the divinity which doth hedge about a judge likely will not accrue to the new-fangled Ombudsman, beyond perhaps a brief honeymoon period. It may be doubted that Parliament, people, or courts would respect a comparably cavalier attitude on his part as to what Parliament was being supreme about.

In practice, aside from the rare malversations in the nature of *détournements de pouvoir*, for which potential controls already exist, charges of administrative irregularity arise as to matters where the administrators profess to be complying with their legislative mandates. Much of the Ombudsman's work would be deciding to interpret Parliament's manifestations of will in a way other than the operating departments and officials had done. One may assume perhaps that the particular parliamentary majority instituting the office meant him to do so. But what of successor Parliaments which might be more concerned with effectuating substantive programmes ? They surely cannot be restrained from whittling down the Ombudsman's dominance. At the very least his status would need to be entrenched by some freeze clause like that in the Canadian Bill of Rights excluding any diminution of his powers by later legislation 'unless it is expressly declared by [the] Act'—and it has been questioned whether even by such procedural impediments a Parliament can hobble its successors.

I do not insist strongly, however, on the incompatibility of the Ombudsman with the dogma of parliamentary supremacy. While they seem not to be fully congenial, their opposition requires somewhat obscure and refined analysis for its discovery. It would in operation almost never come out in the open and can be plausibly verbalized away. It is thus pretty elusive; but that is not true when we turn to the other constitutional premises characteristic of the regimes of Commonwealth countries.

2. *The Rule of Law*

The notion of 'the rule of law' in its primitive Diceyan simplicity vanished even before its sponsor, as he himself recognized. Its current use in some quarters as a rhetorical shorthand for the reign of the 'good guys' has no pretence to Commonwealth constitutional standing. But there is woven into it a conviction as to the role and status of the courts. Whatever offence other emissaries of empire may have given, 'British justice' was generally admired and lingers as a residue throughout the Commonwealth—sometimes more obviously in its ceremonials than in any other way. True, there has been no theory of 'judicial supremacy' corresponding to that in the United States and indeed its rejection is a corollary of parliamentary supremacy. But there has been a popular acquiescence in the temperamental and intellectual qualifications of judges and in the fitness of their established procedures for selecting what claims by subjects deserve recognition and according that recognition by calling the favoured claims 'rights'.

The intricate array of prerogative writs with statutory supplementation, by means of which the courts call in question administrative action, has reserved to the courts an effective although clearly not an efficient control over administrative conduct. Attitudes throughout the Commonwealth are strongly conditioned in favour of this system of court control. Even the civil servants concur in, nay, actually revere judicial supervision of administrative performance, kissing the hand that smites them. If this supervision were regularly and fully exercised, any other, including that of an Ombudsman, would be almost redundant. But the fortuitous way cases get before courts makes its exercise highly irregular. Indeed the existing limitation of available judicial manpower really permits of nothing else.

It would be unthinkable under our constitutional assumptions that the Ombudsman's views would prevail against, granted that they might influence, those of judges, about the administrative behaviour they do examine. In case of a clash, he must expect to find himself simply another bureaucrat open to the same *certioraris* and declaratory orders as the functionaries over whom he rides herd. The judicial emasculation of the privative clauses solemnly pronounced by Parliament, which were designed to exclude the courts from the review of certain decisions, ought to be sufficient warning that this will be so.

But it seems to be contemplated that the primary activity of the Ombudsman will be in respect to matters never coming to court, either because they fall in areas where judges have indicated they do not wish to become involved or because the matters just happen not to be litigated. Here no overt clash with the judiciary would arise. In a country the size of a typical Commonwealth member could an Ombudsman feasibly fill the gaps arising from the randomness of judicial supervision? Supposing he could, his conclusions would perforce have an ambiguous status, since he could not hope they would be taken as authoritatively settling legal rights and duties, that being ultimately a judge's function. Moreover, he would need to be constantly circumspect to refrain from considering anything likely to attract the future attention of a court, at the risk of finding himself cut down to size. One remembers what happened to his precursor, the medieval Chancellor, when he also presumed as keeper of the King's conscience to undertake an active supervision. An Ombudsman shrunk down to an odd-jobs man doing a clean-up operation on administrative action or inaction too trivial or too sensitive for a court to review could peacefully co-exist with the courts. But one who gave signs of becoming truly effective in monitoring administration would, by threatening to challenge the judicial establishment as a power centre, run afoul of 'the rule of law'.

3. *Ministerial Responsibility*

The constitutional postulate of 'ministerial responsibility' is the greatest stumbling block. With it the Ombudsman in anything like his classical form seems to be in grave and necessary conflict.

To whom if anybody a Minister is responsible is not clear. What he is responsible for is the administrative performance of the department entrusted to him and the acts and omissions of all its personnel in that context. The King can do no wrong only on condition that the Minister does every wrong, answering for all maladministration within the ambit of his authority. The Ombudsman would partially relieve him from this onerous liability by ascribing fault to the individual at fault—a fair-seeming proposition but one which could occasion changes of unforeseeable consequences in the internal climate of departments and thereby in cabinet government generally. Aside from the confusion sometimes present as to the extent and nature of the Minister's personal involvement in subordinates' projects, the major flaw might often be the structural arrangements for delegation and communication within a department—and how shall responsibility for hidden defects there be assigned? Operations of central budgetary and personnel authorities have been criticized as intrusions on the particular responsibility of operating departments. Interventions of an Ombudsman censuring things done or left undone would almost certainly be deemed aggravated assaults.

Neither the Franks Committee nor the 'Justice' report ventured to propose arrangements which would trench on ministerial responsibility, the latter even explicitly recognizing that the Ombudsman model would have to be modified *pro tanto*. It resolves nothing to define that responsibility as relating mainly to policy formation, for policy is characteristically formed by a course of conduct, by the ongoing flow of departmental performance. Solemn formal declarations are more obviously but no more essentially policy forming than are routine disposition. Their total impact may even be slighter. The Minister may indeed be jollied into tolerating Ombudsman castigation of his personnel but with serious risk of harm to the institutional web of delegation, communication and confidence without which no department can do its job. Perhaps an independent auditor of line performance to advise 'management', i.e. the Minister, of the adequacy of the system of internal controls might have his place. But that is not, as I understand it, the primary role of the Ombudsman; he will do his job only by adducing instances where the Minister has not done his, under the orthodox theory regarding ministerial responsibility.

The Opposition, moreover, would almost certainly have fewer occasions for initiative. It is sometimes overlooked that a visible Opposition is as integral a part of a functioning Parliamentary system as is a Government. The contemporary view of the primary mission of a legislature as being the ventilation of information and opinion on issues of public concern implies an effective Opposition with a significant function. This implication seems to be confirmed in federal countries of the Commonwealth by the legislatures of some states and provinces where the pitiful Opposition representation, a symptom of public apathy, indicates that the parliamentary system has partly failed. The danger of debilitation of the Opposition is thus a further aspect of inconsistency between the Ombudsman and the organic devices of parliamentary government.

4. *Concluding Comments*

It is no part of my present task to examine how far the constitutional principles specified are valid or realistic. Reassessment or even repudiation of their current relevance may be in order. Each has been questioned by sophisticated critics. Nevertheless they remain at the least vulgar traditions of the constitution and so part of the cultural environment

to which governmental institutions must adapt. It has been my submission that the Ombudsman necessarily affronts each of the three
traditional doctrines with various directness. That confrontation might
hasten re-examination of the tradition and formal abandonment of any
parts found obsolete. But alternatively it might lead to curtailment of
the Ombudsman's functions so that we would have adopted the name
but not the substance, adding a complication of occasional usefulness
but of no great moment to machinery already sufficiently complex.
It seems to me that Ombudsmanship, while clearly now in fashion, is
for the reasons suggested not in the Commonwealth style and that
eventually style moulds fashion, not vice versa. It will be interesting
to observe developments in New Zealand, in many ways the ideal locale
in the Commonwealth for the experiment.

Finally, to turn from observations relevant throughout the Commonwealth, a very considerable number though not all its members share
a structural attribute which could embarrass the working of the
Ombudsman device. They are federal, and therefore operate under
written constitutional instruments allocating competence between the
centre and the provinces, states or regions. There is special difficulty in
accommodating the Ombudsman to a federal arrangement. I am not
now thinking of the problems of scale involved in geographical and
demographical extensions beyond anything with which the Ombudsman
has yet had to cope. The gravity of that problem I by no means discount.
But it has a bearing on the national governments only and it is equally
a problem for unitary systems such as the United Kingdom or Ceylon.
The constituent units of the federations are by and large comparable
in size to the Scandinavian countries so the scale objection would not
apply to state or provincial Ombudsmen. My point is that either level
of government in a federal system must, as to legislation and all official
action claiming legislative warrant, stay within the range of concern
assigned it by the constitution. The obvious immediate consequence
is that claims of administrative misbehaviour which on investigation
turned out to be challenges of constitutional *vires* would be out of
bounds to an Ombudsman. Presumably he would, when that situation
developed, drop the matter and leave it for the ordinary judicial process,
but the lurking taboo on his powers seems bound to give rise to
frictions and frustrations in the course of their use. Conversely, should
he decide to entertain a claim, the *ultra vires* challenge might question
whether the subject's rights claimed to have been infringed or the
remedial measures proposed were properly within the constitutional
sphere of his level of government. These are at bottom situations where
federalism heightens the conflict between the Ombudsman and 'the
rule of law'.

Another difficulty arises where the two levels of government are
collaborating to achieve programme integration through reciprocally
responsive legislation arranging for conjoint or concurrent use of

administrative personnel. Disentangling the sometimes fantastically elaborate interpenetration of each level would baffle the intellectual, and occasionally exceed the legal, powers of an Ombudsman, thus frustrating his effectiveness in an increasingly significant range of matters.

With so much in the Commonwealth constitutional background at odds with the office, it would be a miracle were the Ombudsman to achieve anything like his Continental stature. An Ombudsmanikin, avoiding constitutional collisions by discreet self-limitation on what he undertakes, is not precluded. But for my part, I would not settle for such a modest gain. Instead I favour a fundamental examination of the competing claims of effective government and the rights of the subject, and the devising of a system of administrative supervision that will achieve an optimum balance between them in the specific context of our constitutional assumptions. The second-hand solution, though of admirable cloth and cut, does not comfortably fit our frame.

CONCLUSION

As the evidence presented in this book shows, the Nordic countries and New Zealand are confident that they have developed a worthwhile institution. To other democratic countries of the world considering the desirability of its adoption, the important questions are these: Is it really needed here? How serious are the objections that may be raised against its adoption? Could the institution be adjusted to fit our circumstances and, if so, what adjustments would be needed? The answers to these questions will of course vary somewhat from one country to another according to the type of constitutional and legal system that each possesses. One cannot hope to consider the detailed answers that would have to be developed for each country in turn. This is a job for those who have an intimate knowledge of the inner workings of their own particular political system. However, the countries of the western world, upon which most other democracies have based their institutions, can be divided into three types of constitutional and legal systems, each of which has important characteristics in common. And in trying to answer the above questions, general statements can be made about each type.

First are the countries of western Europe that have a highly developed system of administrative courts, such as France, Italy, Germany and Austria. A common initial reaction of persons from these countries to the Ombudsman scheme, as Mme Questiaux's essay reveals, is to say that it is not needed because administrative courts do the job instead, and, anyway, it could not be fitted into the administrative court system. The reply of Judge Holmgren and Miss Pedersen, however, is that the job of administrative courts is not the same as that of the Ombudsman. He relies upon criticism and publicity rather than the quashing of decisions, and is an agent of Parliament rather than of the executive. Moreover, administrative courts suffer—though admittedly to a lesser extent—from the same shortcomings as ordinary courts in that they can be slow, costly, cumbersome, complex, frightening to the average citizen, and limited in their power to review the merits of decisions. Probably out of modesty, Mme Questiaux did not mention that France has the best system of administrative courts in western Europe. It cannot be taken as typical. In some other European countries the administrative courts are weak, seriously limited in their powers, and subject to the influence of the executive. Judge Holmgren is firm in his conclusion that the parallel existence of a Supreme Administrative Court and an Ombudsman in Sweden does not constitute an unnecessary overlapping or duplication of functions. As to how an

Ombudsman scheme could be fitted into an existing system of administrative courts, the two are so different in function that the former need not be conceived of as an alternative to, or even as part of, the administrative courts. It would be an *additional*, separate institution fulfilling a different need. If it is regarded in this light, many of Mme Questiaux's objections become irrelevant.

Turning now to countries that have inherited the common law and have no system of administrative courts, there is an important distinction between the many that have copied the British cabinet system of government, with a union of executive and legislative powers, and those, like the United States and the Philippines, that have adopted a separation of powers. Regarding the latter countries, the deficiencies in their present legal systems seem to be much the same as in other common-law countries, and speak in favour of an Ombudsman scheme. However, because of the separation of powers and the traditional struggle between the executive and the legislature, it may be objected that an Ombudsman would be regarded with suspicion by the executive departments as a biased agent of Congress. The executive has control over administrative documents and might not be prepared to give him sufficient access to information. Because of the highly politicized nature of the presidency and of the top administrative posts, an Ombudsman would be likely to be caught up in partisan politics. And because of the highly decentralized nature of the political system, pressure groups are strong, and he might be swayed by them in his decisions. It is also said that the separation of powers enhances the role of the Congressman as an agent of his constituents and that an Ombudsman might undesirably reduce the importance of this role. How valid these objections are I am not in a position to say with assurance. But it is significant that several of the authors in this book and an increasing number of knowledgeable persons in the United States have come to doubt their validity and are willing to experiment with the Ombudsman institution at either the federal, state or local levels of government.

Many of the problems raised by the separation of powers might be overcome by creating a plural Ombudsman—a Complaints Commission, whose members would be appointed jointly by the executive and Congress. This could perhaps be a body of three, with one member appointed by the President, one by the Senate and one by the House of Representatives. The experiences of the French *Conseil d'État* and of the Presidential Complaints Committee in the Philippines attest to the fact that such a body need not be exclusively an agent of the legislature as long as it is made sufficiently independent. For its effectiveness would lie not so much in its direct relationship to the legislature as in its easy accessibility to the citizens, its power to investigate, the reasonableness of its opinions on cases, and its ability to bring them to the attention of the public.

Whatever may be the need for Ombudsmen in the United States, it is in the Commonwealth countries that the need is greatest. These countries are steeped in the monarchical tradition and its undesirable implications for bureaucracy. They have not yet succeeded in throwing off the old legal theory that civil servants are servants of the King rather than of the public, that the King can do no wrong and that, by the process of what one might call 'virtue by association', civil servants can never—well, hardly ever—do wrong. Formerly officials acted on behalf of the King, and the old hierarchical myth would even have us believe that when they acted it was really the King who was acting. Hence they had to remain anonymous and their actions secret. These ideas are obviously out of tune with modern democratic government, and we must ask ourselves whether the reasons we now give to defend anonymity and secrecy are not mere rationalizations, whether in reality these characteristics of bureaucracy in the Commonwealth are not preserved mainly for the convenience of the Government in power. For they place serious difficulties in the way of the public's legitimate access to information, its 'right to know', in a democracy.

Clearly, the royal tradition has carried with it legal assumptions about the 'rightness' of executive action and the superiority of the state that have made it difficult for the citizens to secure legitimate redress. Until recent years in Commonwealth countries one could not sue a government agency without the Crown's permission and damages were paid by the Crown only as an act of grace. Even yet in most of these countries the courts are powerless to order the production of official documents because of the doctrine of Crown privilege, and procedures for the Crown's expropriation of private property are often arbitrary. It has been possible for undesirable aspects of executive power such as these to be preserved because Parliament only gradually came to control the executive and because the executive still introduces most of the laws and through its majority still manages to dominate Parliament. Governments have been quite willing to preserve and use prerogative powers that they find convenient and to grant themselves or their agents extensive delegated powers. The previous strength of the royal power has also led the courts to inherit a tradition of no fetters on executive discretion and of reticence about reviewing administrative action. This tradition has been preserved in recent times by the convenient assumption that it is the job of Parliament to control the administration and that therefore any complaint about administrative action, other than its clear illegality, should be left for Parliament to deal with. The courts have only hesitantly entered the arena by marking out a vague area of so-called 'judicial or quasi-judicial' administrative action for review, and the legal procedures used for bringing administrative cases before the courts are hoplessly archaic and complex in most Commonwealth countries. Because of Parliament's inability to cope with the situation, our naïve faith in the doctrine of ministerial responsibility has often resulted in something dangerously close to administrative irresponsibility. An Ombudsman scheme would therefore be a healthy step in the direction of a better balance between the rights of the citizen and the power of the Crown.

Professor Abel has pointed to a number of the common characteristics of the Commonwealth parliamentary systems with which an Ombudsman would have to make his peace. Though these may mean that the Ombudsman scheme would work somewhat differently, it is doubtful whether they can be counted as objections weighty enough to warrant pronouncing judgment against its introduction. Federal systems such as those in India, Canada and Australia would of course require Ombudsmen at both levels of government, and the size and population of some countries might call for a collegial body, a Complaints Commission, as I have dubbed it. Otherwise, as New Zealand's experience to date demonstrates, an Ombudsman can be fitted into the Commonwealth parliamentary system with only minor adjustments, and even some of these, designed to assuage the sensitivity of Ministers, were not necessary. We should hold out strongly against irrelevant arguments about the Ombudsman's supposed interference with ministerial responsibility, for they are likely to result in an undesirable limitation upon his power to investigate and criticize.

More relevant than Professor Abel's objections, it seems to me, is Professor Mitchell's complaint that an Ombudsman would not be enough. Certainly the scheme can be no panacea for curing all bureaucratic ills, nor can it even claim to solve completely the difficult problems of preventing executive arbitrariness and securing redress in the modern democratic state. Many accompanying reforms are needed. Administrative procedures themselves must be improved, parliamentary control must be strengthened, free legal aid must be made more widely available, review by the courts must be simplified and perhaps extended, and much wider opportunities must be provided for appealing administrative decisions. In common-law countries one is tempted to take the view, as does Professor Mitchell, that drastic reform in the direction of the European administrative courts is required. But one need not therefore conclude that the Ombudsman scheme is undesirable because it is only a poor substitute for administrative courts. As I have already suggested, the two may be regarded as half-loaves that together make up a whole.

Unfortunately, many of the reforms that are needed are in the complex realm of administrative and legal procedure and are not easily understood by the public. Hence pressure upon Governments for reform tends to be weak. Yet Governments are not prone to proposing on their own volition measures that limit their own executive powers. One of the great virtues of the Ombudsman idea is that its simplicity gives it tremendous popular appeal. The public enthusiasm engendered by discussing it is likely to overflow into support for other desirable reforms in more legally technical areas.

When one looks comparatively at democratic systems in the modern world one finds a surprising degree of uniformity in their basic governmental machinery and institutions—the secret ballot, the representative assembly, the responsible and/or elected executive, the independent courts, the legislative financial auditor, the public corporation, etc. Machinery that has proved its worth in one country has been gradually adopted in the others. Yet in the modern history of democratic government the invention of new institutional devices has been rare. The public corporation is one of the few that might be said to fall in this category. It is true that technically the Ombudsman system cannot be described as a new invention for it was created in 1809. But as the essay by Mr Bexelius shows, its transformation in recent times into an institution whose primary function is to supervise the administration, and its use exclusively for this purpose in Denmark, Norway and New Zealand, has given it a new dimension and character.

Hence, the Ombudsman should be regarded as an important new addition to the armoury of democratic government. Like the legislative auditor, he enhances the control and prestige of legislatures in a world in which executive power is growing. Indeed, now that New Zealand has paved the way by demonstrating that this Scandinavian scheme can be successfully exported to other countries, one may venture to predict that the Ombudsman institution or its equivalent will become a standard part of the machinery of government throughout the democratic world.

APPENDIX

BIBLIOGRAPHY

BOOKS

CHAPMAN, B., *The Profession of Government: The Public Service in Europe* (London: Allen & Unwin, 1959), Chapter 12.

Inter-Parliamentary Union, *Parliaments* (London: Cassell, 1962), 275–277.

Justice (British Section of the International Commission of Jurists), *The Citizen and the Administration: the Redress of Grievances—a Report* (London: Stevens, 1961), pp. xv, 104; also known as the *Whyatt Report* (Director of Research: Sir John Whyatt). Reviewed in: 5 *Can. Pub. Admin.*, 502; 201 *The Economist*, 413; 4 *Jour. of the I.C. of J.*, 150; 4 *The Lawyer*, 29; 25 *Mod. Law Rev.*, 220; 33 *Pol. Quar.*, 9; 40 *Pub. Admin.*, 125; *Pub. Law* (1961), 1–51, 291.

ROBSON, WILLIAM A., *The Governors and the Governed* (Baton Rouge: Louisiana State Univ. Press, 1964), 22–34.

STRAUSS, ERICH, *The Ruling Servants* (London: Allen & Unwin, 1961), 288–289.

UTLEY, T. E., *Occasion for Ombudsman* (London: C. Johnson, 1961), pp. 160.

ARTICLES AND DOCUMENTS

ABEL, A. S., 'In Search of a Basic Policy', 5 *Canadian Public Administration* (1962), 68–69.

ABRAHAM, H. J., 'People's Watchdog Against Abuse of Power', 20 *Public Administration Review* (1960), 152–157.

ABRAHAMSON, M. W., 'The Grievance Man: In Ireland ?', 8 *Administration* (Dublin, 1960), 238–242.

AGARWAL, J. P., 'Procuratorship', 3 *Journal of the Indian Law Institute* (1961), 71–86.

AIKMAN, C. C., 'The New Zealand Ombudsman', XLII *Canadian Bar Review* (September, 1964), 399–432. (Reprints the New Zealand Act in an Appendix.)

ANDERMAN, S. D., 'The Swedish Justitieombudsman', 11 *American Journal of Comparative Law* (1962), 225–238.

ANDERSON, S. V., 'The Scandinavian Ombudsman', 12 *American-Scandinavian Review* (December 1964), 403–409.

ANDRÉN, NILS, 'The Swedish Office of "Ombudsman"', 33 *Municipal Review* (1962), 820–821.

ANDRÉN, NILS, 'The Swedish Ombudsman', *Anglo-Swedish Review* (London, 1962), 97–103.

BEXELIUS, ALFRED, 'The Swedish Institution of the Justitieombudsman', 27 *International Review of Administrative Sciences* (1961), 243–256; reprinted in 9 *Administration* (Dublin, 1961–1962), 272–290. (Author is Swedish Ombudsman for Civil Affairs.)

BEXELIUS, ALFRED, *The Swedish 'Ombudsman', Special Parliamentary Commissioner for the Judiciary and the Civil Administration 1810–1860* (Stockholm: Royal Ministry for Foreign Affairs, 1961), pp. 34 mimeo.

BLOM-COOPER, L. J., 'An Ombudsman in Britain?', *Public Law* (1960), 145–151.

BLOM-COOPER, L. J., two articles on the Ombudsman in *The Observer* (London, May 31 and June 7, 1959).

BOLANG, C. O., 'But the Ombudsman Thought Otherwise', 57 *American-Swedish Monthly* (1963), 22–24.

CAIDEN, NAOMI, 'An Ombudsman for Australia?' XXIII, *Public Administration* (Australia, June, 1964) 97–116.

Canada, House of Commons, Standing Committee on Privileges and Elections, *Minutes of Proceedings and Evidence*, Nos. 6 and 7 (September 1, 2 and October 1, 1964) on Bill C-7, with Sir Guy Powles and D. C. Rowat as witnesses, 351–467 and 467–513 (Ottawa: Queen's Printer, 1964). No. 6 reprints Sir Guy's annual report for 1963-64, and No. 7 reprints Rowat's article from the *Canadian Journal* and his paper to the American Sociological Association.

CAPELL, LADY IRIS, *The Aggrieved Citizen* (London: The Liberal Publication Department. One of the series: Unservile State Papers), n.d.

CHAPMAN, B., 'The Ombudsman', 38 *Public Administration* (London, 1960), 303–310.

CHRISTENSEN, B., 'The Danish Ombudsman', 109 *University of Pennsylvania Law Review* (1961), 1100–1126 (one of three articles).

'A Council of State for Britain', *The Economist* (August 15, 1964), 623–625.

DAVIS, A. G., 'The Ombudsman in New Zealand', 4 *Journal of the International Commission of Jurists* (1962, 1963), 51–62, 316–322.

DAVIS, K. C., 'Ombudsmen in America', 109 *University of Pennsylvania Law Review* (1961), 1057–1076; excerpted in *Public Law* (1962), 34–42.

EEK, H., 'Protection of News Sources by the Constitution', 5 *Scandinavian Studies in Law* (Stockholm, 1961), 9.

FARLEY, M. C., and FARLEY, 'An American Ombudsman: Due Process in the Administrative State', 16 *Administrative Law Review* (Summer 1964), 212–221.

GELLHORN, WALTER, 'Administrative Procedure Reform: Hardy Perennial', 48 *American Bar Association Journal* (1962), 243–251.

'Germany's Army: Private Verdict', *The Economist* (June 27, 1964), 1466.

GILBERTSON, FORBES, 'Will The Ombudsman Come to Canada ?', *Canadian Business* (July 1964), 29–39.

HANAN, J. R., 'How to be an Ombudsman', 92 *Manchester Guardian Weekly* (January 7, 1965), 15. (Author is New Zealand's Minister of Justice.)

HENKOW, H., *Memorandum on the Institution of the Swedish Procurator of Military Affairs (MO)* (Stockholm, 1959), pp. 18 mimeo. (Author is Swedish Ombudsman for Military Affairs.)

HOLLAND, D. C., 'A British Ombudsman', 1 *Solicitor Quarterly* (1962), 147–158.

HUNTER, A. A. DE C., 'Ombudsman for Britain ?', 4 *Journal of the International Commission of Jurists* (1962), 150–159.

HURWITZ, S., 'Control of the Administration in Denmark: the Danish Parliamentary Commissioner for Civil and Military Government Administration', 1 *Journal of the International Commission of Jurists* (1958), 224–243; also printed in *Public Law* (1958), 236–245. (Author is Danish Ombudsman.)

HURWITZ, S., 'The Danish Ombudsman and his Office', 63 *The Listener* (1960), 835–838 (transcript of a BBC interview).

HURWITZ, S., 'Denmark's Ombudsman: The Parliamentary Commissioner for Civil and Military Government Administration', *Wisconsin Law Review* (1961), 170–199.

HURWITZ, S., 'The Experience of Parliamentary Commissioners in Certain Scandinavian Countries', background paper for the U.N. Seminar on Judicial and Other Remedies Against the Illegal Exercise or Abuse of Administrative Authority (New York: Doc. T E 326/1 (40–7), United Nations, 1959), pp. 28 mimeo.

HURWITZ, S., 'The Folketingets Ombudsman', 12 *Parliamentary Affairs* (1959), 199–208.

HURWITZ, S., *The Ombudsman* (Copenhagen: Det Danske Selskab, 1961), pp. 63.

HURWITZ, S., 'Public Trust in Government Services', 20 *Danish Foreign Office Journal* (1956), 11–15.

HURWITZ, S., 'The Scandinavian Ombudsman', 12 *Political Science* (New Zealand, 1960), 121–142. (A reprint of his 1959 U.N. background paper.)

JÄGERSKIÖLD, S., 'The Swedish Ombudsman', 109 *University of Pennsylvania Law Review* (1961), 1077–1099.

Justice (British Section of the International Commission of Jurists), 'Memorandum on the Whyatt Report' (London, 1962), pp. 4 mimeo.

KASTARI, P., 'The Constitutional Protection of Fundamental Rights in Finland', 34 *Tulane Law Review* (1960), 695–710. (Author was Finnish Ombudsman.)

KENT, GEORGE, 'Watchdog for the Common Man', *Rotarian* (July 1963); condensed in *Reader's Digest* (August 1963), 82–85.

KERSELL, J. E., 'Parliamentary Ventilation of Grievances Arising Out of the Operation of Delegated Legislation', *Public Law* (1959), 152–168.

KJELLIN, BJÖRN (ed.), working paper on Sweden prepared for U.N. Seminar on Judicial and Other Remedies Against Abuse of Administrative Authority (New York: Doc. 62–03518, United Nations, 1962), pp. 40 plus 23, mimeo.

LAWFORD, H. J., 'The Function of Judicial Review', 5 *Canadian Public Administration* (1962), at 52–54.

LAWSON, F. H., 'An Inspector-General of Administration', *Public Law* (1957), 92–95.

LEFOLII, KEN, 'What the Right Ombudsman Would Do for Canada', 77, 8 *Maclean's* (Toronto, April 18, 1964), 6.

LLAMBIAS, H. J., 'The Need for an Ombudsman System in Canada', (M.A. Thesis, Carleton University, Ottawa, 1964), pp. 121.

LLAMBIAS, H. J., 'Wanted—An Ombudsman in Canada', 2 *Edge* (Edmonton, Spring 1964), 81–91.

MARSHALL, GEOFFREY, 'A Critique of the Ombudsman Report', 4 *The Lawyer* (London, 1961), 29–32.

MARSHALL, GEOFFREY, 'Should Britain Have an Ombudsman?', *The Times* (London, April 23, 1963), 13.

MARSHALL, GEOFFREY, 'The New Zealand Parliamentary Commissioner (Ombudsman) Act, 1962', *Public Law* (1963), 20–22.

MCKEOWN, ROBERT, 'Why Canada Needs an Ombudsman', 14, 2 *Weekend Magazine*, 2–3, 24.

MEYER, P., 'The Administrative Aspects of the Constitutions of the Northern Countries', 41 *Nordisk Administrativt Tiddskrift* (Köbenhavn, 1960), 254–265.

MEYER, P., 'The Development of Public Administration in the Scandinavian Countries Since 1945', 26 *International Review of Administrative Sciences* (1960), 135–146.

MIDDLETON, K. W. B., 'The Ombudsman', 5 *Juridical Review* (Edinburgh, 1960), 298–306.

MITCHELL, J. D. B., 'The Ombudsman Fallacy', *Public Law* (1962), 24–33 (one of four articles, with comment by the editor).

MITRANY, DAVID, two articles on the Ombudsman in *The Guardian* (Manchester, August 6 and 7), 1957.

MONTEIRO, J. B., 'The Ombudsman and Its Relevance to India', 111 *Modern Review* (1962), 326–328, 406–411.

MUNDELL, D. W., 'Ombudsman for Canada?', 7 *Canadian Bar Journal* (June, 1964), 179–209.

MURRAY, C. H., 'The Grievance Man: In Scandinavia', 8 *Administration* (1960), 231–237.

NADER, RALPH, 'An Answer to Administrative Abuse', *Harvard Law Record* (December 20, 1962), 13, 15.

NADER, RALPH, 'An Ombudsman for the U.S.?', *Christian Science Monitor* (April 1, 1963), 20.

New Zealand, *Report of the Ombudsman for the Six Months Ended 31 March 1963; and for the Year Ended 31 March 1964* (Wellington: Government Printer, 1963; and 1964).

NORTHEY, J. F., 'A New Zealand Ombudsman?', *Public Law* (1962), 43–51.

'Ombudsman at Work', *The Economist* (London, June 23, 1962), 1222.

'Ombudsmanship', 201 *The Economist* (London, November 4, 1961), 413–414. (On the Whyatt Report.)

OS, AUDVAR, 'Administrative Procedure in Norway', 25 *International Review of Administrative Sciences* (1959), 67–78.

OS, AUDVAR, *The Ombudsman in Norway* (Royal Norwegian Ministry of Justice, No. 71, 1963), pp. 21 mimeo. (A reproduction of the first draft of his essay for this book.)

OS, AUDVAR, working paper on Norway prepared for U.N. Seminar on Judicial and Other Remedies Against the Abuse of Administrative Authority (New York: Doc. SO. 216/3(3) EUR 1962, United Nations, 1962), pp. 19 mimeo.

PATTERSON, A. D., 'The Ombudsman', 1 *U.B.C. Law Review* (April 1963), 777–781.

PEAR, R. H., review of Utley's *Occasion for Ombudsman*, *Public Law* (1962), 123–124.

PEDERSEN, I. M., 'The Danish Parliamentary Commissioner in Action', *Public Law* (1959), 115–127; extracted in Utley, *Occasion for Ombudsman*, 145–160.

PEDERSEN, I. M., 'The Parliamentary Commissioner: A Danish View', *Public Law* (1962), 15–23.

Philadelphia, Mayor's Ad Hoc Committee on Improvement in Municipal Standards and Practices, *Final Report* (1962), Title VIII, 'The Continuing Watchdog Function'.

POWERS, M. R., 'An Ombudsman in New York?' 27 *Albany Law Review* (1963), 84–96. (Reprints Danish Act.)

POWLES, SIR GUY, 'The Citizen's Rights Against the Modern State', 23 *Public Administration* (Australia, 1964), 42–68; reprinted in 13 *International and Comparative Law Quarterly* (July 1964), 761–797. (Author is New Zealand's Ombudsman.)

POWLES, SIR GUY, 'Common Justice', *The Guardian* (May 14, 1964), 10.

PURCHASE, C. E., 'The Parliamentary Commissioner for Investigations', 38 *New Zealand Law Journal* (1962), 321–324, 374–377; see also earlier editorials in 37 (1961), 273–274, 289–291.

RAJASTHAN, *Report of the Administrative Reforms Committee* (Jaipur: Government of Rajasthan, 1963), pp. 235.

REUSS, H. S., 'An "Ombudsman" for America', *New York Times Magazine* (September 13, 1964), 30, 134–135.

RIDLEY, F., 'The Parliamentary Commissioner for Military Affairs in the Federal Republic of Germany', 12 *Political Studies* (1964), 1–20.

ROSENTHAL, A. H., 'The Ombudsman—Swedish "Grievance Man"', 24 *Public Administration Review* (December 1964), 226–229.

ROWAT, D. C., 'Finland's Defenders of the Law', 4 *Canadian Public Administration* (1961), 316–325, 412–415.

ROWAT, D. C., 'How an Aging Admiral Inspired West Germany's Latest Army Scandal', 77, 16 *Maclean's* (Toronto, August 22, 1964), 4.

ROWAT, D. C., 'An Ombudsman Scheme for Canada', 28 *Canadian Journal of Economics and Political Science* (1962), 543–546; reprinted in 30 *Ontario Medical Review* (1963), 213–217, 222 and in Canada, House of Commons, Standing Committee on Privileges and Elections, *Minutes of Proceedings and Evidence*, No. 7 (1964); extracted in 34 *Current* (New York, 1963), 60–64; shortened and revised as 'The Parliamentary Ombudsman: Should the Scandinavian Scheme be Transplanted ?', 28 *International Review of Administrative Sciences* (1962), 399–405; revision reprinted in Macridis, Roy C., and Brown (eds.), *Comparative Politics* (Homewood: Dorsey Press, rev. 1964), 470–479.

ROWAT, D. C., 'The Relevance of the Ombudsman System to the United States and Canada', a paper presented to the annual meeting of the American Sociological Association, September 3, 1964, pp. 18 mimeo; printed in Canada, House of Commons, Standing Committee on Privileges and Elections, *Minutes of Proceedings and Evidence*, No. 7 (1964); revised and condensed as 'Ombudsmen for North America', 24 *Public Administration Review* (December 1964), 230–233.

ROWAT, D. C., 'We Need a New Defense Against So-Called Justice', 74, 1 *Maclean's* (January 7, 1961), 10, 82–83.

SANDERS, MARION K., 'Sweden's Remedy for "Police Brutality"', 229 *Harper's Magazine* (1964), 132–136.

SAWER, GEOFFREY, *Ombudsmen* (Melbourne: Melbourne University Press, 1964), pp. 42.

SHEPPARD, C.-A., 'An Ombudsman for Canada', 10 *McGill Law Journal*, (4, 1964), 291–340.

SIPPONEN, K., Working Paper No. 5 (on Finland) for the United Nations Seminar on Judicial and Other Remedies Against the Abuse of Administrative Authority (New York: Doc SO 216/3(3) EUR 1962, United Nations, 1962), pp. 20 mimeo.

SMITH, AUSTIN, 'What This Country Needs Is An Ombudsman', 15 *Association Management* (1963), 40–42.

SMITH, S. A. DE, 'Anglo-Saxon Ombudsman ?', 33 *Political Quarterly* (1962), 9–19 (on the Whyatt Report).

THORBURN, H. G., 'Ombudsman for Canada ?', 40 *Canadian Forum* (1960), 53.

THORSON, K., 'What About an Ombudsman ?', 28 *Saskatchewan Bar Review* (December, 1963), 169.

Thought (Delhi) 13 (1961) discusses the Ombudsman for India, 2.

United Nations, *1962 Seminar on Judicial and Other Remedies Against the Abuse of Administrative Authority* (New York: U.N., Doc. ST/TAO/HR15, 1962), pp. 34.

United Nations, *Remedies Against the Abuse of Administrative Authority— Selected Studies* (New York: U.N. Doc. ST/TAO/HR/19, 1964). (Reprints earlier papers on the Ombudsman in Sweden and Denmark by A. Bexelius, E. Holmberg, B. Kjellin and S. Hurwitz.)

United States, *Congressional Record*, 88th Congress, 1st Session (1963); the extended remarks of Congressman Reuss on his Bill HR 7593 contain useful information and comment at pp. 2078, A806, A1329, A1367, A1496, A1593, A1690, A1952, A2218.

United States, Senate, Committee on Rules and Administration, Subcommittee on Standing Rules, *Hearings* (88th Congress, 1st Session 1963), 111–124.

'Value of Ombudsman Proved in New Zealand', *The Times* (London, May 15, 1964).

VANDYK, M. D., 'Watchdog at Work', 105 *Solicitor's Journal* (1961), 601–604 (on the Council on Tribunals).

WADE, H. W. R., 'The Council on Tribunals', *Public Law* (1960), 351–366.

WHEARE, K. C., 'The Redress of Grievances', 40 *Public Administration* (London, 1962), 125–128 (on the Whyatt Report).

WOLD, TERJE, 'The Norwegian Parliament's Commissioner for the Civil Administration', 2 *Journal of the International Commission of Jurists* (1960), 23–29.

YAMAMOTO, SHOTARO, 'Ombudsmen in Japan', 12 *Kwansei Gakuin University Annual Studies* (November 1963), 75–91.

Young Conservative and Unionist Organization, *Law, Liberty and Licence* (London: Conservative Political Centre, 1964), pp. 54, at 16–17.

BILLS PROPOSED IN CANADA AND THE UNITED STATES

2nd Session, 26th Parliament, 13 Elizabeth II, 1964.

THE HOUSE OF COMMONS OF CANADA.

BILL C-7.

An Act to establish the Office of Parliamentary Commissioner.

H ER Majesty, by and with the advice and consent of the Senate and House of Commons of Canada, enacts as follows:

SHORT TITLE.

Short title.

1. This Act may be cited as the *Parliamentary Commissioner Act.*　　　　　5

PARLIAMENTARY COMMISSIONER.

Appointment, tenure, and removal.

2. There shall be appointed by joint resolution of the Senate and House of Commons an officer called the Parliamentary Commissioner to hold office during good behaviour until he attains the age of sixty-five years but he is removable by a joint resolution of the Senate and 10 House of Commons.

Expenditure.

3. No public monies shall be expended directly or indirectly in performing the duties of Parliamentary Commissioner set forth in this Act.

Resignation or removal.

4. The Parliamentary Commissioner may at any 15 time resign his office by writing addressed to the Speaker of the House of Commons or to the Speaker of the Senate and he may be removed or suspended for cause from his office upon a joint address of the Senate and the House of Commons.　　　　　20

Filling of
vacancy.

5. If the Parliamentary Commissioner dies, **or** retires, or resigns, or is removed from office the vacancy thereby created shall be filled in accordance with the pre- scriptions of the previous sections if Parliament is in session, and, if not the Governor in Council may appoint a Parlia- 5 mentary Commissioner to fill the vacancy, and the person so appointed shall, unless his office sooner becomes vacant, hold office for one year subject to his appointment being confirmed at the following session of Parliament.

Money, gifts,
etc.

6. The Parliamentary Commissioner may accept 10 money, securities, or other property by gift, bequest, or otherwise, and may, notwithstanding anything in this Act, expend, administer or dispose of any such money, securities or other property (subject to the terms, if any, upon which such money, securities or other property were 15 given), in carrying out the duties of Parliamentary Commis- sioner under this Act, including the retention by himself of such remuneration as may be reasonable for the performance of his own services under this Act.

FUNCTIONS AND DUTIES.

Investigation
of grievances.

7. (1) It is the function and duty of the Parlia- 20 mentary Commissioner to investigate the administration, by a power or authority or officer of such power or authority, of any law of Canada whereby any person is aggrieved or, in the opinion of the Parliamentary Commissioner, may be aggrieved. 25

Who may
petition.

(2) Any person may, in the public interest, apply by petition to the Parliamentary Commissioner to investigate a grievance.

Refusal to
investigate.

8. (1) The Parliamentary Commissioner, in his discretion, may refuse to investigate or may cease to inves- 30 tigate a grievance if

(*a*) a remedy already exists;

(*b*) it is trivial, frivolous, vexatious or is not made in good faith; or

(*c*) upon a balance of convenience between the 35 private interest of the person aggrieved and the public interest, the Parliamentary Commis- sioner is of opinion the grievance should not be investigated.

Notice of
refusal.

(2) Where the Parliamentary Commissioner 40 decides that he will not investigate or that he will cease to investigate a grievance he shall so inform the petitioner and any other interested person.

Notice of investigation.

9. (1) Before investigating a grievance, the Parliamentary Commissioner shall inform the power or authority or officer of such power or authority administering the law of Canada whereby any person is aggrieved or, in his opinion, may be aggrieved, of his intention to investigate. 5

Practice where *prima facie* case.

(2) If the Parliamentary Commissioner is satisfied there is *prima facie* evidence that a power or authority or officer of such power or authority so administered a law of Canada as thereby to cause a grievance or so administers such law as thereby may give cause for griev- 10 ance, he shall so advise the power or authority or officer and shall give it or him an opportunity to be heard.

Breach of duty or misconduct by officer.

(3) If, during or after an investigation, the Parliamentary Commissioner is of opinion there is evidence of a breach of duty or misconduct by an officer of a power or 15 authority, he shall refer the evidence to the power or authority.

Commissioner's power and authority.

10. (1) Subject to this Act and to any rules or orders of Parliament in respect of his office, the Parliamentary Commissioner has power and authority to investigate 20 to the extent and by such means as he deems will best achieve the purpose of this Act.

Inquiries Act.

(2) Without limiting the power and authority of the Parliamentary Commissioner under the preceding subsection, he shall have the powers of a commissioner under 25 the *Inquiries Act*.

Action where grievance adjudged.

11. (1) Where, upon investigation, the Parliamentary Commissioner adjudges that a grievance exists or may exist because a power or authority or officer of such power or authority administered or is administering, as the 30 case may be, a law of Canada

    (*a*) unreasonably, unjustly, oppressively, or in a discriminatory manner, or pursuant to a rule of law, enactment, or practice that so results; or 35

    (*b*) under mistake of law or of fact, in whole or in part; or

    (*c*) wrongly; or

    (*d*) contrary to law; or

    (*e*) by using a discretionary power for an improper 40 purpose, or on irrelevant grounds, or by taking irrelevant considerations into account, or by failing to give reasons for the use of a discretionary power when reasons should have been given; and 45

if the Parliamentary Commissioner is of opinion that

    (*a*) the grievance should be referred to the power or authority or officer of such power or authority for further consideration; or

(b)   an omission should be rectified; or

(c)   a decision should be cancelled or rectified; or

(d)   a practice by reason of which the grievance arose or may arise should be altered; or

(e)   a law by reason of which the grievance arose 5 or may arise should be reconsidered; or

(f)   reasons should be given for the use of a discretionary power; or

(g)   other steps should be taken as he may advise; then 10

the Parliamentary Commissioner shall report his adjudgment with his reasons therefor to the power or authority with such recommendations as he may think fit and, where he so recommends, he may request the power or authority to notify him, within a time limited, what the power or author- 15 ity proposes to do thereon.

Where power or authority fails to remedy.

(2) Where the power or authority, after the lapse of a period deemed reasonable by the Parliamentary Commissioner, does not act upon the Parliamentary Commissioner's recommendations, refuses to act thereon, 20 or acts in a manner unsatisfactory to the Parliamentary Commissioner, he may send a copy of his report and recommendations, with any comment he may wish to add thereto, to the Prime Minister, and may thereafter make such report to Parliament as he thinks fit. 25

Comments of power or authority.

(3) The Parliamentary Commissioner shall include with any report sent or made under subsection (2) a copy of any comment made by the power or authority upon his adjudgment or recommendations.

Opportunity to be heard.

(4) In any report made by him under this 30 Act, the Parliamentary Commissioner shall not make any finding or comment that is adverse to any person unless he gives that person an opportunity to be heard.

Recommendations: petitioner informed.

12.   (1) Where a power or authority does not act to his satisfaction upon his recommendations for the remedy 35 of a grievance, the Parliamentary Commissioner shall inform the petitioner of his recommendations and may add such comment as he wishes.

Findings: petitioner informed.

(2) The Parliamentary Commissioner shall in any case inform the petitioner, in such manner and at 40 such time as he thinks proper, of the result of the investigation.

Annual report.

13.   (1) The Parliamentary Commissioner, within a year after the coming into effect of this Act and thereafter in each succeeding calendar year, shall make a report on 45 the proceedings of his office with his recommendations, if any, as to any measures that should be taken to better implement the intent and achieve the purpose of this Act and shall thereupon lay such report before Parliament.

L

(2) A copy of the report shall be delivered to the Minutes and Journals Office of the Senate and to the Votes and Proceedings Office of the House of Commons respectively; and such copies so delivered on any day during the existence of a Parliament shall be deemed to be for all 5 purposes the laying of the report before Parliament.

(3) Upon receipt of the report, an entry shall that day be made in the respective records of these Offices and, on the day following thereon, the copies of the report shall be deposited in the Library of Parliament. 10

(4) The Parliamentary Commissioner may submit a report to Parliament at any other time.

GENERAL.

Offenses.

14. Every one who

(a) without lawful justification or excuse, wilfully obstructs, hinders, or resists the Parliamentary 15 Commissioner or other person in the exercise of his powers under this Act,

(b) without lawful justification or excuse, refuses or wilfully fails to comply with any lawful requirement of the Parliamentary Commis- 20 sioner or other person under this Act, or

(c) wilfully makes any false statement to or misleads or attempts to mislead the Parliamentary Commissioner or other person in the exercise of his powers under this Act, 25

is guilty of an offense punishable on summary conviction.

Saving of other rights and remedies.

15. This Act shall not abrogate, abridge or infringe or authorize the abrogation, abridgment or infringement of any substantive or procedural right or remedy existing otherwhere or otherwise than in this Act. 30

Act not to apply to Executive in policy capacity nor to Judicature.

16. This Act does not extend or apply to the Governor General acting by and with the aid and advice of the Queen's Privy Council for Canada nor to the Judicature of Canada.

88TH CONGRESS
1ST SESSION
H. R. 7593

IN THE HOUSE OF REPRESENTATIVES

JULY 16, 1963

Mr. REUSS introduced the following bill; which was referred to the Committee on House Administration

---

A BILL

To provide for an Administrative Counsel of the Congress.

1 *Be it enacted by the Senate and House of Representa-*

2 *tives of the United States of America in Congress assembled,*

3 That this Act may be cited as the "Administrative Counsel

4 Act".

5   SEC. 2. The Congress hereby finds and declares that

6 the increasing complexity of the Federal Government has

7 created difficulties on the part of private citizens in dealing

8 with the Government, that there is a clear need for the

9 Congress to be informed of the nature of such difficulties,

10 particularly those of a recurrent nature, in order that reme-

11 dial legislative action may be taken, and that, under existing

I

1 procedures, such information is only sporadically available
2 and frequently is inadequately developed or fails entirely
3 to reach the appropriate legislative committees. The Con-
4 gress further finds that the necessary and proper efforts of
5 its individual Members to deal with these problems have
6 increasingly become so burdensome as to constitute a serious
7 impediment to the discharge of their other legislative duties.

8   SEC. 3. (a) There shall be an officer of the Senate and
9 House of Representatives who shall be known as the Ad-
10 ministrative Counsel of the Congress and shall perform such
11 duties as are prescribed by this Act. He shall be appointed
12 by the Speaker of the House of Representatives and the
13 President pro tempore of the Senate, without reference to
14 political affiliations and solely on the basis of his fitness to
15 perform the duties of his office, for a term which shall expire
16 upon the commencement of the Congress succeeding the
17 Congress during which he was appointed, except that he
18 may continue to act during such succeeding Congress until
19 he has been reappointed or his successor has been appointed.
20 He shall receive a salary at the rate of $22,500 per annum.

21   (b) Subject to the availability of appropriations, the
22 Administrative Counsel may appoint such assistants, clerks,
23 and other personnel as may be necessary to carry on the
24 work of his office.

25   SEC. 4. Upon the request of any Member of either House

1 of Congress, the Administrative Counsel shall review the
2 case of any person who alleges that he believes that he has
3 been subjected to any improper penalty, or that he has been
4 denied any right or benefit to which he is entitled, under
5 the laws of the United States, or that the determination
6 or award of any such right or benefit has been, is being, or
7 will be unreasonably delayed, as a result of any action or
8 failure to act on the part of any officer or employee of the
9 United States other than those exempted under section 6
10 of this Act. The Administrative Counsel may, in his dis-
11 cretion, confine his review of the case to the material sub-
12 mitted to him with the request for review, or may make
13 such further investigation as he may deem appropriate.
14 Upon the completion of his review, he shall report his con-
15 clusions and recommendations, if any, to the Member or
16 committee by whom the claim was referred.

17   SEC. 5. All officers and employees of the United States,
18 except those exempted pursuant to section 6, shall furnish
19 to the Administrative Counsel such information regarding
20 their activities within the scope of their official duties or em-
21 ployment as he may require of them, and the Administra-
22 tive Counsel, or any of his assistants, when duly authorized
23 by him, shall, for the purpose of securing such information,
24 have access to and the right to examine any books, records,
25 files, or other documents, and the right to consult directly

1 any officers or employees of the United States without secur-
2 ing the permission of their superiors.

3 SEC. 6. (a) This Act shall apply to all officers and em-
4 ployees of the United States except the following:

5   (1) The President;

6   (2) Members, officers, and employees of the Senate,
7 the House of Representatives, or any committee or
8 joint committee thereof;

9   (3) Judges, clerks, commissioners, referees in
10 bankruptcy, and other officers (other than attorneys as
11 such) and employees of any court of the United States,
12 regardless of whether such court is legislative or con-
13 stitutional;

14   (4) Officers and employees of the District of Colum-
15 bia or any other local governmental unit not under the
16 supervision or control of some other department or
17 agency of the United States; and

18   (5) Any other officer or employee of the United
19 States whose activities are of such a nature that, in the
20 discretion of the Administrative Counsel, the application
21 of this Act thereto would be contrary to the public
22 interest.

23 (b) For the purposes of this Act, the term "officers and
24 employees of the United States" includes officers and em-

1 ployees of any department, agency, or instrumentality of the
2 United States.

3 SEC. 7. (a) The Administrative Counsel shall make
4 an annual report to the Congress. Such report shall sum-
5 marize his activities, shall include reviews of those indi-
6 vidual cases which, in his judgment, should be brought to
7 the attention of the Congress, and shall set forth such
8 recommendations for legislation or further investigation as
9 he may deem appropriate.

10 (b) The Administrative Counsel may, in his discretion,
11 make an interim report on any occasion when he deems
12 such action appropriate to carry out the purposes of this
13 Act.

14 (c) Any report of the Administrative Counsel pursuant
15 to this section shall be printed as a public document.

90TH CONGRESS
1ST SESSION

S. 1195

IN THE SENATE OF THE UNITED STATES

MARCH 7, 1967

Mr. LONG of Missouri introduced the following bill; which was read twice and referred to the Committee on the Judiciary

---

A BILL

To establish the Office of Administrative Ombudsman to investigate administrative practices and procedures of selected agencies of the United States.

1 *Be it enacted by the Senate and House of Representa-*

2 *tives of the United States of America in Congress assembled,*

3 That subchapter III of chapter 5 of title 5 of the United

4 States Code is amended by renumbering section 576 as

5 section 577, and inserting a new section 576 entitled "Ad-

6 ministrative Ombudsman".

7   SEC. 2. As used in this Act, the term—

8   (a) "Ombudsman" means the Administrative Ombuds-

9 man duly appointed and serving under the provisions of

10 this Act.

L *

1   (b) "Office" means the Office of the Administrative
2 Ombudsman established by this Act.

3   (c) "Agency" shall include the Social Security Admin-
4 istration, Veterans Administration, Internal Revenue Serv-
5 ice, and the Bureau of Prisons, and any officer, employee,
6 or member thereof acting or purporting to act in the exercise
7 of his official duties.

8   (d) "Administrative act" includes any action, omission,
9 decision, recommendation, practice, or procedure.

10   SEC. 3. (a) There is hereby created an establishment
11 of the Government to be known as the Administrative
12 Ombudsman, which shall be independent of the executive
13 department and under the direction and control of the Ad-
14 ministrative Conference. There shall be in the Office an
15 Ombudsman and a Deputy Administrative Ombudsman who
16 shall be appointed by the Ombudsman and shall perform
17 such duties as may be assigned to him by the Ombudsman.
18 During the absence or incapacity of the Ombudsman, or at
19 any time at which there is no Ombudsman, the Deputy shall
20 act as Ombudsman.

21   (b) The Ombudsman shall be appointed by the Presi-
22 dent, by and with the advice and consent of the Senate, for
23 a term of five years. In no case shall any person hold the
24 office for more than four full terms. The Ombudsman shall
25 receive compensation in an amount equal to that of the Chief

Judge of the District of Columbia Court of Appeals. The annual rate of basic compensation of the Deputy Ombudsman shall be $22,500.

(c) The Ombudsman and the Deputy Ombudsman appointed under this Act shall be chosen, without regard to political affiliation, from individuals specially qualified to perform the duties of the office. Each individual so appointed shall be an individual who—

(1) has been admitted to the practice of law before the highest court of any State, possession, territory, Commonwealth, or the District of Columbia, and is a member of the bar of that court in good standing;

(2) is of good moral character, and possesses a good reputation for professional legal competence, personal integrity, diligence in the performance of duty, and freedom from personal bias or prejudice;

(3) has not, within the five-year period immediately preceding his appointment, served as a Member of Congress or as an appointed officer of any agency as defined in this Act;

(4) is a citizen of the United States.

(d) No person may serve as Ombudsman or Deputy Ombudsman while a candidate for or holder of any elected office, whether municipal, State, or Federal, or while engaged in any other business, vocation, or employment.

1   (e) The Congress of the United States, by two-thirds

2 vote in each House, may remove the Ombudsman from office

3 when, in the judgment of the Congress, he has become per-

4 manently incapacitated, or has been guilty of any felony, mis-

5 conduct, or any other conduct involving moral turpitude, and

6 for no other cause and no other manner except by im-

7 peachment.

8   (f) Subject to the civil service laws and the Classifica-

9 tion Act of 1949, the Ombudsman may appoint and fix the

10 compensation of such personnel as may be required for

11 the performance of the duties of the office. The Ombudsman

12 shall promulgate such rules and regulations as may be neces-

13 sary to carry out the duties imposed upon him by this Act,

14 and he may delegate authority for the performance of any

15 such duty, except those specified in section 6 of this Act, to

16 any officer or employee of the office. Such regulations shall

17 include procedures for receiving and processing complaints,

18 conducting investigations, and reporting his findings.

19   (g) The Ombudsman is authorized to charge a nominal

20 fee for the investigation of complaints, and to waive any such

21 fee when, in his opinion, a financial hardship may result to

22 the complainant.

23   SEC. 4. (a) The Ombudsman shall have jurisdiction to

24 investigate the administrative acts, practices, or procedures,

25 of any agency as defined in section 2 (c). Where necessary,

1 the Ombudsman may exercise his powers under this Act

2 without regard to the finality of any administrative act.

3   (b) Upon his own motion or upon any oral or written

4 complaint of any person, the Ombudsman shall conduct or

5 cause to be conducted, in such manner as he shall determine

6 to be appropriate, a full and complete investigation of any

7 matter which is an appropriate subject for investigation under

8 section 5 of this Act, unless, in his opinion—

9   (1) there is presently available an adequate remedy

10   for the grievance stated in the compliant, whether or

11   not complainant has availed himself of it;

12   (2) the complaint relates to a matter that is outside

13   the jurisdiction of the Ombudsman;

14   (3) complainant does not have a sufficient personal

15   interest in the subject matter of the complaint;

16   (4) complainant has had knowledge of the action

17   complained of for too long a period before the complaint

18   was submitted; or

19   (5) the complaint is trivial, frivolous, vexatious, or

20   not made in good faith.

21   (c) If, with respect to any complaint the Ombudsman

22 decides not to investigate, he shall inform the complainant

23 of that decision and his reasons therefor; except that he shall

24 not be required to divulge matters which would invade the

S. 1195——2

1 privacy of any individual, or interfere with legitimate govern-
2 mental activities. In the event he decides to investigate, he
3 shall notify the complainant and the agency concerned in
4 writing of that fact. The Ombudsman shall not be prohibited
5 from making on-the-spot investigations of agency proceed-
6 ings and activities, subject to proper notice to an appropriate
7 official.

8   SEC. 5. (a) For purposes of this Act, an appropriate
9 subject for investigation by the Ombudsman is an adminis-
10 trative act, practice, or procedure, of any agency which
11 might be—

12   (1) contrary to law or regulation;

13   (2) unreasonable, unfair, or oppressive;

14   (3) based wholly or partly on a mistake of law or
15 fact;

16   (4) based on improper or irrelevant grounds;

17   (5) unaccompanied by an adequate statement of
18 reasons;

19   (6) performed in an inefficient manner; or

20   (7) otherwise erroneous.

21   (b) In carrying out his duties under this Act, the
22 Ombudsman may investigate to find an appropriate remedy,
23 or to make routine checks of the operations of any agency or
24 agencies covered under this Act. The Ombudsman may
25 undertake, participate in, or cooperate with general studies

1 or inquiries, whether or not related to any particular adminis-
2 trative agency or any particular administrative act, if he
3 believes that they may enhance knowledge about or lead to
4 improvements in the functioning of administrative agencies.

5 (c) In any investigation under this Act, the Ombuds-
6 man may (1) make inquiries and obtain any and all infor-
7 mation from the agency or agencies as he deems necessary;
8 (2) enter to inspect the premises of an agency; and (3)
9 hold private hearings with both the complaining individual
10 and agency officials.

11 (d) Subject to the privileges which witnesses have in
12 the courts of the United States, the Ombudsman may (1)
13 compel, at a specified time and place, by subpena, the
14 appearance and sworn testimony of any person who the
15 Ombudsman has reasonable cause to believe may be able to
16 give information relating to a matter under investigation;
17 and (2) compel any person to produce documents, papers,
18 or objects which the Ombudsman has reasonable cause to
19 believe may relate to a matter under investigation. The
20 Ombudsman is authorized to bring an action in a district
21 court in which the complainant resides, or has his principal
22 place of business, or in which the agency is situated, in
23 order to enforce the aforementioned powers.

24 SEC. 6. (a) Prior to rendering any opinion or making

1 any recommendation that is critical of any agency or person,

2 the Ombudsman shall consult with that agency or person.

3 The Ombudsman shall allow that agency or person a reason-

4 able period of time to take the necessary or appropriate

5 action indicated, or to file a statement of explanation with

6 the Ombudsman.

7   (b) If, after any investigation conducted by him under

8 this Act, the Ombudsman finds that (1) a matter should be

9 further considered by the agency; (2) an administrative

10 act should be modified, amended, or canceled; (3) a

11 statute or regulation on which an administrative act is based

12 should be amended or repealed; (4) reasons should be given

13 for an administrative act; or (5) any other action should

14 be taken by the agency, he shall submit his views and

15 recommendations to the agency. The Ombudsman may

16 request the agency to notify him within a specified time,

17 of any action taken by the agency on his recommendations.

18 Any agency so requested shall be required to comply with

19 such request.

20   (c) Within sixty days following the submission of his

21 views and recommendations to any agency under subsection

22 (b) of this section, the Ombudsman shall transmit copies

23 thereof, together with copies of the agency's reply, to the

24 head of the concerned agency, to the Chairman of the Ad-

25 ministrative Conference of the United States and to the ap-

1 propriate committees of the Senate and of the House of

2 Representatives. The Ombudsman is further authorized to

3 take such action as he may determine feasible to make such

4 information available to the general public.

5   (d) The Ombudsman shall notify the complainant in

6 writing of any action taken by him and by the agency with

7 respect to his complaint.

8   SEC. 7. (a) If, in carrying out his duties under this

9 Act, the Ombudsman determines that any employee or officer

10 of any agency has been guilty of a breach of duty or miscon-

11 duct in connection with his duties as an employee or officer of

12 such agency, the Ombudsman shall refer the matter to the

13 appropriate authorities in the Department of Justice.

14   (b) The Ombudsman shall, on or before March 1 of

15 each calendar year, submit to the President, to the Congress,

16 and to the head of the Administrative Conference a written

17 report concerning his activities under this Act during the

18 preceding calendar year.

19   SEC. 8. (a) No proceeding, decision, or report of the

20 Ombudsman conducted or made in accordance with the provi-

21 sions of this Act shall be challenged, reviewed, quashed, or

22 called into question in any court. No action, civil or criminal,

23 shall lie against the Ombudsman or against any person hold-

24 ing any office or appointment under the Ombudsman, for

25 anything the Ombudsman or such persons may do, report,

1 say in the course of the exercise or intended exercise of their

2 functions under this Act, unless it is shown that they acted in

3 bad faith. The Ombudsman shall not be called to give evi-

4 dence in any court, or in any proceeding of a judicial investi-

5 gation of his functions.

6   (b) Any letter addressed to the Ombudsman and writ-

7 ten by any person in custody on a charge of, or after con-

8 viction of, any offense under the laws of the United States, or

9 by any inmate of any institution under the control of the

10 Bureau of Prisons, shall be immediately forwarded, un-

11 opened, to the Ombudsman by the institution where the

12 writer of the letter is detained or of which he is an inmate.

13   (c) The provisions of this Act shall be in addition to

14 the provisions of any other law or regulation under which

15 any remedy or right of appeal is provided for any person, or

16 any procedure is provided for the inquiry into or investiga-

17 tion of any matter, and nothing in this Act shall limit or

18 affect any such remedy, right of appeal, or procedure. The

19 powers conferred on the Ombudsman by this Act may be

20 exercised by him notwithstanding any other provision of law

21 to the effect that any administrative action or omission shall

22 be final or that no appeal shall lie in respect thereof.

23   SEC. 9. Any person who willfully obstructs or hinders

24 the Ombudsman in the proper exercise of his powers under

25 this Act, refuses or willfully fails to comply with any lawful

1 requirement of the Ombudsman under this Act, or willfully
2 makes any false statement or misleads or attempts to mislead
3 the Ombudsman in the exercise of his powers under this Act,
4 shall be fined not more than $1,000.

5   SEC. 10. There are hereby authorized to be appropriated
6 such sums as may be necessary, not in excess of $100,000,
7 to carry out the provisions of this Act.

A State Statute to Create
The Office of Ombudsman*

This statute establishes the office of Ombudsman, or commissioner of investigation. The office, new to the United States, has been the object of increasing attention here because of its effective operation in Scandinavia and New Zealand. The Ombudsman, acting on citizens' complaints or on his own initiative, may examine the acts of the ever-growing administrative agencies, probing to find what injustices should be remedied and what procedures should be improved. As liaison between citizen, agency, and legislature, he may publicize his recommendations to help bring to state government long-sought standards of fairness and efficiency.

PART I. SHORT TITLE AND DEFINITIONS

SECTION 101. *Short title.*

This Act may be called "The Ombudsman Act of 1965."

SECTION 102. *Definitions.*

(a) "Agency" includes any permanent governmental entity, department, organization, or institution, and any officer, employee, or member thereof acting or purporting to act in the exercise of his official duties, except

    (1) a court;

    (2) the Legislature, its committees, and its staff;

    (3) a political subdivision of the state or an entity thereof;

    (4) an entity of the federal government;

    (5) a multistate governmental entity; and

    (6) the Governor and his personal staff.

(b) "Administrative act" includes any action, omission, decision, recommendation, practice, or procedure, but does not include the preparation or presentation of legislation.

PART II. ORGANIZATION OF THE OFFICE

SECTION 201. *Establishment.*

The office of Ombudsman is hereby established.

✷ From 2 <u>Harvard Journal on Legislation</u> (June 1965), 213, 221-6. Reprinted, with thanks, by permission of Harvard Student Legislative Research Bureau.

SECTION 202. *Appointment of the Ombudsman.*

The Governor, with the advice and consent of the Senate, shall appoint the Ombudsman.

SECTION 203. *Qualifications.*

No person may serve as Ombudsman

(a) within two years of the last day on which he served as a member of the Legislature,

(b) while he is a candidate for or holds any other state office, or

(c) while he is engaged in any other occupation for reward or profit.

SECTION 204. *Term of Office.*

The term of office of an Ombudsman is six years. An Ombudsman may be reappointed but may not serve more than three terms.

SECTION 205. *Removal.*

The Legislature, by a two-thirds vote in each house, may remove or suspend the Ombudsman from office, but only for neglect of duty, misconduct, or disability.

SECTION 206. *Vacancy.*

If the Ombudsman dies, resigns, becomes ineligible to serve, or is removed or suspended from office, the First Assistant to the Ombudsman becomes the Acting Ombudsman until a new Ombudsman is appointed for a full term.

SECTION 207. *Compensation.*

The Ombudsman is entitled to compensation equal to that of the chief judge of the highest court of the state.

SECTION 208. *Staff and delegation.*

(a) The Ombudsman shall appoint a First Assistant and such other officers and employees as may be necessary to carry out the provisions of this Act.

(b) The Ombudsman may delegate to his appointees any of his duties except those specified in sections 502 and 503.

SECTION 209. *Procedure.*

The Ombudsman may establish procedures for receiving and processing complaints, conducting investigations, and reporting his findings. However, he may not levy fees for the submission or investigation of complaints.

PART III. JURISDICTION AND INITIATION OF INVESTIGATIONS

SECTION 301. *Jurisdiction.*

(a) The Ombudsman has jurisdiction to investigate the administrative acts of agencies.

(b) The Ombudsman may exercise his powers without regard to the finality of any administrative act.

SECTION 302. *Investigation of complaints.*

The Ombudsman shall investigate any complaint indicating an appropriate subject for investigation under section 401, unless he believes that

(a) there is presently available an adequate remedy for the grievance stated in the complaint;

(b) the complaint relates to a matter that is outside the jurisdiction of the Ombudsman;

(c) the complaint relates to an administrative act of which the complainant has had knowledge for too long a time before the complaint was submitted;

(d) the complainant does not have a sufficient personal interest in the subject matter of the complaint;

(e) the complaint is trivial or made in bad faith;

(f) the facilities of the Ombudsman's office are insufficient for adequate investigation; or

(g) there are other complaints more worthy of the Ombudsman's attention.

SECTION 303. *Investigation on the Ombudsman's motion.*

The Ombudsman may investigate on his own motion if he reasonably believes that an appropriate subject for investigation under section 401 exists.

SECTION 304. *Notice to complainant.*

(a) If the Ombudsman decides not to investigate, he shall inform the complainant of that decision and shall state his reasons unless he reasonably believes it is inappropriate to do so.

(b) If the Ombudsman decides to investigate, he shall notify the complainant of his decision.

SECTION 305. *Notice to the agency.*

If the Ombudsman decides to investigate, he shall notify the agency of his intention to investigate.

PART IV. INVESTIGATIONS

SECTION 401. *Appropriate subjects for investigation.*

(a) An appropriate subject for investigation is an administrative act of an agency which might be

(1) contrary to law;

(2) unreasonable, unfair, oppressive, or unnecessarily discriminatory, even though in accordance with law;

(3) based on a mistake of fact;

(4) based on improper or irrelevant grounds;

(5) unaccompanied by an adequate statement of reasons;

(6) performed in an inefficient manner; or

(7) otherwise erroneous.

(b) The Ombudsman may investigate to find an appropriate remedy.

SECTION 402. *Investigation procedures.*

In an investigation, the Ombudsman may

(a) make inquiries and obtain information as he thinks fit;

(b) enter without notice to inspect the premises of an agency; and

(c) hold private hearings.

SECTION 403. *Powers.*

(a) Subject to the privileges which witnesses have in the courts of this state, the Ombudsman may

(1) compel at a specified time and place, by a subpoena, the appearance and sworn testimony of any person who the Ombudsman reasonably believes may be able to give information relating to a matter under investigation; and

(2) compel any person to produce documents, papers, or objects which the Ombudsman reasonably believes may relate to a matter under investigation.

(b) The Ombudsman may bring suit in an appropriate state court to enforce these powers.

Part V. Procedure and Reports after Investigation

Section 501. *Consultation with agency.*

Before giving any opinion or recommendation that is critical of an agency or person, the Ombudsman shall consult with that agency or person.

Section 502. *Procedure after investigation.*

If, after investigation, the Ombudsman finds that

(a) a matter should be further considered by the agency;

(b) an administrative act should be modified or cancelled;

(c) a statute or regulation on which an administrative act is based should be altered;

(d) reasons should be given for an administrative act; or

(e) any other action should be taken by the agency;

he shall report his opinion and recommendations to the agency. He may request the agency to notify him, within a specified time, of any action taken on his recommendations.

Section 503. *Publication of recommendations.*

After a reasonable time has elapsed, the Ombudsman may present his opinion and recommendations to the Governor, the Legislature, the public, or any of these. The Ombudsman shall include with this opinion any reply made by the agency.

Section 504. *Notice to the complainant.*

After a reasonable time has elapsed, the Ombudsman shall notify the complainant of the actions taken by him and by the agency.

Part VI. Miscellaneous

Section 601. *Misconduct by agency personnel.*

If the Ombudsman thinks there is a breach of duty or misconduct by any officer or employee of an agency, he shall refer the matter to the appropriate authorities.

Section 602. *Annual report.*

The Ombudsman shall submit to the Legislature and the public an annual report discussing his activities under this Act.

SECTION 603. *Judicial review.*

No proceeding or decision of the Ombudsman may be reviewed in any court, unless it contravenes the provisions of this Act.

SECTION 604. *Immunity of the Ombudsman.*

The Ombudsman has the same immunities from civil and criminal liability as a judge of this state.

SECTION 605. *Ombudsman's privilege not to testify.*

The Ombudsman and his staff shall not testify in any court with respect to matters coming to their attention in the exercise or purported exercise of their official duties except as may be necessary to enforce the provisions of this Act.

SECTION 606. *Agencies may not open letters to Ombudsman.*

A letter to the Ombudsman from a person held in custody by an agency shall be forwarded immediately, unopened, to the Ombudsman.

SECTION 607. *Penalty for obstruction.*

A person who willfully hinders the lawful actions of the Ombudsman or his staff, or willfully refuses to comply with their lawful demands, shall be fined not more than one thousand dollars.

STATISTICS ON EXISTING OMBUDSMAN SYSTEMS

SWEDEN'S OMBUDSMAN FOR CIVIL AFFAIRS*

1. *Cases arising from complaints and his own initiative, ten-year intervals, 1910–60, and 1960–63*

	1910	1920	1930	1940	1950	1960	1961	1962	1963
Pending at start	28	215	76	41	68	269	240	278	385
Complaints	347	330	489	333	589	983	983	960	1,224
Own initiative (from inspections, press, etc.)	a	85	82	258	122	226	97	203	172
TOTAL CASES	375[b]	630	647	632	779	1,478	1,320	1,441	1,781

a Not available. b Complaints only.

2. *Disposition of cases, ten-year intervals, 1910–60, and 1960–63*

	1910	1920	1930	1940	1950	1960	1961	1962	1963
Dismissed	207	a	221	133	187	263	190	217	287
Transferred or cancelled	5	14	28	7	18	20	29	19	22
Investigated, no direct action	87	a	247	326	372	669	592	620	746
Criticisms, etc.	31	a	82	103	135	273	208	194	276
Prosecutions	10	19	11	14	6	8	7	4	6
Proposals to government	0	6	2	2	1	5	16[c]	2	14[d]
Pending	35	86	58	47	60	240	278	385	430
TOTAL CASES	375	630	649[b]	632	779	1,478	1,320	1,441	1,781

a Total 505; b Total higher than in Table 1 because of double disposition of two cases; c 7 proposals in 16 cases; d 5 proposals in 14 cases.

* *Source:* A. Bexelius, Justitieombudsman.

3. *Administrative scope of cases, 1960–63[a]*

	1960	1961	1962	1963
Courts	210	171	178	241
Public prosecutors	123	171	81	108
Police	190	101	168	213
Execution of verdicts	40	35	44	55
Prison administration	111	123	106	146
Care of mental cases	91	110	123	102
Other health and welfare	80	76	93	99
Other central administration	40	69	49	73
Other central and local[b]	86	81	134	131
Other county, local and municipal	188	172	190	191
Public utilities	8	13	14	17
Ecclesiastical authorities	20	32	14	19
King in Council and Parliament	10	8	6	6
Private associations and persons	56	38	22	59
Inquiries, unclear complaints, etc.	52	71	58	65

a Several cases are included in more than one category; hence the columns should not be totalled.

b Activities involving not only central but also county, local and municipal administration: construction and housing, rent control, land surveying, education, and tax assessment.

SWEDEN'S OMBUDSMAN FOR MILITARY AFFAIRS*

4. *Cases arising from complaints and his own initiative, 1953 and 1960–63*

	1953	1960	1961	1962	1963
Complaints	100	79	72	81	76
Own initiative					
Reports by military prisons	203	258	170	147	148
Reports in the press	20	54	22	31	25
Inspections	367	210	401	382	382
Other	45	37	34	28	30
TOTAL	735	638	699	669	661

5. *Disposition of cases, 1962 and 1963*

	1962	1963
Dismissed, or investigated but no direct action, etc.	376	346
Criticisms, etc.	261	301
Prosecutions	6	4
Proposals to government	0	3
Pending	140	148
TOTAL	783	802

* *Source:* H. Henkow, Militieombudsman.

6. *Types of complainant, 1962 and 1963*

	1962	1963
Conscripts	42	38
Other military	18	21
Civil	21	17
TOTAL	81	76

7. *Types of complaint, 1962 and 1963*

	1962	1963
Insults, etc.	14	13
Other action by superiors	27	29
Conditions of service	40	34
TOTAL	81	76

SWEDEN'S CHANCELLOR OF JUSTICE

8. *Main groups of cases, 1960–63**

	1960	1961	1962	1963
Legal advice requested by the Cabinet or a Minister	179	216	228	202
Representation of the Crown in civil proceedings	33	27	42	40
Complaints lodged against offices and officials, including matters taken up on his own initiative	235	168	264	300
Review of disciplinary actions against advocates	111	110	105	133
TOTAL	558	521	639	675

* *Source:* S. Rudholm, Chancellor of Justice.

FINLAND'S CHANCELLOR OF JUSTICE*

9. *Main groups of cases, 1960–63*

	1960	1961	1962	1963
Statements of opinion to government authorities	45	25	33	32
Representation of the state in the highest courts	50	50	58	49
Appointments, discharges and deputy-ships of prosecuting and investigating authorities	90	95	78	121
Cases arising from complaints or his own or other authorities' initiative, which ended in a prosecution, disciplinary procedure or recommendation	264	164	190	256
Similar cases which ended in no action by the CJ	748	576	684	502
Others (ex. pending)	487	481	491	553
TOTAL	1684	1391	1534	1513

FINLAND'S OMBUDSMAN

10. *Cases arising from complaints and his own initiative, 1963**

Pending at start	226
Complaints to the Ombudsman	1,029
Complaints transferred by the Chancellor of Justice to the Ombudsman	73
Own initiative (inspections, from press, etc.)	110
Other	3
TOTAL	1,441

11. *Disposition of cases, 1963**

Declined for want of jurisdiction, or cancelled	124
Dismissed, or investigated but no direct action, etc.	726[a]
Criticisms, etc.	25
Prosecutions	6
Proposals to government	16
Pending	544
TOTAL	1,441

a Includes 89 inspections, 21 cases in which the authority itself made the correction after the Ombudsman required the explanation, and 29 cases pending in the courts.

* *Source:* P. Kastari, author of essay on Finland.

12. *Disposition of cases, ten-year intervals, 1920–60*★

	1920	1930	1940	1950	1960
Prosecutions, criticisms, etc.	3	6	17	17	12
Dismissed, proposals to government and other	70	155	327	1,025	943
TOTAL (ex. cases pending at end)	73	161	344	1,042	955

13. *Administrative scope of complaints, 1963*†

Courts	
Sentences too severe or wrong	215
Other procedural faults	51
Public prosecutors and police	82
Execution of punishments	102
Prison administration	105
Ordering into institutional care	18
Other health and welfare	11
Other administration	96
Conduct of military officials	5
Private associations and persons	72
Other	30
TOTAL	787

DENMARK'S OMBUDSMAN‡

14. *Disposition of cases initiated during year, 1960–63*

	1960	1961	1962	1963
Dismissed without investigation	603	584	689	725
Dismissed after summary investigation	288	307	239	254
Formally investigated (incl. direct action)	209	174	152	151
TOTAL	1,100	1,065	1,080	1,130
Criticisms, etc.[a]	49	48	36	53
Recommendations, etc.[a]	12	16	14	10

a Cases closed, but not necessarily initiated, during year.

★ *Source:* K. Sipponen, Working Paper for the United Nations Seminar on Judicial and Other Remedies Against the Abuse of Administrative Authority (New York, 1962), 16.

† *Source:* P. Kastari.

‡ *Source:* Office of the Danish Ombudsman and Miss Pedersen, author of essay on Denmark; compiled by D. C. Rowat.

15. Types of case formally investigated, totals for 1959–63

	Ministries	Police and Prosecution	Other	TOTAL
General questions	42	5	29	76
Subject matter of case	196	22	113	331
Rights of public employees	57	0	26	83
Administrative procedure	41	51	91	183
Delay	19	10	76	105
Conduct of officials	2	37	50	89
TOTAL	357	125	385	867

16. Administrative scope of cases formally investigated, 1960–63

MINISTRIES	1960	1961	1962	1963
Ministry of Justice and Prison Directorate	21	21	16	11
Ministry of Finance, Taxation and Customs	11	22	25	15
Minstry of Housing	8	3	3	7
Ministry of Fisheries	3	1	0	0
Ministry of Defence	6	3	9	5
Ministry of Trade	3	4	3	1
Ministry of the Interior	7	1	5	1
Ministry of Ecclesiastical Affairs	2	0	0	1
Ministry of Agriculture	4	0	2	1
Ministry for Greenland	1	2	4	6
Ministry for Public Works and Traffic	3	3	0	2
Ministry of Cultural Affairs	0	0	1	1
Ministry of Social Affairs, etc.	5	4	2	4
Prime Minister's Department	1	2	0	1
Ministry of Foreign Affairs	3	0	1	0
Ministry of Education	10	4	4	8
	88	70	75	64
POLICE AND PROSECUTION AUTHORITIES	35	32	9	15
OTHER AUTHORITIES	86	72	68	72
TOTAL	209	174	152	151

NORWAY'S OMBUDSMAN FOR CIVIL AFFAIRS*

17. Cases arising from complaints and his own initiative, 1963

Complaints	1,257
Own initiative	18
TOTAL CASES	1,275

* Source: A. Os, author of essay on Norway's Ombudsman for Civil Affairs.

18. *Disposition of cases, 1963*

Dismissed	868
Investigated but no direct action	240[a]
Decision changed while case pending	39
Criticisms, etc.	48
Pending	80
TOTAL	1,275

a Excluding 10 which also fall in next category.

19. *Grounds for dismissal of complaints, 1963*

Outside his competence	
Activities of the courts	147
Previously handled in Storting (Parliament)	20
Decisions by King in Council	13
Municipal matters	98
Other	115
	393
Outdated	97
Did not exhaust administrative appeal	128
Insufficient grounds	91
Withdrawn	48
Anonymous or unintelligible	20
Inquiries, etc.	91
TOTAL	868

20. *Administrative scope of cases formally investigated, 1963*

Ministry for Foreign Affairs	3
Ministry for Education and Ecclesiastical Affairs	31
Ministry of Justice	99
Ministry of Labour and Municipal Affairs	22
Ministry for Social Affairs	101
Ministry for the Family and Consumption	0
Ministry of Industry and Trade	5
Ministry of Fisheries	9
Ministry of Agriculture	21
Ministry of Communication	37
Ministry of Finance	23
Ministry of Wages and Prices	13
Ministry of Commerce and Navigation	5
Ministry of Defence	7
Other administrative agencies	26
TOTAL	402

M

NEW ZEALAND'S PARLIAMENTARY
COMMISSIONER*

21. *Cases arising between October 1, 1962, and March 31, 1964*

Complaints	1,091
Petitions referred by Parliamentary Committee	1
Own initiative	8
TOTAL	**1,100**

22. *Disposition of cases, October 1, 1962–March 31, 1964*

Declined for want of jurisdiction	409
Withdrawn	48
Not proceeded with	58
Dismissed, or investigated but no direct action	398
Criticisms, recommendations	107
Pending	80
TOTAL	**1,100**

23. *Administrative scope of cases proceeded with,
October 1, 1962–March 31, 1964*

Air Department	7
Army Department	1
Customs Department	35
Department of Agriculture	7
Department of Education	36
Department of Health	32
Department of Internal Affairs	10
Department of Justice	17
Department of Labour	30
Department of Lands and Survey	10
Department of Maori Affairs	5
Department of Scientific and Industrial Research	3
Inland Revenue Department	52
Marine Department	9
Mines Department	4
Ministry of Works	24
New Zealand Forest Service	5
New Zealand Government Railways	15
Post Office	15
Social Security Department	106
State Advances Corporation of New Zealand	37
Tourist and Publicity Department	3
Transport Department	7
Treasury	4

Carried forward—

* *Source:* J. F. Northey, author of essay on New Zealand.

Brought forward—

Government Superannuation Board	22
Land Settlement Board	4
National Provident Fund Board	8
National Roads Board	4
Police	16
State Services Commission	25
Rehabilitation Board	9
Other	23
TOTAL	585

EXTRACT FROM 'JUSTICE'
MEMORANDUM OF FEBRUARY 1965 ON THE PROPOSAL TO APPOINT AN OMBUDSMAN*

The Whyatt Report

1. It is understood that the promised Bill to provide for the appointment of a Parliamentary Commissioner (or Ombudsman) will be based, with some modifications, on the proposals contained in the Report, *The Citizen and the Administration*, published by JUSTICE in October 1961.

Immediate Proposals

8. The present Government has so far announced its intention only to appoint a Parliamentary Commissioner, and has given no indication of what it proposes to do about extending the powers of the Council on Tribunals. We regard this as unfortunate, since the Whyatt proposals were designed to provide machinery for the redress of grievance over the whole field of central government administration. It may well mean that the Parliamentary Commissioner will have to be empowered to take a somewhat wider definition of 'maladministration' than the Whyatt report had in mind, as is the case with the New Zealand Ombudsman.

Difficulties Peculiar to England

13. Sir John Whyatt's Committee was faced with two major problems when it came to consider the practical possibilities of introducing the Ombudsman idea in England. The first was the volume of complaints which were likely to be referred to him in a country with over 50 million inhabitants. The second was the fact that the Parliamentary Question has been developed into a far more effective and widely used instrument than in Denmark, and that MP's regard it as one of their duties and privileges to take up grievances on behalf of their constituents.

14. To overcome both these very real difficulties, the Committee suggested that, for an experimental period of five years, complaints should be referred to the Ombudsman only by MP's of both Houses of Parliament, and only after an MP had failed to obtain satisfaction for his constituent, or complainant, by a normal approach to the department concerned or by a Parliamentary Question. When Sir John Whyatt's Committee was reconvened to consider various criticisms that had been made of its Report, this suggestion was re-affirmed, and we regard it as important for the success of the Ombudsman proposals.

* Distributed to Members of British Parliament in March 1965. This extract and the one on page 183, from mimeographed memoranda, are printed here, with thanks, by permission of JUSTICE.

15. It will mean that, so far from the MP having any of his privileges taken away from him, he will have an additional weapon at his disposal if he suspects that the department is covering something up or is being perverse. Equally, he will be free to raise the issue on the adjournment if he wants to do so for political reasons. The weakness of the MP's present position is that, if the Minister decides to defend or conceal an unjust action of his department, the MP cannot challenge him effectively as he has no access to the documents or the information on which the decision was based. This goes to the heart of the matter. As one senior civil servant put it, 'there is no difficulty in answering the questions. The real difficulty arises in questioning the answers.' Further, the mere knowledge that a genuine grievance will be referred to the Ombudsman if a satisfactory answer is not given and any obvious injustice not remedied will of itself raise the standards of administration.

Practical Workings

16. Until the Government's Bill has been published, it is not easy to envisage or discuss the precise way in which the referring of complaints by MP's will work. On the assumption that this major restriction will be accepted, we suggest that an MP, on receipt of a complaint, will write to the Minister in the normal way, and if he fails to get satisfaction may ask a question in the House. He will then inform his constituent and advise him that, if he is still dissatisfied, he may have the case referred to the Ombudsman. The MP will then forward all the correspondence and the Ombudsman will take over the case, and pursue it in his own way, seeing the complainant in person, or through one of his assistants, if this is thought necessary or is requested. If the department readily agrees that a bad decision was made and should be remedied, the complainant can be informed of this through his MP and the matter will be ended. If not, then the Ombudsman will forward his opinion, and recommendation if any, to the Minister and inform the complainant. If the Ombudsman makes a recommendation that the Minister is unwilling to accept, then the MP concerned will be at liberty to raise the matter in the House, and the Minister will have to justify his refusal as he does at present. The Ombudsman will include any noteworthy cases in his periodical reports to Parliament.

17. It is envisaged that a complainant will normally approach his own MP as at present, but he will be free to approach any other MP, for example, if his own MP holds office in the department concerned. He may also approach a member of the House of Lords. One of the advantages of referring complaints through MP's is that they will know, whereas the complainant will not, which complaints are likely to lie within the Ombudsman's jurisdiction. Although general direct access is ideally desirable, this would result in grievances about local authorities, public services and the courts pouring in to the Ombudsman's offices and swamping the machinery, as well as in the by-passing of Parliament.

18.　　Some MP's have expressed anxiety as to the burden of extra work this will entail, and about the unfavourable comparisons that may be made between those who may encourage and assist their constituents to pursue grievances through the Ombudsman, and those who may discourage them. It might be argued that both kinds of MP might suffer—the former from overwork and the latter from unpopularity. Potentially this situation exists already. It is, moreover, unlikely that the mere existence of an Ombudsman would lead to an increase in the number of complaints received by MP's. A pattern would soon be established—recognizable by all MP's—for the kind of complaint that could properly be forwarded to the Ombudsman. Complaints which are no more than requests for information, and complaints about, for example, local authorities, would be customarily rejected by the Ombudsman. All MP's would thus be enabled very quickly to identify a proper complaint for the Obudsman. And, in respect of such complaints, they would find they had an additional and powerful string to their bow, and be spared the sometimes almost impossible task of unravelling the real point in a very complex case.

Scope of Jurisdiction

19.　　The limits of jurisdiction have already been indicated so far as this is possible without a knowledge of the Government's detailed intentions. The JUSTICE Committee has suggested that a list of departments and public authorities be drawn up as an appendix to the Bill, which can be amended from time to time, as was done in New Zealand. Three major problems emerged during the discussion and have been the subject of questions by MP's interested in the proposals. They are local authorities, nationalized industries and the police.

20.　　The Whyatt enquiry included a survey of the areas of discretion exercised by local authorities and of the matters which were most frequently the subject of complaint. The Committee could not reach any positive conclusions, partly because of the number of matters in which the responsibility was shared between local authorities and Ministries. It was felt that, in any event, a newly appointed Ombudsman could not possibly cope with all local government complaints. It therefore recommended that local authorities be encouraged to set up their own independent grievance machinery, and it would be an advantage if the new Bill were to make specific provision for this, and if local authority Ombudsmen were able to look to the Ombudsman for guidance and to consult him in matters where there was joint responsibility.

21.　　A similar difficulty was found in respect of nationalized industries, where the Minister is not liable for day to day running and cannot be questioned upon it in the House, except when he presents his annual report. The suggested solution here is that only those matters should be referred to the Ombudsman on which the Minister can be questioned in the House, and that nationalized industries should be encouraged to set up their own independent grievance machinery, which again could have facilities for consultation with the Ombudsman.

22.   The police present a special problem, partly because there is no national force, and complaints are dealt with by Chief Constables unless the Home Secretary is constrained to intervene. An Ombudsman would find it difficult to cope with all the unsatisfied complaints that are received even if they were filtered through MP's. In Denmark and New Zealand, the Ombudsman has jurisdiction in police matters, but in Denmark only after all normal channels of complaint have been exhausted. JUSTICE has always pressed for the independent investigation of serious complaints against the police and in its evidence to the Royal Commission suggested that this could best be achieved by an independent lawyer being present at local enquiries and disciplinary hearings, and by the appointment of an appeal tribunal presided over by an independent chairman, who could be the Ombudsman if one was appointed. The problem could perhaps be solved by giving one of the Ombudsman's senior assistants a special responsibility for police matters, and special staff, until the provisions of the Police Act, 1964, came to be reviewed.

Parliamentary Commissioner Act 1967

CHAPTER 13

An Act to make provision for the appointment and functions of a Parliamentary Commissioner for the investigation of administrative action taken on behalf of the Crown, and for purposes connected therewith.

[22nd March 1967]

B E IT ENACTED by the Queen's most Excellent Majesty, by and with the advice and consent of the Lords Spiritual and Temporal, and Commons, in this present Parliament assembled, and by the authority of the same, as follows:—

The Parliamentary Commissioner for Administration

1.—(1) For the purpose of conducting investigations in accordance with the following provisions of this Act there shall be appointed a Commissioner, to be known as the Parliamentary Commissioner for Administration. Appointment and tenure of office.

(2) Her Majesty may by Letters Patent from time to time appoint a person to be the Commissioner, and any person so appointed shall (subject to subsection (3) of this section) hold office during good behaviour.

(3) A person appointed to be the Commissioner may be relieved of office by Her Majesty at his own request, or may be removed from office by Her Majesty in consequence of Addresses from both Houses of Parliament, and shall in any case vacate office on completing the year of service in which he attains the age of sixty-five years.

(4) The Commissioner shall not be a member of the House of Commons, or of the Senate or House of Commons of Northern Ireland, and accordingly—

> (a) in Part III of Schedule 1 to the House of Commons Disqualification Act 1957 there shall be inserted, at 1957 c. 20.

M*

the appropriate point in alphabetical order, the entry "The Parliamentary Commissioner for Administration"; and

(b) the like amendment shall be made in the Part substituted for the said Part III by Schedule 3 to that Act in its application to the Senate and House of Commons of Northern Ireland.

(5) The Commissioner shall, by virtue of his office, be a member of the Council on Tribunals, and of the Scottish Committee of that Council, in addition to the persons appointed or designated as such under the Tribunals and Inquiries Act 1958.

1958 c. 66.

Salary and pension.

2.—(1) There shall be paid to the holder of the office of Commissioner a salary at the rate (subject to subsection (2) of this section) of £8,600 a year.

(2) The House of Commons may from time to time by resolution increase the rate of the salary payable under this section, and any such resolution may take effect from the date on which it is passed or such other date as may be specified therein.

(3) The provisions of Schedule 1 to this Act shall have effect with respect to the pensions and other benefits to be paid to or in respect of persons who have held office as Commissioner.

(4) The salary payable to a holder of the office of Commissioner shall be abated by the amount of any pension payable to him in respect of any public office in the United Kingdom or elsewhere to which he had previously been appointed or elected; but any such abatement shall be disregarded in computing that salary for the purposes of the said Schedule 1.

(5) Any salary, pension or other benefit payable by virtue of this section shall be charged on and issued out of the Consolidated Fund.

Administrative provisions.

3.—(1) The Commissioner may appoint such officers as he may determine with the approval of the Treasury as to numbers and conditions of service.

(2) Any function of the Commissioner under this Act may be performed by any officer of the Commissioner authorised for that purpose by the Commissioner.

(3) The expenses of the Commissioner under this Act, to such amount as may be sanctioned by the Treasury, shall be defrayed out of moneys provided by Parliament.

Investigation by the Commissioner

4.—(1) Subject to the provisions of this section and to the notes contained in Schedule 2 to this Act, this Act applies to the government departments and other authorities listed in that Schedule.

Departments and authorities subject to investigation.

(2) Her Majesty may by Order in Council amend the said Schedule 2 by the alteration of any entry or note, the removal of any entry or note or the insertion of any additional entry or note ; but nothing in this subsection authorises the inclusion in that Schedule of any body or authority not being a department or other body or authority whose functions are exercised on behalf of the Crown.

(3) Any statutory instrument made by virtue of subsection (2) of this section shall be subject to annulment in pursuance of a resolution of either House of Parliament.

(4) Any reference in this Act to a government department or other authority to which this Act applies includes a reference to the Ministers, members or officers of that department or authority.

5.—(1) Subject to the provisions of this section, the Commissioner may investigate any action taken by or on behalf of a government department or other authority to which this Act applies, being action taken in the exercise of administrative functions of that department or authority, in any case where—

Matters subject to investigation.

    (*a*) a written complaint is duly made to a member of the House of Commons by a member of the public who claims to have sustained injustice in consequence of maladministration in connection with the action so taken ; and

    (*b*) the complaint is referred to the Commissioner, with the consent of the person who made it, by a member of that House with a request to conduct an investigation thereon.

(2) Except as hereinafter provided, the Commissioner shall not conduct an investigation under this Act in respect of any of the following matters, that is to say—

    (*a*) any action in respect of which the person aggrieved has or had a right of appeal, reference or review to or before a tribunal constituted by or under any enactment or by virtue of Her Majesty's prerogative ;

    (*b*) any action in respect of which the person aggrieved has or had a remedy by way of proceedings in any court of law :

Provided that the Commissioner may conduct an investigation notwithstanding that the person aggrieved has or had such a right or remedy if satisfied that in the particular circumstances it is not reasonable to expect him to resort or have resorted to it.

(3) Without prejudice to subsection (2) of this section, the Commissioner shall not conduct an investigation under this Act in respect of any such action or matter as is described in Schedule 3 to this Act.

(4) Her Majesty may by Order in Council amend the said Schedule 3 so as to exclude from the provisions of that Schedule such actions or matters as may be described in the Order ; and any statutory instrument made by virtue of this subsection shall be subject to annulment in pursuance of a resolution of either House of Parliament.

(5) In determining whether to initiate, continue or discontinue an investigation under this Act, the Commissioner shall, subject to the foregoing provisions of this section, act in accordance with his own discretion ; and any question whether a complaint is duly made under this Act shall be determined by the Commissioner.

Provisions relating to complaints.

6.—(1) A complaint under this Act may be made by any individual, or by any body of persons whether incorporated or not, not being—

> (a) a local authority or other authority or body constituted for purposes of the public service or of local government or for the purposes of carrying on under national ownership any industry or undertaking or part of an industry or undertaking ;

> (b) any other authority or body whose members are appointed by Her Majesty or any Minister of the Crown or government department, or whose revenues consist wholly or mainly of moneys provided by Parliament.

(2) Where the person by whom a complaint might have been made under the foregoing provisions of this Act has died or is for any reason unable to act for himself, the complaint may be made by his personal representative or by a member of his family or other individual suitable to represent him ; but except as aforesaid a complaint shall not be entertained under this Act unless made by the person aggrieved himself.

(3) A complaint shall not be entertained under this Act unless it is made to a member of the House of Commons not later than

twelve months from the day on which the person aggrieved first
had notice of the matters alleged in the complaint; but the
Commissioner may conduct an investigation pursuant to a
complaint not made within that period if he considers that there
are special circumstances which make it proper to do so.

(4) A complaint shall not be entertained under this Act unless
the person aggrieved is resident in the United Kingdom (or, if he
is dead, was so resident at the time of his death) or the complaint
relates to action taken in relation to him while he was present
in the United Kingdom or on an installation in a designated
area within the meaning of the Continental Shelf Act 1964 or on 1964 c. 29.
a ship registered in the United Kingdom or an aircraft so
registered, or in relation to rights or obligations which accrued
or arose in the United Kingdom or on such an installation,
ship or aircraft.

7.—(1) Where the Commissioner proposes to conduct an in- Procedure in
vestigation pursuant to a complaint under this Act, he shall respect of
afford to the principal officer of the department or authority con- investigations.
cerned, and to any other person who is alleged in the complaint
to have taken or authorised the action complained of, an
opportunity to comment on any allegations contained in the
complaint.

(2) Every such investigation shall be conducted in private,
but except as aforesaid the procedure for conducting an investigation shall be such as the Commissioner considers appropriate
in the circumstances of the case ; and without prejudice to the
generality of the foregoing provision the Commissioner may
obtain information from such persons and in such manner, and
make such inquiries, as he thinks fit, and may determine whether
any person may be represented, by counsel or solicitor or otherwise, in the investigation.

(3) The Commissioner may, if he thinks fit, pay to the
person by whom the complaint was made and to any other person
who attends or furnishes information for the purposes of an
investigation under this Act—

  (a) sums in respect of expenses properly incurred by them ;
  (b) allowances by way of compensation for the loss of their
      time,

in accordance with such scales and subject to such conditions
as may be determined by the Treasury.

(4) The conduct of an investigation under this Act shall
not affect any action taken by the department or authority
concerned, or any power or duty of that department or authority
to take further action with respect to any matters subject to

the investigation; but where the person aggrieved has been removed from the United Kingdom under any Order in force under the Aliens Restriction Acts 1914 and 1919 or under the Commonwealth Immigrants Act 1962, he shall, if the Commissioner so directs, be permitted to re-enter and remain in the United Kingdom, subject to such conditions as the Secretary of State may direct, for the purposes of the investigation.

1962 c. 21.

Evidence.

8.—(1) For the purposes of an investigation under this Act the Commissioner may require any Minister, officer or member of the department or authority concerned or any other person who in his opinion is able to furnish information or produce documents relevant to the investigation to furnish any such information or produce any such document.

(2) For the purposes of any such investigation the Commissioner shall have the same powers as the Court in respect of the attendance and examination of witnesses (including the administration of oaths or affirmations and the examination of witnesses abroad) and in respect of the production of documents.

(3) No obligation to maintain secrecy or other restriction upon the disclosure of information obtained by or furnished to persons in Her Majesty's service, whether imposed by any enactment or by any rule of law, shall apply to the disclosure of information for the purposes of an investigation under this Act; and the Crown shall not be entitled in relation to any such investigation to any such privilege in respect of the production of documents or the giving of evidence as is allowed by law in legal proceedings.

(4) No person shall be required or authorised by virtue of this Act to furnish any information or answer any question relating to proceedings of the Cabinet or of any committee of the Cabinet or to produce so much of any document as relates to such proceedings; and for the purposes of this subsection a certificate issued by the Secretary of the Cabinet with the approval of the Prime Minister and certifying that any information, question, document or part of a document so relates shall be conclusive.

(5) Subject to subsection (3) of this section, no person shall be compelled for the purposes of an investigation under this Act to give any evidence or produce any document which he could not be compelled to give or produce in proceedings before the Court.

Obstruction and contempt.

9.—(1) If any person without lawful excuse obstructs the Commissioner or any officer of the Commissioner in the performance of his functions under this Act, or is guilty of any act or omission in relation to an investigation under this Act which, if that investigation were a proceeding in the Court, would constitute contempt of court, the Commissioner may certify the offence to the Court.

(2) Where an offence is certified under this section, the Court may inquire into the matter and, after hearing any witnesses who may be produced against or on behalf of the person charged with the offence, and after hearing any statement that may be offered in defence, deal with him in any manner in which the Court could deal with him if he had committed the like offence in relation to the Court.

(3) Nothing in this section shall be construed as applying to the taking of any such action as is mentioned in subsection (4) of section 7 of this Act.

10.—(1) In any case where the Commissioner conducts an Reports by investigation under this Act or decides not to conduct such an Commissioner. investigation, he shall send to the member of the House of Commons by whom the request for investigation was made (or if he is no longer a member of that House, to such member of that House as the Commissioner thinks appropriate) a report of the results of the investigation or, as the case may be, a statement of his reasons for not conducting an investigation.

(2) In any case where the Commissioner conducts an investigation under this Act, he shall also send a report of the results of the investigation to the principal officer of the department or authority concerned and to any other person who is alleged in the relevant complaint to have taken or authorised the action complained of.

(3) If, after conducting an investigation under this Act, it appears to the Commissioner that injustice has been caused to the person aggrieved in consequence of maladministration and that the injustice has not been, or will not be, remedied, he may, if he thinks fit, lay before each House of Parliament a special report upon the case.

(4) The Commissioner shall annually lay before each House of Parliament a general report on the performance of his functions under this Act and may from time to time lay before each House of Parliament such other reports with respect to those functions as he thinks fit.

(5) For the purposes of the law of defamation, any such publication as is hereinafter mentioned shall be absolutely privileged, that is to say—

(a) the publication of any matter by the Commissioner in making a report to either House of Parliament for the purposes of this Act;

(b) the publication of any matter by a member of the House of Commons in communicating with the Commissioner or his officers for those purposes or by the Commissioner or his officers in communicating with such a member for those purposes ;

(c) the publication by such a member to the person by whom a complaint was made under this Act of a report or statement sent to the member in respect of the complaint in pursuance of subsection (1) of this section ;

(d) the publication by the Commissioner to such a person as is mentioned in subsection (2) of this section of a report sent to that person in pursuance of that subsection.

Provision for secrecy of information. 1911 c. 28.

11.—(1) It is hereby declared that the Commissioner and his officers hold office under Her Majesty within the meaning of the Official Secrets Act 1911.

(2) Information obtained by the Commissioner or his officers in the course of or for the purposes of an investigation under this Act shall not be disclosed except—

(a) for the purposes of the investigation and of any report to be made thereon under this Act ;

(b) for the purposes of any proceedings for an offence under the Official Secrets Acts 1911 to 1939 alleged to have been committed in respect of information obtained by the Commissioner or any of his officers by virtue of this Act or for an offence of perjury alleged to have been committed in the course of an investigation under this Act or for the purposes of an inquiry with a view to the taking of such proceedings ; or

(c) for the purposes of any proceedings under section 9 of this Act ;

and the Commissioner and his officers shall not be called upon to give evidence in any proceedings (other than such proceedings as aforesaid) of matters coming to his or their knowledge in the course of an investigation under this Act.

(3) A Minister of the Crown may give notice in writing to the Commissioner, with respect to any document or information specified in the notice, or any class of documents or information so specified, that in the opinion of the Minister the disclosure of that document or information, or of documents or information of that class, would be prejudicial to the safety of the State or otherwise contrary to the public interest ; and where such a notice is given nothing in this Act shall be construed as authorising or requiring the Commissioner or any officer of the Commissioner to communicate to any person or for any

purpose any document or information specified in the notice, or any document or information of a class so specified.

(4) The references in this section to a Minister of the Crown include references to the Commissioners of Customs and Excise and the Commissioners of Inland Revenue.

Supplemental

12.—(1) In this Act the following expressions have the Interpretation. meanings hereby respectively assigned to them, that is to say—

" action " includes failure to act, and other expressions connoting action shall be construed accordingly ;

" the Commissioner " means the Parliamentary Commissioner for Administration ;

" the Court " means, in relation to England and Wales the High Court, in relation to Scotland the Court of Session, and in relation to Northern Ireland the High Court of Northern Ireland ;

" enactment " includes an enactment of the Parliament of Northern Ireland, and any instrument made by virtue of an enactment ;

" officer " includes employee ;

" person aggrieved " means the person who claims or is alleged to have sustained such injustice as is mentioned in section 5(1)(a) of this Act ;

" tribunal " includes the person constituting a tribunal consisting of one person.

(2) References in this Act to any enactment are references to that enactment as amended or extended by or under any other enactment.

(3) It is hereby declared that nothing in this Act authorises or requires the Commissioner to question the merits of a decision taken without maladministration by a government department or other authority in the exercise of a discretion vested in that department or authority.

13.—(1) Subject to the provisions of this section, this Act Application extends to Northern Ireland. to Northern Ireland.

(2) Nothing in this section shall be construed as authorising the inclusion among the departments and authorities to which this Act applies of any department of the Government of Northern Ireland, or any authority established by or with the authority of the Parliament of Northern Ireland ; but this Act shall apply to any such department or authority, in relation to any action taken by them as agent for a department or authority to which this Act applies, as it applies to the last-mentioned department or authority.

(3) In section 6 of this Act the references to a Minister of the Crown or government department and to Parliament shall include references to a Minister or department of the Government of Northern Ireland and to the Parliament of Northern Ireland.

(4) In section 8 of this Act the references to the Cabinet shall include references to the Cabinet of Northern Ireland, and in relation to that Cabinet for the reference to the Prime Minister there shall be substituted a reference to the Prime Minister of Northern Ireland.

Short title and commencement.

14.—(1) This Act may be cited as the Parliamentary Commissioner Act 1967.

(2) This Act shall come into force on such date as Her Majesty may by Order in Council appoint.

(3) A complaint under this Act may be made in respect of matters which arose before the commencement of this Act; and for the purposes of subsection (3) of section 6 of this Act any time elapsing between the date of the passing and the date of the commencement of this Act (but not any time before the first of those dates) shall be disregarded.

SCHEDULES

SCHEDULE 1   Section 2.

PENSIONS AND OTHER BENEFITS

1. A person appointed to be the Commissioner may, within such period and in such manner as may be prescribed by regulations under this Schedule, elect between the statutory schemes of pensions and other benefits applicable respectively to the judicial offices listed in Schedule 1 to the Judicial Pensions Act 1959 and to the civil service 1959 c. 9 of the State (in this Schedule referred to respectively as the judicial (8 & 9 Eliz. 2). scheme and the civil service scheme), and if he does not so elect shall be treated as having elected for the civil service scheme.

2. Where a person so appointed elects for the judicial scheme, a pension may be granted to him on ceasing to hold office as Commissioner if he has held that office for not less than five years and either—

    (a) has attained the age of sixty-five years ; or

    (b) is disabled by permanent infirmity for the performance of the duties of that office ;

and (subject to regulations under this Schedule) the provisions of the Judicial Pensions Act 1959, other than section 2 (retiring age), and of sections 2 to 8 of the Administration of Justice (Pensions) Act 1950 c. 11 1950 (lump sums and widows and dependants pensions), shall apply (14 & 15 Geo. 6). in relation to him and his service as Commissioner as they apply in relation to the holders of judicial offices listed in Schedule 1 to the said Act of 1959 and service in any such office, this paragraph being the relevant pension enactment for the purposes of that Act.

3. Where a person so appointed elects for the civil service scheme, the Superannuation Act 1965 shall (subject to regulations under 1965 c. 74. this Schedule) apply as if his service as Commissioner were service in an established capacity in the civil service of the State.

4. The Treasury may by statutory instrument make regulations for purposes supplementary to the foregoing provisions of this Schedule ; and such regulations may, without prejudice to section 38 of the Superannuation Act 1965 (employment in more than one public office), make special provision with respect to the pensions and other benefits payable to or in respect of persons to whom the judicial scheme or the civil service scheme has applied or applies in respect of any service other than service as Commissioner, including provision—

    (a) for aggregating other service falling within the judicial scheme with service as Commissioner, or service as Commissioner with such other service, for the purpose of determining qualification for or the amount of benefit under that scheme ;

    (b) for increasing the amount of the benefit payable under the judicial scheme, in the case of a person to whom that scheme applied in respect of an office held by him before appointment as Commissioner, up to the amount which would have been payable thereunder if he had retired from that office on the ground of permanent infirmity immediately before his appointment ;

(c) for limiting the amount of benefit payable under the judicial scheme, in the case of a person to whom the civil service scheme applied in respect of service before his appointment as Commissioner, by reference to the difference between the amount of the benefit granted in his case under the civil service scheme and the amount which would be payable under the judicial scheme if that service had been service as Commissioner.

5. Any statutory instrument made by virtue of this Schedule shall be subject to annulment in pursuance of a resolution of the House of Commons.

Section 4.

SCHEDULE 2

DEPARTMENTS AND AUTHORITIES SUBJECT TO INVESTIGATION

Ministry of Agriculture, Fisheries and Food.
Charity Commission.
Civil Service Commission.
Commonwealth Office.
Crown Estate Office.
Customs and Excise.
Ministry of Defence.
Department of Economic Affairs.
Department of Education and Science.
Export Credits Guarantee Department.
Foreign Office.
Ministry of Health.
Home Office.
Ministry of Housing and Local Government.
Central Office of Information.
Inland Revenue.
Ministry of Labour.
Land Commission.
Land Registry.
Lord Chancellor's Department.
Lord President of the Council's Office.
National Debt Office.
Ministry of Overseas Development.
Post Office.
Ministry of Power.
Ministry of Public Building and Works.
Public Record Office.
Public Trustee.
Department of the Registers of Scotland.
General Register Office.
General Register Office, Scotland.
Registry of Friendly Societies.
Royal Mint.
Scottish Office.
Scottish Record Office.
Ministry of Social Security.
Social Survey.

Stationery Office.
Ministry of Technology.
Board of Trade.
Ministry of Transport.
Treasury.
Treasury Solicitor.
Welsh Office.

NOTES

1. The reference to the Ministry of Defence includes the Defence Council, the Admiralty Board, the Army Board and the Air Force Board.

2. The reference to the Lord President of the Council's Office does not include the Privy Council Office.

3. The reference to the Post Office is a reference to that Office in relation only to the following functions, that is to say : —

   (*a*) functions under the enactments relating to national savings ;

   (*b*) functions exercised as agent of another government department or authority listed in this Schedule ;

   (*c*) functions in respect of the control of public broadcasting authorities and services ; or

   (*d*) functions under the Wireless Telegraphy Act 1949.   1949 c. 54.

4. The reference to the Registry of Friendly Societies includes the Central Office, the Office of the Assistant Registrar of Friendly Societies for Scotland and the Office of the Chief Registrar and the Industrial Assurance Commissioner.

5. The reference to the Board of Trade includes, in relation to administrative functions delegated to any body in pursuance of section 7 of the Civil Aviation Act 1949, a reference to that body. 1949 c. 67.

6. The reference to the Treasury does not include the Cabinet Office, but subject to that includes the subordinate departments of the Treasury and the office of any Minister whose expenses are defrayed out of moneys provided by Parliament for the service of the Treasury.

7. The reference to the Treasury Solicitor does not include a reference to Her Majesty's Procurator General.

8. In relation to any function exercisable by a department or authority for the time being listed in this Schedule which was previously exercisable on behalf of the Crown by a department or authority not so listed, the reference to the department or authority so listed includes a reference to the other department or authority.

SCHEDULE 3

Section 5.

MATTERS NOT SUBJECT TO INVESTIGATION

1. Action taken in matters certified by a Secretary of State or other Minister of the Crown to affect relations or dealings between the Government of the United Kingdom and any other Government or any international organisation of States or Governments.

2. Action taken, in any country or territory outside the United Kingdom, by or on behalf of any officer representing or acting under the authority of Her Majesty in respect of the United Kingdom, or any other officer of the Government of the United Kingdom.

3. Action taken in connection with the administration of the government of any country or territory outside the United Kingdom which forms part of Her Majesty's dominions or in which Her Majesty has jurisdiction.

4. Action taken by the Secretary of State under the Extradition Act 1870 or the Fugitive Offenders Act 1881.

5. Action taken by or with the authority of the Secretary of State for the purposes of investigating crime or of protecting the security of the State, including action so taken with respect to passports.

6. The commencement or conduct of civil or criminal proceedings before any court of law in the United Kingdom, of proceedings at any place under the Naval Discipline Act 1957, the Army Act 1955 or the Air Force Act 1955, or of proceedings before any international court or tribunal.

7. Any exercise of the prerogative of mercy or of the power of a Secretary of State to make a reference in respect of any person to the Court of Appeal, the High Court of Justiciary or the Courts-Martial Appeal Court.

8. Action taken on behalf of the Minister of Health or the Secretary of State by a Regional Hospital Board, Board of Governors of a Teaching Hospital, Hospital Management Committee or Board of Management, or by the Public Health Laboratory Service Board.

9. Action taken in matters relating to contractual or other commercial transactions, whether within the United Kingdom or elsewhere, being transactions of a government department or authority to which this Act applies or of any such authority or body as is mentioned in paragraph (a) or (b) of subsection (1) of section 6 of this Act and not being transactions for or relating to—

(a) the acquisition of land compulsorily or in circumstances in which it could be acquired compulsorily ;

(b) the disposal as surplus of land acquired compulsorily or in such circumstances as aforesaid.

10. Action taken in respect of appointments or removals, pay, discipline, superannuation or other personnel matters, in relation to—

(a) service in any of the armed forces of the Crown, including reserve and auxiliary and cadet forces ;

(b) service in any office or employment under the Crown or under any authority listed in Schedule 2 to this Act ; or

(c) service in any office or employment, or under any contract for services, in respect of which power to take action, or to determine or approve the action to be taken, in such matters is vested in Her Majesty, any Minister of the Crown or any such authority as aforesaid.

11. The grant of honours, awards or privileges within the gift of the Crown, including the grant of Royal Charters.

ALBERTA'S OMBUDSMAN BILL
APPROVED 1967

CHAPTER 59

An Act to Provide for the Appointment of a Commissioner to Investigate Administrative Decisions and Acts of Officials of the Government and its Agencies

(Assented to March 30, 1967)

HER MAJESTY, by and with the advice and consent of the Legislative Assembly of the Province of Alberta, enacts as follows:

Short title

1. This Act may be cited as *The Ombudsman Act.*

Interpretation

2. In this Act,
  (*a*) "agency" means an agency of the Government of Alberta;
  (*b*) "department" means a department of the Government of Alberta;
  (*c*) "Minister" means a member of the Executive Council.

Appointment

3. (1) There shall be appointed, as an officer of the Legislature, a commissioner for investigations to be called the Ombudsman.

(2) Subject to section 7, the Lieutenant Governor in Council shall appoint the Ombudsman on the recommendation of the Assembly.

Restriction as to holding other offices

4. (1) The Ombudsman may not be a member of the Assembly and shall not hold any office of trust or profit, other than his office as Ombudsman, or engage in any occupation for reward outside the duties of his office.

(2) The Ombudsman shall be a Canadian citizen.

Term of office

5. (1) Unless his office sooner becomes vacant, a person appointed as Ombudsman holds office for five years
  (*a*) from the date of his appointment under section 3, or
  (*b*) from the date his appointment under section 7 is confirmed under that section,
and any person, if otherwise qualified, may be reappointed.

(2) The Ombudsman may at any time resign his office by writing addressed to the Speaker of the Assembly or, if

there is no Speaker or if the Speaker is absent from Alberta, to the Clerk of the Assembly.

Suspension or removal from office

6. (1) On the recommendation of the Assembly,. the Lieutenant Governor in Council may, at any time, suspend or remove the Ombudsman from his office for disability, neglect of duty, misconduct or bankruptcy.

(2) At any time the Legislature is not in session, the Lieutenant Governor in Council may suspend the Ombudsman from his office for disability, neglect of duty, misconduct or bankruptcy proved to the satisfaction of the Lieutenant Governor in Council, but the suspension shall not continue in force beyond the end of the next ensuing session of the Legislature.

Vacancy in office

7. (1) If the Ombudsman dies, retires, resigns or is removed from office, the vacancy thereby created shall be filled in accordance with this section.

(2) If a vacancy occurs while the Legislature is in session, but no recommendation is made by the Assembly before the close of that session, subsection (3) applies as if the vacancy had occurred while the Legislature was not in session.

(3) If a vacancy occurs while the Legislature is not in session, the Lieutenant Governor in Council may appoint an Ombudsman to fill the vacancy and unless his office sooner becomes vacant, the person so appointed holds office until his appointment is confirmed by the Assembly.

(4) If an appointment under subsection (3) is not confirmed within one month after the commencement of the next ensuing regular session, the appointment lapses and there shall be deemed to be another vacancy in the office of Ombudsman.

Salary

8. (1) The Ombudsman shall be paid a salary of $20,000 which shall be charged to and paid out of the General Revenue Fund.

(2) There shall be paid to the Ombudsman in respect of time spent in travelling in the exercise of his functions such travelling allowances and expenses as may be prescribed by the Lieutenant Governor in Council.

Oath of office

9. (1) Before entering upon his duties, the Ombudsman shall take an oath that he will faithfully and impartially perform the duties of his office and that he will not, except in accordance with subsection (2) of section 19, divulge any information received by him under this Act.

(2) The oath shall be administered by the Speaker of the Assembly or by the Clerk of the Assembly.

Staff

10. (1) Subject to *The Public Service Act, 1962* there may be appointed such officers and employees as may be necessary to assist the Ombudsman in the efficient carrying out of his functions under this Act.

(2) Every person holding an office or appointment under the Ombudsman shall, before he begins to perform his duties under this Act, take an oath, to be administered by the Ombudsman, that he will not divulge any information received by him under this Act except for the purpose of giving effect to this Act.

Functions and duties

11. (1) It is the function and duty of the Ombudsman to investigate any decision or recommendation made, including any recommendation made to a Minister, or any act done or omitted, relating to a matter of administration and affecting any person or body of persons in his or its personal capacity, in or by any department or agency, or by any officer, employee or member thereof in the exercise of any power or function conferred on him by any enactment.

(2) The Ombudsman may make an investigation either on a complaint made to him by any person or of his own motion, and he may commence an investigation notwithstanding that the complaint may not on its face be against a decision, recommendation, act or omission as mentioned in subsection (1).

(3) The powers and duties conferred on the Ombudsman by this Act may be exercised and performed notwithstanding any provision in any Act to the effect

(*a*) that any decision, recommendation, act or omission mentioned in subsection (1) is final, or

(*b*) that no appeal lies in respect thereof, or

(*c*) that no proceeding or decision of the person or organization whose decision, recommendation, act or omission it is shall be challenged, reviewed, quashed or called in question.

(4) Without limiting subsection (1), any committee of the Assembly may at any time refer to the Ombudsman, for investigation and report by him, any petition that is before that committee for consideration or any matter to which the petition relates, and, in that case, the Ombudsman shall,

(*a*) subject to any special directions of the committee, investigate the matters so referred to him so far as they are within his jurisdiction, and

(*b*) make such report to the committee as he thinks fit,

but nothing in section 14, 20 or 21 applies in respect of any investigation or report made under this subsection.

Jurisdiction restricted

12. (1) Nothing in this Act authorizes the Ombudsman to investigate

(*a*) any decision, recommendation, act or omission in respect of which there is under any Act a right of appeal or objection or a right to apply for a review on the merits of the case to any court or to any tribunal constituted by or under any Act, until after that right of appeal or objection or application has been exercised in the particular case or until after the time prescribed for the exercise of that right has expired, or

(b) any decision, recommendation, act or omission of any person acting as a solicitor for the Crown or acting as counsel for the Crown in relation to any proceedings.

(2) If any question arises as to whether the Ombudsman has jurisdiction to investigate any case or class of cases under this Act, he may, if he thinks fit, apply to the Supreme Court of Alberta for a declaratory order determining the question.

Complaint to Ombudsman

13. (1) Every complaint to the Ombudsman shall be made in writing.

(2) Notwithstanding any Act, where a letter written by

(a) any person in custody on a charge or after conviction of any offence, or

(b) any patient of a hospital within the meaning of *The Mental Health Act,*

is addressed to the Ombudsman, it shall be immediately forwarded, unopened, to the Ombudsman by the person for the time being in charge of the place or institution where the writer of the letter is detained or of which he is a patient.

Refusal to investigate

14. (1) If in the course of the investigation of any complaint it appears to the Ombudsman

(a) that under the law or existing administrative practice there is an adequate remedy, other than the right to petition the Legislature, for the complainant, whether or not he has availed himself of it, or

(b) that, having regard to all the circumstances of the case, any further investigation is unnecessary,

he may in his discretion refuse to investigate the matter further.

(2) The Ombudsman may, in his discretion, refuse to investigate or cease to investigate any complaint

(a) if it relates to any decision, recommendation, act or omission of which the complainant has had knowledge for more than 12 months before the complaint is received by the Ombudsman, or

(b) if in his opinion,

(i) the subject matter of the complaint is trivial, or

(ii) the complaint is frivolous or vexatious or is not made in good faith, or

> (iii) the complainant has not a sufficient personal interest in the subject matter of the complaint.

(3) Where the Ombudsman decides not to investigate or to cease to investigate a complaint, he shall inform the complainant of his decision and he may, if he thinks fit, state his reasons therefor.

15. (1) Before investigating any matter under this Act, the Ombudsman shall inform the deputy minister of the department or the administrative head of the agency affected, as the case may be, of his intention to make the investigation.

(2) The Ombudsman may, in his discretion, at any time during or after an investigation consult any Minister who is concerned in the matter of the investigation.

(3) On the request of any Minister in relation to an investigation or in any case where an investigation relates to any recommendation made to a Minister, the Ombudsman shall consult that Minister after making the investigation and before forming a final opinion on any of the matters referred to in subsection (1) or (2) of section 20.

(4) If, during or after an investigation, the Ombudsman is of opinion that there is evidence of any breach of duty or misconduct on the part of any officer or employee of any department or agency, he shall refer the matter to the deputy minister of the department or the administrative head of the agency, as the case may be.

16. (1) Every investigation by the Ombudsman under this Act shall be conducted in private.

(2) The Ombudsman may hear or obtain information from such persons as he thinks fit and he may make such inquiries as he thinks fit.

(3) It is not necessary for the Ombudsman to hold any hearing and no person is entitled as of right to be heard by the Ombudsman, but, if at any time during the course of an investigation it appears to the Ombudsman that there may be sufficient grounds for his making a report or recommendation that may adversely affect any department, agency or person, he shall give to that department, agency or person an opportunity to be heard, and the department, agency or person is entitled to counsel at the hearing.

(4) Subject to this Act and any rules made under section 27, the Ombudsman may regulate his procedure in such manner as he thinks fit.

17. (1) Subject to this section and section 18, the Ombudsman may require any person who, in his opinion, is able to give any information relating to any matter being investigated by him

> (a) to furnish the information to him, and

Notice of investigation (margin, §15)
Conduct of investigation (margin, §16)
Evidence at investigation (margin, §17)

    (*b*) to produce any document, paper or thing that in his opinion relates to the matter being investigated and that may be in the possession or under the control of that person,

whether or not that person is an officer, employee or member of a department or agency and whether or not the document, paper or thing is in the custody or under the control of a department or agency.

(2) The Ombudsman may summon before him and examine on oath

    (*a*) any person who is an officer or employee or member of any department or agency and who in the Ombudsman's opinion is able to give any information mentioned in subsection (1), and

    (*b*) any complainant, and

    (*c*) any other person who in the Ombudsman's opinion is able to give any information mentioned in subsection (1),

and for that purpose may administer an oath.

(3) Subject to subsection (4), a person who is bound by any Act to maintain secrecy in relation to, or not to disclose, any matter is not required to

    (*a*) supply any information to or answer any question put by the Ombudsman in relation to that matter, or

    (*b*) produce to the Ombudsman any document, paper or thing relating to it,

if compliance with that requirement would be in breach of the obligation of secrecy or non-disclosure.

(4) With the prior consent in writing of a complainant, any person to whom subsection (3) applies may be required by the Ombudsman to supply information or answer any question or produce any document, paper or thing relating only to the complainant, and it is the duty of the person to comply with the requirement.

(5) Every person has the same privileges in relation to the giving of information, the answering of questions and the production of documents, papers and things under this Act as witnesses have in any court.

(6) Except on the trial of a person for perjury, no statement made or answer given by that or any other person in the course of an inquiry by or any proceedings before the Ombudsman is admissible in evidence against any person in any court or at any inquiry or in any other proceedings, and no evidence in respect of proceedings before the Ombudsman shall be given against any person.

(7) No person is liable to prosecution for an offence against any Act by reason of his compliance with any requirement of the Ombudsman under this section.

Disclosures
restricted

18. (1) Where the Attorney General certifies that the giving of any information or the answering of any question or the production of any document, paper or thing might involve the disclosure of

    (*a*) the deliberations of the Executive Council, or

    (*b*) proceedings of the Executive Council, or committee thereof relating to matters of a secret or confidential nature and would be injurious to the public interest,

the Ombudsman shall not require the information or answer to be given or, as the case may be, the document, paper or thing to be produced, but shall report the giving of the certificate to the Legislature.

(2) Subject to subsection (1), the rule of law that authorizes or requires the withholding of any document, paper or thing, or the refusal to answer any question, on the ground that the disclosure of the document, paper or thing or the answering of the question would be injurious to the public interest, does not apply in respect of any investigation by or proceedings before the Ombudsman.

Mainten-
ance of
secrecy

19. (1) The Ombudsman and every person holding an office or appointment under him shall maintain secrecy in respect of all matters that come to their knowledge in the exercise of their functions.

(2) Notwithstanding subsection (1), the Ombudsman may disclose in any report made by him under this Act such matters as in his opinion ought to be disclosed in order to establish grounds for his conclusions and recommendations.

Procedure
after investi-
gation

20. (1) This section applies where, after making an investigation under this Act, the Ombudsman is of opinion that the decision, recommendation, act or omission that was the subject matter of the investigation

    (*a*) appears to have been contrary to law, or

    (*b*) was unreasonable, unjust, oppressive, improperly discriminatory or was in accordance with a rule of law or a provision of any Act or a practice that is or may be unreasonable, unjust, oppressive or improperly discriminatory, or

    (*c*) was based wholly or partly on a mistake of law or fact, or

    (*d*) was wrong.

(2) This section also applies where the Ombudsman is of opinion

    (*a*) that in the making of the decision or recommendation, or in the doing or omission of the act, a discretionary power has been exercised

        (i) for an improper purpose, or

        (ii) on irrelevant grounds, or

  (iii) on the taking into account of irrelevant considerations,
   or

 (*b*) that, in the case of a decision made in the exercise of a discretionary power, reasons should have been given for the decision.

(3) If, where this section applies, the Ombudsman is of opinion

 (*a*) that the matter should be referred to the appropriate authority for further consideration, or

 (*b*) that the omission should be rectified, or

 (*c*) that the decision should be cancelled or varied, or

 (*d*) that any practice on which the decision, recommendation, act or omission was based should be altered, or

 (*e*) that any law on which the decision, recommendation, act or omission was based should be reconsidered, or

 (*f*) that reasons should have been given for the decision, or

 (*g*) that any other steps should be taken,

the Ombudsman shall report his opinion and his reasons therefor to the appropriate Minister and to the department or agency concerned, and may make such recommendations as he thinks fit and in that case he may request the department or agency to notify him within a specified time of the steps, if any, that it proposes to take to give effect to his recommendations.

(4) If within a reasonable time after the report is made no action is taken which seems to the Ombudsman to be adequate and appropriate, the Ombudsman, in his discretion, after considering the comments, if any, made by or on behalf of the department or agency affected, may send a copy of the report and recommendations to the Lieutenant Governor in Council and may thereafter make such report to the Legislature on the matter as he thinks fit.

(5) The Ombudsman shall attach to every report sent or made under subsection (4) a copy of any comments made by or on behalf of the department or agency concerned.

(6) Notwithstanding anything in this section, the Ombudsman shall not, in any report made under this Act, make any comment that is adverse to any person unless the person has been given an opportunity to be heard.

Results of investigation to complainant

21. (1) Where the Ombudsman makes a recommendation under subsection (3) of section 20 and no action that seems to the Ombudsman to be adequate and appropriate is taken thereon within a reasonable time, the Ombudsman shall inform the complainant of his recommendation and make such comments on the matter as he thinks fit.

(2) The Ombudsman shall in any case inform the complainant, in such manner and at such time as he thinks proper, of the result of the investigation.

Proceedings not subject to review

22. No proceedings of the Ombudsman shall be held bad for want of form and, except on the ground of lack of jurisdiction, no proceedings or decision of the Ombudsman shall be challenged, reviewed, quashed or called in question in any court.

Proceedings privileged

23. (1) No proceedings lie against the Ombudsman or against any person holding an office or appointment under the Ombudsman for any thing he may do or report or say in the course of the exercise or intended exercise of his functions under this Act, unless it is shown that he acted in bad faith.

(2) Neither the Ombudsman nor any person holding an office or appointment under the Ombudsman shall be called upon to give evidence in any court or in any proceedings of a judicial nature in respect of any thing coming to his knowledge in the exercise of his functions under this Act.

(3) Any thing said or any information supplied or any document, paper or thing produced by any person in the course of any inquiry by or proceedings before the Ombudsman under this Act is privileged in the same manner as if the inquiry or proceedings were proceedings in a court.

(4) For the purposes of *The Defamation Act* any report made by the Ombudsman under this Act shall be deemed to be privileged and a fair and accurate report thereon in a newspaper or a broadcast shall be deemed to be privileged.

Entry of premises

24. (1) For the purposes of this Act, the Ombudsman may at any time enter upon any premises occupied by any department or agency and inspect the premises and, subject to sections 17 and 18, carry out therein any investigation that is within his jurisdiction.

(2) Before entering upon any premises pursuant to subsection (1), the Ombudsman shall notify the deputy minister of the department or, as the case may require, the administrative head of the agency that occupies the premises of his intention to do so.

Delegation of powers

25. (1) With the prior approval of the Lieutenant Governor in Council, the Ombudsman may, by writing under his hand, delegate to any person holding any office under him any of his powers under this Act, except this power of delegation and the power to make any report under this Act.

(2) A delegation may be made to a specified person or to the holder for the time being of a specified office or to the holders of offices of a specified class.

(3) Every delegation is revocable at will and no delegation prevents the exercise of any power by the Ombudsman.

(4) A delegation may be made subject to such restrictions and conditions as the Ombudsman thinks fit, and may be made either generally or in relation to any particular case or class of cases.

(5) Until a delegation is revoked, it continues in force according to its tenor and, in the event of the Ombudsman by whom it was made ceasing to hold office, continues to have effect as if made by his successor.

(6) Any person purporting to exercise any power of the Ombudsman by virtue of such a delegation shall, when required to do so, produce evidence of his authority to exercise the power.

Annual report **26.** (1) The Ombudsman shall in each year make a report to the Legislature on the exercise of his functions under this Act.

(2) The Ombudsman may, from time to time, in the public interest or in the interests of any person or department or agency publish reports relating

(a) generally to the exercise of his functions under this Act, or

(b) to any particular case investigated by him,

whether or not the matters to be dealt with in any such report have been the subject of a report to the Legislature.

Rules for guidance **27.** The Assembly may,

(a) of its own volition, or

(b) upon the recommendation of the Lieutenant Governor in Council,

make rules for the guidance of the Ombudsman in the exercise of his functions and duties.

Offences and penalties **28.** Any person who,

(a) without lawful justification or excuse, wilfully obstructs, hinders or resists the Ombudsman or any other person in the exercise of his powers under this Act, or

(b) without lawful justification or excuse, refuses or wilfully fails to comply with any lawful requirement of the Ombudsman or any other person under this Act, or

(c) wilfully makes any false statement to or misleads or attempts to mislead the Ombudsman or any other person in the exercise of his powers under this Act,

is guilty of an offence and is liable on summary conviction to a fine of not more than $500 and in default of payment to imprisonment for a term not exceeding three months.

Other laws **29.** The provisions of this Act are in addition to the provisions of any other Act or any rule of law under which (*a*) any remedy or right of appeal or objection is provided for any person, or

(*b*) any procedure is provided for the inquiry into or investigation of any matter,

and nothing in this Act limits or affects any such remedy or right of appeal or objection or procedure.

Coming into force   **30.** This Act comes into force on the first day of July, 1967.

N

HAWAII'S OMBUDSMAN BILL,
APPROVED 1967

Be It Enacted By The Legislature Of The State Of Hawaii:

SECTION 1. *Short title.* This Act may be called "The Ombudsman Act of 1967".

SECTION 2. *Definitions.* (a) "Agency" includes any permanent governmental entity, department, organization, or institution, and any officer, employee, or member thereof acting or purporting to act in the exercise of his official duties, except:

(1) a court;

(2) the legislature, its committees, and its staff;

(3) an entity of the federal government;

(4) a multi-state governmental entity; and

(5) the governor and his personal staff.

(b) "Administrative act" includes any action, omission, decision, recommendation, practice, or procedure, but does not include the preparation or presentation of legislation.

SECTION 3. *Ombudsman; office established, appointment, tenure, removal, qualifications, compensation, vacancy.* The office of ombudsman is established. The legislature, by a majority vote of each house in joint session, shall appoint an ombudsman who shall serve for a period of six years. An ombudsman may be reappointed but may not serve for more than three terms. The legislature, by two-thirds vote of the members in joint session, may remove or suspend the ombudsman from office, but only for neglect of duty, misconduct, or disability.

No person may serve as ombudsman within two years of the last day on which he served as a member of the legislature, or while he is a candidate for or holds any other state office, or while he is engaged in any other occupation for reward or profit.

The compensation of the ombudsman shall be $22,000 per annum. The compensation of the ombudsman shall not be diminished during his term of office, unless by general law applying to all salaried officers of the State.

If the ombudsman dies, resigns, becomes ineligible to serve, or is removed or suspended from office, the first assistant to the ombudsman becomes the acting ombudsman until a new ombudsman is appointed for a full term.

SECTION 4. *Assistance, staff, delegation.* The ombudsman shall appoint a first assistant, and such other officers and employees as may be necessary to carry out this Act. All employees, including the first assistant, shall be hired by the ombudsman and shall serve at his pleasure. In determining the salary of each such employee, the ombudsman shall consult with the department of personnel and shall follow as closely as possible the recommendations of the department. The first assistant's salary shall not exceed the percentage limitation established by law for a deputy director of a department. The ombudsman and his full-time staff shall be entitled to participate in any employee benefit plan.

The ombudsman may delegate to his appointees any of his duties except those specified in sections 13 and 14.

SECTION 5. *Procedure.* The ombudsman may establish procedures for receiving and processing complaints, conducting investigations, and reporting his findings. However, he may not levy fees for the submission or investigation of complaints.

SECTION 6. *Jurisdiction.* The ombudsman has jurisdiction to investigate the administrative acts of agencies and he may exercise his powers without regard to the finality of any administrative act.

SECTION 7. *Investigation of complaints.* (a) The ombudsman shall investigate any complaint which he determines to be an appropriate subject for investigation under section 9.

(b) The ombudsman may investigate on his own motion if he reasonably believes that an appropriate subject for investigation under section 9 exists.

SECTION 8. *Notice to complainant and agency.* If the ombudsman decides not to investigate, he shall inform the complainant of that decision and shall state his reasons.

If the ombudsman decides to investigate, he shall notify the complainant of his decision and he shall also notify the agency of his intention to investigate.

SECTION 9. *Appropriate subjects for investigation.* An appropriate subject for investigation is an administrative act of an agency which might be:

(1) Contrary to law;

(2) Unreasonable, unfair, oppressive, or unnecessarily discriminatory, even though in accordance with law;

(3) Based on a mistake of fact;

(4) Based on improper or irrelevant grounds;

(5) Unaccompanied by an adequate statement of reasons;

(6) Performed in an inefficient manner; or

(7) Otherwise erroneous.

The ombudsman may investigate to find an appropriate remedy.

SECTION 10. *Investigation procedures.* (a) In an investigation,

N*

the ombudsman may make inquiries and obtain information as he thinks fit; enter without notice to inspect the premises of an agency; and hold private hearings.

(b) The ombudsman is required to maintain secrecy in respect to all matters and the identities of the complainants or witnesses coming before him except so far as disclosures may be necessary to enable him to carry out his duties and to support his recommendations.

SECTION 11. *Powers.* Subject to the privileges which witnesses have in the courts of this State, the ombudsman may:

(1) Compel at a specified time and place, by a subpoena, the appearance and sworn testimony of any person who the ombudsman reasonably believes may be able to give information relating to a matter under investigation; and

(2) Compel any person to produce documents, papers, or objects which the ombudsman reasonably believes may relate to a matter under investigation.

The ombudsman may bring suit in an appropriate state court to enforce these powers.

SECTION 12. *Consultation with agency.* Before giving any opinion or recommendation that is critical of an agency or person, the ombudsman shall consult with that agency or person.

SECTION 13. *Procedure after investigation.* If, after investigation, the ombudsman finds that:

(1) A matter should be further considered by the agency;

(2) An administrative act should be modified or cancelled;

(3) A statute or regulation on which an administrative act is based should be altered;

(4) Reasons should be given for an administrative act; or

(5) Any other action should be taken by the agency; he shall report his opinion and recommendations to the agency. He may request the agency to notify him, within a specified time, of any action taken on his recommendations.

SECTION 14. *Publication of recommendations.* After a reasonable time has elapsed, the ombudsman may present his opinion and recommendations to the governor, the legislature, the public, or any of these. The ombudsman shall include with this opinion any reply made by the agency.

SECTION 15. *Notice to the complainant.* After a reasonable time has elapsed, the ombudsman shall notify the complainant of the actions taken by him and by the agency.

SECTION 16. *Misconduct by agency personnel.* If the ombudsman thinks there is a breach of duty or misconduct by any officer or employee of an agency, he shall refer the matter to the appropriate authorities.

SECTION 17. *Annual report.* The ombudsman shall submit to the legislature and the public an annual report discussing his activities under this Act.

SECTION 18. *Judicial review, immunity.* No proceeding or decision of the ombudsman may be reviewed in any court, unless it contravenes the provisions of this Act. The ombudsman has the same immunities from civil and criminal liability as a judge of this State. The ombudsman and his staff shall not testify in any court with respect to matters coming to their attention in the exercise or purported exercise of their official duties except as may be necessary to enforce the provisions of this Act.

SECTION 19. *Agencies may not open letters to ombudsman.* A letter to the ombudsman from a person held in custody by an agency shall be forwarded immediately, unopened, to the ombudsman.

SECTION 20. *Penalty for obstruction.* A person who willfully hinders the lawful actions of the ombudsman or his staff, or willfully refuses to comply with their lawful demands, shall be fined not more than one thousand dollars.

SECTION 21. *Effective date.* This Act shall take effect upon its approval.

PROPOSAL BY INDIAN ADMINISTRATIVE REFORMS COMMISSION 1966*

22. We are of the view that the special circumstances relating to our country can be fully met by providing for two special institutions for the redress of citizens' grievances. There should be one authority dealing with complaints against the administrative acts of Ministers or Secretaries to Government at the Centre and in the States. There should be another authority in each State and at the Centre for dealing with complaints against the administrative acts of other officials. All these authorities should be independent of the executive as well as the legislature and the judiciary. The setting up of these authorities should not, however, be taken to be a complete answer to the problem of redress of citizens' grievances. They only provide the ultimate set-up for such redress as has not been available through the normal departmental or governmental machinery and do not absolve the department from fulfilling its obligations to the citizen for administering its affairs without generating, as far as possible, any legitimate

---

* Extract from *Interim Report* of October 1966, 12-18. Reprinted, with thanks, by permission of the present Chairman, Shri K. Hanumanthaiya.

sense of grievance. Thus, the administration itself must play the
major role in reducing the area of grievances and providing
remedies wherever necessary and feasible. For this purpose, there
should be established in each Ministry or Department, as the case
may be, suitable machinery for the receipt and investigation of
complaints and for setting in motion, where necessary, the
administrative process for providing remedies. A large number of
cases which arise at lower levels of administration should in fact
adequately be dealt with by this in-built departmental machinery.
When this machinery functions effectively, the number of cases
which will have to go to an authority outside the Ministry or the
Department should be comparatively small in number. In some
States and at the Centre, there is now some provision for a Governmental authority to hear grievances and attempt to secure remedial
action through the administration. The tendency is to set up such
authorities independent and outside of the departmental machinery.
After the setting up of the authorities we have recommended above,
there would be no need for these functionaries. We would in these
circumstances strongly advocate that the responsibility of the
departments to deal adequately with public grievances must
squarely be faced by them in the first instance and for this purpose,
we shall be making our recommendations in regard to this matter
at a later date when we deal with the departmental set-up.

Cases of corruption.

23. Public opinion has been agitated for a long time over the
prevalence of corruption in the administration and it is likely that
cases coming up before the independent authorities mentioned above
might involve allegations or actual evidence of corrupt motive and
favouritism. We think that this institution should deal with such
cases as well, but where the cases are such as might involve
criminal charge or misconduct cognisable by a Court, the case
should be brought to the notice of the Prime Minister or the Chief
Minister, as the case may be. The latter would then set the
machinery of law in motion after following appropriate procedures
and observing necessary formalities. The present system of
Vigilance Commissions wherever operative will then become
redundant and would have to be abolished on the setting up of the
institution.

Designation of the authorities of the institution.

24. We suggest that the authority dealing with complaints against
Ministers and Secretaries to Government may be designated
"Lokpal" and the other authorities at the Centre and in the States

empowered to deal with complaints against other officials may be designated "Lokayukta". A word may be said about our decision to include Secretaries' actions along with those of Ministers in the jurisdiction of the Lokpal. We have taken this decision because we feel that at the level at which Ministers and Secretaries function, it might often be difficult to decide where the role of one functionary ends and that of the other begins. The line of demarcation between the responsibilities and influence of the Minister and Secretary is thin; in any case much depends on their personal equation and personality and it is most likely that in many a case the determination of responsibilities of both of them would be involved.

25. The following would be the main features of the institutions of Lokpal and Lokayukta:—

(a) They should be demonstrably independent and impartial.

(b) Their investigations and proceedings should be conducted in private and should be informal in character.

(c) Their appointment should, as far as possible, be non-political.

(d) Their status should compare with the highest judicial functionaries in the country.

(e) They should deal with matters in the discretionary field involving acts of injustice, corruption or favouritism.

(f) Their proceedings should not be subject to judicial interference and they should have the maximum latitude and powers in obtaining information relevant to their duties.

(g) They should not look forward to any benefit or pecuniary advantage from the executive Government.

Bearing in mind these essential features of the institutions, we recommend that the Lokpal be appointed and invested with functions in the manner described in the succeeding paragraphs.

Appointment, conditions of service, etc., of Lokpal.

26. The Lokpal should be appointed by the President on the advice of the Prime Minister, which would be tendered by him after consultation with the Chief Justice of India and the Leader of the Opposition. If there be no such leader, the Prime Minister will instead consult a person elected by the members of the Opposition in the Lok Sabha in such manner as the Speaker may direct. The Lokpal will have the same status as the Chief Justice of India. His tenure will be 5 years subject to eligibility for reappointment for another term of five years in accordance with the same procedure. He may, by writing under his hand, addressed to the President, resign his office. He will not be removable from

office except in the manner prescribed in the Constitution for the removal from office of a Judge of the Supreme Court. His salary and other emoluments will be the same as those of the Chief Justice of India. On appointment as Lokpal, he shall cease to be a Member of any Legislature if he was one before the appointment. He shall also resign from any post or office of profit held by him prior to that date whether in or outside the Government. He shall also sever his connections with all business activities, if any. He shall also resign his membership, if any, of a political party. After retirement from the post of Lokpal he will be ineligible for any appointment under the Government or in a Government Undertaking.

27. The Lokpal would be free to choose his own staff, but their number, categories and conditions of service will be subject to the approval of Government. His budget would be subject to the control of the Parliament.

The jurisdiction of the Lokpal.

28. Subject to the exclusions which are mentioned later on, the Lokpal will have the power to investigate an administrative act done by or with the approval of a Minister or a Secretary to Government at the Centre or in the State, if a complaint is made against such an act by a person who is affected by it and who claims to have suffered an injustice on that account. (In this context, an act would include a failure to take action.) Such a complaint may be made either by an individual or by a corporation. He may in his discretion inquire into a complaint of maladministration involving not only an act of injustice but also an allegation of favouritism to any person (including a corporation) or of the accrual of personal benefit or gain to the administrative authority responsible for the act, namely, a Minister or a Secretary to Government at the Centre or in the States. In addition to making investigations on the basis of complaints received by him, the Lokpal may also *suo motu* investigate administrative acts of the types described above which may come to his notice otherwise than through a complaint of an adversely affected person.

Matters excluded from the purview of the Lokpal.

29. The following matters shall, however, be excluded from the purview of the Lokpal:—

i) Action taken in a matter certified by a Minister as affecting the relations or dealings between the Government of India and any foreign Government or any international organisation of States or Governments.

ii) Action taken under the Extradition Act, 1962 or Foreigners Act, 1946.

iii) Action taken for the purpose of investigating crime or protecting the security of the State including action taken with respect to passports.

iv) Action taken in the exercise of power in relation to determining whether a matter shall go to the Court.

v) Action taken in matters which arise out of the terms of contract governing purely commercial relations of the administration with customers or suppliers except complaints of harassment or delays in the performance of contractual obligations.

vi) Action taken in respect of appointments, removals, pay, discipline, superannuation or other personnel matters.

vii) Grant of honours and awards.

viii) A decision made in exercise of his discretion by an administrative authority unless the elements involved in the exercise of discretion are absent to such an extent that no discretion has been exercised to all.

ix) Any action in respect of which the person aggrieved has or had a right of appeal, reference or review to or before a tribunal.

x) Matters in respect of which a person aggrieved has or had a remedy by way of proceedings in any court of law. (However, he may look into such a matter if he is satisfied that in the particular circumstances it is not reasonable to expect the complainant to take or to have taken proceedings in a court of law).

xi) An administrative decision which was taken more than twelve months before the date of the complaint.

Procedure for dealing with complaints.

30. On receipt of a complaint from a person claiming to have suffered an injustice through an administrative act for which a Minister or a Secretary to Government is finally responsible, the Lokpal will scrutinise it and come to a conclusion as to whether he has jurisdiction to deal with it and if so, whether the case is worth investigation. If his conclusion is in the negative on either of these points, he will reject the complaint and inform the complainant accordingly. If he decides to take up the investigation, he will, in the first instance, communicate the complaint to the administration and invite the administration's comments thereon. At this stage, it may be possible for the administration to rectify, on its own, any faulty decision made by it, or it may seek to establish the correctness or justice of the action taken. The Lokpal on receipt of the administration's comments will decide whether the complaint is actionable and inform the complainant in

case the faulty decision has been rectified or he has decided not to take any further action. In cases in which he decides to proceed with the investigation, if on its completion, the Lokpal is satisfied that there is no cause for grievance, he will inform the complainant accordingly and close the case. If, however, he considers that an injustice has been done to the complainant, he will suggest to the administration remedial action where it is possible for it to provide the remedy. If his recommendation is accepted, the case will then be closed. If, however, the recommendation is not accepted, it will be open to him to make a report on the case to the Prime Minister or Chief Minister of the State as the case may be. The Prime Minister or the Chief Minister will inform the Lokpal of action taken on the reference within two months. Thereafter, he may, if he is dissatisfied with the action taken, bring it to the notice of the Parliament or the Legislature as the case may be through an *ad hoc* report or through the annual report. The administration's explanation in its defence will also be brought out in the report. Also, if the Lokpal considers, as a result of his study of any case or cases, that an amendment of the law would be justified, he can make appropriate recommendations to the Prime Minister or Chief Minister as the case may be. The foregoing procedure will apply *mutatis mutandis* to investigation taken up *suo motu* by the Lokpal.

31. If during his investigations, he finds that a case involves criminal misconduct or would justify criminal proceedings, he will report to the Prime Minister or the Chief Minister as the case may be, who will take further action in the matter within two months of the receipt thereof and inform the Lokpal of the action taken.

Powers for carrying out his functions.

32. The Lokpal will have powers of a court with regard to the calling of witnesses, documents, etc. In regard to information available with Government or subordinate authorities, he shall have access to whatever information, document, etc., he requires and no privilege will be claimed for any such information or document except when it affects the security of the State or foreign relations. However, it is expected that the exercise of the powers as a court will be unnecessary and that the Lokpal's procedure would be as informal as possible. The investigation by the Lokpal will be conducted in private. Nothing relating to the investigations shall be published or caused to be published by him till the enquiry is completed and his findings are communicated to the complainant, or to the Legislature. Publication of any matter pending before the Lokpal or decided by him save to the

extent that it is included in the *ad hoc* or annual report or is permitted by the Lokpal should be an offence under the relevant law.

33. At the beginning of each year the Lokpal will submit a report to the Legislature concerned on his activities during the previous year. Besides giving a summary of the cases disposed of by him, he may indicate the need for amending any law in order to remove occasions for unintended hardship experienced as a result of the administration of the existing law.

34. If any person without lawful excuse obstructs the Lokpal in the performance of his functions or is guilty of any act or omission in relation to an investigation, which, had the investigation been proceeding in a court of law, would have constituted contempt of court, the Lokpal may certify the offence to the Supreme Court. If a person making a complaint of maladministration involving undue favour being shown or to the accrual of a personal benefit, makes a false statement before the Lokpal knowing it to be such, he shall be deemed to be guilty of an act constituting contempt of court. When an offence is certified, as above, the Supreme Court may enquire into the matter and dispose of it as if it related to a charge of contempt of the Supreme Court.

35. We append herewith the draft bill providing for the appointment and functions of the Lokpal. The draft can be suitably adapted for the appointment and functions of the office of Lokayukta.

The Lokayukta.

36. So far as the Lokayukta is concerned, we envisage that he would be concerned with problems similar to those which would face the Lokpal in respect of Ministers and Secretaries though, in respect of action taken at subordinate levels of official hierarchy, he would in many cases have to refer complainants to competent higher levels. We, therefore, consider that his powers, functions and procedures may be prescribed *mutatis mutandis* with those which we have laid down for the Lokpal. His status, position, emoluments, etc., should, however, be analogous to those of a Chief Justice of a High Court and he should be entitled to have free access to Secretary to the Government concerned or to the Head of the Department with whom he will mostly have to deal to secure justice for a deserving citizen. Where he is dissatisfied with the action taken by the department concerned, he should be in a position to seek a quick corrective action from the Minister or the Secretary concerned, failing which he should be able to draw the personal attention of the Prime Minister or the Chief Minister as the case may be. It does not seem necessary for us to spell out

here in more detail the functions and powers of the Lokayukta and the procedures to be followed by him.

Constitutional amendment—whether necessary?

37. We have carefully considered whether the institution of Lokpal will require any constitutional amendment and whether it is possible for the office of the Lokpal to be set up by Central Legislation so as to cover both the Central and State functionaries concerned. We agree that for the Lokpal to be fully effective and for him to acquire power, without conflict with other functionaries under the Constitution, it would be necessary to give a constitutional status to his office, his powers, functions, etc. We feel, however, that it is not necessary for Government to wait for this to materialise before setting up the office. The Lokpal, we are confident, would be able to function in a large number of cases without the definition of his position under the Constitution. The Constitutional amendment and any consequential modification of the relevant statute can follow. In the meantime, Government can ensure that the Lokpal or Lokayukta is appointed and takes preparatory action to set up his office, to lay down his procedures, etc., and commence his work to such extent as he can without the constitutional provisions. We are confident that the necessary support will be forthcoming from the Parliament.

Conclusion.

38. We should like to emphasise the fact that we attach the highest importance to the implementation, at an early date, of the recommendations contained in this our Interim Report. That we are not alone in recognising the urgency of such a measure is clear from the British example we have quoted above. We have no doubt that the working of the institution of Lokpal and Lokayukta that we have suggested for India will be watched with keen expectation and interest by other countries. We hope that this aspect would also be fully borne in mind by Government in considering the urgency and importance of our recommendation. Though its timing is very close to the next Election, we need hardly assure the Government that this has had nothing to do with the necessity of making this interim report. We have felt the need of such a recommendation on merits alone and are convinced that we are making it not a day too soon.

> Signed: Morarji Desai (*Chairman*); Harish Chandra Mathur, H. V. Kamath, V. Shankar (*Members*); V. V. Chari (*Secretary*). 14-10-66.

INDEX